THE

COMPLETE OFFICE

OF

HOLY WEEK

ACCORDING TO THE

𝕽oman 𝕸issal and 𝕭reviary,

IN LATIN AND ENGLISH.

CONTENTS.

MAUNDY THURSDAY.

GOOD FRIDAY.

HOLY SATURDAY.

EASTER DAY.

EASTER MONDAY.

EASTER TUESDAY.

PREFACE.

THE week before Easter has been called by several names, from the great mysteries and various ceremonies celebrated and performed in it. The Greeks and Latins anciently called it *the Great Week, the Holy Week;* sometimes *the Painful Week*—that is, the Week of Austerities; also, the Week of Sorrows, the days *of the Cross* or *of sufferings.* "We call it the Great Week," says S. Chrysostom, *on Ps.* 145, "not that it consists of a greater number of days, or that the days in it are longer; but on account of the great things which God has wrought in it; for on these days was the tyranny of the devil overthrown, death disarmed, sin and its curse taken away, heaven opened and made accessible, and men made fellows with the angels."

The chief object of the Church in this

week is to celebrate the memory of the passion and death of her Redeemer. Every part
of the sacred liturgy is directed to this end;
the Church's offices, more solemn and more
multiplied in this week than in any other during the whole year, are most especially adapt-
ed to excite in the hearts of the Faithful
those various sentiments of love and gratitude,
of compassion for the sufferings of our Lord,
of sorrow and detestation for sin, which every
Christian ought to cherish in this holy time.
It is with the sincere desire of exciting pious
sentiments in the hearts of the faithful that
the whole liturgy of the Church for *Holy
Week* has been collected in this volume, and
is presented to the public, both in the Latin
and English languages. Thus, while the pious
Christian unites his voice with that of the
priest and of the choir, he may also penetrate
the sense of the divine office, and sanction by
the fervor of his heart what he pronounces
with his tongue. For this reason, the editor
flatters himself that this book will not fail to
please all those who still entertain a due sense

of piety and religion ; and may profit even those who, through a want of instruction, seldom or never reflect on the great mysteries which the Church commemorates during Holy Week. The very reading of this most pious and affecting part of the Church's liturgy is capable of exciting in their hearts a true and solid devotion.

THE MASS.

The Asperges.

ASPERGES me Domine hyssopo, et mundabor: lavabis me, et super nivem dealbabor.

THOU shalt sprinkle me with hyssop, O Lord, and I shall be cleansed: thou shalt wash me, and I shall be made whiter than snow.

Ps. Miserere mei Deus, secundum magnam misericordiam tuam.
V. Gloria Patri, etc.
Ant. Asperges me.

Have mercy on me, O God, according to thy great mercy.
V. Glory be, etc.
Ant. Thou shalt sprinkle me.

The Priest, being returned to the foot of the Altar, says:

V. OSTENDE nobis Domine misericordiam tuam.

V. SHOW us, O Lord, thy mercy.

R. Et salutare tuum da nobis.

R. And grant us thy salvation.

V. Domine exaudi orationem meam.

V. O Lord, hear my prayer.

R. Et clamor meus ad te veniat.

R. And let my cry come unto thee.

V. Dominus vobiscum.

V. The Lord be with you.

R. Et cum spiritu tuo.

R. And with thy spirit.

Oremus.

Let us pray.

EXAUDI nos Domine sancte, Pater omnipotens, æterne Deus: et mittere digneris sanctum angelum tuum de cœlis, qui custodiat, foveat, protegat, visitet, atque defendat omnes habitantes in hoc habitaculo. Per Christum Dominum nostrum.

HEAR us, O holy Lord, almighty Father, eternal God; and vouchsafe to send thy holy angel from heaven, to guard, cherish, protect, visit, and defend all that are assembled in this house; through Christ our Lord. Amen.

THE

ORDINARY OF THE MASS.

The Priest at the foot of the Altar makes the sign of the Cross, saying:

IN nomine Patris, et Filii, et Spiritus sancti. Amen.

V. Introibo ad altare Dei.

R. Ad Deum, qui lætificat juventutem meam.

IN the name of the Father, and of the Son, and of the Holy Ghost. Amen.

V. I will go in to the altar of God.

R. To God, who giveth joy to my youth.

PSALM 42.

This Psalm is omitted during Holy Week, except on Holy Saturday.

JUDICA me Deus, et discerne causam meam de gente non sancta : ab homine iniquo et doloso erue me.

Quia tu es Deus fortitudo mea, quare me repulisti? et quare tristis incedo, dum affligit me inimicus?

Emitte lucem tuam et

JUDGE me, O God! and distinguish my cause from the nation that is not holy : deliver me from the unjust and deceitful man.

For thou art God my strength : why hast thou cast me off? and why do I go sorrowful, whilst the enemy afflicteth me?

Send forth thy light

12

veritatem tuam: ipsa me deduxerunt, et adduxerunt in montem sanctum tuum, et in tabernacula tua.

And thy truth: they have conducted me, and brought me unto thy holy hill, and into thy tabernacles.

Et introibo ad altare Dei: ad Deum, qui lætificat juventutem meam.

And I will go in to the altar of God: to God, who giveth joy to my youth.

Confitebor tibi in cithara, Deus, Deus meus: quare tristis es anima mea? et quare conturbas me?

To thee, O Lord my God! I will give praise upon the harp: why art thou sad, O my soul? and why dost thou disquiet me?

Spera in Deo, quoniam adhuc confitebor illi: salutare vultus mei, et Deus meus.

Hope in God, for I will still give praise to him: the salvation of my countenance, and my God.

Gloria Patri, et Filio, et Spiritui sancto.

Glory be to the Father, and to the Son, and to the Holy Ghost.

Sicut erat in principio, et nunc, et semper, et in sæcula sæculorum. Amen.

As it was in the beginning, is now, and ever shall be, world without end. Amen.

V. Introibo ad altare Dei.

V. I will go in to the altar of God.

R. Ad Deum, qui lætificat juventutem meam.

R. To God, who giveth joy to my youth.

V. Adjutorium nostrum in nomine Domini.

V. Our help is in the name of the Lord.

R. Qui fecit cœlum et terram.

Confiteor Deo omnipotenti, etc.

V. Misereatur tui omnipotens Deus, et dimissis peccatis tuis, perducat te ad vitam æternam.

R. Amen.

Confiteor Deo omnipotenti, beatæ Mariæ semper Virgini, beato Michaeli Archangelo, beato Joanni Baptistæ, sanctis Apostolis Petro et Paulo, omnibus Sanctis, et tibi, Pater, quia peccavi nimis cogitatione, verbo, et opere, mea culpa, mea culpa, mea maxima culpa. Ideo precor beatam Mariam semper Virginem, beatum Michaelem Archangelum, beatum Joannem Baptistam, sanctos Apostolos Petrum et Paulum, omnes Sanctos, et te. Pater, orare pro me ad Dominum Deum nostrum.

R. Who made heaven and earth.

I confess to Almighty God, etc.

V. May Almighty God have mercy on thee, forgive thee thy sins, and bring thee to everlasting life.

R. Amen.

I confess to Almighty God, to blessed Mary ever Virgin, to blessed Michael the Archangel, to blessed John the Baptist, to the holy Apostles Peter and Paul, to all the Saints, and to thee, Father, that I have sinned exceedingly in thought, word, and deed, through my fault, through my fault, through my most grievous fault. Therefore I beseech the blessed Mary ever Virgin, the blessed Michael the Archangel, the blessed John the Baptist, the holy Apostles Peter and Paul, all the Saints, and thee, Father, to pray to the Lord our God for me.

V. Misereatur vestri omnipotens Deus, et dimissis peccatis vestris, perducat vos ad vitam æternam.

R. Amen.

V. ✚ Indulgentiam, absolutionem et remissionem peccatorum nostrorum tribuat nobis omnipotens et misericors Dominus.

R. Amen.

V. Deus, tu conversus vivificabis nos.

R. Et plebs tua lætabitur in te.

V. Ostende nobis, Domine, misericordiam tuam.

R. Et salutare tuum da nobis.

V. Domine, exaudi orationem meam.

R. Et clamor meus ad te veniat.

V. Dominus vobiscum.

R. Et cum spiritu tuo.

Oremus.

V. May Almighty God have mercy on you, forgive you your sins, and bring you to everlasting life.

R. Amen.

V. ✚ May the Almighty and merciful Lord give us pardon, absolution, and remission of our sins.

R. Amen.

V. Thou wilt turn, O God! and bring us to life.

R. And thy people shall rejoice in thee.

V. Show us, O Lord thy mercy.

R. And grant us thy salvation.

V. O Lord! hear my prayer.

R. And let my cry come unto thee.

V. The Lord be with you.

R. And with thy spirit.

Let us pray.

The Priest says the following prayers in a low voice:

AUFER a nobis, quæ-sumus, Domine, in-iquitates nostra : ut ad Sancta sanctorum puris mereamur mentibus in-troire. Per Christum Do-minum nostrum. Amen.

TAKE from us our iniquities, we be-seech thee, O Lord! that we may be worthy to enter with pure minds into the Holy of holies: through Christ our Lord. Amen.

Oramus te, Domine, per merita Sanctorum tuorum, quorum reli-quiæ hic sunt, et omni-um Sanctorum : ut in-dulgere digneris omnia peccata mea. Amen.

We beseech thee, O Lord! by the merits of thy Saints, whose relics are here, and of all the Saints, that thou wouldst vouchsafe to forgive me all my sins. Amen.

Then he goes to the Book at the corner of the Altar, and making the sign of the cross, recites the Introit aloud. (For Introit for Palm Sunday, see p. 67; Monday in Holy Week, p. 126; Tuesday in Holy Week, p. 135; Wednesday in Holy Week, p. 157; Holy Thurs-day, p. 252; Easter Sunday, p. 509; Easter Monday, p. 520; Eas-ter Tuesday, p. 529.) Afterwards, returning to the middle of the Altar, he says:

V. KYRIE eleison.

R. Kyrie eleison.

V. Kyrie eleison.

R. Christe eleison.

V. LORD! have mer-cy on us.

R. Lord! have mercy on us.

V. Lord! have mercy on us.

R. Christ! have mer-cy on us

V. Christe eleison.

R. Christe eleison.

V. Kyrie eleison.

R. Kyrie eleison.

V. Kyrie eleison.

V. Christ! have mercy on us.

R. Christ! have mercy on us.

V. Lord! have mercy on us.

R. Lord! have mercy on us.

V. Lord! have mercy on us.

Gloria in excelsis Deo, et in terra pax hominibus bonæ voluntatis. Laudamus te; benedicimus te; adoramus te; glorificamus te. Gratias agimus tibi propter magnam gloriam tuam, Domine Deus, Rex cœlestis, Deus Pater omnipotens. Domine Fili unigenite, Jesu Christe. Domine Deus, Agnus Dei, Filius Patris; qui tollis peccata mundi, miserere nobis; qui tollis peccata mundi, suscipe deprecationem nostram; qui sedes ad dexteram Patris, miserere nobis. Quoniam tu solus sanctus: tu solus Dominus: tu solus altissi-

Glory be to God on high, and peace on earth to men of good will. We praise thee, we bless thee, we adore thee, we glorify thee. We give thee thanks for thy great glory. O Lord God, heavenly King! O God the Father almighty! O Lord Jesus Christ, the only begotten Son! O Lord God, Lamb of God, Son of the Father! O thou who takest away the sins of the world! have mercy on us. O thou who takest away the sins of the world! receive our prayer. O thou who sittest at the right hand of the Father! have mercy on

mus, Jesu Christe, cum Sancto Spiritu, in gloria Dei Patris. Amen.

us. For thou alone art holy ; thou alone art Lord; thou alone art the most high, **O** Jesus Christ! together with the Holy Ghost, in the glory of God the Father. Amen.

The Priest, turning to the people, says :

V. **D**OMINUS vobiscum.
R. Et cum spiritu tuo.

V. **T**HE Lord be with you.
R. And with thy spirit.

The Collect, Epistle, etc., being said—(for Collect and Epistle for Palm Sunday, see p. 68 ; Monday in Holy Week, p. 126 ; Tuesday in Holy Week, p. 135 ; Wednesday in Holy Week, p. 157; Holy Thursday, p. 253 ; Good Friday, p. 340; Holy Saturday, p. 497 ; Easter Sunday, p. 509 ; Easter Monday, p. 520 ; Easter Tuesday, p. 529)—the Priest goes to the middle of the Altar, and says :

MUNDA cor meum ac labia mea, omnipotens Deus, qui labia Isaiæ prophetæ calculo mundasti ignito: ita me tua grata miseratione dignare mundare, ut sanctum evangelium tuum digne valeam nuntiare. Per Christum Dominum nostrum. Amen.

CLEANSE my heart and my lips, O almighty God ! who, with a fiery coal, didst cleanse the lips of the prophet Isaiah ; vouchsafe through thy gracious mercy so to cleanse me that I may worthily declare thy holy gospel ; through Christ our Lord. Amen.

Jube, Domine, benedicere.

Bless me, O Lord !

Dominus sit in corde meo, et in labiis meis; ut digne et competenter annuntiem evangelium suum. Amen.

The Lord be in my heart and on my lips, that I may worthily and in a becoming manner announce his gospel. Amen.

Before reading the Gospel, the Priest says:

V. DOMINUS vobiscum.

R. Et cum spiritu tuo.

V. THE Lord be with you.

R. And with thy spirit.

At the end of the Gospel—(for Gospel for Palm Sunday, see p. 50; Monday in Holy Week, p. 130; Tuesday in Holy Week, p. 137; Wednesday in Holy Week, p. 164; Holy Thursday, p. 256; Good Friday, p. 344; Holy Saturday, p. 499; Easter Sunday, p. 512; Easter Monday, p. 523; Easter Tuesday, p. 532)—the Clerk says:

R. LAUS tibi, Christe.

R. PRAISE be to thee, O Christ!

And the Priest kisses the Book, saying:

PER evangelica dicta deleantur nostra delicta.

BY the words of the gospel may our sins be blotted out.

After which he goes to the middle of the Altar, and says the Nicene Creed aloud:

CREDO in unum Deum, Patrem omnipotentem, Factorum cœli et terræ, visibilium omnium et invisibilium. Et in unum Dominum Jesum Christum, Filium Dei unigenitum, et ex

I BELIEVE in one God, the Father Almighty, Maker of heaven and earth, and of all things visible and invisible. And in one Lord, Jesus Christ, the only begotten Son of God.

Patre natum ante omnia sæcula; Deum de Deo; Lumen de Lumine; Deum verum de Deo vero; genitum non factum, consubstantialem Patri, per quem omnia facta sunt; qui propter nos homines, et propter nostram salutem, descendit de cœlis; et incarnatus est de Spiritu Sancto ex Maria Virgine; ET HOMO FACTUS EST. Crucifixus etiam pro nobis: sub Pontio Pilato passus et sepultus est. Et resurrexit tertia die secundum Scripturas. Et ascendit in cœlum: sedet ad dexteram Patris. Et iterum venturus est cum gloria judicare vivos et mortuos: cujus regni non erit finis. Et in Spiritum Sanctum, Dominum et vivificantem, qui ex Patre Filioque procedit; qui cum Patre et Filio simul adoratur et conglorificatur: qui locutus est per prophetas. Et unam sanctam Catholicam et Apostoli-

and born of the Father before all ages. God of God, Light of Light, true God of true God: begotten, not made; consubstantial with the Father, by whom all things were made. Who for us men, and for our salvation, came down from heaven, and became incarnate by the Holy Ghost of the Virgin Mary; AND WAS MADE MAN. He was also crucified for us: suffered under Pontius Pilate, and was buried. And rose again the third day, according to the Scriptures. And ascended into heaven: sitteth at the right hand of the Father. And he is to come again with glory, to judge the living and the dead: of his kingdom there shall be no end. And in the Holy Ghost, the Lord, and giver of life, who proceedeth from the Father and the Son: who with

cam Ecclesiam. Confiteor unum baptisma in remissionem peccatorum. Et expecto resurrectionem mortuorum, et vitam venturi sæculi. Amen.

the Father and the Son is equally adored and glorified : who spake by the prophets. And one holy Catholic and Apostolic Church. I confess one baptism for the remission of sins. And I expect the resurrection of the dead, and the life of the world to come. Amen.

V. Dominus vobiscum.

　　R. Et cum spiritu tuo.
　　　　Oremus.

V. The Lord be with you.

　　R. And with thy spirit.
　　　　Let us pray.

The Priest says the Offertory and makes the oblation of the Bread that is to be consecrated, saying:

SUSCIPE, sancte Pater, omnipotens, æterne Deus, hanc immaculatam Hostiam, quam ego indignus famulus tuus offero tibi, Deo meo vivo et vero, pro innumerabilibus peccatis et offensionibus et negligentiis meis, et pro omnibus circumstantibus, sed et pro omnibus fidelibus Christianis, vivis atque defunctis: ut

RECEIVE, O holy Father, Almighty and eternal God! this unspotted Host, which I, thy unworthy servant, offer to thee, my true and living God, for my innumerable sins, offences, and negligences, and for all here present; as also for all faithful Christians, both living and dead ; that it may avail me and them unto sal-

mihi et illis proficiat ad salutem in vitam æternam. Amen.

vation, and life everlasting. Amen.

He puts Wine and Water into the chalice, saying:

DEUS, qui humanæ substantiæ dignitatem mirabiliter condidisti, et mirabilius reformasti : da nobis per hujus aquæ et vini mysterium, ejus divinitatis esse consortes, qui humanitatis nostræ fieri dignatus est particeps, Jesus Christus, Filius tuus, Dominus noster: qui tecum vivit et regnat in unitate Spiritus Sancti Deus : per omnia sæcula sæculorum. Amen.

O GOD! who, in creating human nature, didst wonderfully dignify it, and who didst still more wonderfully reform it : grant that by the mystery of this water and wine, we may be made partakers of his divinity, who was graciously pleased to become partaker of our humanity, Jesus Christ thy Son, our Lord : who with thee and the Holy Ghost, liveth and reigneth one God, for ever and ever. Amen.

Oblation of the chalice.

OFFERIMUS tibi, Domine, calicem salutaris, tuam deprecantes clementiam : ut in conspectu divinæ majestatis tuæ, pro nostra et totius mundi salute cum odore suavitatis ascendat. Amen.

WE offer unto thee, O Lord! the chalice of salvation, beseeching thy clemency; that it may ascend before thy divine majesty, as a sweet odor for our salvation, and for that of the whole world. Amen

Then bowing down, he says:

IN spiritu humilitatis, et in animo contrito, suscipiamur a te, Domine: et sic fiat sacrificium nostrum in conspectu tuo hodie, ut placeat tibi, Domine Deus.

IN a spirit of humility and with contrition of heart, we pray thee, O Lord! to make us acceptable to thee; and let our sacrifice be so performed this day, in thy sight, that it may be pleasing·to thee, O Lord our God!

After which, lifting up his eyes to Heaven, he blesses the Bread and Wine, saying:

VENI, sanctificator omnipotens, æterne Deus: et benedic hoc sacrificium tuo sancto nomini præparatum.

COME, O Almighty Sanctifier, eternal God! and bless this sacrifice, prepared` for the honor of thy holy name.

The following blessing of the Incense and the incensing of the Altar, as far as Lavabo, *is omitted in private Masses:*

PER intercessionem beati Michaelis Archangeli, stantis a dextris altaris incensi, et omnium electorum suorum, incensum istud dignetur Dominus benedicere, et in odorem suavitatis accipere. Per Christum Dominum nostrum. Amen.

BY the intercession of blessed Michael the Archangel, standing at the right hand of the altar of incense, and of all the elect, may the Lord bless this incense, and receive it as a sweet odor; through Christ our Lord. Amen.

While he incenses the Offerings, he says:

INCENSUM istud a te benedictum, ascendat ad te, Domine, et descendat super nos misericordia tua.

MAY this incense, which thou hast blessed, ascend to thee, O Lord! and may thy mercy descend upon us.

Then he incenses the Altar, saying:

DIRIGATUR, Domine, oratio mea sicut incensum in conspectu tuo; elevatio manuum mearum sacrificium vespertinum. Pone, Domine, custodiam ori meo, et ostium circumstantiæ labiis meis: ut non declinet cor meum in verba malitiæ, ad excusandas excusationes in peccatis.

LET my prayer, O Lord! be directed as incense in thy sight: the lifting up of my hands, an evening sacrifice. Set a watch, O Lord! before my mouth, and a door round about my lips; that my heart may not incline to evil words, to make excuses in sin.

Giving the censer to the Deacon, he says:

ACCENDAT in nobis Dominus ignem sui amoris, et flammam æternæ charitatis. Amen.

MAY the Lord kindle in us the fire of his love, and the flame of eternal charity. Amen.

Then he goes to the corner of the Altar, and washes his fingers, saying:

LAVABO inter innocentes manus

I WILL wash my hands among the

meas: et circumdabo altare tuum, Domine.

innocent, and will compass thy altar, O Lord.

Ut audiam vocem laudis: et enarrem universa mirabilia tua.

That I may hear the voice of thy praise, and tell all thy wondrous works.

Domine, dilexi decorem domus tuæ, et locum habitationis gloriæ tuæ.

I have loved, O Lord! the beauty of thy house; and the place where thy glory dwelleth.

Ne perdas cum impiis, Deus, animam meam, et cum viris sanguinum vitam meam.

Take not away my soul, O God! with the wicked, nor my life with bloody men.

In quorum manibus iniquitates sunt: dextera eorum repleta est muneribus.

In whose hands are iniquities: their right hand is filled with gifts.

Ego autem in innocentia mea ingressus sum: redime me, et miserere mei.

But as for me, I have walked in my innocence: redeem me, and have mercy on me.

Pes meus stetit in directo: in ecclesiis benedicam te, Domine.

My foot hath stood in the direct way: in the churches I will bless thee, O Lord!

Gloria Patri, etc.

Glory, etc.

Having returned to the middle of the Altar, bowing down, he says:

SUSCIPE, sancta Trinitas, hanc oblationem, quam tibi offerimus, ob memoriam

RECEIVE, O holy Trinity! this oblation, which we make to thee, in memory of

passionis, resurrectionis, et ascensionis Jesu Christi, Domini nostri; et in honorem beatæ Mariæ semper virginis, et beati Joannis Baptistæ, et sanctorum Apostolorum Petri et Pauli, et istorum et omnium sanctorum: ut illis proficiat ad honorem, nobis autem ad salutem; et illi pro nobis intercedere dignentur in cœlis, quorum memoriam agimus in terris. Per eundem Christum Dominum nostrum. Amen.

the passion, resurrection, and ascension of our Lord Jesus Christ; and in honor of the blessed Mary ever Virgin; of blessed John the Baptist; of the holy Apostles Peter and Paul; of these, and of all the Saints; that it may avail to their honor, and to our salvation; and may they vouchsafe to intercede for us in heaven, whose memory we celebrate on earth; through the same Christ, our Lord. Amen.

Then turning to the People, he says:

ORATE, fratres, ut meum ac vestrum sacrificium acceptabile fiat apud Deum Patrem omnipotentem.

PRÁY, brethren, that my sacrifice and yours may be acceptable to God the Father almighty.

The Clerk answers in the name of the People:

SUSCIPIAT Dominus sacrificium de manibus tuis, ad laudem et gloriam nominis sui, ad utilitatem quoque nostram, totiusque Ecclesiæ suæ sanctæ.

MAY the Lord receive this sacrifice from thy hands, to the praise and glory of his name, to our benefit also, and to that of all his holy Church.

The Priest, in a low voice, says:

Amen.   Amen.

Here the appropriate Secreta *are said. That which follows is said aloud.*

PER omnia sæcula sæculorum.

R. Amen.

V. Dominus vobiscum.

R. Et cum spiritu tuo.

V. Sursum corda.

R. Habemus ad Dominum.

V. Gratias agamus Domino Deo nostro. .

R. Dignum et justum est.

WORLD without end.

R. Amen.

V. The Lord be with you.

R. And with thy spirit.

V. Lift up your hearts,

R. We have them lifted up to the Lord.

V. Let us give thanks to the Lord our God.

R. It is meet and just.

The Priest says the Preface, after which is said:

SANCTUS, sanctus, sanctus, Dominus Deus Sabaoth. Pleni sunt cœli et terra gloria tua. Hosanna in excelsis. Benedictus qui venit in nomine Domini. Hosanna in excelsis.

HOLY, holy, holy, Lord God of Hosts! the heavens and the earth are full of thy glory. Hosanna in the highest! Blessed is he that cometh in the name of the Lord. Hosanna in the highest!

THE
CANON OF THE MASS.

Here the Priest begins the Canon of the Mass, which is said in a low voice:

TE igitur, clementissime Pater, per Jesum Christum, Filium tuum Dominum nostrum, supplices rogamus ac petimus, uti accepta habeas, et benedicas hæc dona, hæc munera, hæc sancta sacrificia illibata, in primis, quæ tibi offerimus pro Ecclesia tua sancta Catholica: quam pacificare, custodire, adunare, et regere digneris toto orbe terrarum: una cum famulo tuo Papa nostro N., et Antistite nostro N., et omnibus orthodoxis, atque Catholicæ et Apostolicæ fidei cultoribus.

WE therefore humbly pray and beseech thee, most merciful Father! through Jesus Christ thy Son our Lord, that thou wouldst accept and bless these gifts, these presents, these holy unspotted sacrifices, which, in the first place, we offer to thee for thy holy Catholic Church, to which vouchsafe to grant peace; preserve, unite, and govern it throughout the whole world, together with thy servant N. our Chief Bishop, N. our Prelate, and all orthodox believers and professors of the Catholic and Apostolic Faith.

29

The commemoration of the living.

MEMENTO, Domine, famulorum famularumque tuarum N. et N.

BE mindful, O Lord, of thy servants N. and N.

Here he pauses a little, to call to his mind those he designs to pray for, and then continues :

ET omnium circumstantium, quorum tibi fides cognita est, et nota devotio : pro quibus tibi offerimus, vel qui tibi offerunt hoc sacrificium laudis, pro se, suisque omnibus, pro redemptione animarum suarum, pro spe salutis et incolumitatis suæ; tibique reddunt vota sua æterno Deo, vivo et vero.

AND all here present, whose faith and devotion are known to thee, for whom we offer, or who themselves offer thee this sacrifice of praise, for themselves and all that are dear to them; for the redemption of their souls, for the hope of their salvation and safety; and who now pay their vows to thee, the eternal, living, and true God.

Communicantes, et memoriam venerantes, in primis gloriosæ semper Virginis Mariæ, genitricis Dei et Domini nostri Jesu Christi : sed et beatorum apostolorum ac martyrum tuorum, Petri et Pauli, Andreæ, Jacobi, Joannis, Thomæ,

Communicating with, and honoring the memory, in the first place, of the glorious ever Virgin Mary, Mother of our God and Lord Jesus Christ; and also of thy blessed Apostles and Martyrs, Peter and Paul, Andrew, James, John, Thomas,

Jacobi, Philippi, Bartholomæi, Matthæi, Simonis et Thaddæi, Lini, Cleti, Clementis, Xysti, Cornelii, Cypriani, Laurentii, Chrysogoni, Joannis et Pauli, Cosmæ et Damiani, et omnium Sanctorum tuorum: quorum meritis precibusque concedas, ut in omnibus protectionis tuæ muniamur auxilio. Per eundem Christum Dominum nostrum. Amen.

James, Philip, Bartholomew, Matthew, Simon and Thaddeus, Linus, Cletus, Clement, Xystus, Cornelius, Cyprian, Lawrence, Chrysogonus, John and Paul, Cosmas and Damian, and of all thy Saints; by whose merits and prayers grant that we may, in all things, be defended by the help of thy protection: through the same Christ our Lord. Amen.

The Priest spreads his hands over the offerings.

HANC igitur oblationem servitutis nostræ, sed et cunctæ familiæ tuæ, quæsumus, Domine, ut placatus accipias: diesque nostros in tua pace disponas, atque ab æterna damnatione nos eripi, et in electorum tuorum jubeas grege numerari. Per Christum Dominum nostrum. Amen.

WE therefore beseech thee, O Lord! graciously to accept this oblation of our servitude, which is also that of thy whole family; dispose our days in thy peace; preserve us from eternal damnation, and place us in the number of thy elect; through Christ our Lord. Amen.

Quam oblationem tu Deus in omnibus, quæ-

Vouchsafe, we beseech thee, O God! to make this

sumus, benedictam, adscriptam, ratam, rationabilem, acceptabilemque facere digneris : ut nobis corpus et sanguis fiat dilectissimi filii tui Domini nostri Jesu Christi.

Qui pridie quam pateretur, accepit panem in sanctas ac venerabiles manus suas ; et elevatis oculis in cœlum, ad te Deum Patrem suum omnipotentem, tibi gratias agens, benedixit, fregit, deditque discipulis suis, dicens : Accipite, et manducate ex hoc omnes : HOC EST ENIM CORPUS MEUM.

oblation in all things blessed, approved, ratified, reasonable, and acceptable ; that it may be made for us the body and blood of thy most beloved Son, our Lord, Jesus Christ.

Who, on the day before he suffered, took bread in his sacred and venerable hands, and with his eyes lifted up towards heaven, to thee, O God! his almighty Father, giving thee thanks, blessed it, broke it, and gave it to his disciples, saying : Take and eat ye all of this ; FOR THIS IS MY BODY.

Here he adores the Sacrament on his knee, and then elevates it for the adoration of the people. After which he proceeds to the consecration of the chalice, saying:

SIMILI modo postquam cœnatum est, accipiens et hunc præclarum calicem in sanctas ac venerabiles manus suas, item tibi gratias agens, benedixit, deditque discipulis suis, di-

IN like manner, after he had supped, taking this ineffable chalice in his sacred and venerable hands, again giving thee thanks, he blessed it, and gave it to his disciples, saying : Take

cens : Accipite, et bibite ex eo omnes :

and drink ye all of this :

HIC EST ENIM CALIX SANGUINIS MEI, NOVI ET ÆTERNI TESTAMENTI: MYSTERIUM FIDEI : QUI PRO VOBIS ET PRO MUL-TIS EFFUNDETUR IN REMISSIONEM PECCATO-RUM.

FOR THIS IS THE CHAL-ICE OF MY BLOOD, OF THE NEW AND EVERLASTING TESTAMENT: A MYSTERY OF FAITH, WHICH SHALL BE SHED FOR YOU, AND FOR MANY, FOR THE RE-MISSION OF SINS.

Then he adores the sacred Blood, saying:

HÆC quotiescum-que feceritis, in mei memoriam facietis.

AS often as ye shall do these things, ye shall do them in re-membrance of me.

After this he elevates it for the adoration of the people, and con-tinues:

UNDE et memores, Domine, nos servi tui, sed et plebs tua sancta, ejusdem Christi Filii tui, Domini nostri, tam beatæ passionis, necnon et ab inferis re-surrectionis, sed et in cœlos gloriosæ ascen-sionis, offerimus præcla-ræ majestati tuæ de tuis donis ac datis, Hostiam puram, Hostiam sanc-tam, Hostiam immacu-

WHEREFORE, O Lord! we thy servants, as also thy holy people, being mindful of the blessed passion of the same Christ, thy Son our Lord, and of his re-surrection from hell, as also of his glorious as-cension into heaven, of-fer to thy most excellent majesty of thy own gifts and favors, a pure Host, a holy Host, an unspotted

latam, panem sanctum vitæ æternæ, et calicem salutis perpetuæ.

Supra quæ propitio ac sereno vultu respicere digneris, et accepta.habere, sicuti accepta habere dignatus es munera pueri tui justi Abel, et sacrificium patriarchæ nostri Abrahæ, et quod tibi obtulit summus sacerdos tuus Melchisedech, sanctum sacrificium, immaculatam hostiam.

Supplices te rogamus, omnipotens Deus, jube hæc perferri per manus sancti angeli tui in sublime altare tuum, in conspectu divinæ majestatis tuæ, ut quotquot ex hac altaris participatione, sacrosanctum Filii tui corpus et sanguinem sumpserimus, omni benedictione cœlesti, et gratia repleamur. Per eundem Christum Dominum nostrum. Amen.

Host, the holy bread of eternal life, and the chalice of everlasting salvation.

Upon which vouchsafe to look with a propitious and serene countenance, and to accept them, as thou wert pleased to accept the offerings of thy just servant Abel, and the sacrifice of our patriarch Abraham, and that which thy high priest Melchisedech offered to thee, a holy sacrifice, and unspotted victim.

We humbly beseech thee, O Almighty God! command these to be carried by the hands of thy holy angel to thy altar above, in the presence of thy divine majesty, that as many as shall receive the most sacred body and blood of thy Son, from this altar, may be filled with every heavenly blessing and grace; through the same Christ our Lord. Amen.

The Commemoration of the Dead.

MEMENTO etiam, Domine, famulorum famularumque tuarum N. et N. qui nos præcesserunt cum signo fidei, et dormiunt in somno pacis.

REMEMBER also, O Lord, thy servants, N. and N., who are gone before us with the sign of faith, and repose in the sleep of peace.

Here he pauses a little, to pray for particular persons.

IPSIS, Domine, et omnibus in Christo quiescentibus, locum refrigerii, lucis et pacis, ut indulgeas deprecamur. Per eundem Christum Dominum nostrum. Amen.

TO these, O Lord! and to all that rest in Christ, grant, we beseech thee, a place of refreshment, light, and peace; through the same Christ our Lord. Amen.

He strikes his breast, saying aloud the first words of the following Prayer :

NOBIS quoque peccatoribus, famulis tuis, de multitudine miserationum tuarum sperantibus, partem aliquam et societatem donare digneris cum tuis sanctis Apostolis et Martyribus : cum Joanne, Stephano, Matthia, Barnaba, Ignatio, Alexandro, Marcellino, Petro,

TO us sinners also, thy servants, hoping in the multitude of thy mercies, vouchsafe to grant some part and fellowship with thy holy Apostles and Martyrs, with John, Stephen, Matthias, Barnaby, Ignatius, Alexander, Marcellinus, Peter, Felicitas, Perpetua, Agatha, Lucy,

Felicitate, Perpetua, Agatha, Lucia, Agnete, Cæcilia, Anastasia, et omnibus Sanctis tuis; intra quorum nos consortium, non æstimator meriti, sed veniæ, quæsumus, largitor admitte. Per Christum Dominum nostrum.

Agnes, Cecilia, Anastasia, and all thy Saints; into whose company we beseech thee to admit us, not regarding our merit, but thy own gratuitous favor; through Christ our Lord.

Per quem hæc omnia, Domine, semper bona creas, sanctificas, vivificas, benedicis, et præstas nobis. Per ipsum, et cum ipso, et in ipso, est tibi Deo Patri omnipotenti, in unitate Spiritus Sancti, omnis honor et gloria.

By whom, O Lord! thou dost always create, sanctify, quicken, bless, and give us all these good things. By him, and with him, and in him, is to thee, God the Father Almighty, in the unity of the Holy Ghost, all honor and glory.

Here he says aloud:

V. PER omnia sæcula sæculorum.
R. Amen.
Oremus.
Præceptis salutaribus moniti, et divina institutione formati, audemus dicere:

Pater noster, qui es in cœlis, santificetur

V. WORLD without end.
R. Amen.
Let us pray.
Instructed by thy wholesome precepts, and following thy divine institution, we presume to say:

Our Father, who art in heaven, hallowed be

nomen tuum : adveniat regnum tuum : fiat voluntas tua, sicut in cœlo, et in terra : panem nostrum quotidianum da nobis hodie : et dimitte nobis debita nostra, sicut et nos dimittimus debitoribus nostris : et ne nos inducas in tentationem.

R. Sed libera nos a malo.

thy name ; thy kingdom come ; thy will be done on earth as it is in heaven. Give us this day our daily bread ; and forgive us our trespasses, as we forgive them that trespass against us. And lead us not into temptation.

R. But deliver us from evil.

The Priest, in a low voice, says:

Amen.

Amen.

LIBERA nos, quæsumus Domine, ab omnibus malis, præteritis, præsentibus et futuris : et intercedente beata et gloriosa semper Virgine Dei Genitrice Maria, cum beatis apostolis tuis Petro et Paulo, atque Andrea, et omnibus Sanctis, da propitius pacem in diebus nostris; ut ope misericordiæ tuæ adjuti, et a peccato simus semper liberi, et ab omni perturbatione securi.

DELIVER us, we beseech thee, O Lord! from all evils, past, present, and to come ; and by the intercession of the blessed and glorious ever Virgin Mary, Mother of God, of thy blessed Apostles Peter and Paul, and of Andrew, and all the Saints, mercifully grant peace in our days ; that by the assistance of thy mercy, we may be always free from sin, and secure from all disturbance.

Breaking the Host, he says:

PER eundem Dominum nostrum Jesum Christum, Filium tuum, qui tecum vivit et regnat in unitate Spiritus Sancti Deus. Per omnia sæcula sæculorum.

R. Amen.

V. Pax Domini sit semper vobiscum.

R. Et cum spiritu tuo.

THROUGH the same Jesus Christ our Lord, thy Son, who liveth and reigneth with thee in the unity of the Holy Ghost, one God. World without end.

R. Amen.

V. The peace of the Lord be always with you.

R. And with thy spirit.

He puts a particle of the Host into the chalice, saying:

HÆC commixtio et consecratio Corporis et Sanguinis Domini nostri Jesu Christi, fiat accipientibus nobis in vitam æternam. Amen.

MAY this mixture and consecration of the body and blood of our Lord Jesus Christ be to us that receive them effectual to eternal life. Amen.

After this, bowing down, he strikes his breast, saying aloud:

AGNUS Dei, qui tollis peccata mundi, miserere nobis.

Agnus Dei, qui tollis peccata mundi, miserere nobis.

LAMB of God, who takest away the sins of the world, have mercy on us.

Lamb of God, who takest away the sins of the world, have mercy on us.

Agnus Dei, qui tollis peccata mundi, dona nobis pacem.

Lamb of God, who takest away the sins of the world, grant us peace.

The following Prayers are said in a low voice:

DOMINE Jesu Christe, qui dixisti Apostolis tuis : Pacem relinquo vobis, pacem meam do vobis ; ne respicias peccata mea, sed fidem Ecclesiæ tuæ: eamque secundum voluntatem tuam pacificare, et coadunare digneris. Qui vivis et regnas Deus, per omnia sæcula sæculorum. Amen.

LORD Jesus Christ, who didst say to thy Apostles, I leave you peace, my peace I give you ; look not on my sins, but on the faith of thy Church; and vouchsafe to grant it that peace and union which are according to thy will : who livest and reignest God for ever and ever. Amen.

In solemn Masses, after this Prayer, the Priest gives the kiss of peace to the Deacon, saying:

V. Pax tecum.

V. Peace be with thee.

To which the Deacon answers:

R. Et cum spiritu tuo.

R. And with thy spirit.

DOMINE Jesu Christe, Fili Dei vivi, qui ex voluntate Patris, co-operante Spiritu Sancto, per mortem tuam mundum vivificasti : libera me per hoc sacrosanctum Corpus et

LORD Jesus Christ, Son of the living God, who, according to the will of the Father, and by the co-operation of the Holy Ghost, hast through thy death given life to the world ; deliver

Sanguinem tuum ab omnibus iniquitatibus meis, et universis malis; et fac me tuis semper inhaerere mandatis, et a te nunquam separari permittas : qui cum eodem Deo Patre et Spiritu Sancto vivis et regnas Deus in saecula saeculorum. Amen.

Perceptio corporis tui, Domine Jesu Christe, quod ego indignus sumere praesumo, non mihi proveniat in judicium et condemnationem : sed pro tua pietate prosit mihi ad tutamentum mentis et corporis, et ad medelam percipiendam : qui vivis et regnas cum Deo Patre, in unitate Spiritus Sancti, Deus per omnia saecula saeculorum. Amen.

me by this thy most sacred Body and Blood from all iniquities, and from all evils : make me always obedient to thy commandments, and never suffer me to be separated from thee ; who with the same God the Father and Holy Ghost livest and reignest God for ever and ever. Amen.

Let not the participation of thy body, O Lord Jesus Christ ! which, though unworthy, I presume to receive, turn to my judgment and condemnation; but, through thy mercy, let it be for me an effectual safeguard and remedy of soul and body ; who with God the Father and the Holy Ghost livest and reignest one God for ever and ever. Amen.

Taking the Host in his hands, he says :

PANEM coelestem accipiam, et nomen Domini invocabo.

I WILL take the heavenly bread, and invoke the name of the Lord.

Then striking his breast thrice, he says :

DOMINE, non sum dignus, ut intres sub tectum meum; sed tantum dic verbo, et sanabitur anima mea.

LORD, I am not worthy that thou shouldst enter under my roof; but only say the word, and my soul shall be healed.

After this, he receives the Blessed Sacrament, saying :

CORPUS Domini nostri Jesu Christi custodiat animam meam in vitam æternam. Amen.

THE body of our Lord Jesus Christ preserve my soul to life everlasting. Amen.

After a little pause, he gathers the fragments, and takes the chalice, saying :

QUID retribuam Domino pro omnibus quæ retribuit mihi? Calicem salutaris accipiam, et nomen Domini invocabo. Laudans invocabo Dominum, et ab inimicis meis salvus ero.

WHAT return shall I make to the Lord for all that he has given me? I will take the chalice of salvation, and call upon the name of the Lord. Praising I will call upon the Lord, and I shall be safe from my enemies.

Then he receives the sacred Blood, saying :

SANGUIS Domini nostri Jesu Christi custodiat animam meam in vitam æternam. Amen.

THE blood of our Lord Jesus Christ preserve my soul to life everlasting. Amen.

Whilst the Clerk pours wine into the chalice, he says:

QUOD ore sumpsimus, Domine, pura mente capiamus ; et de munere temporali, fiat nobis remedium sempiternum.

GRANT, O Lord ! that what we have taken with our mouth, we may receive with a pure mind ; and that of a temporal gift, it may prove an everlasting remedy.

Whilst he washes his fingers over the chalice with wine and water, he says:

CORPUS tuum, Domine, quod sumpsi, et sanguis quem potavi, adhæreat visceribus meis : et præsta, ut in me non remaneat scelerum macula, quem pura et sancta refecerunt sacramenta. Qui vivis et regnas in sæcula sæculorum. Amen.

MAY thy body, O Lord ! which I have received, and thy blood, which I have drunk, cleave to my bowels ; and grant that no stain of sin may remain in me, who have been nourished with thy pure and holy sacrament. Who livest and reignest, for ever and ever. Amen.

The Book is moved to the Epistle side of the Altar, where he says aloud the Communion. (For Communion and Post-Communion for Palm Sunday, see p. 95; Monday in Holy Week, p. 133; Tuesday in Holy Week, p. 155; Wednesday in Holy Week, p. 182; Holy Thursday, p. 262; Easter Sunday, p. 516; Easter Monday, p. 527; Easter Tuesday, p. 534.) Then turning to the middle of the Altar, he turns towards the people, and says:

V. DOMINUS vobiscum.

V. THE Lord be with you.

R. Et cum spiritu tuo. *R.* And with thy spirit.

He says the prayer called Post-Communion, and turning again to the people, says :

V DOMINUS vo- biscum.

V. THE Lord be with you.

R. Et cum spiritu tuo.
V. Benedicamus Domino.
R. Deo gratias.

R. And with thy spirit.
V. Let us bless the Lord.
R. Thanks be to God.

After this, bowing in the middle of the Altar, he says in a low voice :

PLACEAT tibi, sancta Trinitas, obsequium servitutis meæ : et præsta, ut sacrificium quod oculis tuæ majestatis indignus obtuli, tibi sit acceptabile, mihique, et omnibus pro quibus illud obtuli, sit, te miserante, propitiabile. Per Christum Dominum nostrum. Amen.

LET this acknowledgment of my subjection, O holy Trinity! be pleasing to thee, and grant that this sacrifice, which I, though unworthy, have offered to thy divine majesty, may be acceptable to thee, and through thy mercy be propitiatory for me, and for all those for whom it hath been offered ; through Christ our Lord. Amen.

Then the Priest having kissed the Altar, blesses the people, saying :

BENEDICAT vos omnipotens Deus, Pater, et Filius, et Spiritus Sanctus. Amen.

MAY Almighty God the Father, Son, and Holy Ghost, bless you. Amen.

And going to the Gospel side, he says:

V. DOMINUS vo-
biscum.

R. Et cum spiritu tuo.

V. Initium   sancti
Evangelii   secundum
Joannem.

R. Gloria tibi, Domi-
ne.

In principio erat Ver-
bum, et Verbum erat
apud Deum, et Deus
erat Verbum. Hoc erat
in principio apud Deum.
Omnia per ipsum facta
sunt, et sine ipso factum
est nihil, quod factum
est. In ipso vita erat, et
vita erat lux hominum,
et lux in tenebris lucet,
et tenebræ eam non
comprehenderunt. Fuit
homo missus a Deo, cui
nomen   erat   Joannes.
Hic venit in testimo-
nium, ut testimonium
perhiberet de lumine, ut
omnes crederent per il-
lum.   Non erat ille lux,
sed ut testimonium per-
hiberet de lumine. Erat
lux vera, quæ illuminat
omnem hominem veni-

V. THE Lord
with you.

R. And with thy spirit

V. The beginning of
the Holy Gospel, accord·
ing to St. John.

R. Glory be to thee.
O Lord !

In the beginning was
the Word, and the Word
was with God, and the
Word was God.   The
same was in the begin-
ning with God.   All
things were made by
him, and without him
was made nothing that
was made.   In him was
life, and the life was the
light of men ; and the
light shineth in dark-
ness, and the darkness
did not comprehend it.
There was a man sent
from God, whose name
was John.   This man
came for a witness, to
bear witness of the light,
that all men might be-
lieve through him.   He
was not the light, but
was to bear witness of

entem in hunc mundum. In mundo erat, et mundus per ipsum factus est, et mundus eum non cognovit. In propria venit, et sui eum non receperunt : quotquot autem receperunt eum, dedit eis potestatem filios Dei fieri, his, qui credunt in nomine ejus : qui non ex sanguinibus, neque ex voluntate carnis, neque ex voluntate viri, sed ex Deo nati sunt. [*Hic genuflectitur.*] Et Verbum caro factum est, et habitavit in nobis : et vidimus gloriam ejus, gloriam quasi Unigeniti a Patre, plenum gratiæ et veritatis.

the light. That was the true light, which en lighteneth every man that cometh into this world. He was in the world, and the world was made by him, and the world knew him not. He came unto his own, and his own received him not. But as many as received him, to them he has given power to be made the sons of God, to them that believe in his name; who are born not of blood, nor of the will of flesh, nor of the will of man, but of God. [*Here kneel down.*] And the Word was made flesh, and dwelt among us; and we saw his glory, the glory as of the only-begotten Son of the Father, full of grace and truth.

R. Deo gratias.

R. Thanks be to God.

PALM SUNDAY.

THE first day of this Week is called *Palm Sunday*, being appointed to honor the triumphant entry of Jesus Christ into Jerusalem, when many of the Jews cut off branches from the trees, and strewed them in the way through which he was to pass. It is in memory of this triumph that the *Palms* are blessed, distributed to the faithful, and carried by them in solemn procession. They hold them also in their hands, while the history of the Passion is read out of St. Matthew's Gospel, to signify by that ceremony that they are to partake of the triumph of Jesus Christ by the virtue of his death and passion.

In the benediction of the Palms are mentioned the branches of the Palm-tree, Olive-tree, and other trees, which are made use of in countries where these trees grow; but in our northern countries we supply that defect with any sort of green boughs, which are called Palms, from the original ceremony, and they are intended to represent to us our Saviour's victory over the prince of death, and the riches of his mercies; the Palm branches being emblems of victory, and the Olive branches of mercy.

We may also observe, that Christ enters Jerusalem on a day that answers to the tenth day of the moon; when the Jews brought to their house (Exod. xii.) the lambs that were to be killed and eaten on the Passover, in memory of their deliverance from the slavery of Egypt, and of their entrance into the Land of Promise, by their miraculous passage over the Red Sea. Hence, in the procession of this day, the opening of the door of the Church by knocking with the foot of the Cross, signifies not only the triumphant entry into Jerusalem, but also that the gates of the celestial Jerusalem were opened for us by Christ, the true Paschal Lamb, dying on the Cross, to redeem us from the slavery of sin.

THE BLESSING OF THE PALMS.

After the Sprinkling of Holy Water, the Palms are blessed as follows. The Choir sings:

HOSANNA filio David: benedictus qui venit in nomine Domini. O rex Israel! Hosanna in excelsis.

HOSANNA to the Son of David! blessed is he that comes in the name of the Lord. O king of Israel! Hosanna in the highest

Then the Priest says:

V. DOMINUS vobiscum.

R. Et cum spiritu tuo.

Oremus.

Deus, quem diligere et amare justitia est, ineffabilis gratiæ tuæ in nobis dona multiplica: et qui fecisti nos in morte Filii tui sperare quæ credimus; fac nos eodem resurgente pervenire quo tendimus: qui tecum vivit et regnat in unitate Spiritus Sancti Deus, per, etc.

V. THE Lord be with you.

R. And with thy spirit.

Let us pray.

O God! whom to love is righteousness, multiply in our hearts the gifts of thy unspeakable grace, and as by the death of thy Son thou hast made us hope for those things which we believe, grant that by his resurrection we may arrive at the happy end of our journey; who liveth and reigne'h, etc.

After this, the Subdeacon sings the following lesson:

Lectio libri Exodi, cap. xv. et xvi.

IN diebus illis: Venerunt filii Israel in

The lesson from the book of Exodus, xv. and xvi.

IN those days, the children of Israel

Elim, ubi erant duodecim fontes aquarum, et septuaginta palmæ; et castrametati sunt juxta aquas. Profectique sunt de Elim, et venit omnis multitudo filiorum Israel in desertum Sin, quod est inter Elim et Sinai; quintodecimo die mensis secundi, postquam egressi sunt de terra Ægypti. Et murmuravit omnis congregatio filiorum Israel contra Moysen et Aaron in solitudine. Dixeruntque filii Israel ad eos: Utinam mortui essemus per manum Domini in terra Ægypti, quando sedebamus super ollas carnium, et comedebamus panem in saturitate: cur eduxistis nos in desertum istud, ut occideretis omnem multitudinem fame? Dixit autem Dominus ad Moysen: Ecce, ego pluam vobis panes de cœlo; egrediatur populus, et colligat quæ sufficiunt per sin-

came to Elim, where there were twelve fountains of water and seventy palm-trees; and they encamped by the waters. And they set forward from Elim, and all the multitude of the children of Israel came into the desert of Sin, which is between Elim and Sinai, the fifteenth day of the second month after they came out of the land of Egypt. And all the congregation of the children of Israel murmured against Moses and Aaron in the wilderness. And the children of Israel said to them: Would to God we had died by the hand of the Lord in the land of Egypt, when we sat over the flesh pots and eat bread to the full; why have you brought us into this desert, that you might destroy all the multitude with famine? And the Lord said to Moses, Behold

gulos dies: ut tentem eum, utrum ambulet in lege mea, an non. Die autem sexto parent quod inferant, et sit duplum quam colligere solebant per singulos dies. Dixeruntque Moyses et Aaron ad omnes filios Israel: Vespere scietis, quod Dominus eduxerit vos de terra Ægypti: et mane videbitis gloriam Domini.

I will rain bread from heaven for you; let the people go forth and gather what is sufficient for every day, that I may prove them whether they will walk in my law, or no. But the sixth day let them provide for to bring in; and let it be double to that they were wont to gather every day. And Moses and Aaron said to the children of Israel: In the evening you shall know that the Lord hath brought you forth out of the land of Egypt; and in the morning ye shall see the glory of the Lord.

R. Collegerunt Pontifices et Pharisæi concilium, et dixerunt: Quid facimus, quia hic homo multa signa facit? Si dimittimus eum sic, omnes credunt in eum: * Et venient Romani, et tollent nostrum locum et gentem.

R. The Chief Priests and the Pharisees gathered a council and said: What do we, for this man doth many miracles? If we let him alone so, all men will believe in him; * and the Romans will come and take away our place and nation.

V. Unus autem ex illis, Caiphas nomine, cum esset pontifex anni illius, prophetavit, dicens: Expedit vobis, ut unus moriatur homo pro populo, et non tota gens pereat. Ab illo ergo die cogitaverunt interficere eum, dicentes: * Et venient, etc.

V. But of them, named Caiphas, being the high priest that year, said to them: It is expedient for you that one man die for the people, and that the whole nation perish not. From that day therefore they devised to put him to death, saying: * And the Romans, etc.

Aliud R. In monte Oliveti oravit ad Patrem: Pater, si fieri potest, transeat a me calix iste. * Spiritus quidem promptus est, caro autem infirma: fiat voluntas tua.

Another R. On Mount Olivet he prayed to his Father: O Father! if it is possible, let this chalice pass from me. * The spirit indeed is willing, but the flesh is weak; thy will be done.

V. Vigilate, et orate, ut non intretis in tentationem. * Spiritus quidem, etc.

V. Watch ye and pray, that ye enter not into temptation. * The spirit, etc.

Then the Deacon sings the following Gospel, with the usual ceremonies:

Sequentia Sancti Evangelii, secundum Matthæum, cap. xxi. 1–9.

A continuation of the Holy Gospel, according to St. Matthew, xxi. 1–9.

IN illo tempore: cum appropinquasset Je-

AT that time, when Jesus drew nigh

ius Jerosolymis, et venisset Bethphage ad montem Oliveti ; tunc misit duos discipulos suos, dicens eis : Ite in castellum, quod contra vos est, et statim invenietis asinam alligatam, et pullum cum ea : solvite, et adducite mihi ; et si quis vobis aliquid dixerit, dicite, quia Dominus his opus habet, et confestim dimittet eos. Hoc autem totum factum est, ut adimpleretur, quod dictum est per prophetam dicentem : Dicite filiæ Sion : ecce, rex tuus venit tibi mansuetus, sedens super asinam, et pullum filium subjugalis. Euntes autem discipuli fecerunt, sicut præcepit illis Jesus. Et adduxerunt asinam et pullum ; et imposuerunt super eos vestimenta sua, et eum desuper sedere fecerunt. Plurima autem turba straverunt vestimenta sua in via : alii autem

to Jerusalem, and was come to Bethphage, unto Mount Olivet ; then he sent two disciples, saying to them : Go ye into the village that is over against you, and immediately ye will find an ass tied, and a colt with her ; loose them, and bring them to me ; and if any man shall say anything to you, say ye that the Lord hath need of them, and forthwith he will let them go. Now all this was done, that the word might be fulfilled, which was spoken by the prophet, saying : Tell ye the daughter of Sion, behold thy king cometh to thee, meek, and sitting upon an ass, and a colt, the foal of her that is used to the yoke. And the disciples going, did as Jesus commanded them. And they brought the ass and the colt, and laid their garments upon them, and made him sit

cædebant ramos de arboribus, et sternebant in via; turbæ autem, quæ præcedebant, et quæ sequebantur, clamabant, dicentes : Hosanna filio David : benedictus, qui venit in nomine Domini.

thereon. And a very great multitude spread their garments in the way; and others cut down boughs from the trees, and strewed them in the way; and the multitude that went before and that followed, cried, saying : Hosanna to the Son of David ! blessed is he that cometh in the name of the Lord.

The Blessing of the Palms. The Priest, standing at the corner of the Epistle, says :

V. DOMINUS vobiscum.

R. Et cum spiritu tuo.

Oremus.

Auge fidem in te sperantium, Deus, et supplicum preces clementer exaudi: veniat super nos multiplex misericordia tua : benedicantur et hi palmites palmarum, seu olivarum : et sicut in figura Ecclesiæ multiplicasti Noe egredientem de arca, et Moysen exeuntem de Ægypto cum filiis Israel ; ita nos portantes palmas et ramos

V. THE Lord be with you.

R. And with thy spirit.

Let us pray.

Increase, O God ! the faith of them that hope in thee, and mercifully hear the prayers of thy suppliants ; let thy manifold mercy come upon us, and let these branches of palm-trees, or olive-trees, be blessed ; and, as in a figure of the Church, thou didst multiply, Noah going out of the Ark, and Moses going out of Egypt with

olivarum, bonis actibus occurramus obviam Christo, et per ipsum in gaudium introeamus æternum: qui tecum vivit et regnat in unitate Spiritus Sancti Deus, per omnia sæcula sæculorum.

R. Amen.

V. Dominus vobiscum.

R. Et cum spiritu tuo.

V. Sursum corda.

R. Habemus ad Dominum.

V. Gratias agamus Domino Deo nostro.

R. Dignum et justum est.

Vere dignum et justum est, æquum et salutare, nos tibi semper et ubique gratias agere; Domine sancte, Pater omnipotens, æterne Deus: qui gloriaris in consilio Sanctorum tuorum. Tibi enim serviunt creaturæ tuæ, quia te solum auctorem et Deum cognoscunt: et omnis fac-

the children of Israel; so let us, carrying palms and branches of olive-trees, go and meet Christ with good works, and enter through him into eternal joy: who with thee and the Holy Ghost liveth and reigneth, one God, world without end.

R. Amen.

V. The Lord be with you.

R. And with thy spirit.

V. Lift up your hearts.

R. We have them lifted up to the Lord.

V. Let us give thanks to the Lord our God.

R. It is meet and just.

It is truly meet and just, right and profitable to salvation, that we should at all times, and in all places, give thee thanks, O holy Lord, almighty Father, and eternal God! who art glorious in the assembly of thy Saints. For thy creatures serve thee, because they acknowledge

tura tua te collaudat, et benedicunt te sancti tui: quia illud magnum, Unigeniti tui nomen coram regibus et potestatibus hujus sæculi, libera voce confitentur. Cui assistunt angeli et archangeli, throni et dominationes; cumque omni militia cœlestis exercitus hymnum gloriæ tuæ concinunt, sine fine dicentes:

thee for their only Creator and God. The whole creation praiseth thee, and thy Saints bless thee; because they confess with freedom before the kings and powers of this world, the great name of thy only begotten Son: before whom the angels and archangels, the thrones and dominations stand, and, with all the troops of the heavenly host, sing the hymn of thy glory, saying without ceasing:

The Choir sings:

SANCTUS, sanctus, sanctus Dominus Deus Sabaoth. Pleni sunt cœli et terra gloria tua. Hosanna in excelsis. Benedictus qui venit in nomine Domini: Hosanna in excelsis.

HOLY, holy, holy is the Lord God of hosts! The heavens and the earth are full of thy glory. Hosanna in the highest! Blessed is he that cometh in the name of the Lord: Hosanna in the highest!

Then the Priest says:

V. DOMINUS vobiscum.
R. Et cum spiritu tuo.

V. THE Lord be with you.
R. And with thy spirit

Oremus. Let us pray.

Petimus, Domine sancte, Pater omnipotens, æterne Deus, ut hanc creaturam olivæ, quam ex ligni materia prodire jussisti, quamque columba rediens ad arcam proprio pertulit ore, benedicere et sanctificare digneris: ut quicumque ex ea receperint, accipiant sibi protectionem animæ et corporis, fiatque, Domine, nostræ salutis remedium, et tuæ gratiæ sacramentum. Per Dominum, etc.

We beseech thee, O holy Lord, almighty Father, eternal God! that thou wouldst be pleased to bless and sanctify these branches which thou hast caused to spring from the olive-tree, and which the dove, returning to the ark, brought in its bill; that whoever receiveth it may find protection of soul and body; and that it may prove, O Lord! the remedy of our salvation, and a sacred sign of thy grace; through our Lord, etc.

R. Amen.

R. Amen.

Oremus. Let us pray.

Deus, qui dispersa congregas, et congregata conservas; qui populis obviam Jesu ramos portantibus benedixisti: benedic etiam hos ramos palmæ et olivæ, quos tui famuli ad honorem no-

O God! who gatherest what is dispersed and preservest what is gathered: who didst bless the people that carried boughs to meet Jesus; bless also these branches of the palm-tree and

minis tui fideliter susci- olive-tree, which thy ser-
piunt; ut in quemcum- vants take with faith, for
que locum introducti the honor of thy name,
fuerint, tuam benedic- that into whatever place
tionem habitatores loci they may be carried, the
illius consequantur: et inhabitants of that place
omni adversitate effu- may obtain thy blessing;
gata, dextera tua prote- and thy right hand pre-
gat quos redemit Jesus serve from all adversity,
Christus, Filius tuus, Do- and protect those that
minus noster: qui tecum have been redeemed by
vivit et regnat, etc. our Lord Jesus Christ,
thy Son, who liveth and
reigneth, etc.

Oremus.   Let us pray.

Deus, qui miro dispo- O God! who by the
sitionis ordine, ex rebus wonderful order of thy
etiam insensibilibus dis- providence wouldst even
pensationem nostræ sa- in insensible things show
lutis ostendere voluisti: us the manner of our
da quæsumus, ut devota salvation, grant, we be-
tuorum corda fidelium seech thee, that the de-
salubriter intelligant, vout hearts of thy faith-
quid mystice designet ful may savingly un-
in facto, quod hodie derstand the mystical
cœlesti lumine efflata, meaning of that cere-
Redemptori obviam pro- mony, which the multi-
cedens, palmarum atque tude performed, when
olivarum ramos vestigiis by direction from hea-
ejus turba substravit. ven, going this day to
Palmarum igitur rami meet our Redeemer, they

de mortis principe triumphos expectant: surculi vero olivarum spiritualem unctionem advenisse quodammodo clamant. Intellexit enim jam tunc illa hominum beata multitudo præfigurari, quia Redemptor noster humanis condolens miseriis, pro totius mundi vita cum mortis principe esset pugnaturus, ac moriendo triumphaturus. Et ideo talia obsequens administravit, quæ in illo et triumphos victoriæ, et misericordiæ pinguedinem declararent. Quod nos quoque plena fide, et factum et significatum retinentes, te Domine sancte, Pater omnipotens, æterne Deus, per eundem Dominum nostrum Jesum Christum suppliciter exoramus ; ut in ipso, atque per ipsum, cujus nos membra fieri voluisti, de mortis imperio victoriam reportantes, ipsius gloriosæ

strewed under his feet palm and olive branches —the palms represent his triumph over the prince of death; and the olive-branches proclaim, in some manner, the spreading of a spiritual unction. For that pious multitude knew even then what was signified by them ; that our Redeemer, compassionating the miseries of mankind, was to combat for the life of the whole world with the prince of death, and to triumph over him by his own death. Hence it was they made use of such emblems as might declare both the triumph of his victory, and the riches of his mercy. We, also, with a firm faith retaining both the ceremony and its signification, humbly beseech thee, O holy Lord, almighty Father, eternal God ! through the same Lord, Jesus Christ; that

resurrectionis participes esse mereamur : qui tecum vivit et regnat, etc.

we, whom thou hast made his members, gaining by him, and in him, a victory over the empire of death, may deserve to be partakers of his glorious resurrection ; who liveth and reigneth with thee, etc.

Oremus,

Let us pray.

Deus, qui per olivæ ramum pacem terris columbam nuntiare jussisti: præsta, quæsumus, ut hos olivæ, cæterarumque arborum ramos, cœlesti benedictione sanctifices, ut cuncto populo tuo proficiant ad salutem. Per Christum Dominum nostrum.

O God ! who by an olive branch didst command the dove to proclaim peace to the world; grant us, we beseech thee, thy grace to sanctify by thy heavenly benediction these branches of the olive and other trees ; that they may be serviceable to all thy people for their salvation ; through Christ our Lord.

R. Amen.

R. Amen.

Oremus.

Let us pray.

Benedic, quæsumus Domine, hos palmarum seu olivarum ramos : et præsta, ut quod populus tuus in tui venerationem hodierna die corporaliter agit, hoc spiritualiter

Bless, O Lord ! we beseech thee, these branches of the palm-tree or olive-tree ; and grant that what thy people this day corporally perform for the honor of

summa devotione perficiat, de hoste victoriam reportando, et opus misericordiæ summopere diligendo. Per Dominum nostrum, etc.

thy name, they may with the greatest devotion spiritually accomplish, by gaining a victory over their enemy, and ardently loving works of mercy; through our Lord, etc.

The Priest sprinkles the Palms with Holy Water, and fumes them with Incense, and says:

V. DOMINUS vobiscum.
R. Et cum spiritu tuo.
Oremus.

Deus, qui Filium tuum Jesum Christum, Dominum nostrum, pro salute nostra in hunc mundum misisti, ut se humiliaret ad nos, et nos revocaret ad te: cui etiam, dum Jerusalem veniret, ut adimpleret Scripturas, credentium populorum turba, fidelissima devotione vestimenta sua cum ramis palmarum in via sternebant: præsta, quæsumus, ut illi fidei viam præparemus, de qua remoto lapide offensionis et petra scandali,

V. THE Lord be with you.
R. And with thy spirit.
Let us pray.

O God! who for our salvation didst send into this world thy Son, Jesus Christ, our Lord, that humbling himself to our condition he might recall us to thee: who, also, as he was going to Jerusalem to fulfil the Scriptures, was met by a multitude of faithful people, with zealous devotion, spreading their garments together with branches of palm-trees in his path; grant, we beseech thee, that we may prepare him the

frondeant apud te opera nostra justitiæ ramis; ut ejus vestigia sequi mereamur: qui tecum vivit et regnat, etc.

way of faith from which the stone of offence and the rock of scandal being removed, our actions may flourish with branches of justice, so that we may be able to follow his steps : who liveth and reigneth, etc.

The Palms being blessed, they are distributed by the Priest to the clergy, and to the laity. The Palms are received kneeling. The receiver kisses the Palm and the Priest's hand. During the distribution the following Antiphons are sung:

Ant. PUERI Hebræorum portantes ramos olivarum obviaverunt Domino, clamantes et dicentes: Hosanna in excelsis.

Ant. THE Hebrew children carrying olive-branches met our Lord, crying out, and saying: Hosanna in the highest.

Alia Ant. Pueri Hebræorum vestimenta prosternebant in via, et clamabant dicentes : Hosanna filio David : benedictus qui venit in nomine Domini.

Another Ant. The Hebrew children spread their garments in the way, and cried out, saying: Hosanna to the Son of David ! blessed is he that cometh in the name of the Lord.

Then the Priest says:

V. DOMINUS vobiscum.
R. Et cum spiritu tuo.

V. THE Lord be with you.
R. And with thy spirit.

Oremus.   Let us pray.

Omnipotens sempiter- ne Deus, qui Dominum nostrum Jesum Chris- tum super pullum asinæ sedere fecisti, et turbas populorum vestimenta, vel ramos arborum in via sternere, et Hosanna decantare in laudem ip- sius docuisti : da, quæ- sumus, ut illorum inno- centiam imitari possi- mus, et eorum meritum consequi mereamur. Per eundem Christum Do- minum nostrum.
R. Amen.

Omnipotent and eter. nal God ! who wouldst have our Lord, Jesus Christ, ride on the colt of an ass, and didst in- spire crowds of people to spread their garments, or the branches of trees, in his way, and to sing Hosanna in his praise ; grant, we beseech thee, that we may imitate their innocence, and deserve to partake of their merit; through the same Christ our Lord.
R. Amen.

Next follows the procession. First the Priest puts incense in the censer, and the Deacon, turning to the people, says :

V. **P**ROCEDAMUS in pace.
R. In nomine Christi. Amen.

V. **L**ET us go in peace.
R. In the name of Christ. Amen.

The Thurifer walks first with the censer smoking; then the Sub- Deacon, with the Cross, between two Acolytes with their candles burning; next the Clergy in order ; and last of all the Priest with the Deacon at his left, all bearing Palms in their hands During the procession, the following Anthems are sung :

Ant. **C**UM appropin- quaret Do-

Ant. **W**HEN the Lord drew

minus Jerosolymam, misit duos ex discipulis suis, dicens : Ite in castellum quod contra vos est, et invenietis pullum asinæ alligatum, super quem nullus hominum sedit : solvite, et adducite mihi. Si quis vos interrogaverit, dicite : Opus Domino est. Solventes adduxerunt ad Jesum ; et imposuerunt illi vestimenta sua, et sedit super eum : alii expandebant vestimenta sua in via : alii ramos de arboribus sternebant : et qui sequebantur, clamabant : Hosanna, benedictus qui venit in nomine Domini : benedictum regnum patris nostri David : Hosanna in excelsis : miserere nobis, Fili David.

Alia Ant. Cum audis-

nigh to Jerusalem, he sent two of his disciples, saying · Go ye into the village that is over against you, and you shall find the colt of an ass tied, on which no man hath ever sat; loose him and bring him to me. If any man shall ask you : Why do you loose him? you shall say thus unto him : Because the Lord hath need of his service. They loosing him brought him to Jesus, and laid their garments on him, and he seated himself upon him. Some spread their garments in the way; others strewed branches, cut from trees ; and they that followed cried out : Hosanna ! blessed is he that comes in the name of our Lord ! blessed is the kingdom of our father David ! Hosanna in the highest ! have mercy on us, O Son of David !

Another Ant. Wher

set populus, quia Jesus venit Jerosolymam, acceperunt ramos palmarum, et exierunt ei obviam, et clamabant pueri, dicentes : Hic est qui venturus est in salutem populi. Hic est salus nostra, et redemptio Israel. Quantus est iste, cui throni et dominationes occurrunt ? Noli timere, filia Sion : ecce Rex tuus venit tibi sedens super pullum asinæ, sicut scriptum est. Salve, Rex, fabricator mundi, qui venisti redimere nos.

the people heard that Jesus was coming to Jerusalem, they took palm-branches and went out to meet him ; and the children cried out, saying : This is he that is to come for the salvation of the people. He is our salvation, and the redemption of Israel. How great is he, whom the thrones and dominations go out to meet ? Fear not, O daughter of Sion ! behold thy King cometh to thee sitting on an ass's colt ; as it is written. Hail, O King, the Creator of the world, who art come to redeem us !

Alia Ant. Ante sex dies solemnis paschæ, quando venit Dominus in civitatem Jerosolyman, occurrerunt ei pueri; et in manibus portabant ramos palmarum; et clamabant voce magna, dicentes : Hosanna in excelsis: benedictus qui venisti in multitudine

Another Ant. Six days before the solemnity of the passover, when the Lord was coming into the city of Jerusalem, the children met him, and carried palm-branches in their hands ; and they cried with a loud voice, saying, Hosanna in the highest ! blessed art

misericordiæ tuæ : Hosanna in excelsis.

thou, who art come in the multitude of thy mercy ! Hosanna in the highest !

Alia Ant. Occurrunt turbæ cum floribus et palmis Redemptori obviam, et victori triumphans digna dant obsequia : Filium Dei ore gentes prædicant ; et in laudem Christi voces tonant per nubila ; Hosanna in excelsis.

Another Ant. The multitude go out to meet the Redeemer with flowers and palms, and pay the homage due to a triumphant conqueror : nations proclaim the Son of God ; and their voices rend the skies in the praise of Christ : Hosanna in the highest !

Alia Ant. Cum angelis et pueris fideles inveniamur, triumphatori mortis clamantes : Hosanna in excelsis.

Another Ant. Let us faithfully join the angels and children, singing to the conqueror of death : Hosanna in the highest !

Alia Ant. Turba multa quæ convenerat ad diem festum, clamabat Domino : Benedictus qui venit in nomine Domini : Hosanna in excelsis.

Another Ant. A great multitude, which had assembled for the festival, cried out to the Lord : Blessed is he that cometh in the name of the Lord ! Hosanna in the highest !

At the return of the procession, two or four singers go into the Church, and, shutting the door, stand with their faces towards the procession, singing the two first verses, Gloria, laus, *which are repeated by the Priest, and the others without the Church. Then. they that are within sing the other following verses, and they that are without, at every second verse, answer* Gloria, laus, *etc.*

GLORIA. laus, et honor tibi sit, rex Christe, redemptor :
Cui puerile decus promp-sit Hosanna pium.
R. Gloria, etc.
Israel es tu rex, Davidis et inclita proles :
Nomine qui in Domini, rex, benedicte, venis.

R. Gloria, etc.
Cœtus in excelsis te lau-dat cœlicus omnis,
Et mortalis homo, et cuncta creata simul.
R. Gloria, etc.
Plebs Hebræa tibi cum palmis obvia venit .

Cum prece, voto, hym-nis adsumus ecce tibi.
R. Gloria, etc.
Hi tibi passuro solvebant munia laudis :

TO thee, O Christ ! be glory, praises loud :
To thee, Hosanna, cried the Jewish crowd.
R. To thee, etc.
We Israel's monarch, David's Son proclaim :
Thou com'st, blest king! in God's most holy name.
R. To thee, etc.
Angels and men, in one harmonious choir,
To sing thy everlasting praise conspire.
R. To thee, etc.
Thee Israel's children met with conquering palms :
To thee our vows we pay in loudest psalms.
R. To thee, etc.
For thee, on earth, with boughs they strewed the ways :

Nos tibi regnanti pangi-
nius ecce melos.
  R. Gloria, etc.
Hi placuere tibi : pla-
ceat devotio nostra,
Rex bene, rex clemens,
cui bona cuncta pla-
cent.
  R Gloria, etc.

To thee, in heaven, we
sing melodious praise.
  R. To thee, etc.
Accept this tribute which
to thee we bring,
As thou didst theirs, O
good and gracious
king !
  R. To thee, etc.

*After this, the Subdeacon knocks at the door with the foot of the
  Cross, which being opened, the procession goes into the Church
  singing :*

R. INGREDIENTE
Domino in sanc-
tam civitatem, Hebræ-
orum pueri resurrec-
tionem vitæ pronuntian-
tes : * cum ramis palma-
rum Hosanna clamabant
in excelsis.
  V. Cum audisset po-
pulus, quod Jesus veniret
Jerosolymam, exierunt
obviam ei : * cum ramis,
etc.

R. AS our Lord en-
tered the holy
city, the Hebrew chil-
dren declaring the re-
surrection of life : * with
palm-branches, cried
out, Hosanna in the
highest !
  V. When the people
heard that Jesus was
coming to Jerusalem,
they went out to meet
him, and * with palm-
branches, etc.

*At Mass, all hold the Palms in their hands during the reading or
tinging of the Passion.*

THE MASS.

The Priest begins the Mass at the foot of the Altar, as at page 13, to Peccata mea, *p.* 17.

THE INTROIT.

DOMINE, ne longe facias auxilium tuum a me : ad defensionem meam aspice : libera me de ore leonis, et a cornibus unicornium humilitatem meam.

Psal. Deus, Deus meus, respice in me, quare me dereliquisti? longe a salute mea verba delictorum meorum. Domine, ne longe, etc.

O LORD ! remove not thy help to a distance from me; look towards my defence ; save me from the lion's mouth, and my lowness from the horns of the unicorns.

The Psalm. O God, my God ! look on me, why hast thou forsaken me ? Far from my salvation are the words of my sins. O Lord ! remove not, etc.

Kyrie, Gloria, Dominus vobiscum, *pp.* 17-19.

THE COLLECT.

Oremus.

Let us pray.

OMNIPOTENS sempiterne Deus, qui humano generi ad imitandum humilitatis exemplum. Salvatorem nostrum carnem sumere.

ALMIGHTY and everlasting God ! who didst vouchsafe to send thy Son, our Saviour, to take upon him our flesh, and to suffer

et crucem subire fecisti : concede propitius, ut et patientiæ ipsius habere documenta, et resurrectionis consortia mereamur. Per eundem, etc.

death upon the cross, to give mankind an example of humility ; mercifully grant that we may both follow the example of his patience, and be made partakers of his resurrection ; through the same Jesus Christ our Lord, etc.

THE EPISTLE.

Lectio Epistolæ beati Pauli Apostoli ad Philippenses, cap. ii. 5–11.

The Lesson from the Epistle of St. Paul, the Apostle, to the Philippians, chap. ii. 5–11.

FRATRES, hoc enim sentite in vobis, quod et in Christo Jesu : qui cum in forma Dei esset, non rapinam arbitratus est esse se æqualem Deo; sed semetipsum exinanivit, formam servi accipiens, in similitudinem hominum factus, et habitu inventus ut homo. Humiliavit semetipsum, factus obediens usque ad mortem, mortem autem crucis. Propter quod et

BRETHREN, let this mind be in you, which was also in Christ Jesus; who being in the form of God, thought it no robbery himself to be equal to God ; but debased himself, taking the form of a servant, being made to the likeness of men, and in shape found as a man. He humbled himself, becoming obedient unto death, even the death of the cross.

Deus exaltavit illum; et donavit illi nomen, quod est super omne nomen [*hic genuflectitur*]: ut in nomine Jesu omne genu flectatur cœlestium, terrestrium, et infernorum; et omnis lingua confiteatur, quia Dominus Jesus Christus in gloria est Dei Patris.

Wherefore, God also hath exalted him, and hath given him a name, which is above every name [*here kneel down*]: that in the name of Jesus every knee should bow, of those that are in heaven, on earth, and under the earth ; and that every tongue should confess that the Lord, Jesus Christ, is in the glory of God the Father.

THE GRADUAL.

TENUISTI manum dexteram meam, et in voluntate tua deduxisti me, et cum gloria assumpsisti me.

THOU hast held me by my right hand; and by thy will thou hast conducted me; and with glory thou hast received me.

V. Quam bonus Israel Deus rectis corde ! mei autem pene moti sunt pedes, pene effusi sunt gressus mei : quia zelavi in peccatoribus, pacem peccatorum videns.

V. How good is God to Israel, to them that are of a right heart ! but my feet were almost moved, my steps had well-nigh slipped, because I had a zeal on occasion of the wicked, seeing the prosperity of sinners.

THE TRACT.

DEUS, Deus meus, respice in me: quare me dereliquisti?

V. Longe a salute mea verba delictorum meo-rum.

V. Deus meus, clama-bo per diem, nec exau-dies; in nocte, et non ad insipientiam mihi.

V. Tu autem in sanc-to habitas, laus Israel.

V. In te speraverunt patres nostri: sperave-runt, et liberasti eos.

V. Ad te clamaverunt, et salvi facti sunt: in te speraverunt, et non sunt confusi.

V. Ego autem sum vermis, et non homo: opprobrium hominum, et abjectio plebis.

V. Omnes qui vide-bant me, aspernabantur me: locuti sunt labiis, et moverunt cuput.

V. Speravit in Domi-

O GOD, my God! look on me: why hast thou forsaken me?

V. Far from my sal-vation are the words of my sins.

V. O my God! I shall cry by day, and thou wilt not hear; and by night, and it shall not be reputed as folly in me.

V. But thou dwellest in the holy place, the praise of Israel.

V. In thee have our fathers hoped; they have hoped, and thou hast de-livered them.

V. They cried to thee, and they were saved; they trusted in thee, and were not confounded.

V. But I am a worm, and no man; the re-proach of men, and the outcast of the people.

V. All they that saw me, have laughed me to scorn; they have spoken with the lips, and wagged the head.

V. He hoped in the

no, eripiat eum : salvum faciat eum, quoniam vult eum.

Lord, let him deliver him ; let him save him, seeing he delighteth in him.

V. Ipsi vero consideraverunt, et conspexerunt me : diviserunt sibi vestimenta mea, et super vestem meam miserunt sortem.

V. And they have looked and stared upon me : they parted my garments amongst them, and upon my vesture they cast lots.

V. Libera me de ore leonis, et a cornibus unicornium humilitatem meam.

V. Save me from the lion's mouth ; and my lowness from the horns of the unicorns.

V. Qui timetis Dominum, laudate eum : universum semen Jacob magnificate eum.

V. Ye that fear the Lord, praise him : all ye the seed of Jacob, glorify him.

V. Annuntiabitur Domino generatio ventura, et annuntiabunt cœli justitiam ejus.

V. There shall be declared to the Lord, a generation to come : and the heavens shall show forth his justice.

V. Populo qui nascetur, quem fecit Dominus.

V. To a people that shall be born, which the Lord hath made.

Passio Domini nostri Jesu Christi, secundum Matthæum, cap. xxvi., xxvii.

The passion of our Lord Jesus Christ, according to St. Matthew, chap. xxvi., xxvii.

IN illo tempore: Dixit Jesus discipulis

AT that time, Jesus said to his disci-

suis: Scitis, quia post
biduum pascha fiet, et
Filius hominis tradetur,
ut crucifigatur.   Tunc
congregati sunt princi-
pes sacerdotum, et seni-
ores populi in atrium
principis sacerdotum,
qui dicebatur Caiphas:
et concilium fecerunt, ut
Jesum dolo tenerent, et
occiderent.   Dicebant
autem: Non in die festo,
ne forte tumultus fieret
in populo.   Cum autem
esset Jesus in Bethania
in domo Simonis leprosi,
accessit ad eum mulier
habens alabastrum un-
guenti pretiosi, et effudit
super caput ipsius re-
cumbentis.   Videntes
autem discipuli, indig-
nati sunt, dicentes: Ut
quid perditio hæc? po-
tuit enim istud venum-
dari multo, et dari pau-
peribus.   Sciens autem
Iesus, ait illis: Quid
molesti estis huic mu-
lieri? opus enim bonum
operata est in me.   Nam
semper pauperes habetis

ples   You know that
after two days shall be
the pasch, and the Son
of Man shall be deliv-
ered up to be crucified.
Then were gathered to-
gether the chief priests,
and the ancients of the
people, into the palace
of the high priest, who
was called Caiphas. And
they consulted together,
that, by subtilty, they
might apprehend Jesus
and put him to death.
But they said: Not on
the festival day, lest
there should be a tumult
among the people. And
when Jesus was in Be-
thania, in the house of
Simon the leper, there
came to him a woman
having an alabaster-box
of precious ointment,
and poured it on his
head, as he was at table
And the disciples seeing
it, had indignation, say-
ing: To what purpose
is this waste? For this
might have been sold for
much, and given to the

vobiscum, me autem non semper habetis. Mittens enim hæc unguentum hoc in corpus meum, ad sepeliendum me fecit. Amen dico vobis, ubicumque prædicatum fuerit hoc evangelium in toto mundo, dicetur et quod hæc fecit in memoriam ejus. Tunc abiit unus de duodecim, qui dicebatur Judas Iscariotes, ad principes sacerdotum, et ait illis: Quid vultis mihi dare, et ego vobis eum tradam? At illi constituerunt ei triginta argenteos. Et exinde quærebat opportunitatem ut eum traderet.

poor. And Jesus knowing it, said to them: Why do you trouble this woman? for she hath wrought a good work upon me. For the poor you have always with you: but me you have not always. For she, in pouring this ointment upon my body, hath done it for my burial. Amen, I say to you, wheresoever this gospel shall be preached in the whole world, that also which she hath done shall be told for a memory of her. Then went one of the twelve, who was called Judas Iscariot, to the chief priests, and said to them: What will you give me, and I will deliver him unto you? But they appointed for him thirty pieces of silver. And from thenceforth he sought opportunity to betray him.

Prima autem die Azymorum, accesserunt dis-

And on the first day of the Azymes, the disci-

cipuli ad Jesum, dicentes : Ubi vis paremus tibi comedere pascha? At Jesus dixit : Ite in civitatem ad quemdam, et dicite ei : Magister dicit : Tempus meum prope est, apud te facio pascha cum discipulis meis. Et fecerunt discipuli, sicut constituit illis Jesus, et paraverunt pascha. Vespere autem facto, discumbebat cum duodecim discipulis suis. Et edentibus illis, dixit: Amen dico vobis, quia unus vestrum me traditurus est. Et contristati valde, cœperunt singuli dicere : Numquid ego sum, Domine? At ipse respondens, ait : Qui intingit mecum manum in paropside, hic me tradet. Filius quidem hominis vadit, sicut scriptum est de illo : væ autem homini illi, per quem Filius hominis tradetur; bonum erat ei, si natus non fuisset homo ille. Respondens au-

ples came to Jesus, saying : Where wilt thou that we prepare for thee to eat the pasch? But Jesus said : Go ye into the city to a certain man, and say to him : The master saith, My time is near at hand; I will keep the pasch at thy house with my disciples. And the disciples did as Jesus had appointed them, and they prepared the pasch. Now when it was evening, he sat down with his twelve disciples. And whilst they were eating, he said : Amen, I say to you, that one of you is about to betray me. And they being very much troubled, began every one to say: Is it I, Lord? But he answering, said : He that dippeth his hand with me in the dish, the same shall betray me. The Son of Man indeed goeth as it is written of him; but woe to that man by whom the Son of Man shall be betrayed : it

tem Judas, qui tradidit eum, dixit : Numquid ego sum, Rabbi ? Ait illi : Tu dixisti. Cœnantibus autem eis, accepit Jesum panem, et benedixit, ac fregit, deditque discipulis suis, et ait : Accipite, et comedite : hoc est corpus meum. Et accipiens calicem, gratias egit, et dedit illis, dicens : Bibite ex hoc omnes. Hic est enim sanguis meus novi testamenti, qui pro multis effundetur in remissionem peccatorum. Dico autem vobis : non bibam amodo de hoc genimine vitis, usque in diem illum, cum illud bibam vobiscum novum in regno Patris mei. Et hymno dicto, exierunt in montem Oliveti.

were better for that man if he had not been born. And Judas that betrayed him, answering, said : Is it I, Rabbi ? He said to him : Thou hast said it. And whilst they were at supper, Jesus took bread, and blessed and broke, and gave to his disciples, and said : Take ye and eat : this is my body. And taking the chalice he gave thanks : and gave to them, saying : Drink ye all of this. For this is my blood of the New Testament, which shall be shed for many for the remission of sins. And I say to you, I will not drink from henceforth of the fruit of the vine, until that day when I shall drink it new with you in the kingdom of my Father. And when they had sung a hymn, they went out to Mount Olivet.

Tunc dicit illis Jesus : Omnes vos scandalum

Then Jesus saith to them : All you shall be

patiemini in me, in ista nocte. Scriptum est enim : Percutiam pastorem, et dispergentur oves gregis. Postquam autem resurrexero, præcedam vos in Galilæam. Respondens autem Petrus, ait illi : Etsi omnes scandalizati fuerint in te, ego nunquam scandalizabor. Ait illi Jesus: Amen dico tibi, quia in hac nocte, antequam gallus cantet, ter me negabis. Ait illi Petrus : Etiamsi opportuerit me mori tecum, non te negabo. Similiter et omnes discipuli dixerunt. Tunc venit Jesus cum illis in villam, quæ dicitur Gethsemani, et dixit discipulis suis : Sedete hic, donec vadam illuc, et orem. Et assumpto Petro, et duobus filiis Zebedæi, cœpit contristari et mœstus esse. Tunc ait illis : Tristis est anima mea usque ad mortem : sustinete hic, et vigila'e mecum. Et

scandalized in me this night. For it is written. I will strike the shepherd, and the sheep of the flock shall be dispersed. But after I shall be risen again, I will go before you into Galilee. And Peter answering, said to him : Though all shall be scandalized in thee, I will never be scandalized. Jesus said to him : Amen I say to thee, that in this night, before the cock crow, thou wilt deny me thrice. Peter saith to him : Though I should die with thee, I will not deny thee. And in like manner said all the disciples. Then Jesus came with them to a country place which is called Gethsemani, and he said to his disciples : Sit you here, till I go yonder and pray. And taking with him Peter and the two sons of Zebedee, he began to grow sorrowful and to be sad. Then he saith

progressus pusillum, pro-
cidit in faciem suam,
orans et dicens : Pater
mi, si possibile est, transeat a me calix iste : verumtamen non sicut ego
volo, sed sicut tu. Et
venit ad discipulos suos,
et invenit eos dormien-
tes, et dicit Petro : Sic
non potuistis una hora
vigilare mecum ? Vigi-
late, et orate ut non in-
tretis in tentationem.
Spiritus quidem promp-
tus est, caro autem in-
firma. Iterum secundo
abiit, et oravit, dicens :
Pater mi, si non potest
hic calix transire nisi bibam illum, fiat voluntas
tua. Et venit iterum,
et invenit eos dormien-
tes : erant enim oculi
eorum gravati. Et re-
lictis illis, iterum abiit,
et oravit tertio, eundem
sermonem dicens. Tunc
venit ad discipulos suos,
et dicit illis : Dormite
jam, et requiescite : ecce
appropinquavit hora, et
Filius hominis tradetur

to them : My soul is sor-
rowful even unto death;
stay you here, and watch
with me. And going a
little further he fell upon
his face, praying, and
saying : O my Father !
if it is possible, let this
chalice pass from me.
Nevertheless not as I
will but as thou wilt.
And he cometh to his
disciples, and findeth
them asleep; and he
saith to Peter : What !
could you not watch one
hour with me ? Watch
ye, and pray that ye en-
ter not into temptation.
The spirit indeed is
willing, but the flesh is
weak. Again he went
the second time, and
prayed, saying : O my
Father ! if this chalice
cannot pass away except
I drink it, thy will be
done. And he cometh
again, and findeth them
asleep; for their eyes
were heavy. And leav-
ing them, he went away
again, and he prayed the

in manus peccatorum. Surgite, eamus : ecce appropinquavit qui me tradet.

third time, saying the same words. Then he cometh to his disciples, and saith to them : Sleep on now, and take your rest; behold the hour is at hand, and the Son of Man shall be betrayed into the hands of sinners. Rise, let us go; behold, he is at hand that will betray me.

Adhuc eo loquente, ecce Judas unus de duodecim venit, et cum eo turba multa cum gladiis et fustibus, missi a principibus sacerdotum, et senioribus populi. Qui autem tradidit eum, dedit illis signum, dicens : Quemcumque osculatus fuero, ipse est, tenete eum. Et confestim accedens ad Jesum, dixit : Ave Rabbi, et osculatus est eum. Dixitque illi Jesus : Amice, ad quid venisti ? Tunc accesse runt, et manus injece runt in Jesum, et tenue runt eum. Et ecce unus ex his qui erant cum

As he yet spoke, behold, Judas, one of the twelve, came, and with him a great multitude with swords and clubs, sent from the chief priests, and the ancients of the people. And he that betrayed him, gave them a sign, saying : Whomsoever I shall kiss, that is he: hold him fast. And forthwith coming to Jesus, he said : Hail, Rabbi ! And he kissed him. And Jesus said to him : Friend, whereto art thou come ? Then they came up and laid hands on Jesus and held him. And behold one

Jesu, extendens manum, exemit gladium suum, et percutiens servum principis sacerdotum, amputavit auriculam ejus. Tunc ait illi Jesus : Converte gladium tuum in locum suum : omnes enim, qui acceperint gladium, gladio peribunt. An putas, quia non possum rogare patrem meum, et exhibebit mihi modo plusquam duodecim legiones Angelorum ? Quomodo ergo implebuntur scripturæ, quia sic oportet fieri ? In illa hora dixit Jesus turbis : Tanquam ad latronem existis cum gladiis et fustibus comprehendere me : quotidie apud vos sedebam docens in templo, et non me tenuistis. Hoc autem totum factum est, ut adimplerentur scripturæ prophetarum, Tunc discipuli omnes, relicto eo, fugerunt.

of the. 1 that were with Jesus, stretching forth his hand, drew out his sword ; and striking the servant of the high priest, cut off his ear. Then Jesus saith to him : Put up again thy sword into its place : for all that take the sword shall perish by the sword. Thinkest thou that I cannot ask my Father, and he will give me presently more than twelve legions of angels ? How then shall the scriptures be fulfilled, that so it must be done ? In that same hour Jesus said to the multitude : You are come out as against a robber with swords and clubs to apprehend me. I sat daily with you teaching in the temple, and you laid not hands on me. Now all this was done, that the scriptures of the prophets might be fulfilled. Then the disciples all leaving him, fled away

At illi tenentes Jesum duxerunt ad Caipham, principem sacerdotum, ubi scribæ et seniores convenerant. Petrus autem sequebatur eum a longe, usque in atrium principis sacerdotum. Et ingressus intro, sedebat cum ministris, ut videret finem. Principes autem sacerdotum, et omne concilium, quærebant falsum testimonium contra Jesum, ut eum morti traderent : et non invenerunt, cum multi falsi testes accessissent. Novissime autem venerunt duo falsi testes, et dixerunt : Hic dixit : Possum destruere templum Dei, et post triduum reædificare illud. Et surgens princeps sacerdotum, ait illi. Nihil respondes ad ea, quæ isti adversum te testificantur? Jesus autem tacebat. Et princeps sacerdotum ait illi : Adjuro te per Deum vivum, ut dicas nobis si tu es

But they holding Jesus, led him to Caiphas. the high priest, where the scribes and the ancients were assembled. But Peter followed him afar off to the high priest's palace. And going in, he sat with the servants, to see the end. Now the chief priests and whole council sought false witness against Jesus that they might put him to death : and they found not, though many false witnesses had come in. And last of all, there came two false witnesses. And they said : This man said, I am able to destroy the temple of God, and in three days to rebuild it. And the high priest rising up, said to him : Answerest thou nothing to the things which these witness against thee. But Jesus held his peace. And the high priest said to him : I adjure thee by the living God. that thou

Christus, filius Dei. Dicit illi Jesus: Tu dixisti Verumtamen dicc vobis, amodo videbitis 1 ilium hominis sedentem a dextrix virtutis Dei, et venientem in nubibus cœli. Tunc princeps sacerdotum scidit vestimenta sua, dicens: Blasphemavit: quid adhuc egemus testibus? ecce nunc audistis blasphemiam: quid vobis videtur? At illi respondentes dixerunt: Reus est mortis. Tunc expuerunt in faciem ejus, et colaphis eum ceciderunt, alii autem palmas in faciem ejus dederunt, dicentes: Prophetiza nobis Christe, quis est qui te percussit? Petrus vero sedebat foris in atrio: et accessit ad eum una ancilla, dicens: Et tu cum Jesu Galilæo eras. At ille negavit coram omnibus, dicens: Nescio quid dicis. Exeunte autem illo januam, vidit eum alia ancilla, et ait his qui erant ibi: Et

tell us if thou be the Christ, the Son of God. Jesus saith to him: Thou hast said it. Nevertheless I say to you, hereafter you shall see the Son of Man, sitting on the right hand of the power of God, and coming in the clouds of heaven. Then the high priest rent his garments, saying: He hath blasphemed, what further need have we of witnesses? Behold, now you have heard the blasphemy. What think you? But they answering, said: He is guilty of death. Then they spit in his face, and buffeted him, and others struck his face with the palms of their hands, saying: Prophesy unto us, O Christ! who is he that struck thee? But Peter sat without in the palace, and there came to him a servant maid, saying: Thou also wast with Jesus the Galilean

hic erat cum Jesu Nazareno. Et iterum negavit cum juramento : Quia non novi hominem. Et post pusillum accesserunt qui stabant, et dixerunt Petro : Vere et tu ex illis es ; nam et loquela tua manifestum te facit. Tunc cœpit detestari, et jurare quia non novisset hominem. Et continuo gallus cantavit. Et recordatus est Petrus verbi Jesu, quod dixerat : Priusquam gallus cantet, ter me negabis. Et egressus foras, flevit amare.

But he denied before them all, saying : I know not what thou sayest. And as he went out of the gate, another maid saw him, and she saith to them that were there : This man also was with Jesus of Nazareth. And again he denied with an oath : I do not know the man. And after a little while they that stood by came and said to Peter : Surely thou also art one of them ; for even thy speech doth discover thee. Then he began to curse and to swear that he knew not the man. And immediately the cock crew. And Peter remembered the word of Jesus which he had said : Before the cock crow, thou wilt deny me thrice. And going forth, he wept bitterly.

Mane autem facto, consilium inierunt omnes principes sacerdotum et seniores populi

And when the morning was come, all the chief priests and ancients of the people held a

adversus Jesum, ut eum morti traderent. Et vinctum adduxerunt eum, et tradiderunt Pontio Pilato præsidi. Tunc videns Judas, qui eum tradidit, quod damnatus esset, pœnitentia ductus, retulit triginta argenteos principibus sacerdotum, et senioribus, dicens: Peccavi tradens sanguinem justum: At illi dixerunt: Quid ad nos? Tu videris. Et projectis argenteis in templo, recessit; et abiens, laqueo se suspendit. Principes autem sacerdotum, acceptis argenteis, dixerunt: Non licet eos mittere in corbonam, quia pretium sanguinis est. Consilio autem inito, emerunt ex illis agrum figuli, in sepulturam peregrinorum Propter hoc vocatus est ager ille, Haceldama, hoc est, ager sanguinis, usque in hodiernum diem. Tunc impletum est, quod dictum est per

council against Jesus, to put him to death. And they brought him bound, and delivered him to Pontius Pilate, the governor. Then Judas, who betrayed him, seeing that he was condemned, repenting himself, brought back the thirty pieces of silver to the chief priests and the ancients, saying: I have sinned, in betraying innocent blood. But they said: What is that to us? look thou to it. And casting down the pieces of silver in the temple, he departed: and went and hanged himself with a halter. But the chief priests having taken the pieces of silver, said: It is not lawful to put them into the corbona, because it is the price of blood. And having consulted together, they bought with them the potter's field, to be a burying-place for strangers.

Jeremiam Prophetam, dicentem : Et accepe- runt triginta argenteos pretium appretiati, quem appretiaverunt a filiis Israel, et dederunt eos in agrum figuli, sicut con- stituit mihi Dominus. Jesus autem stetit ante præsidem, et interroga- vit eum præses, dicens : Tu es rex Judæorum. Dicit illi Jesus : Tu di- cis. Et cum accusare- tur a principibus sacer- dotum, et senioribus, nihil respondit. Tunc dicit illi Pilatus : Non audis quanta adversum te dicunt testimonia ? Et non respondit ei ad ullum verbum, ita ut miraretur præses vehe- menter.

Wherefore that field was called Haceldama, that is, the field of blood, even to this day. Then was fulfilled that which was spoken by Jeremias the prophet, saying : And they took the thirty pieces of silver, the price of him that was valued, whom they prized of the children of Israel. And they gave them unto the potter's field, as the Lord appointed to me. And Jesus stood before the governor, and the governor asked him, say- ing : Art thou the king of the Jews? Jesus saith to him : Thou sayest it. And when he was ac- cused by the chief priests and ancients, he an- swered nothing. Then Pilate saith to him : Dost thou not hear how great testimonies they allege against thee ? And he answered him not to any word : so that the governor won- dered exceedingly.

Per diem autem solemnem consueverat præses populo dimittere unum vinctum, quem voluissent. Habebat autem tunc vinctum insignem, qui dicebatur Barabbas. Congregatis ergo illis, dixit Pilatus: Quem vultis dimittam vobis: Barabbam, an Jesum, qui dicitur Christus? Sciebat enim quod per invidiam tradidissent eum. Sedente autem illo pro tribunali, misit ad eum uxor ejus, dicens: Nihil tibi, et justo illi; multa enim passa sum hodie per visum propter eum. Principes autem sacerdotum, et seniores persuaserunt populis ut peterent Barabbam, Jesum vero perderent. Respondens autem præses, ait illis: Quem vultis vobis de duobus dimitti? At illi dixerunt: Barabbam. Dicit illis Pilatus: Quid igitur faciam de Jesu, qui dicitur Christus?

Now upon the solemn day the governor was accustomed to release to the people one prisoner, whom they would. And he had then a notorious prisoner, that was called Barabbas. They, therefore, being gathered together, Pilate said: Whom will you that I release to you, Barabbas, or Jesus, who is called Christ? For he knew that through envy they had delivered him up. And as he was sitting on the judgment-seat, his wife sent to him, saying: Have thou nothing to do with that just man. For I have suffered many things this day in a dream on account of him. But the chief priests and ancients persuaded the people, that they should ask Barabbas, and make Jesus away. And the governor answering, said to them: Which will you have of the two to be

Dicunt omnes : Crucifigatur. Ait illis præses : Quid enim mali fecit ? At illi magis clamabant, dicentes : Crucifigatur. Videns autem Pilatus quia nihil proficeret, sed magis tumultus fieret, accepta aqua, lavit manus coram populo, dicens : Innocens ego sum a sanguine justi hujus : vos videritis. Et respondens universus populus, dixit : Sanguis ejus super nos, et super filios nostros. Tunc dimisit illis Barabbam : Jesum autem flagellatum tradidit eis, ut crucifigeretur. Tunc milites præsidis suscipientes Jesum in prætorium, congregaverunt ad eum universam cohortem : et exeuntes eum, chlamydem coccineam circumdederunt ei ; et plectentes coronam de spinis, posuerunt super caput ejus, et arundinem in dextera ejus. Et genuflexo ante eum, lludebant ei, dicentes :

released unto you ? But they said, Barabbas. Pilate saith to them : What shall I do then with Jesus that is called Christ ? They all say Let him be crucified The governor said to them : Why, what evil hath he done ? But they cried out the more, saying : Let him be crucified. And Pilate seeing that he prevailed nothing, but that rather a tumult was made, having taken water, washed his hands before the people, saying : I am innocent of the blood of this just man : look you to it. And all the people answering, said . His blood be upon us, and upon our children Then he released to them Barabbas, and having scourged Jesus, delivered him to them to be crucified. Then the soldiers of the governor, taking Jesus into the hall, gathered together

Ave rex Judæorum. Et expuentes in eum, acceperunt arundinem, et percutiebant caput ejus. Et postquam illuserunt ei, exuerunt eum chlamyde, et induerunt eum vestimentis ejus, et duxerunt eum ut crucifigerent.

unto him the whole band. And stripping him, they put a scarlet cloak about him. And platting a crown of thorns, they put it upon his head, and a reed in his right hand. And bowing the knee before him, they mocked him saying: Hail, king of the Jews! And spitting upon him, they took the reed, and struck his head. And after they had mocked him, they took off the cloak from him, and put on him his own garments, and led him away to crucify him.

Exeuntes autem invenerunt hominem Cyrenæum, nomine Simonem: hunc angariaverunt ut tolleret crucem ejus. Et venerunt in locum, qui dicitur Golgotha, quod est, Calvariæ locus. Et dederunt ei vinum bibere cum felle mistum. Et cum gustasset, noluit bibere.

And going out, they found a man of Cyrene, named Simon; him they forced to take up his cross. And they came to the place that is called Golgotha, which is, the place of Calvary. And they gave him wine to drink mingled with gall. And when he had tasted, he would not drink. And

Postquam autem crucifixerunt eum, diviserunt vestimenta ejus, sortem mittentes : ut impleretur quod dictum est per prophetam, dicentem : Diviserunt sibi vestimenta mea, et super vestem meam miserunt sortem. Et sedentes servabant eum. Et imposuerunt super caput ejus causam ipsius scriptam : Hic est Jesus Rex Judæorum. Tunc crucifixi sunt cum eo duo latrones, unus a dextris, et unus a sinistris. Prætereuntes autem blasphemabant eum, moventes capita sua, et dicentes : Vah qui destruis templum Dei, et in triduo illud reædificas, salva temetipsum. Si filius Dei es, descende de cruce. Similiter et principes sacerdotum illudentes cum scribis et senioribus, dicebant : Alios salvos fecit, seipsum non potest salvum

after they had crucified him, they parted his garments, casting lots ; that the word might be fulfilled which was spoken by the prophet, saying : They divided my garments among them ; and upon my vesture they cast lots. And they sat down, and watched him. And they put over his head his cause written : This is Jesus, the King of the Jews. Then were there crucified with him two thieves ; the one on the right hand, and the other on the left. And they that passed by blasphemed him, wagging their heads, and saying : Vah, thou who destroyest the temple of God, and in three days buildest it up again, save thy ownself : if thou be the Son of God, come down from the cross. In like manner, also, the chief priests with the scribes and ancients, mocking, said : He saved others ; him-

facere : si rex Israel est, descendat nunc de cruce, et credimus ei : confidit in Deo ; liberet nunc, si vult, eum : dixit enim : Quia Filius Dei sum. Idipsum autem et latrones qui crucifixi erant cum eo, improperabant ei. A sexta autem hora, tenebræ factæ sunt super universam terram, usque ad horam nonam. Et circa horam nonam ciamavit Jesus voce magna, dicens : Eli, Eli, lamma sabacthani ? Hoc est : Deus meus, Deus meus, ut quid dereliquisti me ? Quidam autem illic stantes, et audientes, dicebant : Eliam vocat iste. Et continuo currens unus ex eis, acceptam spongiam implevit aceto et imposuit arundini, et dabat ei bibere. Cæteri vero dicebant : Sine videamus an veniat Elias liberans eum. Jesus autem iterum cla-

self he cannot save ; if he be the king of Israel, let him now come down from the cross, and we will believe him. He trusted in God, let him deliver him now if he will save him : for he said : I am the Son of God. And the selfsame thing the thieves also, that were crucified with him, reproached him with. Now from the sixth hour, there was darkness over all the earth, until the ninth hour. And about the ninth hour, Jesus cried with a loud voice, saying : Eli, Eli, lamma sabacthani ? that is, my God ! my God ! why hast thou forsaken me ? And some of them that stood there and heard, said : This man calleth for Elias. And immediately one of them running, took a sponge, and filled it with vinegar ; and put it on a reed and gave him to drink. And the others said : Stay, let us see

mans voce magna, emisit spiritum.

whether Elias will come to deliver him. And Jesus again crying with a loud voice, yielded up the ghost.

Here all kneel down, and after a little pause (to meditate on the redemption of mankind) they rise, and the Deacon proceeds :

ET ecce velum templi scissum est in duas partes a summo usque deorsum, et terra mota est, et petræ scissæ sunt, et monumenta aperta sunt, et multa corpora sanctorum, qui dormierant, surrexerunt. Et exeuntes de monumentis post resurrectionem ejus, venerunt in sanctam civitatem, et apparuerunt multis. Centurio autem, et qui cum eo erant, cusiodientes Jesum, viso terræ motu, et his quæ fiebant, timuerunt valde, dicentes: Vere filius Dei erat iste. Erant autem ibi mulieres multæ a longe, quæ secutæ erant Jesum a Galilæa, ministrantes ei; inter quas erat Maria

AND behold the veil of the temple was rent in two, from the top even to the bottom, and the earth quaked, and the rocks were rent; and the graves were opened : and many bodies of the saints that had slept arose : and coming out of the tombs after his resurrection, came into the holy city, and appeared to many. Now the centurion, and they that were with him, watching Jesus, having seen the earthquake, and the things that were done, were greatly afraid, saying: Indeed this was the Son of God. And there were there many women afar off, who had fol

Magdalene, et Maria Jacobi, et Joseph mater, et mater filiorum Zebedæi Cum autem sero factum esset, venit quidam homo dives ab Arimathæa, nomine Joseph, qui et ipse discipulus erat Jesu. Hic accessit ad Pilatum, et petiit corpus Jesu. Tunc Pilatus jussit reddi corpus. Et accepto corpore, Joseph involvit illud in sindone munda. Et posuit illud in monumento suo novo, quod exciderat in petra. Et advolvit saxum magnum ad ostium monumenti, et abiit. Erat autem ibi Maria Magdalene, et altera Maria, sedentes contra sepulchrum.

lowed Jesus from Galilee, ministering unto him. Among whom was Mary Magdalene, and Mary, the mother of James and Joseph, and the mother of the sons of Zebedee. And when it was evening, there came a certain rich man of Arimathea, named Joseph, who also himself was a disciple of Jesus. He went to Pilate and begged the body of Jesus. Then Pilate commanded that the body should be delivered. And Joseph taking the body, wrapped it up in a clean linen cloth. And laid it in his own new monument, which he had hewed out in a rock ; and he rolled a great stone to the door of the monument, and went his way. And there was Mary Magdalene and the other Mary sitting over against the sepulchre.

Here is said the prayer, Munda cor meum, *p.* 19.

ALTERA autem die, quæ est post Parasceven, convenerunt principes sacerdotum et Pharisæi ad Pilatum, dicentes : Domine, recordati sumus quia seductor ille dixit adhuc vivens : Post tres dies resurgam. Jube, ergo, custodiri sepulchrum usque in diem tertium : ne forte veniant discipuli ejus, et furentur eum, et dicant plebi : Surrexit a mortuis ; et erit novissimus error pejor priore. Ait illis Pilatus : Habetis custodiam ; ite, custodite sicut scitis. Illi autem abeuntes, munierunt sepulchrum, signantes lapidem, cum custodibus.

AND the next day, which followed the day of the preparation, the chief priests and the Pharisees came together to Pilate, saying : Sir, we have remembered that seducer said, while he was yet alive : After three days I will rise again. Command, therefore, the sepulchre to be guarded until the third day ; lest his disciples come and steal him away, and say to the people : He is risen from the dead ; so the last error shall be worse than the first. Pilate said to them : You have a guard, go guard it as you know. And they departing, made the sepulchre sure, with guards, sealing the stone.

The Credo, *p.* 20.

Oremus.   Let us pray.

THE OFFERTORY.

IMPROPERIUM expectavit cor meum, et miseriam: et sustinui qui simul mecum contristaretur, et non fuit; consolantem me quæsivi, et non inveni: et dederunt in escam meam fel, et in siti mea potaverunt me aceto.

MY heart hath expected reproach and misery; and I looked for one that would grieve together with me, but there was none; and for one that would comfort me, and I found none; and they gave me gall for my food, and in my thirst they gave me vinegar to drink.

Suscipe—Receive, etc., *p.* 26, *to* Then the Priest says Amen, *p.* 28,

THE SECRET.

CONCEDE, quæsumus Domine, ut oculis tuæ majestatis munus oblatum, et gratiam nobis devotionis obtineat, et effectum beatæ perennitatis acquirat. Per Dominum nostrum Jesum Christum, Filium tuum, qui tecum vivit et regnat in unitate Spiritus Sancti Deus.

GRANT, we beseech thee, O Lord! that this offering made in the presence of thy majesty, may procure us the grace of devotion, and effectually obtain a blessed eternity. through our Lord Jesus Christ, thy Son, who with thee and the Holy Ghost liveth and reigneth one God.

That which follows is said aloud :

V. PER omnia sæcu-
la sæculorum.

R. Amen.

V. Dominus vobis-
cum.

R. Et cum spiritu tuo.

V. Sursum corda.

R. Habemus ad Do-
minum.

V. Gratias agamus
Domino Deo nostro.

R. Dignum et justum
est.

Vere dignum et jus-
tum est, æquum et salu-
tare, nos tibi semper et
ibique gratias agere,
Domine sancte, Pater
omnipotens, æterne De-
us. Qui salutem hu-
mani generis in ligno
crucis constituisti, ut
unde mors oriebatur,
inde vita resurgeret ; et
qui in ligno vincebat, in
ligno quoque vinceretur.
per Christum Dominum
nostrum. Per quem ma-
jestatem tuam laudant
Angeli, adorant Domi-
nationes, tremunt Potes-
tates. Cœli, cœlorum-

V. WORLD with-
out end.

R. Amen.

V. The Lord be with
you.

R. And with thy spirit.

V. Lift up your hearts.

R. We have them lift-
ed up to the Lord.

V. Let us give thanks
to the Lord our God.

R. It is meet and just.

It is truly meet and
just, right and profitable
to salvation, that we
should at all times, and
in all places, give thanks
to thee, O holy Lord,
almighty Father, and
eternal God ! who hast
appointed that the salva-
tion of mankind should
be wrought on the tree
of the cross ; that life
might spring whence
death had arisen ; and
he that had overcome
by a tree, might also
by a tree be overcome ;
through Christ our Lord,
by whom the Angels

que virtutes, ac beata Seraphim, socia exultatione concelebrant. Cum quibus et nostras voces, ut admitti jubeas deprecamur, supplici confessione dicentes :

Sanctus, sanctus, sanctus, Dominus Deus Sabaoth. Pleni sunt cœli et terra gloria tua: Hosanna in excelsis. Benedictus qui venit in nomine Domine : Hosanna in excelsis.

praise thy majesty, the Dominations adore it, the Powers tremble before it, the Heavens and heavenly Virtues, and the blessed Seraphim with united exultation glorify it. With whom, also, we beseech thee, admit our voices with humble praise, saying :

Holy, holy, holy is the Lord God of hosts ! the Heavens and the earth are full of thy glory; Hosanna in the highest ! Blessed is he that cometh in the name of the Lord, Hosanna in the highest !

The Canon of the Mass, p. 20, *to end of prayer,* Corpus tuum—May thy, p. 42.

THE COMMUNION.

PATER, si non potest hic calix transire, nisi bibam illum, fiat voluntas tua.

V. Dominus vobiscum.

R. Et cum spiritu tuo.

FATHER, if this chalice cannot pass away except I drink it, thy will be done.

V. The Lord be with thee.

R. And with thy spirit

THE POST-COMMUNION.

Oremus.

PER hujus, Domine, operationem mysterii, et vitia nostra purgentur, et justa desideria compleantur. Per Dominum nostrum, Jesum Christum, Filium tuum, qui tecum vivit et regnat in unitate Spiritus Sancti Deus, per omnia sæcula sæculorum.

R. Amen.

Let us pray.

BY the virtue of this mystery, O Lord! let our vices be destroyed, and our just desires fulfilled; through our Lord Jesus Christ, thy Son, who with thee and the Holy Ghost, liveth and reigneth one God, world without end.

R. Amen.

The rest of the Mass from Dominus vobiscum, *as on p.* 43.

In private Masses, the Gospel as above in the Blessing of the Palms, p. 90, is here read instead of the ordinary Gospel.

THE VESPERS.

PATER noster, etc.
Ave Maria, etc.

V. Deus, in adjuto-
rium meum intende.

R. Domine, ad adju-
vandum me festina.

V. Gloria Patri, et Fi-
lio, et Spiritui Sancto.

R. Sicut erat in prin-
cipio, et nunc, et sem-
per, et in sæcula sæcu-
lorum. Amen.

Laus tibi, Domine, Rex
æternæ gloriæ.

Antiphona. Dixit Do-
minus.

OUR Father, etc.
Hail Mary, etc.

V. Incline unto my
aid, O God!

R. O Lord! make
haste to help me.

V. Glory be to the
Father, and to the Son,
and to the Holy Ghost.

R. As it was in the
beginning, is now, and
ever shall be, world without end. Amen.

Praise be to thee, O
Lord! King of eternal
glory.

The Antiphon. The
Lord said.

PSALM 109.

DIXIT Dominus
Domino meo : *
Sede a dextris meis :

Donec ponam inimi-
cos tuos * scabellum pe-
dum tuorum.

Virgam virtutis tuæ
emittet Dominus ex Sion:

THE Lord said to
my Lord: Sit thou
at my right hand :

Until I make thy ene-
mies thy footstool.

The Lord will send
forth the sceptre of thy

* dominare in medio inimicorum tuorum.

power out of Sion : rule thou in the midst of thy enemies.

Tecum principium in die virtutis tuæ in splendoribus sanctorum : * ex utero ante luciferum genui te.

With thee is the principality in the day of thy strength ; in the brightness of the saints : from the womb, before the day-star, I begat thee.

Juravit Dominus, et non pœnitebit eum : * Tu es sacerdos in æternum, secundum ordinem Melchisedech.

The Lord hath sworn, and he will not repent : Thou art a priest for ever, according to the order of Melchisedech.

Dominus a dextris tuis, * confregit in die iræ suæ reges.

The Lord at thy right hand hath broken kings in the day of his wrath.

Judicabit in nationibus, implebit ruinas : * conquassabit capita in terra multorum.

He shall judge among nations ; he shall fill ruins : he shall crush the heads in the land of many.

De torrente in via bibet : * propterea exaltabit caput.

He shall drink of the torrent in the way : therefore shall he lift up the head.

Gloria Patri, etc.

Glory, etc.

Ant. Dixit Dominus Domino meo : Sede a dextris meis.

Ant. The Lord said to my Lord : Sit thou at my right hand.

Ant. Fidelia.

Ant. All his commandments.

PSALM 110.

CONFITEBOR tibi Domine, in toto corde meo : * in consilio justorum, et congregatione.

Magna opera Domini : * exquisita in omnes voluntates ejus.

Confessio et magnificentia opus ejus : * et justitia ejus manet in sæculum sæculi.

Memoriam fecit mirabilium suorum, misericors et miserator Dominus : * escam dedit timentibus se.

Memor erit in sæculum testamenti sui : * virtutem operum suorum annuntiabit populo suo.

Ut det illis hæreditatem gentium : * opera manuum ejus, veritas et judicium.

Fidelia omnia mandata ejus, confirmata in

I WILL praise thee, O Lord ! with my whole heart ; in the council of the just, and in the congregation.

Great are the works of the Lord : sought out according to all his wills.

His work is praise and magnificence : and his justice continueth for ever and ever.

He hath made a remembrance of his wonderful works, being a merciful and gracious Lord : he hath given food to them that fear him.

He will be mindful for ever of his covenant : he will show forth to his people the power of his works.

That he may give them the inheritance of the Gentiles : the works of his hands are truth and judgment.

All his commandments are faithful, confirmed

sæculum sæculi : * facta in veritate et æquitate.

for ever and ever : made in truth and equity.

Redemptionem misit populo suo : * mandavit in æternum testamentum suum.

He hath sent redemption to his people : he hath commanded his covenant for ever.

Sanctum et terribile nomen ejus : * initium sapientiæ timor Domini.

Holy and terrible is his name : the fear of the Lord is the begin ning of wisdom.

Intellectus bonus omnibus facientibus eum : * laudatio ejus manet in sæculum sæculi.

A good understanding to all that do it : his praise continueth for ever and ever.

Gloria Patri, etc.

Glory, etc.

Ant. Fidelia omnia mandata ejus, confirmata in sæculum sæculi.

Ant. All his commandments are faithful. confirmed for ever and ever.

Ant. In mandatis.

Ant. He shall delight.

PSALM III.

BEATUS vir, qui timet Dominum : * in mandatis ejus volet nimis.

BLESSED is the man that feareth the Lord : he shall delight exceedingly in his commandments.

Potens in terra erit semen ejus : * generatio rectorum benedicetur.

His seed shall be mighty upon earth : the generation of the righteous shall be blessed.

Gloria et divitiæ in domo ejus : * et justitia ejus manet in sæculum sæculi.

Glory and wealth shall be in his house : and his justice remaineth for ever and ever.

Exortum est in tenebris lumen rectis : * misericors et miserator et justus.

To the righteous a light is risen up in darkness : he is merciful, and compassionate, and just.

Jucundus homo qui miseretur et commodat, disponet sermones suos in judicio : * quia in æternum non commovebitur.

Acceptable is the man that showeth mercy and lendeth : he shall order his words with judgment : because he shall not be moved for ever.

In memoria æterna erit justus : * ab auditione mala non timebit.

The just shall be in everlasting remembrance : he shall not fear the evil hearing.

Paratum cor ejus sperare in Domino, confirmatum est cor ejus : * non commovebitur donec despiciat inimicos suos.

His heart is ready to hope in the Lord ; his heart is strengthened ; he shall not be moved until he look over his enemies.

Dispersit, dedit pauperibus : justitia ejus manet in sæculum sæculi, * cornu ejus exaltabitur in gloria.

He hath distributed, he hath given to the poor: his justice remaineth for ever and ever ; his horn shall be exalted in glory.

Peccator videbit et irascetur, dentibus suis fremet et tabescet : *

The wicked shall see, and shall be angry ; he shall gnash with his

desiderium peccatorum peribit.

teeth, and pine away: the desire of the wicked shall perish.

Gloria Patri, etc.

Glory, etc.

Ant. In mandatis ejus cupit nimis.

Ant. He shall delight exceedingly in his commandments.

Ant. Sit nomen Domini.

Ant. Blessed be.

PSALM 112.

LAUDATE pueri Dominum : * laudate nomen Domini.

PRAISE the Lord, ye children! praise ye the name of the Lord.

Sit nomen Domini benedictum, * ex hoc nunc, et usque in sæculum.

Blessed be the name of the Lord, from henceforth, now and for ever.

A solis ortu usque ad occasum, * laudabile nomen Domini.

From the rising of the sun unto the going down of the same, the name of the Lord is worthy of praise.

Excelsus super omnes gentes Dominus, * et super cœlos gloria ejus.

The Lord is high above all nations, and his glory above the heavens.

Quis sicut Dominus Deus noster, qui in altis habitat, * et humilia respicit in cœlo et in terra?

Who is as the Lord, our God, who dwelleth on high ; and looketh down on the low things in heaven, and in earth?

Suscitans a terra in-

Raising up the needy

opem, * et de stercore erigens pauperem.

from the earth, and lifting up the poor out of the dunghill.

Ut collocet eum cum principibus, * cum principibus populi sui.

That he may place him with princes, with the princes of his people.

Qui habitare facit sterilem in domo, * matrem filiorum lætantem.

Who maketh a barren woman to dwell in a house, the joyful mother of children.

Gloria Patri, etc.

Glory, etc.

Ant. Sit nomen Domini benedictum in sæcula.

Ant. Blessed be the name of the Lord for ever.

Ant. Nos qui vivimus.

Ant. We that live.

PSALM 113.

IN exitu Israel de Ægypto, * domus Jacob de populo barbaro :

WHEN Israel went out of Egypt, the house of Jacob from a barbarous people :

Facta est Judæa sanctificatio ejus, * Israel potestas ejus.

Judea was made his sanctuary, Israel his dominion.

Mare videt et fugit : * Jordanis conversus est retrorsum.

The sea saw and fled : Jordan was turned back.

Montes exaltaverunt ut arietes, * et colles sicut agni ovium.

The mountains skipped like rams, and the hills like the lambs of the flock.

Quid est tibi, mare,

What ailed thee, O

quod fugisti ? * et tu Jordanis, quia conversus es retrorsum ?

thou sea? that thou didst flee, and thou, O Jordan, that thou wast turned back ?

Montes exultastis sicut arietes, * et colles sicut agni ovium.

Ye mountains, that ye skipped like rams ? and ye hills, like lambs of the flock ?

A facie Domini mota est terra, * a facie Dei Jacob.

At the presence of the Lord the earth was moved, at the presence of the God of Jacob.

Qui convertit petram in stagna aquarum, * et rupem in fontes aquarum.

Who turned the rock into pools of water, and the stony hill into fountains of waters.

Non nobis, Domine, non nobis : * sed nomini tuo da gloriam.

Not to us, O Lord, not to us ; but to thy name, give glory.

Super misericordia tua, et veritate tua : * nequando dicant gentes : Ubi est Deus eorum ?

For thy mercy and for thy truth's sake, lest the Gentiles should say, where is their God ?

Deus autem noster in cœlo: * omnia quæcumque voluit, fecit.

But our God is in heaven : he hath done all things whatsoever he would.

Simulacra gentium argentum et aurum, * opera manuum hominum.

The idols of the Gentiles are silver and gold, the works of the hands of men.

Os habent, et non lo-

They have mouths and

quentur: * oculos habent, et non videbunt.

Aures habent, et non audient: * nares habent, et non odorabunt.

Manus habent, et non palpabunt ; pedes habent, et non ambulabunt : * non clamabunt in gutture suo.

Similes illis fiant qui faciunt ea : * et omnes qui confidunt in eis.

Domus Israel speravit in Domino : * adjutor eorum et protector eorum est.

Domus Aaron speravit in Domino : * adjutor eorum et protector eorum est.

Qui timent Dominum, speraverunt in Domino : * adjutor eorum et protector eorum est.

Dominus memor fuit nostri : * et benedixit nobis.

Benedixit domui Israel : * benedixit domui Aaron.

speak not ; they have eyes and see not.

They have ears and hear not ; they have noses and smell not.

They have hands and feel not ; they have feet and walk not ; neither shall they cry out through their throat.

Let them that make them become like unto them ; and all such as trust in them.

The house of Israel hath hoped in the Lord: he is their helper, and their protector.

The house of Aaron hath hoped in the Lord: he is their helper, and their protector.

They that fear the Lord have hoped in the Lord : he is their helper, and their protector.

The Lord hath been mindful of us, and hath blessed us.

He hath blessed the house of Israel: he hath blessed the house of Aaron.

Benedixit omnibus qui timent Dominum, * pusillis cum majoribus.

He hath blessed all that fear the Lord, both little and great.

Adjiciat Dominus super vos : * super vos, et super filios vestros.

May the Lord add blessings upon you : upon you, and upon your children.

Benedicti vos a Domino, * qui fecit cœlum et terram.

Blessed be you of the Lord, who made heaven and earth.

Cœlum cœli Domino : * terram autem dedit filiis hominum.

The heaven of heavens is the Lord's ; but the earth he hath given to the children of men.

Non mortui laudabunt te Domine : * neque omnes qui descendunt in infernum.

The dead shall not praise thee, O Lord, nor any of them that go down to hell.

Sed nos qui vivimus, benedicimus Domino, * ex hoc nunc et usque in sæculum.

But we that live bless the Lord, from this time, now and for ever.

Gloria Patri, etc.

Glory, etc.

Ant. Nos qui vivimus, benedicimus Domino.

Ant. We that live, bless the Lord.

Capitulum, Philip. ii.

FRATRES, hoc enim sentite in vobis, quod et in Christo Jesu : qui cum in forma Dei esset, non rapinam arbitratus est esse se æqua-

BRETHREN, let this mind be in you, which was also in Christ Jesus ; who being in the form of God, thought it no robbery,

lem Deo ; sed semetip- himself to be equal to
sum exinanivit, formam God ; but he debased
servi accipiens, in simi- himself, taking the form
litudinem hominum fac- of a servant, being made
tus, et habitu inventus to the likeness of men,
ut homo. and in shape found as a
man.

R. Deo gratias. *R*. Thanks be to God.

THE HYMN.

Vexilla regis prodeunt,
Fulget Crucis mysterium
Qua vita mortem pertulit
Et morte vitam protulit.

Quæ vulnerata lanceæ
Mucrone diro criminum,
Ut nos lavaret sordibus,
Manavit unda et sanguine.

Impleta sunt quæ concinit,
David fideli carmine,
Dicendo nationibus,
Regnavit a ligno Deus.

Arbor decora et fulgida,
Ornata Regis purpura,
Electa digno stipite
Tam sancta membra **tangere.**

Beata, cujus brachiis
Pretium pependit seculi,
Statera facta corporis,
Tulit prædamque tartari.

O Crux, ave, spes unica,
Hoc passionis tempore,
Piis ad auge gratium,
Reisque dele crimina.

Te, fons salutis, Trinitas,
Collaudet omnis spiritus :
Quibus crucis victoriam
Largiris, adde præmium.   **Amen**

V. Eripe me, Domine, ab homine **malo.**
R. A viro iniquo eripe me.

The same in English.

Behold the royal ensigns fly,
Bearing the Cross's mystery ;
Where life itself did death endure,
And, by that death, did life procure.

A cruel spear let out a flood
Of water, mixed with saving blood,
Which, gushing from the Saviour's side
Drown'd our offences in the tide.

The mystery we now unfold,
Which David's faithful verse foretold,
Of our Lord's kingdom, whilst we see
God ruling nations from a tree.

O lovely tree, whose branches wore
The royal purple of his gore !
How glorious does thy body shine,
Supporting members so divine ı

The world's blest balance thou art made,
On thee, our ransom, Christ is weigh'd,
Our sins, though great. his pains outweigh,
And rescue hell's expected prey.

Hail, holy cross ! Hail, mournful tree,
Our hope, with Christ, is nailed on thee;
Grant to the just increase of grace,
And every sinner's crimes efface.

Blest Trinity ! we praises sing
To thee from whom all graces spring .
Celestial crowns on those bestow
Who conquer by the cross below.   **Amen.**

V. Deliver me, O Lord, from the wicked man,
R. Rescue me from the unjust man.

Ant. Scriptum   est   *Ant.* For it is written,
enim.

The Canticle of the Blessed Virgin Mary, St. Luke i.

MAGNIFICAT * anima mea Dominum.

MY soul doth magnify the Lord.

Et exultavit spiritus meus * in Deo salutari meo.

And my spirit has rejoiced in God, my Saviour.

Quia respexit humilitatem ancillæ suæ : * ecce enim ex hoc, beatam me dicent omnes generationes.

Because he hath regarded the humility of his handmaid ; for behold, from henceforth, all generations shall call me blessed.

Quia fecit mihi magna qui potens est: * et sanctum nomen ejus.

For he that is mighty hath done great things to me ; and holy is his name.

Et misericordia ejus a progenie in progenies, * timentibus eum.

And his mercy is from generation to generation, to them that fear him.

Fecit potentiam in brachio suo : * dispersit superbos mente cordis sui.

He hath showed might in his arm ; he hath scattered the proud in the conceit of their heart.

Deposuit potentes de sede, * et exaltavit humiles.

He hath put down the mighty from their seat, and hath exalted the humble.

Esurientes implevit bonis : * et divites dimisit inanes.

He hath filled the hungry with good things ; and the rich he hath sent empty away.

Suscepit Israel puerum suum, * recordatus misericordiæ suæ.

He hath received Israel, his servant ; being mindful of his mercy.

Sicut locutus est ad patres nostros, * Abraham, et semini ejus in sæcula.

As he spoke to our fathers ; to Abraham, and to his seed for ever.

Gloria Patri, etc.

Glory, etc.

Ant. Scriptum est enim : Percutiam pastorem, et dispergentur oves gregis : postquam

Ant. For it is written : I will strike the Shepherd, and the sheep of the flock shall be dis

autem resurrexero, præcedam vos in Galilæam; ibi me videbitis, dicit Dominus.

Oremus.

Omnipotens sempiterne Deus, qui humano generi, ad imitandum humilitatis exemplum, Salvatorem nostrum, carnem sumere et crucem subire fecisti: concede propitius; ut et patientiæ ipsius habere documenta, et resurrectionis consortia mereamur. Per eundem Dominum, etc.

V. Dominus vobiscum.

R. Et cum spiritu tuo.

V Benedicamus Domino.

R. Deo gratias.

V. Fidelium animæ per misericordiam Dei requiescant in pace.

R. Amen.

persed; but after I shall be risen again, I will go before you into Galilee; there you shall see me, saith the Lord.

Let us pray.

Almighty and everlasting God, who didst vouchsafe to send thy Son, our Saviour, to take upon himself our flesh, and to suffer death upon a cross, to give mankind an example of humility: mercifully grant that we may both follow the example of his patience, and be made partakers of his resurrection; through the same Lord, etc.

V. The Lord be with you.

R. And with thy spirit.

V. Let us bless our Lord.

R. Thanks be to God.

V. May the souls of the faithful, through the mercy of God, rest in peace.

R. Amen

When Complin is not said, conclude thus:

PATER noster, se-creto.

OUR Father, *privately.*

V. Dominus det nobis suam pacem.

V. Our Lord grant us his peace.

R. Et vitam æternam. Amen.

R. And life everlasting. Amen.

Then the Anthem Ave Regina, etc., *p. 124.*

COMPLINE.

Lector incipit : Jube, Domne, benedicere. *Benedictio :* Noctem quietam, et finem perfectum concedat nobis Dominus omnipotens.

The reader begins : Pray, Father, give me your blessing. *The blessing :* May the Almighty Lord grant us a quiet night, and a happy end.

R. Amen.

R. Amen.

Lectio brevis. 1 Pet v. 5.

FRATRES, Sobrii estote, et vigilate : quia adversarius vester diabolus tanquam leo rugiens circuit, quærens quem devoret : cui resistite fortes in fide. Tu autem Domine, miserere nobis.

BRETHREN, be sober, and watch, because your adversary, the devil, as a roaring lion, goeth about seeking whom he may devour ; whom resist ye, strong in faith. And thou, O Lord! have mercy on us.

R. Deo gratias.

R. Thanks be to God.

V. Adjutorium nostrum in nomine Domini.

V. Our help is in the name of the Lord.

R. Qui fecit cœlum et terram. Pater noster, secreto.

R. Who made heaven and earth. Our Father, *privately.*

Then the Priest recites the Confiteor, *and the Choir answers:*

MISEREATUR tui omnipotens Deus, et dimissis peccatis tuis, perducat te ad vitam æternam.

R. Amen.

MAY the Almighty God have mercy on you, forgive you your sins, and bring you to everlasting life.

R Amen.

The Choir repeats the Confiteor.

CONFITEOR Deo omnipotenti, beatæ Mariæ semper Virgini, beato Michaeli Archangelo, beato Joanni Baptistæ, sanctis Apostolis Petro et Paulo, omnibus Sanctis, et tibi, Pater, quia peccavi nimis cogitatione, verbo et opere: mea culpa, mea culpa, mea maxima culpa. Ideo precor beatam Mariam, semper Virginem, beatum Michaelem, Archangelum, beatum Joannem Baptistam, sanctos Apostolos Petrum et Paulum, omnes Sanctos, et te, Pater, orare pro me ad Dominum Deum nostrum

I CONFESS to Almighty God, to blessed Mary ever Virgin, to blessed Michael the Archangel, to blessed John the Baptist, to the holy Apostles Peter and Paul, to all the Saints, and to you, Father, that I have sinned exceedingly in thought, word, and deed, through my fault, through my fault, through my most grievous fault. Therefore I beseech the blessed Mary ever Virgin, the blessed Michael the Archangel, the blessed John the Baptist, the holy Apostles Peter and Paul, all the Saints, and you, Father, to pray for me to the Lord our God.

MISEREATUR vestri omnipotens Deus, et dimissis peccatis vestris, perducat vos ad vitam æternam.

R. Amen.

Indulgentiam, absolutionem, et remissionem peccatorum nostrorum tribuat nobis omnipotens et misericors Dominus.

R. Amen.

V. Converte nos, Deus, salutaris noster.

R. Et averte iram tuam a nobis.

V. Deus, in adjutorium meum intende.

R. Domine, ad adjuvandum me festina.

Gloria Patri, etc.

Laus tibi, etc.

Ant. Miserere.

MAY the Almighty God have mercy on you, forgive you your sins, and bring you to everlasting life.

R. Amen.

May the almighty and merciful Lord give us pardon, absolution, and remission of our sins.

R. Amen.

V. Convert us, O God, our Saviour!

R. And turn off thy anger from us.

V. Incline unto my aid, O God!

R. O Lord! make haste to help me.

Glory be to the Father, etc.

Praise to thee, etc.

Ant. Have mercy

PSALM 4.

CUM invocarem, exaudivit me Deus justitiæ meæ : * in tribulatione dilatasti mihi.

WHEN I called upon him, the God of my justice heard me : when I was in distress, thou hast enlarged me.

Miserere mei, * et exaudi orationem meam.

Have mercy on me, and hear my prayer.

Filii hominum, usquequo gravi corde? * ut quid diligitis vanitatem, et quæritis mendacium?

O ye sons of men! how long will you be dull of heart? why do you love vanity, and seek after lying?

Et scitote quoniam mirificavit Dominus sanctum suum: * Dominus exaudiet me, cum clamavero ad eum.

Know ye also that the Lord hath made his holy one wonderful: the Lord will hear me when I shall cry unto him.

Irascimini et nolite peccare: * quæ dicitis in cordibus vestris, in cubilibus vestris compungimini.

Be ye angry, and sin not: the things you say in your hearts, be sorry for them upon your beds.

Sacrificate sacrificium justitiæ, et sperate in Domino. * Multi dicunt: Quis ostendit nobis bona?

Offer up the sacrifice of justice, and trust in the Lord: many say, Who showeth us good things?

Signatum est super nos lumen vultus tui, Domine: * dedisti lætitiam in corde meo.

The light of thy countenance, O Lord, is signed upon us: thou hast given gladness in my heart.

A fructu frumenti, vini et olei sui, * multiplicati sunt.

By the fruit of their corn, their wine and oil, they are multiplied.

In pace in idipsum * dormiam, et requiescam,

In peace, in the selfsame, I will sleep, and I will rest.

Quoniam tu, Domine, singulariter in spe * constituisti me.

For thou, O Lord, singularly hast settled me in hope.

Gloria Patri, etc.

Glory, etc.

PSALM 30.

IN te Domine speravi, non confundar in æternum : * in justitia tua libera me.

IN thee, O Lord, have I hoped, let me never be confounded : deliver me in thy justice.

Inclina ad me aurem tuam, * accelera ut eruas me.

Bow down thine ear to me : make haste to deliver me.

Esto mihi in Deum protectorem, et in domum refugii, * ut salvum me facias.

Be thou unto me a God, a protector, and a house of refuge, to save me.

Quoniam fortitudo mea, et refugium meum es tu : * et propter nomen tuum deduces me, et enutries me.

For thou art my strength and my refuge : and for thy name's sake, thou wilt lead me, and nourish me.

Educes me de laqueo hoc quem absconderunt mihi : * quoniam tu es protector meus.

Thou wilt bring me out of this snare, which they have hidden for me : for thou art my protector.

In manus tuas commendo spiritum meum : * redemisti me, Domine Deus veritatis.

Into thy hands I commend my spirit . thou hast redeemed me, O Lord, the God of truth !

Gloria Patri, etc,

Glory, etc.

PSALM 90:

QUI habitat in adjutorio Altissimi, * in protectione Dei cœli commorabitur.

Dicet Domino : Susceptor meus es tu, et refugium meum : * Deus meus, sperabo in eum.

Quoniam ipse liberavit me de laqueo venantium, * et a verbo aspero.

Scapulis suis obumbrabit tibi : * et sub pennis ejus sperabis.

Scuto circumdabit te veritas ejus : * non timebis a timore nocturno.

A sagitta volante in die, a negotio perambulante in tenebris, * ab incursu, et dæmonio meridiano.

Cadent a latere tuo mille, et decem millia a

HE that dwelleth in the aid of the Most High, shall abide under the protection of the God of Jacob.

He shall say to the Lord : Thou art my protector, and my refuge : my God, in him will I trust.

For he hath delivered me from the snare of the hunters, and from the sharp word.

He will overshadow thee with his shoulders: and under his wings thou shalt trust.

His truth shall compass thee with a shield : thou shalt not be afraid of the terror of the night ;

Of the arrow that flieth in the day ; of the business that walketh about in the dark; of invasion, or of the noon-day devil.

A thousand shall fall at thy side, and ten

dextris tuis : * ad te autem non appropinquabit.

Verumtamen oculis
tuis considerabis, * et
retributionem peccato-
rum videbis.

Quoniam tu es Do-
mine, spes mea : * altis-
simum posuisti refugium
tuum.

Non accedet ad te
malum : * et flagellum
non appropinquabit ta-
bernaculo tuo.

Quoniam angelis suis
mandavit de te : * ut
custodiant te in omni-
bus viis tuis.

In manibus portabunt
te : * ne forte offendas ad
lapidem pedem tuum.

Super aspidem et ba-
siliscum ambulabis : * et
conculcabis leonem et
draconem.

Quoniam in me spera-
vit, liberabo eum : * pro-
tegam eum, quoniam cog-
novit nomen meum.

thousand at thy right
hand : but it shall not
come nigh thee.

But thou shalt consi-
der with thy eyes : and
shalt see the reward of
the wicked.

Because thou, O Lord,
art my hope ; thou hast
made the Most High thy
refuge.

There shall no evil
come to thee ; nor shall
the scourge come near
thy dwelling.

For he hath given his
angels charge over thee :
to keep thee in all thy
ways.

In their hands they
shall bear thee up : lest
thou dash thy foot
against a stone.

Thou shalt walk upon
the asp and the basilisk :
and thou shalt trample
under foot the lion and
the dragon.

Because he hath hoped
in me, I will deliver him :
I will protect him, be-
cause he hath known my
name.

Clamabit ad me, et ego exaudiam eum : * cum ipso sum in tribulatione; eripiam eum, et glorificabo eum.

He shall cry to me, and I will hear him : I am with him in his trouble : I will deliver him, and I will glorify him.

Longitudine dierum replebo eum : * et ostendam illi salutare meum.

I will fill him with length of days : and I will show him my salvation.

Gloria Patri, etc.

Glory, etc.

PSALM 133.

ECCE nunc benedicite Dominum, * omnes servi Domini.

BEHOLD now, bless ye the Lord, all ye servants of the Lord,

Qui statis in domo Domini, * in atriis domus Dei nostri.

Who stand in the house of the Lord, in the courts of the house of our God.

In noctibus extollite manus vestras in sancta, * et benedicite Dominum.

In the nights, lift up your hands to the holy places, and bless ye the Lord.

Benedicat te Dominus ex Sion, * qui fecit cœlum et terram.

May the Lord out of Sion bless thee : he that made heaven and earth.

Gloria Patri, etc.

Glory, etc.

Ant. Miserere mihi, Domine, et exaudi orationem meam.

Ant. Have mercy on me, O Lord, and hear my prayer.

THE HYMN.

Te lucis ante terminum,
Rerum Creator, poscimus,
Ut pro tua clementia
Sis præsul et custodia.

Procul recedant somnia,
Et noctium phantasmata ;
Hostemque nostrum comprime,
Ne polluantur corpora.

Præsta, Pater piissime,
Patrique compar Unice,
Cum Spiritu Paraclito,
Regnans per omne sæculum **Amen**

The same in English.

Ere fades the evening's light away,
Creator of the world, we pray,
Thy wonted clemency extend,
And be our guardian and our friend.

From dreams our peaceful slumbers keep,
And all the phantasies of sleep :
The midnight enemy restrain,
Preserve our bodies free from stain.

Almighty Parent ! deign to hear,
Through Jesus Christ, our humble prayer
Who, with the Holy Ghost and Thee,
Shall live and reign eternally. **Amen**

TU autem in nobis es, Domine, et nomen sanctum tuum invocatum est super nos: ne derelinquas nos, Domine Deus noster.

R. Deo gratias.

R. In manus tuas Domine, commendo spiritum meum. In manus tuas Domine, commendo spiritum meum.

V. Redemisti nos, Domine Deus veritatis. Commendo spiritum meum. In manus tuas Domine, commendo spiritum meum.

V. Custodi nos, Domine, ut pupillam oculi.

R. Sub umbra alarum tuarum protege nos.

Ant. Salva nos.

THOU, O Lord! art among us, and thy holy name is called upon us; **forsake us not, O Lord our God!**

R. Thanks be to God.

R. Into thy hands, O Lord! I commend my spirit. Into thy hands, O Lord! I commend my spirit.

V. Thou hast redeemed us, O Lord, the God of truth! I commend my spirit. Into thy hands, O Lord! I commend my spirit.

V. Keep us, O Lord, as the apple of thy eye.

R. Protect us under the shadow of thy wings.

Ant. Save us.

The song of Simeon, St. Luke ii. 29-32.

NUNC dimittis servum tuum Domine, * secundum verbum tuum, in pace:

Quia viderunt oculi mei * salutare tuum,

Quod parasti * ante

NOW thou dost dismiss thy servant, O Lord! according to thy word, in peace.

Because my eyes have seen thy salvation;

Which thou hast pre-

faciem omnium populorum,

pared before the face of all people

Lumen ad revelationem gentium, * et gloriam plebis tuæ Israel.

A light to the revelation of the Gentiles, and to the glory of thy people, Israel.

Gloria, etc.

Glory, etc.

Ant. Salva nos Domine, vigilantes, custodi nos, dormientes, ut vigilemus cum Christo, et requiescamus in pace.

Ant. Save us, O Lord. waking, and keep us sleeping, that we may watch with Christ, and rest in peace.

Kyrie eleison. Christe eleison. Kyrie eleison. Pater noster, *secreto.*

Lord! have mercy on us. Christ! have mercy on us. Lord! have mercy on us. Our Father, *privately.*

V. Et ne nos inducas in tentationem.

V. And lead us not into temptation.

R. Sed libera nos a malo. Credo in Deum, etc., *secreto.*

R. But deliver us from evil. I believe in God, etc., *privately.*

V. Carnis resurrectionem.

V. The resurrection of the body.

R. Vitam æternam. Amen.

R. Life everlasting. Amen.

V. Benedictus es, Domine, Deus patrum nostrorum.

V. Blessed art thou, O Lord, the God of our fathers!

R. Et laudabilis, et gloriosus in sæcula.

R. And worthy to be praised, and glorified for ever.

V. Benedicamus Pa-

V. Let us bless the

trem et Filium cum Sancto Spiritu.

R. Laudemus, et superexaltemus eum in sæcula.

V. Benedictus es, Domine, in firmamento cœli.

R. Et laudabilis, et gloriosus, et superexaltatus in sæcula.

V. Benedicat et custodiat nos omnipotens et misericors Dominus.

R. Amen.

V. Dignare, Domine, nocte ista.

R. Sine peccato nos custodire.

V. Miserere nostri, Domine.

R. Miserere nostri.

V. Fiat misericordia tua, Domine, super nos.

R. Quemadmodum speravimus in te.

V. Domine, exaudi orationem meam.

R. Et clamor meus ad te veniat.

V. Dominus vobiscum.

R. Et cum spiritu tuo.

Father and the Son, with the Holy Ghost.

R. Let us praise and exalt him for ever.

V. Blessed art thou, O Lord! in the firmament of heaven.

R. And worthy to, be praised, and glorified, and exalted for ever.

V. May the almighty and merciful Lord bless and preserve us.

R. Amen.

V. Vouchsafe, O Lord' this night,

R. To keep us without sin.

V. Have mercy on us, O Lord!

R. Have mercy on us.

V. Let thy mercy, O Lord! be upon us.

R. As we have hoped in thee.

V. O Lord! hear my prayer.

R. And let my cry come unto thee.

V The Lord be with you.

R. And with thy spirit.

Oremus.

Visita, quæsumus Domine, habitationem istam, et omnes insidias inimici ab ea longe repelle : Angeli tui sancti habitent in ea, qui nos in pace custodiant; et benedicto tua sit super nos semper. Per Dominum, etc.

V. Dominus vobiscum.

R. Et cum spiritu tuo.

V. Benedicamus Domino.

R. Deo gratias. *Benedictio :* Benedicat et custodiat nos, omnipotens et misericors Dominus, Pater, et Filius, et Spiritus Sanctus.

R. Amen.

Let us pray.

Visit, we beseech thee, O Lord ! this habitation, and drive from it all the snares of the enemy : let thy holy angels dwell in it, to preserve us in peace : and may thy blessing be upon us for ever; through our Lord, etc.

V. The Lord be with you.

R. And with thy spirit.

V. Let us bless the Lord.

R. Thanks be to God. *The blessing :* May the almighty and merciful Lord, the Father, Son, and Holy Ghost, bless and preserve us.

R. Amen.

THE ANTHEM.

AVE, Regina cœlorum,

Ave, Domina angelorum :

Salve radix, salve porta,

HAIL, Mary, Queen of heavenly spheres !

Hail, whom the angelic host reveres !

Hail, fruitful root ! hail, sacred gate !

Ex qua mundo lux est orta.

Whence the world's light derives its date.

Gaude. Virgo gloriosa,

O glorious maid, with beauty blessed !

Super omnes speciosa :

May joys eternal fill thy breast !

Vale, o valde decora.

Thus crown'd with beauty and with joy,

Et pro nobis, Christum exora.

Thy prayers with Christ for us employ.

V. Dignare me laudare te, Virgo sacrata.

V. Vouchsafe, O sacred Virgin ! to accep my praises.

R. Da mihi virtutem contra hostes tuos.

R. Give me power against thy enemies.

Oremus.

Let us pray.

Concede, misericors Deus, fragilitati nostræ præsidium : ut, qui sanctæ Dei genitricis memoriam agimus, intercessionis ejus auxilio, a nostris iniquitatibus resurgamus. Per eundem Christum Dominum nostrum.

Grant us, O merciful God ! strength against all our weakness ; that we, who celebrate the memory of the holy mother of God, may, by the help of her intercession, rise again from our iniquities ; through the same Christ our Lord.

R. Amen.

R. Amen.

V. Divinum auxilium maneat semper nobiscum.

V. May the divine assistance always remain with us.

R. Amen.

R. Amen.

Pater noster. Ave Maria, and Credo, *privately*.

MONDAY IN HOLY WEEK.

The Mass.

The Priest begins the Mass at the foot of the Altar, as at page 13, down to Peccata mea—My sins, *p. 17.*

THE INTROIT.

JUDICA, Domine, nocentes me, expugna impugnantes me : apprehende arma et scutum, et exurge in adjutorium meum, Domine virtus salutis meæ. *Psal.* Effunde frameam, et conclude adversus eos qui persequuntur me : dic animæ meæ, salus tua ego sum. Judica, Domine, etc.

JUDGE thou, O Lord! them that wrong me ; overthrow them that fight against me : take hold of arms and shield, and rise up to help me, O Lord, the strength of my salvation! *Psalm.* Bring out the sword, and shut up the way against them that persecute me: say to my soul, I am thy salvation. Judge thou, O Lord! etc.

Kyrie eleison, Dominus vobiscum, *as at p.* 17.

THE COLLECT.

Oremus.

DA, quæsumus, omnipotens Deus: ut qui in tot adversis ex nostra infirmitate deficimus, intercedente unige-

Let us pray.

GRANT, we beseech thee, O Almighty God! that we who, through our weakness, faint under so many ad-

niti Filii tui passione, respiremus. Qui tecum vivit et regnat in unitate Spiritus Sancti Deus, per omnia sæcula sæculorum.

R. Amen.

versities, may recover by the passion of thy only begotten Son : who with thee and the Holy Ghost, liveth and reigneth one God, world without end.

R. Amen.

Then is said one of the following prayers :

For the Church.

ECCLESIÆ tuæ, quæsumus, Domine, preces placatus admitte : ut destructis adversitatibus et erroribus universis, secura tibi serviat libertate. Per Dominum nostrum, etc.

MERCIFULLY hear, we beseech thee, O Lord! the prayers of thy Church ; that all adversity and errors being removed, she may serve thee in perfect liberty ; through our Lord. etc.

Or for the Pope.

DEUS, omnium fidelium pastor et rector, famulum tuum *N.* quem pastorem Ecclesiæ tuæ præesse voluisti, propitius respice : da ei, quæsumus, verbo et exemplo, quibus præest, proficere ; ut ad vitam, una cum grege sibi credito, perveniat sempiternam. Per Dominum

O GOD! the Pastor and Governor of all the faithful, look down, in thy mercy, upon thy servant *N.*, whom thou hast been pleased to appoint pastor of thy Church: grant him, we beseech thee, that both by word and example he may edify all those that are under

nostrum Jesum Chris-
tum, etc.

his charge ; that with
the flock entrusted to
him, he may arrive to
life everlasting; through
our Lord, etc.

THE EPISTLE.

Lectio Isaiæ Prophetæ,
cap. l. 5.

The Lesson from the Pro-
phet Isaias, chap. l. 5.

IN diebus illis : Dixit
Isaias : Dominus
Deus aperuit mihi au-
rem, ego autem non con-
tradico : retrorsum non
abii. Corpus meum dedi
percutientibus, et genas
meas vellentibus; faciem
meam non averti ab in-
crepantibus, et conspu-
entibus in me. Dominus
Deus, auxiliator meus,
ideo non sum confusus :
ideo posui faciem meam
ut petram durissimam,
et scio quoniam non
confundar.   Juxta   est
qui justificat me, quis
contradicet mihi ? Ste-
mus simul, quis est ad-
versarius meus? accedat
ad me. Ecce Dominus
Deus, auxiliator meus :
quis est, qui condemnet

IN those days, Isaias
said : The Lord
God hath opened my
ear, and I do not resist:
I have not gone back ;
I have given my body
to the strikers, and my
cheeks to them that
plucked them. I have
not turned away my face
from them that rebuked
me, and spit upon me.
The Lord God is my
helper, therefore am I
not confounded : there-
fore have I set my face
as a most hard rock, and
I know that I shall not
be confounded. He is
near that justifieth me,
who will contend with
me ? let us stand to-
gether. Who is my ad-
versary ? let him come

me ? Ecce omnes quasi vestimentum conterentur, tinea comedit eos. Quis ex vobis timens Dominum, audiens vocem servi sui? Qui ambulavit in tenebris, et non est lumen ei, speret in nomine Domini, et innitatur super Deum suum.

near to me. Behold the Lord God is my helper: who is he that shall condemn me ? Lo, they shall all be destroyed as a garment, the moth shall eat them up. Who is there among you that feareth the Lord, that heareth the voice of his servant, that hath walked in darkness, and hath no light ? Let him hope in the name of the Lord, and lean upon his God.

THE GRADUAL.

EXURGE, Domine, et intende judicio meo : Deus meus et Dominus meus, in causam meam.

V. Effunde frameam, et conclude adversus eos qui me persequuntur.

ARISE, O Lord! and be attentive to my judgment, to my cause, my God and my Lord !

V. Bring out the sword, and shut up the way against them that persecute me.

THE TRACT.

DOMINE, non secundum peccata nostra, quæ fecimus nos ; neque secundum iniquitates nostras retribuas nobis.

O LORD! deal not with us according to the sins we have committed, nor reward us according to our iniquities

V. Domine, ne memineris iniquitatum nostrarum antiquarum ; cito anticipent nos misericordiæ tuæ, quia pauperes facti sumus nimis.

V. [*Hic genuflectitur.*] Adjuva nos, Deus salutaris noster, et propter gloriam nominis tui, Domine, libera nos ; et propitius esto peccatis nostris, propter nomen tuum.

Munda cor meum, *etc.*, *p.* 19.

V. O Lord ! remember not our former iniquities : let thy mercies speedily prevent us ; for we are become exceeding poor.

V. [*Here kneel down.*] Help us, O God our Saviour ! and for the glory of thy name, O Lord ! deliver us ; and forgive us our sins, for thy name's sake.

Cleanse my heart, *etc.*, *p.* 19.

THE GOSPEL.

Sequentia Sancti Evangelii secundum Joannem, cap. xii. 1–9.

ANTE sex dies paschæ, venit Jesus Bethaniam, ubi Lazarus fuerat mortuus, quem suscitavit Jesus. Fecerunt autem ei cœnam ibi : et Martha ministrabat, Lazarus vero unus erat ex discumbentibus cum eo. Maria ergo accepit libram unguenti nardi pistici pretiosi, et unxit pedes Jesu, et ex-

A continuation of the Holy Gospel according to St. John, xii. 1–9.

NOW Jesus, six days before the pasch, came to Bethania, where Lazarus had been dead, whom Jesus raised to life. And they made him a supper there ; and Martha served, but Lazarus was one of them that were at table with him. Mary therefore took a pound of ointment of right spikenard,

tersit pedes ejus capillis suis : et domus impleta est ex odore unguenti. Dixit ergo unus ex discipulis ejus, Judas Iscariotes, qui erat eum traditurus : Quare hoc unguentum non væniit trecentis denariis, et datum est egenis ? Dixit autem hoc, non quia de egenis pertinebat ad eum, sed quia fur erat, et loculos habens, ea quæ mittebantur, portabat. Dixit ergo Jesus : Sinite illam, ut in diem sepulturæ meæ servet illud. Pauperes enim semper habetis vobiscum ; me autem non semper habetis. Cognovit ergo turba multa ex Judæis quia illic est : et venerunt, non propter Jesum tantum, sed ut Lazarum viderent, quem suscitavit a mortuis.

of great price, and anointed the feet of Jesus, and wiped his feet with her hair : and the house was filled with the odor of the ointment. Then one of his disciples, Judas Iscariot, he that was about to betray him, said : Why was not this ointment sold for three hundred pence, and given to the poor ? Now he said this not because he cared for the poor, but because he was a thief, and having the purse, carried what was put therein. But Jesus said : Let her alone, that she may keep it against the day of my burial. For the poor you have always with you ; but me you have not always. A great multitude therefore of the Jews knew that he was there : and they came, not for Jesus' sake only, but that they might see Lazarus, whom he had raised from the dead.

THE OFFERTORY.

ERIPE me de inimicis meis, Domine: ad te confugi, doce me facere voluntatem tuam, quia Deus meus es tu.

DELIVER me from my enemies, O Lord! to thee have I fled, teach me to do thy will, for thou art my God.

Suscipe, *etc.*, *as at p.* 26, *to* Then the Priest says Amen, *p.* 28.

THE SECRET.

HÆC sacrificia nos, omnipotens Deus, potenti virtute mundatos, ad suum faciant puriores venire principium. Per Dominum nostrum, etc.

GRANT, O Almighty God! that, being purified by the powerful virtue of these sacrifices, we may arrive with greater purity to the fountain thereof; through our Lord, etc.

For the Church.

PROTEGE nos, Domine, tuis mysteriis servientes: ut divinis rebus inhærentes, et corpore tibi famulemur et mente. Per Dominum nostrum, etc.

PROTECT us, O Lord! whilst we assist at thy mysteries. that, our minds being applied to divine things, we may serve thee both in soul and body: through our Lord, etc.

Or for the Pope.

OBLATIS, quæsumus, Domine placare muneribus: et famulum tuum N. quem

BE appeased, O Lord we beseech thee, by these offerings: and cease not to protect thy

pastorem Ecclesiæ tuæ præesse voluisti, assidua protectione guberna. Per Dominum nostrum, etc.

servant N., whom thou hast been pleased to appoint pastor over thy church; through our Lord, etc.

The Preface, p. 94. The Canon down to end of prayer Corpus tuum *—May thy, etc., p. 42.*

THE COMMUNION.

ERUBESCANT, et revereantur simul, qui gratulantur malis meis: induantur pudore et reverentia, qui maligna loquuntur adversus me.

LET them blush and be ashamed together, who rejoice at my evils: let them be clothed with confusion and shame, that speak malicious things against me.

V. Dominus vobiscum.

R. Et cum spiritu tuo.

V. The Lord be with you.

R. And with thy spirit.

THE POST-COMMUNION.

Oremus.

PRÆBEANT nobis, Domine, divinum tua sancta fervorem: quo eorum pariter et actu delectemur, et fructu. Per Dominum nostrum, etc.

Let us pray.

LET thy holy mysteries, O Lord! inspire us with a divine fervor; that we may delight both in their effect and celebration; through our Lord, etc.

For the Church.

QUÆSUMUS, Domine, Deus noster, ut quos di-

O LORD our God! we beseech thee to protect those, whom

vina tribuis participa-
tione gaudere, humanis
non sinas subjacere pe-
riculis. Per Dominum
nostrum, etc.

thou hast permitted to
partake of these divine
mysteries, from the dan-
gers incident to human
life; through our Lord,
etc.

Or for the Pope.

H ÆC nos, quæsu-
mus, Domine, di-
vini sacramenti percep-
tio protegat: et famulum
tuum N., quem pastorem
Ecclesiæ tuæ præesse
voluisti, una cum com-
misso sibi grege salvet
semper et muniat. Per
Dominum nostrum, etc.

L ET the participa-
tion of the divine
sacrament protect us, we
beseech thee, O Lord'
and always save and
strengthen thy servant
N., whom thou hast ap-
pointed pastor over thy
church, together with
the flock entrusted to
his charge; through our
Lord, etc.

The Prayer over the People.

Oremus.

H UMILIATE ca-
pita vestra Deo.
Adjuva nos, Deus sa-
lutaris noster: et ad be-
neficia recolenda, quibus
nos instaurare dignatus
es, tribue venire gauden-
tes. Per Dominum nos-
trum, etc.

Let us pray.

B OW down your
heads to God.
Help us, O God, our
salvation! and grant
that we may celebrate
with joy the memory of
those benefits by which
thou hast been pleased
to redeem us; through
our Lord, etc.

The rest of the Mass from Dominus vobiscum, *as on p. 17.*

TUESDAY IN HOLY WEEK.

The Mass.

The Priest begins the Mass at the foot of the Altar, as at page 13
down to Peccata mea—My sins, p. 17.

THE INTROIT.

NOS autem gloriari oportet in cruce Domini nostri, Jesu Christi, in quo est salus, vita, et resurrectio nostra: per quem salvati et liberati sumus. *Psalmus.* Deus misereatur nostri, et benedicat nobis: illuminet vultum suum super nos, et misereatur nostri. Nos autem, etc.

WE ought to glory in the cross of our Lord Jesus Christ; in whom is our salvation, life, and resurrection: by whom we have been saved and delivered. *Psalm.* May God have mercy on us, and bless us; may he make the light of his countenance to shine upon us, may he have mercy on us. We ought, etc.

Kyrie eleison *and* Dominus vobiscum, *as at p.* 17.

THE COLLECT.

Oremus.

OMNIPOTENS sempiterne Deus, da nobis ita Dominicæ passionis sacramenta peragere, ut indulgentiam

Let us pray.

ALMIGHTY and everlasting God! grant that we may so celebrate the mysteries of our Lord's passion as

percipere mereamur. Per eundem Dominum nostrum, etc.

to obtain thy pardon; through the same Lord, etc.

Then is said the Prayer for the Church, or for the Pope, as at p 127

THE EPISTLE.

Lectio Jeremiæ Prophetæ, cap. xi. 18–20.

The Lesson from the Prophet Jeremias, xi. 18–20.

IN diebus illis : Dixit Jeremias : Domine, demonstrasti mihi, et cognovi : tunc ostendisti mihi studia eorum. Et ego quasi agnus mansuetus, qui portatur ad victimam : et non cognovi quia cogitaverunt super me consilia, dicentes : Mittamus lignum in panem ejus, et eradamus eum de terra viventium, et nomen ejus non memoretur amplius. Tu autem, Domine Sabaoth, qui judicas juste, et probas renes et corda, videam ultionem tuam ex eis : tibi enim revelavi causam meam, Domine, Deus meus.

IN those days, Jeremias said : Thou, O Lord ! hast showed me, and I have known : then thou showedst me their doings. And I was as a meek lamb, that is carried to be a victim : and I knew not that they had devised counsels against me, saying, Let us put wood on his bread, and cut him off from the land of the living, and let his name be remembered no more. But thou, O Lord of Sabaoth ! who judgest justly, and triest the reins and the hearts, let me see thy revenge on them : for to thee have I revealed my cause, O Lord, my God !

THE GRADUAL.

EGO autem, dum mihi molesti essent, induebam me cilicio, et humiliabam in jejunio animam meam : et oratio mea in sinu meo convertetur.

V. Judica, Domine, nocentes me, expugna impugnantes me : apprehende arma et scutum, et exurge in adjutorium mihi.

Passio Domini nostri Jesu Christi secundum Marcum, cap. xiv. et xv.

IN illo tempore : Erat Pascha et Azyma post biduum ; et quærebant summi sacerdotes et Scribæ, quomodo Jesum dolo tenerent, et occiderent. Dicebant autem : Non in die festo, ne forte tumultus fieret in populo. Et cum esset Jesus Bethaniæ in domo Simonis leprosi, et re-

BUT as for me, when they were troublesome to me, I was clothed with hair-cloth, and I humbled my soul with fasting ; and my prayer shall be turned into my bosom.

V. Judge thou, O Lord ! them that wrong me, overthrow them that fight against me ; take hold of arms and shield, and rise up to help me.

The Passion of our Lord Jesus Christ according to St. Mark, chap. xiv. and xv.

AT that time, the feast of the pasch and of the azyms was after two days : and the chief priests and the Scribes sought how they might by some wile lay hold on him and kill him ; but they said : Not on the festival day, lest there should be a tumult among the people. And when

cumberet, venit mulier habens alabastrum unguenti nardi spicati pretiosi, et fractro alabastro, effudit super caput ejus. Erant autem quidam indigne ferentes intra semetipsos, et dicentes: Ut quid perditio ista unguenti facta est? Poterat enim unguentum istud venumdari plusquam trecentis denariis, et dari pauperibus: et fremebant in eam. Jesus autem dixit: Sinite eam, quid illi molesti estis? Bonum opus operata est in me. Semper enim pauperes habetis vobiscum; et cum volueritis, potestis illis benefacere: me autem non semper habetis. Quod habuit hæc, fecit: prævenit ungere corpus meum in sepulturam. Amen dico vobis: Ubicumque prædicatum fuerit Evangelium istud in universo mundo, et quod fecit hæc, narrabitur in memoriam ejus. Et Judas

he was in Bethania in the house of Simon, the leper, and was at meat: there came a woman having an alabaster box of ointment of precious spikenard: and breaking the alabaster box, she poured it out upon his head. Now there were some that had indignation within themselves, and said: Why was this waste of the ointment made? For this ointment might have been sold for more than three hundred pence, and given to the poor. And they murmured against her. But Jesus said: Let her alone, why do you molest her? She hath wrought a good work upon me. For the poor you have always with you; and whensoever you will, you may do them good; but me you have not always. She hath done what she could: she is come beforehand to anoint my

Iscariotes, unus de duodecim, abiit ad summos sacerdotes, ut proderet eum illis. Qui audientes, gavisi sunt, et promiserunt ei pecuniam se daturos. Et quærebat quomodo illum opportune traderet. Et primo die Azymorum quando Pascha immolabant, dicunt ei discipuli : Quo vis eamus, et paremus tibi ut manduces Pascha ? Et mittit duos ex discipulis suis, et dicit eis : Ite in civitatem : et occurret vobis homo lagenam aquæ bajulans : sequimini eum, et quocumque introierit, dicite domino domus, quia magister dicit : Ubi est refectio mea, ubi Pascha cum discipulis meis manducem ? Et ipse vobis demonstrabit connaculum grande, stratum : et illic parate nobis. Et abierunt discipuli ejus, et venerunt in civitatem : et invenerunt sicut dixerat illis, et paraverunt

body for the burial. Amen, I say to you, wheresoever this gospel shall be preached in the whole world, that also which she hath done shall be told for a memorial of her. And Judas Iscariot, one of the twelve, went to the chief priests, to betray him to them. And they hearing it, were glad ; and promised to give him money. And he sought how he might conveniently betray him. Now on the first day of the unleavened bread, when they sacrificed the pasch, the disciples say to him : Whither wilt thou that we go, and prepare for thee to eat the pasch? And he sendeth two of his disciples and saith to them : Go ye into the city ; and there shall meet you a man carrying a pitcher of water, follow him : And whithersoever he shall go in, say to the master of the house

Pascha. Vespere autem facto, venit cum duodecim. Et discumbentibus eis, et manducantibus, ait Jesus : Amen dico vobis, quia unus ex vobis tradet me, qui manducat mecum. At illi cœperunt contristari, et dicere ei singulatim : Numquid ego ? Qui ait illis : Unus ex duodecim, qui intingit mecum manum in catino. Et Filius quidem hominis vadit, sicut scriptum est de eo : væ autem homini iili, per quem Filius hominis tradetur. Bonum erat ei, si non esset natus homo ille. Et manducantibus illis, accepit Jesus panem : et benedicens fregit, et dedit eis, et ait : Sumite, hoc est corpus meum. Et accepto calice, gratias agens, dedit eis : et biberunt ex illo omnes. Et ait illis : Hic est sanguis meus novi testamenti, qui pro multis effundetur. Amen dico vobis,

The Master saith : Where is my refectory, where I may eat the pasch with my disciples ? And he will show you a large dining-room furnished ; and there prepare ye for us. And his disciples went their way, and came into the city ; and they found as he had told them, and they prepared the pasch. And when evening was come, he cometh with the twelve. And when they were at table and eating, Jesus saith : Amen I say to you, one of you that eateth with me shall betray me. But they began to be sorrowful, and to say to him one by one : Is it I ? And he said to them : One of the twelve who dippeth his hand in the dish with me. And the Son of Man indeed goeth, as it is written of him ; but woe to that man by whom the Son of Man shall be betrayed. It were better

quia jam non bibam de hoc genimine vitis, usque in diem illum, cum illud bibam novum in regno Dei.

for him if that man had not been born. And whilst they were eating, Jesus took bread : and blessing, broke, and gave to them, and said : Take ye, this is my body. And having taken the chalice, giving thanks he gave it to them ; and they all drank of it. And he said to them : This is my blood of the New Testament which shall be shed for many. Amen I say unto you, that I will drink no more of this fruit of the vine, until that day when I shall drink it new in the kingdom of God.

Et hymno dicto, exierunt in montem Olivarum. Et ait eis Jesus : Omnes scandalizabimini in me in nocte ista, quia scriptum est: Percutiam pastorem, et dispergentur oves. Sed postquam resurrexero, præcedam vos in Galilæam. Petrus autem ait illi : Et si om-

And when they had sung a hymn, they went forth to the Mount of Olives. And Jesus saith unto them : You will all be scandalized in me this night; for it is written : I will strike the shepherd, and the sheep shall be dispersed. But after I shall be risen

nes scandalizati fuerint in te, sed non ego. Et ait illi Jesus : Amen dico tibi, quia tu hodie in nocte hac, priusquam gallus vocem bis dederit, ter me es negaturus. At ille amplius loquebatur : Et si oportuerit me simul commori tibi, non te negabo. Similiter autem et omnes dicebant. Et veniunt in prædium, cui nomen Gethsemani. Et ait discipulis suis : Sedete hic donec orem. Et assumit Petrum, et Jacobum, et Joannem secum : et cœpit pavere, et tædere. Et ait illis : Tristis est anima mea usque ad mortem : sustinete hic, et vigilate. Et cum processisset paululum, procidit super terram : et orabat ut, si fieri posset, transiret ab eo hora, et dixit : Abba, Pater, omnia tibi possibilia sunt : transfer calicem hunc a me ; sed non quod ego volo, sed quod tu. Et venit, et

again, I will go before you into Galilee. But Peter saith to him : Although all shall be scandalized in thee, yet not I. And Jesus saith to him : Amen I say to thee, to-day, even in this night, before the cock crow twice, thou shalt deny me thrice. But he spoke the more vehemently : Although I should die together with thee, I will not deny thee. And in like manner also said they all. And they came to a farm called Gethsemani. And he saith to his disciples Sit you here while I pray And he taketh Peter, and James, and John with him : and he began to fear, and to be heavy. And he saith to them : My soul is sorrowful even unto death ; stay you here, and watch. And when he had gone forward a little, he fell flat on the ground ; and he prayed that if it were

invenit eos dormientes. Et ait Petro : Simon, dormis ? non potuisti una hora vigilare ? Vi- gilate, et orate ut non intretis in tentationem. Spiritus quidem promp- tus est, caro vero infir- ma. Et iterum abiens, oravit eundem sermo- nem dicens. Et rever- sus denuo invenit eos dormientes (erant enim oculi eorum gravati), et ignorabant quid respon- derent ei. Et venit ter- tio, et ait illis : Dormite jam, et requiescite. Suf- ficit ; venit hora ; ecce Filius hominis tradetur in manus peccatorum. Surgite, eamus : ecce qui me tradet, prope est. Et, adhuc eo lo- quente, venit Judas Iscariotes, unus de duodecim, et cum eo turba multa cum gla- diis et lignis, a sum- mis sacerdotibus, et Scribis, et senioribus. Dederat autem tradi- tor ejus signum eis.

possible the hour might pass from him. And he said : Abba, Father! all things are possible to thee, take away this chal- ice from me : but not what I will, but what thou wilt. And he com- eth and findeth them sleeping. And he saith to Peter : Simon! sleep- est thou ? couldst thou not watch one hour ? Watch ye, and pray, that you enter not into temp- tation. The spirit in- deed is willing, but the flesh is weak. And going away again, he prayed, saying the same words. And when he returned, he found them again asleep (for their eyes were heavy), and they knew not what to answer him. And he cometh the third time, and saith to them : Sleep ye now, and take your rest. It is enough ; the hour is come ; behold the Son of Man shall be betrayed into the hands of sinners.

dicens : Quemcumque osculatus fuero, ipse est, tenete eum, et ducite caute. Et cum venisset, statim accedens ad eum, ait : Ave, Rabbi ; et osculatus est eum. At illi manus injecerunt in eum, et tenuerunt eum. Unus autem quidam de circumstantibus educens gladium, percussit servum summi sacerdotis, et amputavit illi auriculam. Et respondens Jesus, ait illis : Tamquam ad latronem existis cum gladiis et lignis comprehendere me ? Quotidie eram apud vos in templo docens, et non me tenuistis. Sed ut impleantur Scripturæ. Tunc discipuli ejus relinquentes eum, omnes fugerunt. Adolescens autem quidam sequebatur eum amictus sindone super nudo : et tenuerunt eum. At ille, rejecta

Rise up, let us go. Behold, he that will betray me is at hand. And while he was yet speaking, cometh Judas Iscariot, one of the twelve, and with him a great multitude, with swords and staves, from the chief priests and the Scribes and the ancients. And he that betrayed him had given them a sign, saying : Whomsoever I shall kiss, that is he, lay hold on him, and lead him away cautiously. And when he was come, immediately going up to him, he saith : Hail, Rabbi ! and he kissed him. But they laid hands on him, and held him. And one of them that stood by, drawing a sword, struck the servant of the chief priest, and cut off his ear. And Jesus answering, said to them : Are you come out as against a robber, with swords and staves to apprehend me ? I was daily

sindone, nudus profugit ab eis.

with you in the temple teaching, and you did not lay hands on me. But, that the Scriptures may be fulfilled. Then his disciples leaving him, all fled away. And a certain young man followed him, having a linen cloth cast about his naked body, and they laid hold on him. But he casting off the linen cloth, fled from them naked.

Et adduxerunt Jesum ad summum sacerdotem: et convenerunt omnes sacerdotes, et Scribæ, et seniores. Petrus autem a longe secutus est eum usque intro in atrium summi sacerdotis, et sedebat cum ministris ad ignem, et calefaciebat se. Summi vero sacerdotes, et omne concilium quærebant adversus Jesum testimonium, ut eum morti traderent, nec inveniebant. Multi enim testimonium falsum dicebant adversus eum: et convenientia testimonia

And they brought Jesus to the high priest: and all the priests and the scribes and the ancients were assembled together. And Peter followed him afar off, even into the palace of the high priest: and he sat with the servants at the fire and warmed himself. And the chief priests and all the council sought for evidence against Jesus, that they might put him to death, and they found none. For many bore false witness against him, and their evidence did

non erant. Et quidam surgentes, falsum testimonium ferebant adversus eum, dicentes: Quoniam nos audivimus eum dicentem: Ego dissolvam templum hoc manufactum, et per triduum aliud non manufactum ædificabo. Et non erat conveniens testimonium illorum. Et exurgens summus sacerdos in medium, interrogavit Jesum, dicens: Non respondes quidquam ad ea, quæ tibi objiciunter ab his? Ille autem tacebat, et nihil respondit. Rursum summus sacerdos interrogabat eum, et dixit ei: Tu es Christus Filius Dei benedicti? Jesus autem dixit illi: Ego sum. Et videbitis Filium hominis sedentem a dextris virtutis Dei, et venientem cum nubibus cœli. Summus autem sacerdos scindens vestimenta sua, ait: Quid adhuc desideramus testes? Audistis

not agree. And some rising up, bore false witness against him, saying: We heard him say, I will destroy this temple made with hands, and within three days I will build another not made with hands. And their testimony did not agree. And the high priest rising up in the midst, asked Jesus, saying: Answerest thou nothing to the things that are laid to thy charge by these men? But he held his peace and answered nothing. Again the high priest asked him and said unto him: Art thou the Christ, the Son of the blessed God? And Jesus said to him, I am. And you shall see the Son of Man sitting on the right hand of the power of God, and coming with the clouds of heaven. Then the high priest rending his garments, saith: What need we any farther witness-

blasphemiam : quid vobis videtur ? Qui omnes condemnaverunt eum esse reum mortis. Et cœperunt quidam conspuere eum, et velare faciem ejus, et colaphis eum cædere, et dicere ei : Prophetiza. Et ministri alapis eum cædebant. Et cum esset Petrus in atrio deorsum, venit una ex ancillis summi sacerdotis : et cum vidisset Petrum calefacientem se, aspiciens illum, ait : Et tu cum Jesu Nazareno eras. At ille negavit, dicens : Neque scio, neque novi quid dicas. Et exiit foras ante atrium, et gallus cantavit. Rursus autem cum vidisset illum ancilla, cœpit dicere circumstantibus : Quia hic ex illis est. At ille iterum negavit. Et post pusillum rursus qui astabant, dicebant Petro : Vere ex illis es ; nam et Galilæus es. Ille autem cœpit anathematizare et

es ? You have heard the blasphemy. What think you ? And they all condemned him to be guilty of death. And some began to spit on him, and to cover his face, and to buffet him, and to say to him, Prophesy : and the servants struck him with the palms of their hands. Now when Peter was in the court below, there cometh one of the maid servants of the high priest. And when she had seen Peter warming himself, looking on him she aith : Thou also wast with Jesus of Nazareth. But he denied, saying : I neither know nor understand what thou sayest. And he went forth before the court, and the cock crew. And again a maid servant seeing him, began to say to the bystanders : This is one of them. But he denied again. And after a while they that stood by, said

jurare : Quia nescio hominem istum, quem dicitis. Et statim gallus iterum cantavit. Et recordatus est Petrus verbi quod dixerat ei Jesus : Priusquam gallus cantet bis, ter me negabis. Et cœpit flere.

again to Peter : Surely thou art one of them, for thou art also a Galilean. But he began to curse and to swear, saying : I know not this man of whom you speak. And immediately the cock crew again. And Peter remembered the word that Jesus had said to him : Before the cock crow twice, thou shalt deny me thrice. And he began to weep.

Et confestim mane consilium facientes summi sacerdotes, cum senioribus, et Scribis, et universo concilio, vincientes Jesum, duxerunt, et tradiderunt Pilato. Et interrogavit eum Pilatus : Tu es Rex Judæorum ? At ille respondens, ait illi : Tu dicis. Et accusabant eum summi sacerdotes in multis. Pilatus autem rursus interrogavit eum, dicens. Non respondes quidquam ? vide in quantis te accusant. Jesus au-

And straightway in the morning the chief priests holding a consultation with the ancients and the Scribes and the whole council, bound Jesus and led him away, and delivered him to Pilate. And Pilate asked him : Art thou the King of the Jews ? But he answering, saith to him : Thou sayest it. And the chief priests accused him in many things. And Pilate again asked him, saying : Answerest thou nothing ? behold in how

tem amplius nihil respondit, ita ut miraretur Pilatus. Per diem autem festum solebat dimittere illis unum ex vinctis, quemcumque petiissent. Erat autem qui dicebatur Barabbas, qui cum seditiosis erat vinctus, qui in seditione fecerat homicidium. Et cum ascendisset turba, cœpit rogare, sicut semper faciebat illis. Pilatus autem respondit eis, et dixit : Vultis dimittam vobis regem Judæorum ? Sciebat enim quod per invidiam tradidissent eum summi sacerdotes. Pontifices autem concitaverunt turbam, ut magis Barabbam dimitteret eis. Pilatus autem iterum respondens, ait illis: Quid ergo vultis faciam regi Judæorum ? At illi iterum clamaverunt : Crucifige eum. Pilatus vero dicebat illis: Quid enim mali fecit ? At illi magis clamabant : Crucifige eum.

many things they accuse thee. But Jesus still answered nothing, so that Pilate wondered. Now on the festival day, he was wont to release unto them one of the prisoners, whomsoever they demanded. And there was one called Barabbas, who was put in prison with seditious men, who in the sedition had committed murder. And when the multitude was come up, they began to desire that he would do as he had always done to them. And Pilate answered them, and said : Will you that I release to you the King of the Jews ? For he knew that the chief priests had delivered him up out of envy. But the chief priests moved the people, that he should rather release Barabbas to them. And Pilate again answering, saith to them : What will you then that I do

Pilatus autem volens populo satisfacere, dimisit illis Barabbam, et tradidit Jesum flagellis cæsum, ut crucifigeretur. Milites autem duxerunt eum in atrium prætorii, et convocant totam cohortem, et induunt eum purpura, et imponunt ei plectentes spineam coronam. Et cœperunt salutare eum : Ave Rex Judæorum. Et percutiebant caput ejus arundine, et conspuebant eum, et ponentes genua, adorabant eum.

to the King of the Jews? But they again cried out: Crucify him. And Pilate saith to them : Why, what evil hath he done ? But they cried out the more : Crucify him. So Pilate being willing to satisfy the people, released to them Barabbas, and delivered up Jesus, when he had scourged him, to be crucified. And the soldiers led him into the court of the palace, and they call together the whole band : and they clothe him with purple, and plaiting a crown of thorns, they put it upon him. And they began to salute him, Hail, King of the Jews ! And they struck his head with a reed : and they did spit on him, and bowing their knees, they worshipped him.

Et postquam illuserunt ei, exuerunt illum purpura, et induerunt eum vestimentis suis :

And after they had mocked him, they took off the purple from him, and put his own gar-

et educunt illum, ut crucifigerent eum. Et angariaverunt prætereuntem quempiam, Simonem Cyrenæum, venientem de villa, patrem Alexandri et Rufi, ut tolleret crucem ejus. Et perducunt illum in Golgotha locum, quod est interpretatum Calvariæ locus. Et dabant ei bibere myrrhatum vinum : et non accepit. Et crucifigentes eum, diviserunt vestimenta ejus, mittentes sortem super eis, quis quid tolleret. Erat autem hora tertia : et crucifixerunt eum. Et erat titulus causæ ejus inscriptus : Rex Judæorum. Et cum eo crucifigunt duos latrones ; unum a dextris, et alium a sinistris ejus. Et impleta est Scripturæ, quæ dicit : Et cum iniquis reputatus est. Et prætereuntes blasphemabant eum, moventes capita sua, et dicentes : Vah, qui destruis tem-

ments on him, and they led him out to crucify him. And they forced one Simon, a Cyrenian, who passed by, coming out of the country, the father of Alexander and of Rufus, to take up his cross. And they bring him into the place called Golgotha, which being interpreted, is the place of Calvary. And they gave him to drink wine mingled with myrrh ; but he took it not. And crucifying him, they divided his garments, casting lots upon them, what every man should take. And it was the third hour, and they crucified him. And the inscription of his cause was written over : The King of the Jews. And with him they crucify two thieves, the one on his right hand, and the other on his left. And the Scripture was fulfilled which saith : And with the wicked he was

plum Dei, et in tribus diebus reædificas : salvum fac temetipsum, descendens de cruce. Similiter et summi sacerdotes illudentes, ad alterutrum cum Scribis dicebant : alios salvos fecit, seipsum non potest salvum facere. Christus rex Israel descendat nunc de cruce, ut videamus, et credamus. Et qui cum eo crucifixi erant, convitiabantur ei. Et facta hora sexta, tenebræ factæ sunt per totam terram, usque in horam nonam. Et hora nona, exclamavit Jesus voce magna, dicens ; Eloi, Eloi, lamma sabacthani ? Quod est interpretatum : Deus meus, Deus meus, ut quid dereliquisti me ? Et quidam de circumstantibus audientes, dicebant: Ecce Eliam vocat. Currens autem unus, et implens spongiam aceto circumponensque calamo, potum dabat ei, di-

reputed. And they that passed by blasphemed, him, wagging their heads, and saying : Vah ! thou that destroyest the temple of God, and in three days buildest it up again : save thyself, coming down from the cross. In like manner also the chief priests, with the Scribes, mocking, said to one another : He saved others, himself he cannot save. Let Christ, the King of Israel, come down now from the cross that we may see and believe. And they that were crucified with him reviled him. And when the sixth hour was come, there was darkness over the whole earth until the ninth hour. And at the ninth hour Jesus cried out with a loud voice, saying : Eloi, Eloi, lamma sabacthani ! Which is, being interpreted : My God, my God ! why hast thou forsaken me ? And some

cens : Sinite, videamus si veniat Elias ad deponendum eum. Jesus autem emissa voce magna expiravit.

of the bystanders hearing, said : Behold he calleth Elias. And one running and filling a sponge with vinegar, and putting it upon a reed, gave him to drink, saying : Stay, let us see if Elias will come to take him down. And Jesus having cried out with a loud voice, gave up the ghost.

Here all kneel, to meditate on the redemption of mankind: and after a little pause, they rise, and the Deacon goes on :

ET velum templi scissum est in duo, a summo usque deorsum. Videns autem centurio, qui ex adverso stabat, quia sic clamans expirasset, ait : Vere hic homo Filius Dei erat. Erant autem et mulieres de longe aspicientes, inter quas erat Maria Magdalene, et Maria Jacobi minoris et Joseph mater, et Salome : et cum esset in Galilæa, sequebantur eum, et ministrabant ei ;

AND the veil of the temple was rent in two from the top to the bottom. And the centurion who stood over against him seeing that crying out in this manner he had given up the ghost, said : Indeed this man was the Son of God. And there were also women looking on afar off ; among whom was Mary Magdalene, and Mary the mother of James the less, and

et aliæ multæ, quæ simul cum eo ascenderant Jerosolymam,

of Joseph, and Salome: who also, when he was in Galilee, followed him and ministered to him; and many other women that came up with him to Jerusalem.

Here is said Munda, *etc., as at p. 19.*

ET cum jam sero esset factum (quia erat Parasceve quod est ante Sabbatum) venit Joseph ab Arimathæa nobilis decurio, qui et ipse erat expectans regnum Dei, et audacter introivit ad Pilatum, et petiit corpus Jesu. Pilatus autem mirabatur si jam obiisset. Et accersito centurione, interrogavit eum si jam mortuus esset. Et cum cognovisset a centurione, donavit corpus Joseph. Joseph autem mercatus sindonem, et deponens eum involvit sindone, et posuit eum in monumento, quod erat excisum de petra, et advol-

AND when the evening was now come, because it was the Parasceve, that is the day before the Sabbath, Joseph of Arimathea, a noble counsellor, who was also himself looking for the kingdom of God, came and went in boldly to Pilate, and begged the body of Jesus. But Pilate wondered that he should be already dead. And sending for the centurion, he asked him if he were already dead. And when he had understood it by the centurion, he gave the body to Joseph. And Joseph buying fine linen and taking him down, wrapped him

vit lapidem ad ostium monumenti.

up in the fine linen, and laid him in a sepulchre which was hewed out of a rock, and he rolled a stone to the door of the sepulchre.

THE OFFERTORY.

CUSTODI me, Domine, de manu peccatoris, et ab hominibus iniquis eripe me.

KEEP me, O Lord! from the hand of the wicked, and from unjust men deliver me.

Suscipe, *etc.*, *as at p.* 26, *down to* **Then the Priest says Amen**, *p.* 28.

THE SECRET.

SACRIFICIA nos, quæsumus, Domine, propensius ista restaurent, quæ medicinalibus sunt instituta jejuniis. Per Dominum nostrum, etc.

LET these sacrifices, O Lord! we beseech thee, which are accompanied with healing fasts, mercifully reform us; through our Lord, etc.

The other Secret, **Protege,** *or* **Oblatis,** *as at p.* 132; *The Preface, p* 94; *and the Canon, down to end of prayer,* **Corpus tuum—May thy,** *etc., p.* 42.

THE COMMUNION.

ADVERSUM me exercebantur, qui sedebant in porta; et in me psallebant, qui bibebant vinum : ego vero orationem meam ad te

THEY that sat in the gate spoke against me : and they that drank wine made me their songs; but, as for me, my prayer is to

Domine : tempus bene- thee, O Lord ! for the placiti, Deus, in multitu- time of thy good plea- dine misericordiæ tuæ. sure, O God ! in the multitude of thy mercy.

THE POST-COMMUNION.

Oremus.   Let us pray.

SANCTIFICATI-ONIBUS tuis, om-nipotens Deus, et vitia nostra curentur, et re-media nobis sempiterna proveniant. Per Domi-num nostrum, etc.

MAY these thy holy sacrifices, Al-mighty God ! both cure our vices, and become an eternal remedy to us ; through our Lord, etc.

The other Post-communion : Quæsumus, *or* Hæc nos, *as at p.* 133.

The Prayer over the People.

Oremus.   Let us pray.

Humiliate capita vestra Deo.

Bow down your heads to God.

TUA nos misericor-dia, Deus, et ab omni subreptione vetus-tatis expurget, et capaces sanctæ novitatis efficiat. Per Dominum nostrum, etc.

MAY thy mercy, O God ! purify us from the corruption of the old man and enable us to put on the new ; through our Lord, etc.

The rest of the Mass from Dominus vobiscum, *as on p.* 17.

WEDNESDAY IN HOLY WEEK.

The Mass.

The Priest begins the Mass at the foot of the Altar, as at page 13, down to Peccata mea—My sins, *p. 17.*

THE INTROIT.

IN nomine Jesu omne genu flectatur, cœlestium, terrestrium, et infernorum: quia Dominus factus est obediens usque ad mortem, mortem autem crucis: ideo Dominus Jesus Christus in gloria est Dei Patris. *Psal.* Domine, exaudi orationem meam, et clamor meus ad te veniat. In nomine, etc,

IN the name of Jesus every knee should bow, of those that are in heaven, on earth, and under the earth : because the Lord became obedient unto death, even the death of the cross : Wherefore the Lord Jesus Christ is in the glory of God, the Father. *The Psalm.* Hear, O Lord! my prayer, and let my cry come to thee. In the name, etc.

Kyrie eleison *and* Dominus vobiscum, *as at p.* 17.

THE FIRST COLLECT.

Oremus.
Flectamus genua.
R. Levate.

Let us pray.
Let us bend our knees.
R. Rise up.

PRÆSTA, quæsumus, omnipotens

GRANT, we beseech thee, O Almighty

Deus : ut, qui nostris excessibus incessanter affligimur, per unigeniti Filii tui passionem liberemur. Qui tecum vivit, etc.

God ! that we, who are continually punished for our excesses, may be delivered by the passion of thy only begotten Son ; who with thee and the Holy Ghost, etc.

THE FIRST EPISTLE.

Lectio Isaiæ Prophetæ, cap. lxii. 11 ; lxiii. 1–7.

The Lesson from the Prophet Isaias, chap. lxii. 11 ; lxiii. 1–7.

HÆC dicit Dominus Deus : Dicite filiæ Sion : Ecce Salvator tuus venit ; ecce merces ejus cum eo. Quis est iste, qui venit de Edom, tinctis vestibus de Bosra ? Iste formosus in stola sua, gradiens in multitudine fortitudinis suæ. Ego, qui loquor justitiam, et propugnator sum ad salvandum. Quare ergo rubrum est indumentum tuum, et vestimenta tua sicut calcantium in torculari ? torcular calcavi solus, et de gentibus non est vir mecum ; calcavi

THUS saith the Lord God : Tell the daughter of Sion ; behold thy Saviour cometh ; behold his reward is with him. Who is this that cometh from Edom, with dyed garments from Bosra, this beautiful one in his robe, walking in the greatness of his strength ? I, that speak justice, and am a defender to save. Why then is thy apparel red, and thy garments like theirs that tread in the wine-press ? I have trodden the wine-press alone, and of the Gentiles there

eos in furore meo ; et conculcavi eos in ira mea : et aspersus est sanguis eorum super vestimenta mea, et omnia indumenta mea inquinavi. Dies enim ultionis in corde meo, annus redemptionis meæ venit. Circumspexi, et non erat auxiliator ; quæsivi, et non fuit qui adjuvaret : et salvavit mihi brachium meum, et indignatio mea ipsa auxiliata est mihi. Et conculcavi populos in furore meo, et inebriavi eos in indignatione mea, et detraxi in terram virtutem eorum. Miserationum Domini recordabor, laudem Domini super omnibus, quæ reddidit nobis Dominus Deus noster.

is not a man with me: I have trampled on them in my indignation, and have trodden them down in my wrath, and their blood is sprinkled upon my garments, and I have stained all my apparel. For the day of vengeance is in my heart, the year of my redemption is come. I looked about, and there was none to help : I sought, and there was none to give aid : and my own arm hath saved for me, and my indignation itself hath helped me. And I have trodden down the people in my wrath, and have made them drunk in my indignation, and have brought down their strength to the earth. I will remember the tender mercies of the Lord, the praise of the Lord for all things, that the Lord our God hath bestowed on us.

THE GRADUAL.

N E avertas faciem tuam a puero tuo, quoniam tribulor : velociter exaudi me.

V. Salvum me fac, Deus, quoniam intraverunt aquæ usque ad animam meam : infixus sum in limo profundi, et non est substantia.

V. Dominus vobiscum.

R. Et cum spiritu tuo.

T URN not away thy face from thy servant, for I am in trouble ; hear me speedily.

V. Save me, O God ! for waters are come in even unto my soul : I stick fast in the mire of the deep, and there is no sure standing.

V. The Lord be with you.

R. And with thy spirit.

THE SECOND COLLECT.

Oremus.

D EUS, qui pro nobis Filium tuum crucis patibulum subire v - luisti, ut inimici a nobis expelleres potestatem concede nobis famulis cuis, ut resurrectionis gratiam consequamur. Per eundem Dominum nostrum, etc.

Let us pray.

O GOD! who wouldst have thy Son suffer death for us on the cross, to deliver us from the power of the enemy ; grant to us, thy servants, that we may obtain the grace of his resurrection ; through the same Lord, etc.

The Prayer for the Church, or for the Pope, as at p 127.

THE SECOND EPISTLE.

Lectio Isaiæ Prophetæ, cap. liii.

I N diebus illis : Dixit Isaias: Domine, quis

The Lesson from the Pro phet Isaias, chap. liii.

I N those days Isaias said : Lord ! who

credidit auditui nostro? hath believed our report? et brachium Domini cui And to whom is the arm revelatum est? Et as- of the Lord revealed? cendet sicut virgultum And he shall grow up coram eo, et sicut radix as a tender plant before de terra sitienti; non est him, and as a root out of species ei, neque decor: a thirsty ground : there et vidimus eum, et non is no beauty in him, erat aspectus, et deside- nor comeliness : and we ravimus eum ; despec- have seen him, and tum, et novissimum vi- there was no sightliness, rorum, virum dolorum, that we should be desir- et scientem infirmita- ous of him. Despised, tem: et quasi abscon- and the most abject of ditus vultus ejus et de- men, a man of sorrows, spectus, unde nec re- and acquainted with putavimus eum. Vere infirmity ; and his look languores nostros ipse was as it were hidden tulit, et dolores nostros and despised, whereupon ipse portavit: et nos pu- we esteemed him not. tavimus eum quasi lepro- Surely he hath borne our sum, et percussum a Deo, infirmities, and carried our et humiliatum. Ipse au- sorrows : and we have tem vulneratus est propter thought him as it were a iniquitates nostras, attritus leper, and as one struck est propter scelera nostra. by God and afflicted. But disciplina pacis nostræ he was wounded for our super eum, et livore ejus iniquities, he was bruised sanati sumus. Omnes nos for our sins : the chastise- quasi oves erravimus, un- ment of our peace was usquisque in viam suam upon him, and by his declinavit : et posuit Do- bruises we are healed. All minus in eo iniquitatem we like sheep have gone

omnium nostrum. Obla-
tus est, quia ipse voluit,
et non aperuit os suum:
sicut ovis ad occisionem
ducetur, et quasi agnus
coram tondente se obmu-
tescet, et non aperiet os
suum. De angustia et de
judicio sublatus est: generationem ejus quis enar-
rabit? quia abscissus est
de terra viventium: prop-
ter scelus populi mei percussi eum. Et dabit im-
pios pro sepultura, et di-
vitem pro morte sua: eo
quod iniquitatem non fe-
cerit, neque dolus fuerit
in ore ejus. Et Domi-
nus voluit conterere eum
in infirmitate: si posu-
erit pro peccato animam
suam, videbit semen
longævum, et voluntas
Domini in manu ejus
dirigetur. Pro eo quod
laboravit anima ejus,
videbit, et saturabitur:
in scientia sua justifi-
cabit ipse justus servus
meus multos, et iniqui-
tates eorum ipse porta-
bit. Ideo dispertiam ei

astray, every one hath
turned aside into his own
way: and the Lord hath
laid on him the iniquity
of us all. He was offered
because it was his own
will, and he opened not
his mouth: he shall be led
as a sheep to the slaugh-
ter, and shall be dumb as
a lamb before his shearer,
and he shall not open his
mouth. He was taken
away from distress and
from judgment: who shall
declare his generation?
Because he is cut off out
of the land of the living,
for the wickedness of
my people have I struck
him. And he shall give
the ungodly for his bu-
rial, and the rich for his
death; because he hath
done no iniquity, neither
was there deceit in his
mouth. And the Lord
was pleased to bruise
him in infirmity: if he
shall lay down his life
for sin, he shall see a
long-lived seed, and the
will of the Lord shall be

plurimos, et fortium dividet spolia, pro eo quod tradidit in mortem animam suam, et cum sceleratis reputatus est: et ipse peccata multorum tulit, et pro transgressoribus rogavit.

prosperous in his hand. Because his soul had labored, he shall see, and be filled : by his knowledge shall this, my just servant, justify many: and he shall bear their iniquities. Therefore will I distribute to him very many, and he shall divide the spoils of the strong; because he hath delivered his soul unto death, and was reputed with the wicked; and he hath borne the sins of many, and hath prayed for the transgressors.

THE TRACT.

DOMINE, exaudi orationem meam, et clamor meus ad te veniat.

HEAR, O Lord! my prayer, and let my cry come to thee.

V. Ne avertas faciem tuam a me : in quacumque die tribulor, inclina ad me aurem tuam.

V. Turn not away thy face from me in the day when I am in trouble : incline thy ear to me.

V. In quacumque die invocavero te, velociter exaudi me.

V. In what day soever I shall call upon thee, hear me speedily.

V. Quia defecerunt sicut fumus dies mei: et ossa mea sicut in frixorio confrixa sunt.

V. Percussus sum sicut fœnum, et aruit cor meum: quia oblitus sum manducare panem meum.

V. Tu exurgens, Domine, misereberis Sion: quia venit tempus miserendi ejus.

Passio Domini nostri Jesu Christi secundum Lucam, cap. xxii. et xxiii.

I N illo tempore: Appropinquabat dies festus Azymorum, qui dicitur pascha; et quærebant principes sacerdotum et scribæ, quomodo Jesum interficerent: timebant vero plebem. Intravit autem satanas in Judam, qui cognominabatur Iscariotes, unum de duodecim. Et abiit, et locutus est

V. For my days are vanished like smoke; and my bones are as if they were fried in a frying pan.

V. I am smitten as grass, and my heart is withered, because I forgot to eat my bread.

V. Thou shalt arise, O Lord! and have mercy on Sion: for it is time to have mercy on it, for the time is come.

The Passion of our Lord Jesus Christ according to St. Luke chap. xxii. and xxiii.

A T that time the feast of unleavened bread, which is called the pasch, was at hand. And the chief priests and the scribes sought how they might put Jesus to death: but they feared the people. And Satan entered into Judas, who was surnamed Iscariot, one of the twelve. And he

cum principibus sacerdotum, et magistratibus, quemadmodum illum traderet eis. Et gavisi sunt, et pacti sunt pecuniam illi dare. Et spopondit. Et quærebat opportunitatem ut traderet illum sine turbis. Venit autem dies Azymorum, in qua necesse erat occidi pascha. Et misit Petrum et Joannem, dicens: Euntes parate nobis pascha, ut manducemus. At illi dixerunt: Ubi vis paremus? Et dixit ad eos: Ecce introeuntibus vobis in civitatem, occurret vobis homo quidam amphoram aquæ portans: sequimini eum in domum, in quam intrat, et dicetis patrifamilias domus: Dicit tibi Magister: Ubi est diversorium, ubi pascha cum discipulis meis manducem? Et ipse ostendet vobis cœnaculum magnum stratum, et ibi parate. Euntes autem in-

went and discoursed with the chief priests, and the magistrates, how he might betray him to them. And they were glad, and covenanted to give him money. And he promised. And he sought for an opportunity to betray him in the absence of the multitude. And the day of the unleavened bread came, on which it was necessary that the pasch should be killed. And he sent Peter and John, saying: G ᴗnd repare us the pasch that we may eat. But they said: Where wilt thou that we prepare? And he said to them: Behold, as you go into the city, there shall meet you a man carrying a pitcher of water: follow him into the house which he entereth into, and you shall say to the master of the house: The Master saith to thee: Where is the guest-chamber, where I

venerunt sicut dixit illis, et paraverunt pascha.

may eat the pasch with my disciples? And he will show you a large dining-room, furnished; and there prepare. And they going, found as he had said to them: and they made ready the pasch.

Et cum facta esset hora, discubuit, et duodecim Apostoli cum eo. Et ait illis: Desiderio desideravi hoc pascha manducare vobiscum, antequam patiar. Dico enim vobis, quia ex hoc non manducabo illud, donec impleatur in regno Dei. Et accepto calice, gratias egit, et dixit: Accipite, et dividite inter vos. Dico enim vobis, quod non bibam de generatione vitis, donec regnum Dei veniat. Et accepto pane, gratias egit, et fregit, et dedit eis, dicens: Hoc est corpus meum, quod pro vobis datur: hoc facite in meam commemorationem. Similiter

And when the hour was come, he sat down, and the twelve apostles with him. And he said to them: With desire I have desired to eat this pasch with you before I suffer. For I say to you, that from this time I will not eat it, till it be fulfilled in the kingdom of God. And having taken the chalice, he gave thanks and said: Take, and divide it among you. For I say to you, that I will not drink of the fruit of the vine till the kingdom of God come. And taking bread, he gave thanks, and brake, and gave to them, saying: This is my body which is given

et calicem, postquam cœnavit, dicens : Hic est calix novum testamentum in sanguine meo, qui pro vobis fundetur. Verumtamen ecce manus tradentis me, mecum est in mensa. Et quidem Filius hominis, secundum quod definitum est, vadit : verumtamen væ homini illi, per quem tradetur. Et ipsi cœperunt quærere inter se, quis esset ex eis, qui hoc facturus esset. Facta est autem et contentio inter eos, quis eorum videretur esse major. Dixit autem eis : Reges gentium dominantur eorum ; et qui potestatem habent super eos, benefici vocantur. Vos autem non sic : sed qui major est in vobis, fiat sicut minor ; et qui præcessor est, sicut ministrator. Nam quis major est, qui recumbit, an qui ministrat ? Nonne qui recumbit ? Ego autem in

for you : Do this for a commemoration of me. In like manner the chalice also, after he had supped, saying : This is the chalice, the new testament in my blood, which shall be shed for you. But yet behold, the hand of him that betrayeth me is with me on the table. And the Son of Man indeed goeth, according to that which is determined : but woe to that man by whom he shall be betrayed. And they began to enquire among themselves, which of them it was that should do this thing. And there was also a strife amongst them, which of them seemed to be greater. And he said to them : The kings of the Gentiles lord it over them ; and they that have power over them are called beneficent. But you not so : but he that is the greatest among

medio vestrum sum, sicut qui ministrat: vos autem estis, qui permansistis mecum in tentationibus meis. Et ego dispono vobis sicut disposuit mihi Pater meus regnum, ut edatis et bibatis super mensam meam in regno meo, et sedeatis super thronos, judicantes duodecim tribus Israel. Ait autem Dominus: Simon, Simon, ecce satanas expetivit vos ut cribraret sicut triticum; ego autem rogavi pro te, ut non deficiat fides tua; et tu aliquando conversus, confirma fratres tuos. Qui dixit ei: Domine, tecum paratus sum et in carcerem, et in mortem ire. At ille dixit: Dico tibi, Petre, non cantabit hodie gallus, donec ter abneges nosse me. Et dixit eis: Quando misi vos sine sacculo, et pera, et calceamentis, numquid aliquid defuit vobis? At illi dixerunt: Nihil. Dixit

you, let him be as the least: and he that is the leader, as he that serveth. For which is greater, he that sitteth at table, or he that serveth? Is not he that sitteth at table? but I am in the midst of you as he that serveth: and you are they who have continued with me in my temptations. And I appoint to you, as my Father hath appointed to me, a kingdom. That you may eat and drink at my table in my kingdom: and may sit upon thrones, judging the twelve tribes of Israel. And the Lord said: Simon, Simon, behold Satan hath desired to have you, that he may sift you as wheat, but I have prayed for thee, that thy faith fail not; and thou being once converted, confirm thy brethren. And he said to him: Lord! I am ready to go with thee, both into prison and to

ergo eis : Sed nunc qui habet sacculum, tollat similiter et peram : et qui non habet, vendat tunicam suam, et emat gladium. Dico enim vobis, quoniam adhuc hoc quod scriptum est, oportet impleri in me : Et cum iniquis deputatus est. Etenim ea, quæ sunt de me, finem habent. At illi dixerunt : Domine, ecce duo gladii hic. At ille dixit eis : Satis est.

death. And he said : I say to thee, Peter, the cock shall not crow this day, till thou, thrice, deny that thou knowest me. And he said to them : When I sent you without purse, and scrip, and shoes, did you want anything ? But they said : Nothing. Then said he to them : But now, he that hath a purse, let him take it, and likewise a scrip : and he that hath no sword, let him sell his coat and buy one. For I say to you that this that is written must yet be fulfilled in me : And with the wicked he was reputed. For the things concerning me have an end. But they said : Lord ! behold here are two swords. And he said to them : It is enough.

Et egressus ibat, secundum consuetudinem, in montem Olivarum. Secuti sunt autem illum

And going out, he went according to his custom to the mount of Olives. And his disci-

et discipuli. Et cum pervenisset ad locum, dixit illis : Orate ne intretis in tentationem. Et ipse avulsus est ab eis, quantum jactus est lapidis ; et positis genibus orabat, dicens : Pater, si vis, transfer calicem istum a me: verumtamen non mea voluntas, sed tua fiat. Apparuit autem illi Angelus de cœlo, confortans eum. Et factus in agonia, prolixius orabat. Et factus est sudor ejus, sicut guttæ sanguinis decurrentis in terram. Et cum surrexisset ab oratione, et venisset ad discipulos suos, invenit eos dormientes præ tristitia. Et ait illis: Quid dormitis? Surgite, orate ne intretis in tentationem. Adhuc eo loquente, ecce turba ; et qui vocabatur Judas, unus de duodecim, antecedebat eos: et appropinquavit Jesu et oscularetur eum. Jesus autem dixit illi : Juda,

ples also followed him. And when he was come to the place he said to them : Pray, lest ye enter into temptation. And he was withdrawn away from them a stone's cast: and kneeling down, he prayed, saying : Father! if thou wilt, remove this chalice from me : nevertheless, not my will but thine be done. And there appeared to him an angel from heaven, strengthening him. And being in an agony, he prayed the longer. And his sweat became as drops of blood trickling down upon the ground. And when he rose up from prayer, and was come to his disciples, he found them sleeping for sorrow. And he said to them : Why sleep you? Arise, pray, lest you enter into temptation. As he was yet speaking, behold a multitude ; and he that was called Judas, one of the twelve, went

osculo Filium hominis tradis? Videntes autem hi, qui circa ipsum erant, quod futurum erat, dixerunt ei : Domine, si percutimus in gladio? Et percussit unus ex illis servum principis sacerdotum, et amputavit auriculam ejus dexteram. Respondens autem Jesus, ait : Sinite usque huc. Et cum tetigisset auriculam ejus, sanavit eum. Dixit autem Jesus ad eos qui venerant ad se, principes sacerdotum, et magistratus templi, et seniores: Quasi ad latronem existis cum gladiis et fustibus? Cum quotidie vobiscum fuerim in templo, non extendistis manus in me: sed hæc est hora vestra, et potestas tenebrarum. Comprehendentes autem eum, duxerunt ad domum principis sacerdotum: Petrus vero sequebatur a longe. Accenso autem igne in medio atrii, et circumsedenti-

before them, and drew near to Jesus, to kiss him. And Jesus said to him : Judas ! dost thou betray the Son of Man with a kiss? And they that were about him, seeing what would follow, said to him : Lord ! shall we strike with the sword? And one of them struck the servant of the high priest, and cut off his right ear. But Jesus answering, said : Suffer ye thus far. And when he had touched his ear, he healed him. And Jesus said to the chief priests, and magistrates of the temple, and the ancients that were come to him : Are you come out as it were against a thief, with swords and clubs? When I was daily with you in the temple, you did not stretch forth your hands against me : but this is your hour, and the power of darkness. Then they laid hold on him, and led

bus illis, erat Petrus in medio eorum. Quem cum vidisset ancilla quædam sedentem ad lumen, et eum fuisset intuita, dixit: Et hic cum illo erat. At ille negavit eum, dicens: Mulier, non novi illum. Et post pusillum alius videns eum, dixit: Et tu de illis es. Petrus vero ait: O homo, non sum. Et intervallo facto quasi horæ unius, alius quidam affirmabat, dicens: Vere et hic cum illo erat: nam et Galilæus est. Et ait Petrus: Homo, nescio quid dicis. Et continuo adhuc illo loquente cantavit gallus. Et conversus Dominus respexit Petrum. Et recordatus est Petrus verbi Domini, sicut dixerat: Quia priusquam gallus cantet, ter me negabis. Et egressus

him to the high priest's house: but Peter followed afar off. And when they had kindled a fire in the midst of the hall, and were sitting about it, Peter was in the midst of them. And when a certain servant-maid had seen him sitting at the light, and had looked upon him, she said: This man was also with him. But he denied him, saying: Woman! I know him not. And after a little while, another seeing him, said: Thou also art one of them. But Peter said: O man! I am not. And about the space of one hour after, another man affirmed, saying: Of a truth this man was also with him: for he is also a Galilean. And Peter said: Man! I know not what thou sayest. And immediately while he was yet speaking the cock crew. And the Lord turning

foras Petrus flevit amare.

Et viri qui tenebant illum, illudebant ei, cædentes. Et velaverunt eum, et percutiebant faciem ejus : et interrogabant eum, dicentes : Prophetiza, quis est qui te percussit? Et alia multa blasphemantes dicebant in eum. Et ut factus est dies, convenerunt seniores plebis, et principes sacerdotum, et scribæ, et duxerunt illum in concilium suum, dicentes : Si tu es Christus, dic nobis. Et ait illis : Si vobis dixero, non credetis mihi : si autem et interrogavero, non respondebitis mihi, neque dimittetis. Ex hoc au-

looked on Peter. And Peter remembered the word of the Lord, how he had said : Before the cock crow, thou shalt deny me thrice. And Peter went out and wept bitterly.

And the men that held him, mocked him and struck him. And they blindfolded him, and smote him on the face. And they asked him, saying : Prophesy, who is it that struck thee ? And many other things, blaspheming, they said against him. And as soon as it was day, the ancients of the people and the chief priests and scribes came together, and they brought him into their council, saying : If thou be the Christ, tell us. And he said to them : If I shall tell you, you will not believe me : and if I shall also ask you, you will not answer me, nor let me go But here-

tem erit Filius hominis sedens a dextris virtutis Dei. Dixerunt autem omnes : Tu ergo es Filius Dei ? Qui ait : Vos dicitis, quia ego sum. At illi dixerunt : Quid adhuc desideramus testimonium ? ipsi enim audivimus de ore ejus. Et surgens omnis multitudo eorum, duxerunt illum ad Pilatum. Cœperunt autem illum accusare, dicentes : Hunc invenimus subvertentem gentem nostram, et prohibentem tributa dare Cæsari, et dicentem se Christum regem esse. Pilatus autem interrogavit eum, dicens : Tu es Rex Judæorum ? At ille respondens, ait : Tu dicis. Ait autem Pilatus ad principes sacerdotum, et turbas : Nihil invenio causæ in hoc homine. At illi invalescebant, dicentes : Commovet po-

after the Son of Man shall be sitting on the right hand of the power of God. Then said they all : Art thou then the Son of God ? And he said : You say that I am. Then they said : What need we any further testimony? For we ourselves have heard it from his own mouth. And the whole multitude of them rose up, and led him away to Pilate. And they began to accuse him, saying : We have found this man perverting our nation, and forbidding to give tribute to Cæsar, and saying that he is Christ, the king. And Pilate asked him, saying : Art thou the King of the Jews? And he answered and said : Thou sayest it. Then Pilate said to the chief priests and to the multitude : I find no cause in this man. But they were more earnest, saying : He stirreth up

pulum, docens per universam Judæam, incipiens a Galilæa usque huc. Pilatus autem audiens Galilæam, interrogavit si homo Galilæus esset. Et ut cognovit quod de Herodis potestate esset, remisit eum ad Herodem, qui et ipse Jerosolymis erat illis diebus. Herodes autem viso Jesu, gavisus est valde : erat enim cupiens ex multo tempore videre eum, eo quod audierat multa de eo, et sperabat signum aliquod videre ab eo fieri. Interrogabat autem eum multis sermonibus. At ipse nihil illi respondebat. Stabant autem principes sacerdotum et scribæ constanter accusantes eum. Sprevit autem illum Herodes cum exercitu suo : et illusit indutum veste alba, et remisit ad Pilatum. Et facti sunt amici Herodes

the people, teaching throughout all Judea, beginning from Galilee to this place. And Pilate hearing of Galilee, asked if the man was a Galilean. And when he understood that he belonged to Herod's jurisdiction, he sent him away to Herod, who himself was also at Jerusalem in those days. And Herod, seeing Jesus, was very glad, for he was desirous of a long time to see him, because he had heard many things of him ; and he hoped to see some miracle wrought by him. And he questioned him with many words. But he answered him nothing. And the chief priests and the scribes stood by, earnestly accusing him. And Herod with his soldiers despised him ; and mocked him, putting on him a white garment, and sent him back

et Pilatus in ipsa die; nam antea inimici erant ad invicem.

Pilatus autem, convocatis principibus sacerdotum, et magistratibus, et plebe, dixit ad illos: Obtulistis mihi hunc hominem, quasi avertentem populum, et ecce ego coram vobis interrogans, nullam causam inveni in homine isto ex his, in quibus eum accusatis. Sed neque Herodes: nam remisi vos ad illum, et ecce nihil dignum morte actum est ei. Emendatum ergo illum dimittam. Necesse autem habebat dimittere eis per diem festum, unum. Exclamavit autem simul universa turba, dicens: Tolle hunc, et dimitte nobis Barabbam. Qui erat propter seditionem quamdam factam in civitate et homicidium, missus in carcerem. Iterum au-

to Pilate. And Herod and Pilate were made friends that same day; for before they were enemies one to another.

Then Pilate, calling together the chief priests, and the magistrates, and the people, said to them: You have brought this man to me, as one that perverteth the people, and behold I, having examined him before you, find no cause in this man touching those things, wherein you accuse him. No, nor Herod neither: for I sent you to him, and behold nothing worthy of death is done to him. I will chastise him therefore, and release him. Now of necessity he was to release to them one upon the feast day. But the whole multitude cried out at once, saying: Away with this man, and release unto us Barabbas; who for a certain sedition, made in the city, and for murder, had been

tem Pilatus locutus est ad eos, volens dimittere Jesum. At illi succlamabant dicentes : Crucifige, crucifige eum. Ille autem tertio dixit ad illos : Quid enim mali fecit iste ? nullam causam mortis invenio in eo : corripiam ergo illum, et dimittam. At illi instabant vocibus magnis postulantes ut crucifigeretur ; et invalescebant voces eorum. Et Pilatus adjudicavit fieri petitionem eorum. Dimisit autem illis eum, qui propter homicidium et seditionem missus fuerat in carcerem, quem petebant ; Jesum vero tradidit voluntati eorum. Et cum ducerent eum, apprehenderunt Simonem quemdam Cyrenensem, venientem de villa ; et imposuerunt illi crucem portare post Jesum.

cast into prison. And Pilate spoke to them again, desiring to release Jesus. But they cried out, saying : Crucify him, crucify him. And he said to them the third time : Why, what evil hath this man done ? I find no cause of death in him ; I will chastise him therefore, and let him go. But they were instant with loud voices requiring that he might be crucified ; and their voices prevailed. And Pilate gave sentence, that their petition should be granted. And he released unto them him, who, for murder and sedition, had been cast into prison, whom they had desired ; but Jesus he delivered up to their will. And as they led him away, they laid hold on one Simon of Cyrene, that was coming out of the country : and they laid the cross on him to carry after Jesus.

Sequebatur autem illum multa turba populi, et mulierum quæ plangebant et lamentabantur eum. Conversus autem ad illas Jesus, dixit: Filiæ Jerusalem, nolite flere super me, sed super vos ipsas flete, et super filios vestros. Quoniam ecce venient dies, in quibus dicent: Beatæ steriles, et ventres qui non genuerunt, et ubera quæ non lactaverunt. Tunc incipient dicere montibus: Cadite super nos; et collibus. Operite nos. Quia si in viridi ligno hæc faciunt, in arido quid fiet? Ducebantur autem et alii duo nequam cum eo, ut interficerentur. Et postquam venerunt in locum, qui vocatur Calvariæ, ibi crucifixerunt eum; et latrones, unum a dextris, et alterum a sinistris. Jesus autem dicebat; Pater, dimitte illis: non enim sciunt quid faciunt. Dividentes vero vesti-

And there followed him a great multitude of people, and of women; who bewailed and lamented him. But Jesus turning to them, said: Daughters of Jerusalem! weep not over me, but weep for yourselves, and for your children. For behold the days shall come, wherein they will say: Blessed are the barren, and the wombs that have not borne, and the breasts that have not given suck. Then shall they begin to say to the mountains: Fall upon us; and to the hills: Cover us. For if in the green wood they do these things, what shall be done in the dry? And there were also two other malefactors led with him, to be put to death. And when they were come to the place, which is called Calvary, they crucified him there; and the robbers, one on the right hand, and the other on the left. And

menta ejus, miserunt sortes. Et stabat populus spectans, et deridebant eum principes cum eis, dicentes : Alios salvos fecit : se salvum faciat, si hic est Christus Dei electus. Illudebant autem ei et milites accedentes, et acetum offerentes ei, et dicentes : Si tu es Rex Judæorum, salvum te fac. Erat autem et superscriptio scripta super eum litteris Græcis, et Latinis, et Hebraicis : Hic est Rex Judæorum. Unus autem de his, qui pendebant, latronibus, blasphemabat eum, dicens : Si tu es Christus, salvum fac temetipsum, et nos. Respondens autem alter, increpabat eum, dicens : Neque tu times Deum, quod in eadem damnatione es. Et nos quidem juste, nam digna factis recipimus ; hic vero nihil mali gessit. Et dicebat ad Jesum : Domine, memento mei, cum ve-

Jesus said : Father ! forgive them, for they know not what they do. But they divided his garments, and cast lots. And the people stood beholding, and the rulers with them derided him, saying : He saved others, let him save himself, if he be Christ, the chosen of God. And the soldiers also mocked him, coming to him, and offering him vinegar, and saying : If thou be the King of the Jews, save thyself. And there was also a superscription written over him in Greek, and Latin, and Hebrew letters : This is the King of the Jews. And one of these robbers, who were hanging, blasphemed him, saying : If thou be Christ, save thyself, and us. But the other answering, rebuked him, saying : Neither dost thou fear God, seeing thou art under the same con-

neris in regnum tuum. Et dixit illi Jesus: Amen dico tibi, hodie mecum eris in paradiso. Erat autem fere hora sexta, et tenebræ factæ sunt in universam terram usque in horam nonam. Et obscuratus est sol, et velum templi scissum est medium. Et clamans voce magna Jesus ait : Pater, in manus tuas commendo spiritum meum. Et hæc dicens, expiravit.

demnation. And we indeed justly, for we receive the due reward of our deeds ; but this man hath done no evil. And he said to Jesus : Lord ! remember me when thou shalt come into thy kingdom. And Jesus said to him : Amen I say to thee, this day thou shalt be with me in paradise. And it was almost the sixth hour ; and there was darkness over all the earth until the ninth hour. And the sun was darkened ; and the veil of the temple was rent in the midst. And Jesus, crying with a loud voice, said : Father ! into thy hands I commend my spirit. And saying this he gave up the ghost.

Here all kneel, and after a little pause, to meditate on the redemption of mankind, they rise, and the Deacon goes on :

VIDENS autem centurio quod factum fuerat, glorificavit Deum, dicens : Vere hic homo

NOW the centurion seeing what was done, glorified God, saying : Indeed this was a

justus erat. Et omnis turba eorum, qui simul aderant ad spectaculum istud, et videbant quæ fiebant, percutientes pectora sua revertebantur. Stabant autem omnes noti ejus a longe, et mulieres quæ secutæ eum erant a Galilæa, hæc videntes.

just man. And all the multitude of them that were come together to that sight, and saw the things that were done, returned, striking their breasts. And all his acquaintances and the women, that had followed him from Galilee, stood afar off beholding these things.

Here is said the prayer Munda cor meum, *p.* 19.

ET ecce vir nomine Joseph, qui erat decurio, vir bonus et justus : hic non consenserat consilio et actibus eorum, ab Arimathæa civitate Judææ, qui expectabat et ipse regnum Dei. Hic accessit ad Pilatum, et petiit corpus Jesu : et depositum involvit sindone, et posuit eum in monumento exciso, in quo nondum quisquam positus fuerat.

AND behold, a man by name Joseph, who was a counsellor, a good and a just man : the same had not consented to their counsel and doings. He was of Arimathea, a city of Judea, who also himself looked for the kingdom of God. This man went to Pilate, and begged the body of Jesus. And taking him down, he wrapped him in fine linen, and laid him in a sepulchre, that was hewn in stone, wherein never yet any man had been lain.

THE OFFERTORY.

DOMINE, exaudi orationem meam, et clamor meus ad te perveniat : ne avertas faciem tuam a me.

HEAR, O Lord ! my prayer, and let my cry come to thee : turn not away thy face from me.

Suscipe, *as at p.* 26, *down to* Then the Priest says Amen, *p.* 28.

THE SECRET.

SUSCIPE, quæsumus Domine, munus oblatum, et dignanter operare, ut quod passionis Filii tui Domini nostri mysterio gerimus, piis affectibus consequamur. Per eundem Dominum nostrum, etc.

ACCEPT, O Lord ! we beseech thee, this offering, and mercifully grant that we may receive with pious sentiments what we celebrate in the mystery of the passion of thy Son our Lord ; through the same Lord, etc.

*The Preface, p.*94, *and the Canon, down to end of prayer* Corpus tuum—Let thy, *etc., p.* 42. *The other Secret, as at p.* 132 : Protege, *or* Oblatis.

THE COMMUNION.

POTUM meum cum fletu temperabam ; quia elevans allisisti me : et ego sicut fœnum arui. Tu autem, Domine, in æternum permanes : tu exurgens misereberis

I MINGLED my drink with weepings ; for having lifted me up, thou hast thrown me down ; and I withered like grass ; but thou, O Lord ! endurest for ever ;

Sion, quia venit tempus miserendi ejus.

thou shalt arise, and have mercy on Sion, for it is time to have mercy on it, for the time is come.

THE POST-COMMUNION.

LARGIRE sensibus nostris, omnipotens Deus ; ut per temporalem Filii tui mortem, quam mysteria veneranda testantur, vitam te nobis dedisse perpetuam confidamus. Per eundem, etc.

GRANT, O Almighty God ! that we may firmly believe, and hope, that thou hast given us eternal life, by the temporal death of thy Son, represented in these adorable mysteries ; through the same Lord, etc.

The other Post-communion : Quæsumus, *or* Hæc nos, *as at p.* 133.

The Prayer over the People.

Oremus.

Let us pray.

Humiliate capita vestra Deo.

Bow down your heads to God.

RESPICE, quæsumus Domine, super hanc familiam tuam, pro qua Dominus noster Jesus Christus non dubitavit manibus tradi nocentium, et crucis subire tormentum. Qui tecum vivit et regnat, etc.

LOOK down, we beseech thee, O Lord! on this thy family, for which our Lord Jesus Christ was pleased to be delivered into the hands of the wicked, and to suffer the torment of the cross ; who liveth and reigneth, etc.

The rest of the Mass from Dominus vobiscum, *as on p.* 43.

THE TENEBRÆ.

In the evening of Wednesday, Thursday, and Friday, the Church performs a solemn office commonly called the *Tenebræ*, which, in the following translation, is ranged under the titles of Maundy Thursday, Good Friday, and Holy Saturday, being the Matins and Lauds assigned to those days. The name of *Tenebræ* is given to it from the circumstance of extinguishing, during the course of it, all the candles which have been prepared in the sanctuary for the ceremony.

The rites of the Church upon these three days declare her concern and her trouble for the sufferings of her Redeemer and the sins of men. She lays aside every expression of joy and festivity. Her offices are not commenced with those impressive invocations by which she beseeches the Lord to open her lips to sing his praises, and to come to her assistance, to enable her to render him a homage worthy of his majesty. The sacred doxology, *Gloria Patri*, is omitted at the end of the Psalms. No hymns of divine praise are sung. No *Dominus vobiscum* is said, to ask the blessing of God upon the people. The Psalms and the Lessons that constitute her office breathe scarcely anything else but sighs and lamentations. Her canonical hours are terminated by the same prayer, imploring God to look with an eye of pity on those for whom his Son our Lord has vouchsafed to suffer death. At every other time, before she offers up a prayer, the people are invited to unite with her in spirit, and at the conclusion express their assent by the acclamation *amen ;* but upon this occasion, to evince still more the greatness of her sorrow, the invitation and the acclamation are both omitted.

The six candles on the Altar, and the fifteen candles placed on the epistle side, all burning at the beginning of the office, signify the lights of faith preached by the Prophets and Jesus Christ ; of which faith the fundamental article is the mystery of the Blessed Trinity, represented by the triangular candlestick. At the repetition of the fourteen Antiphons in the Matins and Lauds, fourteen of the candles in the triangular candlestick are extinguished, and at the last six verses of the *Benedictus* those on the Altar are put out, to teach us that the Jews were totally deprived of the light of faith when they put our Saviour to death. But the fifteenth candle, that represents the light of the world, Jesus Christ, is only hidden for a time under the Altar, and afterwards brought out again, still burning ; to signify that, though Christ, according to his humanity, died, and was laid in the sepulchre, yet he was always alive according to his Divinity, by which he raised his body again to life

The darkness which pervades the sanctuary while the *Miserere* and Prayer are said naturally puts us in mind of the darkness that covered the whole earth at his death; and the noise made at the end of the prayer represents the confusion of nature for the loss of its Author, when the earth trembled, the rocks were rent, the graves opened, and the veil of the temple was torn from the top to the bottom.

TENEBRÆ ON WEDNESDAY,

BEING THE MORNING OFFICE OF

MAUNDY THURSDAY.

The Matins.

Aperi Domine, Pater noster, Ave Maria, *and* Credo *are said in a low voice.*

THE FIRST NOCTURN.

Antiphona. ZELUS domus tuæ comedit me, et opprobria exprobrantium tibi ceciderunt super me.

The Antiphon. THE zeal of thy house hath eaten me up, and the reproaches of them that reproached thee are fallen upon me.

PSALM 68.

SALVUM me fac Deus: * quoniam intraverunt aquæ usque ad animam meam.

Infixus sum in limo profundi: * et non est substantia.

Veni in altitudinem

SAVE me, O God for the waters are come even into my soul.

I am stuck fast in the mire of the deep: and there is no sure standing.

I am come into the

maris : * et tempestas demersit me.

depth of the sea : and a tempest hath over-whelmed me.

Laboravi clamans, raucæ factæ sunt fauces meæ : * defecerunt oculi mei, dum spero in Deum meum.

I have labored with crying out, my jaws are become hoarse ; my eyes have failed whilst I hope in my God.

Multiplicati sunt super capillos capitis mei, * qui oderunt me gratis.

They are multiplied above the hairs of my head, who hate me with-out cause.

Confortati sunt qui persecuti sunt me inimici mei injuste : * quæ non rapui, tunc exolvebam.

My enemies are grown strong, who have wrong-fully persecuted me : then I paid that which I took not away.

Deus, tu scis insipientiam meam : * et delicta mea a te non sunt abscondita.

O God ! thou knowest my foolishness : and my offences are not hidden from thee.

Non erubescant in me qui expectant te Domine, * Domine virtutum.

Let not them be ashamed for me, who look for thee, O Lord, the Lord of hosts !

Non confundantur super me, * qui quærunt te, Deus Israel.

Let them not be con-founded on my account, who seek thee, O God of Israel !

Quoniam propter te sustinui opprobrium : * operuit confusio faciem meam.

Because for thy sake I have borne reproach ; shame hath covered my face.

Extraneus factus sum fratribus meis, * et peregrinus filiis matris meæ.

I am become a stranger to my brethren, and an alien to the sons of my mother.

Quoniam zelus domus tuæ comedit me : * et opprobria exprobrantium tibi ceciderunt super me.

For the zeal of thy house hath eaten me up ; and the reproaches of them that reproached thee are fallen upon me.

Et operui in jejunio animam meam : * et factum est in opprobrium mihi.

And I covered my soul in fasting : and it was made a reproach to me.

Et posui vestimentum meum cilicium : * et factus sum illis in parabolam.

And I made haircloth my garment : and I became a by-word to them.

Adversum me loquebantur qui sedebant in porta : * et in me psallebant qui bibebant vinum.

They that sat in the gate spoke against me : and they that drank wine made me their song.

Ego vero orationem meam ad te Domine : * tempus beneplaciti Deus.

But as for me, my prayer is to thee, O Lord ! for the time of thy good pleasure, O God !

In multitudine misericordiæ tuæ exaudi me, * in veritate salutis tuæ.

In the multitude of thy mercy hear me, in the truth of thy salvation.

Eripe me de luto, ut non infigar : * libera me

Draw me out of the mire, that I may not

ab iis qui oderunt me, et de profundis aquarum.

stick fast : deliver me from them that hate me : and out of the deep waters.

Non me demergat tempestas aquæ, neque absorbeat me profundum : * neque urgeat super me puteus os suum.

Let not the tempest of water drown me, nor the deep swallow me up and let not the pit shut her mouth upon me.

Exaudi me Domine, quoniam benigna est misericordia tua : * secundum multitudinem miserationum tuarum respice in me.

Hear me, O Lord! for thy mercy is kind ; look upon me according to the multitude of thy tender mercies.

Et ne avertas faciem tuam a puero tuo : * quoniam tribulor, velociter exaudi me.

And turn not away thy face from thy servant : for I am in trouble, hear me speedily.

Intende animæ meæ et libera eam : * propter inimicos meos eripe me.

Attend to my soul, and deliver it : save me because of my enemies.

Tu scis improperium meum, et confusionem meam, * et reverentiam meam.

Thou knowest my reproach, and my confusion, and my shame.

In conspectu tuo sunt omnes qui tribulant me : * improperium expectavit cor meum, et miseriam.

In thy sight are all they that afflict me : my heart hath expected reproach and misery.

Et sustinui qui simul

And I looked for one

contristaretur, et non fuit : * et qui consolaretur, et non inveni.

Et dederunt in escam meam fel; * et in siti mea potaverunt me aceto.

Fiat mensa eorum coram ipsis in laqueum, * et in retributiones, et in scandalum.

Obscurentur oculi eorum ne videant : * et dorsum eorum semper incurva.

Effunde super eos iram tuam : * et furor iræ tuæ comprehendat eos.

Fiat habitatio eorum deserta : * et in tabernaculis eorum non sit qui inhabitet.

Quoniam quem tu percussisti, persecuti sunt : * et super dolorem vulnerum meorum addiderunt.

Appone iniquitatem super iniquitatem eo-

that would grieve together with me, but there was none ; and for one, that would comfort me, and I found none.

And they gave me gall for my food, and in my thirst, they gave me vinegar to drink.

Let their table become as a snare before them, and a recompense, and a stumbling block.

Let their eyes be darkened, that they see not ; and their back bow thou down always.

Pour out thy indignation upon them : and let thy wrathful anger take hold of them.

Let their habitation be made desolate ; and let there be none to dwell in their tabernacles.

Because they have persecuted him whom thou hast smitten ; and they have added to the grief of my wounds.

Add thou iniquity upon their iniquity ; and

rum : * et non intrent in justitiam tuam.

Deleantur de libro viventium : * et cum justis non scribantur.

Ego sum pauper et dolens : * salus tua Deus suscepit me.

Laudabo nomen Dei cum cantico : * et magnificabo eum in laude.

Et placebit Deo super vitulum novellum, * cornua producentem et ungulas.

Videant pauperes et lætentur : * quærite Deum, et vivet anima vestra.

Quoniam exaudivit pauperes Dominus : * et vinctos suos non despexit.

Laudent illum cœli et terra, * mare, et omnia reptilia in eis.

Quoniam Deus salvam faciet Sion : * et ædificabuntur civitates Juda.

let them not come into thy justice.

Let them be blotted out of the book of the living; and with the just let them not be written.

But I am poor and sorrowful : thy salvation, O God ! hath set me up.

I will praise the name of God with a canticle : and I will magnify him with praise.

And it shall please God better than a young calf, that bringeth forth horns and hoofs.

Let the poor see and rejoice : seek ye God, and your soul shall live.

For the Lord hath heard the poor ; and hath not despised his prisoners.

Let the heavens and the earth praise him ; the sea, and everything that creepeth therein.

For God will save Sion, and the cities of Juda shall be built up.

Et inhabitabunt ibi, * et hæreditate acquirent eam.

And they shall dwell there, and acquire it by inheritance.

Et semen servorum ejus possidebit eam, * et qui diligunt nomen ejus, habitabunt in ea.

And the seed of his servants shall possess it; and they that love his name shall dwell therein.

Here the lowest candle on the left side of the triangle is extinguished.

Ant. Zelus domus tuæ comedit me, et opprobria exprobrantium tibi ceciderunt super me.

Ant. The zeal of thy house hath eaten me up, and the reproaches of them that reproached thee, are fallen upon me.

Ant. Avertantur retrorsum, et erubescant, qui cogitant mihi mala.

Ant. Let them be turned backward and blush for shame, that desire evils to me.

PSALM 69.

DEUS in adjutorium meum intende : * Domine, ad adjuvandum me festina.

O GOD ! come to my assistance : O Lord ! make haste to help me.

Confundantur et revereantur, * qui quærunt animam meam.

Let them be confounded and ashamed that seek my soul.

Avertantur retrorsum, et erubescant, * qui volunt mihi mala.

Let them be turned backward and blush for shame, that desire evils to me.

Avertantur statim erubescentes, * qui dicunt mihi : Euge, euge.

Exultent et lætentur in te omnes qui quærunt te, * et dicant semper : Magnificetur Dominus, qui diligunt salutare tuum.

Ego vero egenus et pauper sum : * Deus adjuva me.

Adjutor meus, et liberator meus es tu : * Domine ne moreris.

Let them be presently turned away blushing for shame that say to me : 'Tis well, 'tis well.

Let all that seek thee, rejoice and be glad in thee, and let such as love thy salvation say always : The Lord be magnified.

But I am needy and poor; O God! help me.

Thou art my helper, and my deliverer ; O Lord! make no delay.

Here the lowest candle on the right of the triangle is extinguished.

Ant. Avertantur retrorsum, et erubescant, qui cogitant mihi mala.

Ant. Deus meus eripe me de manu peccatoris.

Ant. Let them be turned backward and blush for shame, that desire evils to me.

Ant. Deliver me, O my God! out of the hand of the sinner.

PSALM 70.

IN te Domine speravi, non confundar in æternum : * in justitia tua libera me, et eripe me.

Inclina ad me aurem tuam, * et salva me.

IN thee, O Lord! I have hoped, let me never be put to confusion. Deliver me in thy justice, and rescue me.

Incline thy ear unto me, and save me.

Esto mihi in Deum protectorem, et in locum munitum : * ut salvum me facias.

Be thou unto me a God, a protector, and a place of strength, that thou mayest make me safe.

Quoniam firmamentum meum, * et refugium meum es tu.

For thou art my firmament and my refuge.

Deus meus eripe me de manu peccatoris, * et de manu contra legem agentis, et iniqui.

. Deliver me, O my God! out of the hand of the sinner, and out of the hand of the transgressor of the law, and of the unjust.

Quoniam tu es patientia mea, Domine : * Domine spes mea a juventute mea.

For thou art my patience, O Lord! my hope, O Lord! from my youth.

In te confirmatus sum ex utero : * de ventre matris meæ tu es protector meus.

By thee have I been confirmed from the womb; from my mother's womb, thou art my protector.

In te cantatio mea semper : * tamquam prodigium factus sum multis ; et tu adjutor fortis.

Of thee shall I continually sing ; I am become unto many as a wonder ; but thou art a strong helper.

Repleatur os meum laude, ut cantem gloriam tuam : * tota die magnitudinem tuam.

Let my mouth be filled with praise, that I may sing thy glory ; thy greatness all the day long.

Ne projicias me in tempore senectutis : * cum defecerit virtus mea, ne derelinquas me.

Cast me not off in the time of old age ; when my strength shall fail, do not thou forsake me.

Quia dixerunt inimici mei mihi : * et qui custodiebant animam meam, consilium fecerunt in unum.

For my enemies have spoken against me : and they that watched my soul have consulted together.

Dicentes : Deus dereliquit eum, persequimini et comprehendite eum : * quia non est qui eripiat.

Saying : God hath forsaken him, pursue, and take him : for there is none to deliver him.

Deus ne elongeris a me : * Deus meus in auxilium meum respice.

O God ! be not thou far from me : O my God ! make haste to my help.

Confundantur et deficiant detrahentes animæ meæ : * operiantur confusione et pudore, qui quærunt mala mihi.

Let them be confounded and come to nothing, that detract my soul ; let them be covered with confusion and shame that seek my hurt.

Ego autem semper sperabo : * et adjiciam super omnem laudem tuam.

But I will always hope ; and will add to all thy praise.

Os meum annuntiabit Justitiam tuam ; * tota die salutare tuum.

My mouth shall show forth thy justice ; thy salvation, all the day long.

Quoniam non cognovi litteraturam, introibo in potentias Domini: * Domine memorabor justitiæ tuæ solius.

Because I have not known learning, I will enter into the powers of the Lord: O Lord! I will be mindful of thy justice alone.

Deus docuisti me a juventute mea: * et usque nunc pronuntiabo mirabilia tua.

Thou hast taught me, O God! from my youth; and till now, I will declare thy wonderful works.

Et usque in senectam et senium: * Deus ne derelinquas me,

And unto old age and gray hairs, O God! forsake me not.

Donec annuntiem brachium tuum * generationi omni, quæ ventura est.

Until I show forth thy arm to all the generation that is to come.

Potentiam tuam, et justitiam tuam Deus, usque in altissima, quæ fecisti magnalia: * Deus quis similis tibi?

Thy power, and thy justice, O God! even to the highest great things, thou hast done; O God! who is like to thee?

Quantas ostendisti mihi tribulationes multas et malas: et conversus vivificasti me: * et de abyssis terræ iterum reduxisti me.

How great troubles hast thou showed me, many and grievous? and turning thou hast brought me to life; and hast brought me back again from the depths of the earth.

Multiplicasti magnificentiam tuam: * et

Thou hast multiplied thy magnificence; and

conversus consolatus es me.

turning to me, thou hast comforted me.

Nam et ego confitebor tibi in vasis psalmi veritatem tuam : * Deus psallam tibi in cithara, sanctus Israel.

For I will also confess to thee, thy truth with the instruments of Psaltery; O God! I will sing to thee with the harp, thou holy one of Israel.

Exultabunt labia mea cum cantavero tibi; * et anima mea, quam redemisti.

My lips shall greatly rejoice when I shall sing to thee; and my soul, which thou hast redeemed.

Sed et lingua mea tota die meditabitur justitiam tuam : * cum confusi et reveriti fuerint qui quærunt mala mihi.

Yea, and my tongue shall meditate on thy justice all the day; when they shall be confounded and put to shame, that seek evils to me.

Here a candle is extinguished.

Ant. Deus meus eripe me de manu peccatoris.

Ant. Deliver me, O my God! out of the hand of the sinner.

V. Avertantur retrorsum, et erubescant.

V. Let them be turned backward and blush for shame.

R. Qui cogitant mihi mala.

R. That desire evils to me.

Pater noster, *secreto.*

Our Father, *privately.*

THE FIRST LESSON.

Incipit lamentatio Jeremiæ Prophetæ, cap. i.

Aleph. QUOMODO sedet sola civitas plena populo : facta est quasi vidua domina gentium : princeps provinciarum facta est sub tributo.

Beth. Plorans ploravit in nocte, et lacrymæ ejus in maxillis ejus : non est qui consoletur eam ex omnibus charis ejus : omnes amici ejus spreverunt eam, et facti sunt ei inimici.

Ghimel. Migravit Judas propter afflictionem, et multitudinem servitutis : habitavit inter gentes, nec invenit requiem : omnes persecutores ejus apprehenderunt eam inter angustias.

The beginning of the lamentation of Jeremias, the Prophet, chap. i.

Aleph. HOW doth the city sit solitary that was full of people ? how is the mistress of the nations become as a widow ; the princess of provinces made tributary ?

Beth. Weeping, she hath wept in the night, and her tears are on her cheeks ; there is none to comfort her among them all that were dear to her: all her friends have despised her, and are become her enemies.

Ghimel. Juda hath removed her dwelling place, because of her affliction, and the greatness of her bondage: she hath dwelt among the nations, and she hath found no rest ; all her persecutors have taken her in the midst of straits.

Daleth. Viæ Sion lugent, eo quod non sint qui veniant ad solemnitatem : omnes portæ ejus destructæ, sacerdotes ejus gementes, virgines ejus squalidæ, et ipsa oppressa amaritudine.

He. Facti sunt hostes ejus in capite, inimici ejus locupletati sunt ; quia Dominus locutus est super eam propter multitudinem iniquitatum ejus : parvuli ejus ducti sunt in captivitatem, ante faciem tribulantis.

Jerusalem, Jerusalem, convertere ad Dominum Deum tuum.

R. In monte Oliveti oravit ad Patrem : Pater, si fieri potest, transeat a me calix iste : * Spiritus quidem promptus est, caro autem infirma.

V. Vigilate, et orate, ut non intretis in tentationem. * Spiritus quidem, etc.

Daleth. The ways of Sion mourn, because there are none that come to the solemn feast; all her gates are broken down : her priests sigh : her virgins are in affliction, and she is oppressed with bitterness.

He. Her adversaries are become her lords, her enemies are enriched : because the Lord hath spoken against her for the multitude of her iniquities; her children are led into captivity, before the face of the oppressor.

Jerusalem! Jerusalem! be converted to the Lord, thy God.

R. He prayed to his Father on Mount Olivet: Father! if it is possible, let this chalice pass from me. * The Spirit indeed is willing, but the flesh is weak.

V. Watch and pray, that ye enter not into temptation. * The Spirit indeed, etc.

THE SECOND LESSON.

Vau. ET egressus est a filia Sion omnis decor ejus: facti sunt principes ejus velut arietes non invenientes pascua, et abierunt absque for*t*itudine ante faciem subsequentis.

Zain. Recordata est *t*erusalem dierum afflic*t*ionis suæ, et prævaricationis omnium desiderabilium suorum, quæ habuerat a diebus antiquis, cum caderet populus ejus in manu hostili, et non esset auxiliator: viderunt eam hostes, et deriserunt sabbata ejus.

Heth. Peccatum peccavit Jerusalem, propterea instabilis facta est: omnes qui glorificabant eam, spreverunt illam, quia viderunt ignominiam ejus: ipsa autem gemens conversa est retrorsum.

Teth. Sordes ejus in

Vau. AND from the daughter of Sion all her beauty is departed: her princes are become like rams, that find no pastures: and they are gone away without strength before the face of the pursuer.

Zain. Jerusalem hath remembered the days of her affliction, and transgression of all her desirable things, which she had from the days of old, when her people fell in the enemy's hand · and there was no helper: the enemies have seen her, and have mocked at her sabbaths.

Heth. Jerusalem hath grievously sinned, therefore is she become vagabond: all that honored her, have despised her, because they have seen her shame: but she sighed and turned backward.

Teth. Her filthiness is

pedibus ejus, nec recordata est finis sui: deposita est vehementer, non habens consolatorem; vide Domine afflictionem meam, quoniam erectus est inimicus.

on her feet, and she hath not remembered her end: she is wonderfully cast down, not having a comforter: behold, O Lord! my affliction. because the enemy is lifted up.

Jerusalem, Jerusalem, convertere ad Dominum Deum tuum.

Jerusalem! Jerusalem! be converted to the Lord, thy God.

R. Tristis est anima mea usque ad mortem: sustinete hic, et vigilate mecum: nunc videbitis turbam, quæ circumdabit me. * Vos fugam capietis, et ego vadam immolari pro vobis.

R. My soul is sorrowful even unto death; stay you here, and watch with me. Now ye shall see a multitude, that will surround me. * Ye shall run away, and I will go to be sacrificed for you.

V. Ecce appropinquat hora, et Filius hominis tradetur in manus peccatorum. * Vos.

V. Behold the hour is at hand, and the Son of Man shall be betrayed into the hands of sinners. * Ye shall.

THE THIRD LESSON.

Iod. MANUM suam misit hostis ad omnia desiderabilia ejus: quia vidit gentes ingressas sanctuarium suum, de quibus

Jod. THE enemy hath put out his hand to all her desirable things: for she hath seen the Gentiles enter into her sanctuary

præceperas ne intrarent in ecclesiam tuam.

Caph. Omnis populus ejus gemens, et quærens panem : dederunt pretiosa quæque pro cibo ad refocillandam animam. Vide Domine, et considera, quoniam facta sum vilis.

Lamed. O vos omnes, qui transitis per viam, attendite, et videte si est dolor sicut dolor meus : quoniam vindemiavit me, ut locutus est Dominus in die iræ furoris sui.

Mem. De excelso misit ignem in ossibus meis, et erudivit me : expandit rete pedibus meis, convertit me retrorsum : posuit me desolatam, tota die mœrore confectam.

Nun. Vigilavit jugum iniquitatum mearum : in manu ejus convolutæ

of whom thou gavest commandment that they should not enter into the church.

Caph. All her people sigh, they seek bread : they have given all their precious things for food to relieve the soul : see, O Lord ! and consider, for I am become vile.

Lamed. Oh ! all ye, that pass by the way, attend, and see if there be any sorrow like to my sorrow : for he hath made a vintage of me, as the Lord spoke in the day of his fierce anger.

Mem. From above he hath sent fire into my bones, and hath chastised me : he hath spread a net for my feet, he hath turned me back : he hath made me desolate, and spent with sorrow all the day long.

Nun. The yoke of my iniquities hath watched for me : they are folded

sunt, et impositæ collo meo: infirmata est virtus mea: dedit me Dominus in manu, de qua non potero surgere.

Jerusalem, Jerusalem, convertere ad Dominum Deum tuum.

R. Ecce vidimus eum non habentem speciem, neque decorem: aspectus ejus in eo non est: hic peccata nostra portavit et pro nobis dolet: ipse autem vulneratus est propter iniquitates nostras, * cujus livore sanati sumus.

V. Vere languores nostros ipse tulit, et dolores nostros ipse portavit. * Cujus livore, etc. Ecce vidimus, etc.

together in his hand, and put upon my neck: my strength is weakened: the Lord hath delivered me into a hand, out of which I am not able to rise.

Jerusalem! Jerusalem! be converted to the Lord, thy God.

R. Behold we have seen him having neither beauty, nor comeliness; there is no sightliness in him; he hath borne our sins, and suffers for us; and he was wounded for our iniquities, * and by his bruises we are healed.

V. He hath truly borne our iniquities and carried our sorrows. * And by his bruises, etc. Behold we have seen him, etc.

THE SECOND NOCTURN.

Ant. LIBERAVIT Dominus pauperem a potente, et inopem, cui non erat adjutor.

Ant. THE Lord hath delivered the poor from the mighty, and the needy that had no helper.

PSALM 71.

DEUS, judicium tuum regi da : * et ustitiam tuam filio regis.

Judicare populum tuum in justitia : * et pauperes tuos in judicio.

Suscipiant montes pacem populo, * et colles justitiam.

Judicabit pauperes populi, et salvos faciet filios pauperum : * et humiliabit calumniatorem.

Et permanebit cum sole, et ante lunam, * in generatione et generationem.

Descendet sicut pluvia in vellus : * et sicut stillicidia stillantia super terram.

Orietur in diebus ejus justitia, et abundantia pacis : * donec auferatur luna.

Et dominabitur a mari usque ad mare : * et a

GIVE to the king thy judgment, O God ! and to the king's son, thy justice.

To judge thy people with justice, and thy poor with judgment.

Let the mountains receive peace for the people, and the hills justice.

He shall judge the poor of the people, and he shall save the children of the poor ; and he shall humble the oppressor.

And he shall continue with the sun, and before the moon ; throughout all generations.

He shall come down like rain upon the fleece, and like snow as falling greatly upon the earth.

In his days shall justice spring up, and abundance of peace, till the moon be taken away.

And he shall rule from sea to sea, and from the

flumine usque ad terminos orbis terrarum.

Coram illo procident Æthiopes, * et inimici ejus terram lingent.

Reges Tharsis et insulæ munera offerent: * reges Arabum et Saba dona adducent.

Et adorabunt eum omnes reges terræ : * omnes gentes servient ei.

Quia liberabit pauperem a potente: * et pauperem, cui non erat adjutor.

Parcet pauperi et inopi : * et animas pauperum salvas faciet.

Ex usuris et iniquitate redimet animas eorum : * et honorabile nomen eorum coram illo.

Et vivet, et dabitur ei de auro Arabiæ, et adorabunt de ipso semper : * tota die benedicent ei.

river unto the ends of the earth.

Before him the Ethiopians shall fall down : and his enemies shall lick the ground.

The kings of Tharsis and the islands shall offer presents : the kings of the Arabians and of Saba shall bring gifts.

And all kings of the earth shall adore him : all nations shall serve him.

For he shall deliver the poor from the mighty; and the needy that had no helper.

He shall spare the poor and needy, and he shall save the souls of the poor.

He shall redeem their souls from usuries and iniquity: and their name shall be honorable in his sight.

And he shall live; and to him shall be given of the gold of Arabia ; for him they shall always adore, they shall bless him all the day

Et erit firmamentum in terra in summis montium, superextolletur super Libanum fructus ejus : * et florebunt de civitate sicut fœnum terræ.

And there shall be a firmament on the earth, on the tops of mountains above Libanus shall the fruit thereof be exalted : and they of the city shall flourish like grass of the earth.

Sit nomen ejus benedictum in sæcula : * ante solem permanet nomen ejus.

Let his name be blessed for evermore : his name continueth before the sun.

Et benedicentur in ipso omnes tribus terræ : * omnes gentes magnificabunt eum.

And in him shall all the tribes of the earth be blessed : all nations shall magnify him.

Benedictus Dominus Deus Israel, * qui facit mirabilia solus.

Blessed be the Lord, the God of Israel, who alone doth wonderful things.

Et benedictum nomen majestatis ejus in æternum : * et replebitur majestate ejus omnis terra : fiat, fiat.

And blessed be the name of his majesty for ever, and the whole earth shall be filled with his majesty. So be it, so be it.

Here a candle is extinguished.

Ant. Liberavit Dominus pauperem a potente, et inopem, cui non erat adjutor.

Ant. The Lord hath delivered the poor from the mighty, and the needy that had no helper.

Ant. Cogitaverunt impii, et locuti sunt nequitiam : iniquitatem in excelso locuti sunt.

Ant. The impious have thought and spoken wickedness; they have spoken iniquity on high.

PSALM 72.

QUAM bonus Israel Deus, * his qui recto sunt corde!

Mei autem pene moti sur.t pedes : * pene effusi sunt gressus mei.

Quia zelavi super iniquos, * pacem peccatorum videns.

Quia non est respectus morti eorum : * et firmamentum in plaga eorum.

In labore hominum non sunt, * et cum hominibus non flagellabuntur.

Ideo tenuit eos superbia, * operti sunt iniquitate et impietate sua.

Prodiit quasi ex adipe iniquitas eorum : * tran-

HOW good is God to Israel, to them that are of a right heart !

But my feet were almost moved ; my steps had well nigh slipt.

Because I had a zeal on occasion of the wicked ; seeing the prosperity of sinners.

For there is no regard to their death, nor is there strength in their stripes.

They are not in the labor of men : neither shall they be scourged like other men.

Therefore pride hath held them fast : they are covered with their iniquity and their wickedness.

Their iniquity hath come forth, as it were

sierunt in affectum cordis.

Cogitaverunt, et locuti sunt nequitiam : * iniquitatem in excelso locuti sunt.

Posuerunt in cœlum os suum : * et lingua eorum transivit in terra.

Ideo convertetur populus meus hic : * et dies pleni invenientur in eis.

Et dixerunt : Quomodo scit Deus, * et si est scientia in Excelso ?

Ecce ipsi peccatores, et abundantes in sæculo, * obtinuerunt divitias.

Et dixi : Ergo sine causa justificavi cor meum, * et lavi inter innocentes manus meas.

Et fui flagellatus tota die, * et castigatio mea in matutinis.

from fatness : they have passed into the affection of the heart.

They have thought and spoken wickedness : they have spoken iniquity on high.

They have set their mouth against heaven . and their tongue hath passed through the earth.

Therefore will my people return here : and full days shall be found in them.

And they said : How doth God know ? and is there knowledge in the Most High ?

Behold these are sinners : and yet abounding in the world, they have obtained riches.

And I said : Then have I in vain justified my heart, and washed my hands among the innocent.

And I have been scourged all the day ; and my chastisement hath been in the morn ings.

Si dicebam : Narrabo sic : * ecce nationem filiorum tuorum repro-bavi.

Existimabam ut cog-noscerem hoc, * labor est ante me.

Donec intrem in sanc-tuarium Dei : * et intel-ligam in novissimis eo-rum.

Verumtamen propter dolos posuisti eis : * de-jecisti eos dum alleva-rentur.

Quomodo facti sunt in desolationem ? subito defecerunt : * perierunt propter iniquitatem su-am.

Velut somnium sur-gentium Domine : * in civitate tua imaginem ipsorum ad nihilum re-diges.

Quia inflammatum est cor meum, et renes mei commutati sunt : * et ego ad nihilum redactus sum, et nescivi.

If I said : I will speak thus ; behold I should condemn the generation of thy children.

I studied that I might know this thing : it is a labor in my sight.

Until I go into the sanctuary of God, and understand concerning their last ends.

But indeed for deceits, thou hast put it to them : when they were lifted up, thou hast cast them down.

How are they brought to desolation ? they have suddenly ceased to be ; they have perished by reason of their ini-quity.

As the dream of them that awake, O Lord ! so in thy city thou shalt bring their image to nothing.

For my heart hath been inflamed ; and my reins have been changed, and I am brought to nothing, and I knew not.

Ut jumentum factus sum apud te : * et ego semper tecum.

Tenuisti manum dexteram meam : et in voluntate tua deduxisti me, * et cum gloria suscepisti me.

Quid enim mihi est in cœlo? * et a te quid volui super terram ?

Defecit caro mea, et cor meum : * Deus cordis mei, et pars mea Deus in æternum.

Quia ecce, qui elongant se a te, peribunt : * perdidisti omnes, qui fornicantur abs te.

Mihi autem adhærere Deo bonum est : * ponere in Domino Deo spem meam.

Ut annuntiem omnes prædicationes tuas, * in portis filiæ Sion.

I am become as a beast before thee, and am always with thee.

Thou hast held me by my right hand ; and by thy will thou hast conducted me, and with glory thou hast received me.

For what have I in heaven ? And besides thee, what do I desire upon earth ?

For thee my flesh and my heart have fainted away : thou art the God of my heart, and the God that is my portion for ever.

For behold, they that go far from thee shall perish : thou hast destroyed all them that are disloyal to thee.

But it is good for me to stick close to God ; to put my hope in the Lord God.

That I may declare all thy praises, in the gates of the daughter of Sion.

Here a candle is extinguished.

Ant. Cogitaverunt impii, et locuti sunt nequitiam : iniquitatem in excelso locuti sunt.

Ant. The impious have thought and spoken wickedness; they have spoken iniquity on high.

Ant. Exurge Domine, et judica causam meam.

Ant. Arise, O Lord! and judge my cause.

PSALM 73.

UT quid Deus repulisti in finem : * iratus est furor tuus super oves pascuæ tuæ ?

O GOD! why hast thou cast us off, unto the end ? Why is thy wrath enkindled against the sheep of thy pasture ?

Memor esto congregationis tuæ, * quam possedisti ab initio.

Remember thy congregation, which thou hast possessed from the beginning.

Redemisti virgam hæreditatis tuæ : * mons Sion, in quo habitasti in eo.

The sceptre of thy inheritance, which thou hast redeemed : Mount Sion in which thou hast dwelt.

Leva manus tuas in superbias eorum in finem : * quanta malignatus est inimicus in sancto !

Lift up thy hands against their pride unto the end ; see what things the enemy hath done wickedly in the sanctuary.

Et gloriati sunt qui oderunt te, * in medio solemnitatis tuæ.

And they that hate thee, have made their boasts in the midst of thy solemnity.

Posuerunt signa sua, signa : * et non cognoverunt, sicut in exitu super summum.

Quasi in silva lignorum securibus exciderunt januas ejus in idipsum : * in securi et ascia dejecerunt eam.

Incenderunt igni sanctuarium tuum : * in terra polluerunt tabernaculum nominis tui.

Dixerunt in corde suo cognatio eorum simul : * Quiescere faciamus omnes dies festos Dei a terra.

Signa nostra non vidimus, jam non est propheta : * et nos non cognoscet amplius.

Usquequo Deus improperabit inimicus : * irritat adversarius nomen tuum in finem ?

Ut quid avertis manum tuam, et dexteram

They set up their ensigns for signs, and they knew not ; both in the going out, and on the highest top.

As with axes in a wood of trees they have cut down at once the gates thereof ; with axe and hatchet they have brought it down.

They have set fire to thy sanctuary : they have defiled the dwelling place of thy name on the earth.

They said in their heart, the whole kindred of them together : Let us abolish all the festival days of God from the land.

Our signs we have not seen, there is now no prophet : and he will know us no more.

How long, O God ! shall the enemy reproach ? is the adversary to provoke thy name for ever ?

Why dost thou turn away thy hand : and thy

tuam, * de medio sinu tuo in finem ?

right hand out of the midst of thy bosom for ever ?

Deus autem rex noster ante sæcula, * operatus est salutem in medio terræ.

But God is our king before ages : he hath wrought salvation in the midst of the earth.

Tu confirmasti in virtute tua mare : * contribulasti capita draconum in aquis.

Thou by thy strength didst make the sea firm : thou didst crush the heads of the dragons in the waters.

Tu confregisti capita draconis : * dedisti eum escam populis Æthiopum.

Thou hast broken the heads of the dragon : thou hast given him to be meat for the people of the Ethiopians.

Tu dirupisti fontes, et torrentes : * tu siccasti fluvios Ethan.

Thou hast broken up the fountains and the torrents: thou hast dried up the Ethan rivers.

Tuus est dies, et tua est nox : * tu fabricatus es auroram et solem.

Thine is the day, and thine is the night : thou hast made the morn and the sun.

Tu fecisti omnes terminos terræ : * æstatem et ver tu plasmasti ea.

Thou hast made all the borders of the earth : the summer and the spring were formed by thee.

Memor esto hujus, inimicus improperavit Domino : * et populus

Remember this, the enemy hath reproached the Lord ; and a foolish

insipiens incitavit no-men tuum.

Ne tradas bestiis animas confitentes tibi, * et animas pauperum tuorum ne obliviscaris in finem.

Respice in testamentum tuum : * quia repleti sunt, qui obscurati sunt terræ domibus iniquitatum.

Ne avertatur humilis factus confusus : * pauper et inops laudabunt nomen tuum.

Exurge Deus, judica causam tuam : * memor esto improperiorum tuorum, eorum quæ ab in-sipiente sunt tota die.

Ne obliviscaris voces inimicorum tuorum : * superbia eorum, qui te oderunt, ascendit semper.

people hath provoked thy name.

Deliver not up to beasts the souls that confess to thee : and forget not to the end, the souls of thy poor.

Have regard to thy covenant : for they that are the obscure of the earth have been filled with dwellings of iniquity.

Let not the humble man be turned away with confusion ; the poor and needy shall praise thy name.

Arise, O God ! judge thy own cause : remember thy reproaches with which the foolish man hath reproached thee all the day.

Forget not the voices of thy enemies : the pride of them that hate thee ascendeth continu· ally.

Here a candle is extinguished.

Ant. Exurge Domine, et judica causam meam.

Ant. Arise, O Lord and judge my cause.

V. Deus meus eripe me de manu peccatoris.

V. Deliver me, O my God! out of the hand of the sinner.

R. Et de manu contra legem agentis, et iniqui.

R. And out of the hand of the transgressor of the law and the unjust.

Pater noster, *secreto.*

Our Father, *privately.*

THE FOURTH LESSON.

Ex Tractatu sancti Augustini Episcopi super Psalmos. In Psal. 54.

From the treatise of Saint Augustin, the Bishop, on the Psalms. On the 54th Psalm.

EXAUDI Deus orationem meam, et ne despexeris deprecationem meam : intende mihi, et exaudi me. Satagentis, solliciti, in tribulatione positi, verba sunt ista. Orat multa patiens, de malo liberari desiderans. Superest ut videamus in quo malo sit ; et cum dicere cœperit, agnoscamus ibi nos esse : ut communicata tribulatione, conjungamus orationem. Contristatus sum, inquit, in exercitatione mea, et

HEAR, O God! my prayer, and despise not my supplication: be attentive to me, and hear me. These are the words of a man in trouble, solicitude, and affliction. He prays in his great sufferings, desiring to be freed from some evil. Let us now see what evil he lies under; and having told us, let us acknowledge ourselves in it; that by partaking of the affliction, we may join in his prayer. I am grieved

conturbatus sum. Ubi contristatus ? ubi conturbatus ? In exercitatione mea, inquit. Homines malos, quos patitur, commemoratus est: eamdemque passionem malorum hominum, exercitationem suam dixit. Ne putetis gratis esse malos in hoc mundo, et nihil boni de illis agere Deum. Omnis malus aut ideo vivit, ut corrigatur ; aut ideo vivit, ut per illum bonus exerceatur.

R. Amicus meus osculi me tradidit signo : quem osculatus fuero, ipse est, tenete eum. Hoc malum fecit signum, qui per osculum adimplevit homicidium. * Infelix prætermisit pretium sanguinis, et in fine laqueo se suspendit.

V. Bonum erat ei, si natus non fuisset homo ille. * Infelix prætermisit.

in my exercise, says he. and am troubled. Where is he grieved ? where is he troubled ? He says : In my exercise. He speaks of the wicked men, whom he suffers,. and calls such sufferings of wicked men his exercise. Think not that the wicked are in this world for nothing, and that God does no good with them. Every wicked man lives, either to amend his life or to exercise the good.

R. The sign by which my friend betrayed me was a kiss: whomsoever I shall kiss, that is he ; hold him fast. He that committed murder by a kiss, gave this wicked sign. * The unhappy wretch returned the price of blood, and in the end hanged himself.

V. It were better for that man, if he had not been born. * The unhappy wretch.

THE FIFTH LESSON.

UTINAM ergo qui nos modo exercent, convertantur et nobiscum exerceantur : tamen quamdiu ita sunt ut exerceant, non eos oderimus; quia in eo quod malus est quis eorum, utrum usque in finem perseveraturus sit ignoramus. Et plerumque, cum tibi videris odisse inimicum, fratrem odisti, et nescis. Diabolus, et angeli ejus in Scripturis sanctis manifestati sunt nobis, quod ad ignem æternum sint destinati. Ipsorum tantum desperanda est correctio, contra quos habemus occultam luctam; ad quam luctam nos armat Apostolus, dicens: Non est nobis colluctatio adversus carnem et sanguinem; id est, non adversus homines, quos videtis, sed adversus principes, et potestates, et rectores

WOULD to God, then, they that now exercise us, were converted and exercised with us; but let us not hate them, though they continue to exercise us; for we know not whether they will persevere to the end in their wickedness. And many times, when you imagine that you hate your enemy, it is your brother you hate, though you are ignorant of it. The Holy Scriptures plainly show us, that the devil and his agents are doomed to eternal fire. It is only their amendment we may despair of, with whom we wage an invisible war; for which the Apostle arms us, saying: Our conflict is not with flesh and blood, that is, not with the men you see before your eyes, but with the princes, and powers,

mundi, tenebrarum harum. Ne forte cum dixisset, mundi, intelligeres dæmones esse rectores cœli et terræ. Mundi dixit, tenebrarum harum ; mundi dixit, amatorum mundi ; mundi dixit, impiorum et iniquorum ; mundi dixit, de quo dicit Evangelium : Et mundus eum non cognovit.

and rulers of the world, of this darkness. And lest, by his saying of the world, you might think perhaps that the devils are the rulers of heaven and earth, he added, of this darkness. By the world, then, he meant the lovers of the world : by the world, he meant the impious and the wicked ; by the world, he meant that which the gospel speaks of : And the world knew him not.

R. Judas, mercator pessimus, osculo petiit Dominum : ille ut agnus innocens non negavit Judæ osculum : * Denariorum numero Christum Judæis tradidit.

R. The wicked merchant, Judas, kissed the Lord ; he, like an innocent lamb, refused not the kiss to Judas. For a few pence, he delivered Christ to the Jews.

V. Melius illi erat, si natus non fuisset. * Denariorum.

V. It were better for that man if he had not been born. * For a few pence.

THE SIXTH LESSON.

QUONIAM vidi iniquitatem, et contradictionem in civitate. Attende gloriam crucis ipsius. Jam in fronte regum crux illa fixa est, cui inimici insultaverunt. Effectus probavit virtutem : domuit orbem non ferro, sed ligno. Lignum crucis contumeliis dignum visum est inimicis, et ante ipsum lignum stantes caput agitabant, et dicebant : Si Filius Dei est, descendat de cruce. Extendebat ille manus suas ad populum non credentem, et contradicentem. Si enim justus est qui ex fide vivit, iniquus est qui non habet fidem. Quod ergo hic ait iniquitatem, perfidiam intellige. Videbat ergo Dominus in civitate iniquitatem et contradictionem, et extendebat manus suas ad populum non credentem,

FOR I nave seen injustice and strife in the city. See the glory of the cross. That cross, that was the derision of his enemies, is now placed on the fore-heads of kings. The effect is a proof of his power ; he conquered the world, not by the sword, but by the wood. The wood of the cross was thought a subject of scorn by his enemies, who as they stood before it, shook their heads and said : If he is the Son of God, let him come down from the cross. He stretched forth his hands to an unbelieving and seditious people. For if he is just that lives by faith, he is unjust that hath not faith. By injustice, then, here you must understand infidelity. The Lord, therefore, saw injustice and strife in the

et contradicentem ; et tamen et ipsos expectans dicebat : Pater, ignosce illis, quia nesciunt quid faciunt.

city, and stretched forth his hands to an unbelieving and seditious people ; and yet, he waited for them too, saying : Father ! forgive them, for they know not what they do.

R. Unus ex discipulis meis tradet me hodie : væ illi per quem tradar ego ; * Melius illi erat, si natus non fuisset.

R. One of my disciples will this day betray me : woe to him by whom I shall be betrayed. * It were better for that man if he had not been born.

V. Qui intingit mecum manum in paropside, hic me traditurus est in manus peccatorum. * Melius illi. Unus ex discipulis, etc.

V. He that dippeth his hand with me in the dish, the same shall betray me into the hands of sinners. * It were. One of my disciples, etc.

THE THIRD NOCTURN.

Ant. DIXI iniquis : Nolite loqui adversus Deum iniquitatem.

Ant. I SAID to the wicked : Speak not iniquity against God.

PSALM 74.

CONFITEBIMUR tibi Deus : confitebimur, et invocabimus nomen tuum.

WE will praise thee, O God ! we will praise, and we will call upon thy name.

Narrabimus mirabilia tua : * cum accepero tempus, ego justitias judicabo.

Liquefacta est terra, et omnes qui habitant in ea : * ego confirmavi columnas ejus.

Dixi iniquis : Nolite inique agere; * et delinquentibus : Nolite exaltare cornu.

Nolite extollere in altum cornu vestrum : * nolite loqui adversus Deum iniquitatem.

Quia neque ab oriente, neque ab occidente, neque a desertis montibus: * quoniam Deus judex est.

Hunc humiliat, et hunc exaltat : * quia calix in manu Domini, vini meri plenus misto.

Et inclinavit ex hoc in hoc : verumtamen fæx ejus non est exinanita : * bibent omnes peccatores terræ.

We will relate thy wondrous works : when I shall take a time, I will judge justices.

The earth is melted, and all that dwell therein ; I have established the pillars thereof.

I said to the wicked : Do not act wickedly; and to the sinner : Lift not up the horn.

Lift not up your horn on high ; speak not iniquity against God.

For neither from the east, nor from the west, nor from the desert hills ; for God is the judge.

One he putteth down, and another he lifteth up : for in the hand of the Lord there is a cup of strong wine, full of mixture.

And he hath poured it out from this to that ; but the dregs thereof are not emptied ; all the sinners of the earth shall drink.

Ego autem annuntiabo in sæculum : * cantabo Deo Jacob.

But I will declare for ever ; I will sing to the God of Jacob.

Et omnia cornua peccatorum confringam : * et exaltabuntur cornua justi.

And I will break all the horns of sinners ; but the horns of the just shall be exalted.

Here a candle is extinguished.

Ant. Dixi iniquis : Nolite loqui adversus Deum iniquitatem.

Ant. I said to the wicked : Speak not iniquity against God.

Ant. Terra tremuit et quievit, dum exurgeret in judicio Deus.

Ant. The earth trembled and was still, when God arose in judgment.

PSALM 75.

NOTUS in Judæa Deus: * in Israel magnum nomen ejus.

IN Judea God is known, his name is great in Israel.

Et factus est in pace locus ejus : * et habitatio ejus in Sion.

And his place is in peace, and his abode in Sion.

Ibi confregit potentias arcuum, * scutum, gladium, et bellum.

There hath he broken the powers of bows, the shield, the sword, and the battle.

Illuminans tu mirabiliter a montibus æternis: * turbati sunt omnes insipientes corde.

Thou enlightenest wonderfully from the everlasting hills : all the foolish of heart were troubled.

Dormierunt somnum suum : * et nihil inve-

They have slept their sleep : and all the men

nerunt omnes viri divitiarum in manibus suis.

of riches have found nothing in their hands.

Ab increpatione tua Deus Jacob : * dormitaverunt qui ascenderunt equos.

At thy rebuke, O God of Jacob ! they have all slumbered that mounted on horseback.

Tu terribilis es, et quis resistet tibi ? * ex tunc ira tua.

Thou art terrible, and who shall resist thee ? from that time thy wrath.

De cœlo auditum fecisti judicium : * terra tremuit et quievit.

Thou hast caused judgment to be heard from heaven : the earth trembled and was still.

Cum exurgeret in judicium Deus, * ut salvos faceret omnes mansuetos terræ.

When God arose in judgment, to save all the meek of the earth.

Quoniam cogitatio hominis confitebitur tibi : * et reliquiæ cogitationis diem festum agent tibi.

For the thought of man shall give praise to thee ; and the remainders of the thought shall keep holyday to thee.

Vovete, et reddite Domino Deo vestro : * omnes qui in circuitu ejus affertis munera.

Vow ye, and pay to the Lord, your God ; all you that round about him bring presents.

Terribili et ei qui aufert spiritum principium, * terribili apud reges terræ.

To him that is terrible, even to him who taketh away the spirit of princes, to the terrible with the kings of the earth.

Here a candle is extinguished.

Ant. Terra tremuit et quievit, dum exurgeret in judicio Deus.

Ant. The earth trembled and was still, when God arose in judgment.

Ant. In die tribulationis meæ, Deum exquisivi manibus meis.

Ant. In the day of my tribulation, I sought God, with my hands lifted up to him.

PSALM 76.

VOCE mea ad Dominum clamavi : * voce mea ad Deum, et intendit mihi.

I CRIED to the Lord with my voice : to God with my voice, and he gave ear to me.

In die tribulationis meæ Deum exquisivi, manibus meis nocte contra eum : * et non sum deceptus.

In the day of my trouble, I sought God, with my hands lifted up to him in the night ; and I was not deceived.

Renuit consolari anima mea, * memor fui Dei, et delectatus sum et exercitatus sum : et defecit spiritus meus.

My soul refused to be comforted : I remembered God, and was delighted, and was exercised, and my spirit swooned away.

Anticipaverunt vigilias oculi mei : * turbatus sum, et non sum locutus.

My eyes prevented the watches ; I was troubled, and I spoke not.

Cogitavi dies antiquos : * et annos æternos in mente habui.

I thought upon the days of old : and I had in my mind the eternal years.

Et meditatus sum nocte cum corde meo, * et exercitabar, et scopebam spiritum meum.

And I meditated in the night with mine own heart : and I was exercised, and I swept my spirit.

Numquid in æternum projiciet Deus : * aut non apponet ut complacitior sit adhuc ?

Will God then cast off for ever ? or will he never be more favorable again ?

Aut in finem misericordiam suam abscindet, * a generatione in generationem ?

Or will he cut off his mercy for ever, from generation to generation ?

Aut obliviscetur misereri Deus ? * aut continebit in ira sua misericordias suas ?

Or will God forget to show mercy ? or will he in his anger shut up his mercies ?

Et dixi : Nunc cœpi : * hæc mutatio dexteræ Excelsi.

And I said : Now have I begun : this is the change of the right hand of the Most High.

Memor fui operum Domini : * quia memor ero ab initio mirabilium tuorum.

I remembered the works of the Lord : for I will be mindful of thy wonders from the beginning.

Et meditabor in omnibus operibus tuis : * et in adinventionibus tuis exercebor.

And I will meditate on all the works, and will be employed in thy inventions.

Deus, in sancto via tua : quis Deus magnus sicut Deus noster ? * tu

Thy way, O God ! is in the holy place ; who is the great God like our

es Deus qui facis mirabilia.

Notam fecisti in populis virtutem tuam : * redemisti in brachio tuo populum tuum, filios Jacob et Joseph.

Viderunt te aquæ, Deus, viderunt te aquæ: * et timuerunt, et turbatæ sunt abyssi.

Multitudo sonitus aquarum : * vocem dederunt nubes.

Etenim sagittæ tuæ transeunt : * vox tonitrui tui in rota.

Illuxerunt coruscationes tuæ orbi terræ : * commota est, et contremuit terra.

In mari via tua, et semitæ tuæ in aquis multis : * et vestigia tua non cognoscentur.

Deduxisti sicut oves populum tuum, * in manu Moysi et Aaron.

God? Thou art the God that dost wonders.

Thou hast made thy power known amongst the nations : with thy arm thou hast redeemed thy people, the children of Jacob, and of Joseph.

The waters saw thee, O God ! the waters saw thee ; and they were afraid and the depths were troubled.

Great was the noise of the waters ; the clouds sent out a sound.

For thy arrows pass ; the voice of thy thunder is a wheel.

Thy lightnings enlightened the world ; the earth shook, and trembled.

Thy way is in the sea, and thy paths in many waters ; and thy footsteps shall not be known.

Thou hast conducted thy people like sheep, by the hand of Moses and Aaron.

Here a candle is extinguished.

Ant. In die tribulationis meæ, Deum exquisivi manibus meis.

Ant. In the day of my trouble I sought God with my hands lifted up to him.

V. Exurge Domine.
R. Et judica causam meam.

V. Arise, O Lord!
R. And judge my cause.

Pater noster, *secreto.*

Our Father, *privately.*

THE SEVENTH LESSON.

De Epistola prima beati Pauli Apostoli ad Corinthios, cap. xi.

Out of the first Epistle of St. Paul the Apostle to the Corinthians, chap. xi.

HOC autem præcipio, non laudans quod non in melius, sed in deterius convenitis. Primum quidem convenientibus vobis in ecclesiam, audio scissuras esse inter vos, et ex parte credo. Nam oportet et hæreses esse, ut et qui probati sunt, manifesti fiant in vobis. Convenientibus ergo vobis in unum, jam non est Dominicam cœnam manducare : unusquisque enim suam cœnam præsumit ad manducandum. Et alius qui-

NOW this I ordain ; not praising you, that you come together not for the better, but for the worse. For first of all I hear that when you come together in the church, there are divisions among you, and in part I believe it. For there must be also heresies ; that they also, who are approved, may be made manifest among you. When you come together therefore into one place, it is not now to eat the Lord's supper. For every one taketh

dem esurit, alius autem ebrius est. Numquid domos non habetis ad manducandum et bibendum? Aut ecclesiam Dei contemnitis, et confunditis eos qui non habent? Quid dicam vobis? Laudo vos? in hoc non laudo.

before his own supper to eat. And one indeed is hungry, and another is drunk. What! have you not houses to eat and to drink in? Or despise ye the church of God; and put them to shame that have not? What shall I say to you? Do I praise you? In this I praise you not.

R. Eram quasi agnus innocens: ductus sum ad immolandum, et nesciebam: consilium fecerunt inimici mei adversum me, dicentes: * Venite, mittamus lignum in panem ejus, et eradamus eum de terra viventium.

R. I was like an innocent lamb; I was led to be sacrificed, and I knew it not: my enemies conspired against me, saying: Come, let us put wood on his bread, and cut him off from the land of the living.

V. Omnes inimici mei adversum me cogitabant mala mihi: verbum iniquum mandaverunt adversum me, dicentes: * Venite, etc.

V. All my enemies contrived evils to me; they determined against me an unjust word, saying: Come, etc.

THE EIGHTH LESSON.

EGO enim accepi a Domino quod et tradidi vobis, quoniam

FOR I have received of the Lord that which also I delivered

Dominus Jesus, in qua nocte tradebatur, accepit panem, et gratias agens fregit, et dixit: Accipite, et manducate : hoc est corpus meum, quod pro vobis tradetur : hoc facite in meam commemorationem. Similiter et calicem, postquam coenavit, dicens : Hic calix novum testamentum est in meo sanguine. Hoc facite, quotiescumque bibetis, in meam commemorationem. Quotiescumque enim manducabitis panem hunc, et calicem bibetis, mortem Domini annuntiabitis donec veniat.

to you, that the Lord Jesus, the same night in which he was betrayed, took bread, and giving thanks, broke, and said : Take ye, and eat : this is my body which shall be delivered for you ; this do for the commemoration of me. In like manner also the chalice, after he had supped, saying : This chalice is the new testament in my blood : this do ye, as often as you shall drink it, for the commemoration of me. For as often as you shall eat this bread, and drink this chalice, you shall show the death of the Lord, until he come.

R. Una hora non potuistis vigilare mecum, qui exhortabamini mori pro me ? * Vel Judam non videtis, quomodo non dormit, sed festinat tradere me Judæis ?

R. Could you not watch one hour with me, you that were resolved to die for me? Or do you not see Judas, how he sleeps not, but makes haste to betray me to the Jews ?

V. Quid dormitis? surgite et orate, ne intretis

V. Why do ye sleep? Arise and pray, that ye

in tentationem. * Vel Judam, etc.

enter not into temptation. Or do ye not see, etc.

THE NINTH LESSON.

ITAQUE quicumque manducaverit panem hunc, vel biberit calicem Domini indigne, reus erit corporis et sanguinis Domini. Probet autem seipsum homo, et sic de pane illo edat, et de calice bibat. Qui enim manducat et bibit indigne, judicium sibi manducat et bibit, non dijudicans corpus Domini. Ideo inter vos multi infirmi et imbecilles, et dormiunt multi. Quod si nosmetipsos dijudicaremus, non utique judicaremur. Dum judicamur autem, a Domino corripimur, ut non cum hoc mundo damnemur. Itaque, fratres mei, cum convenitis ad manducandum, invicem expectate. Si quis esurit, domi manducet ; ut non in judicium conveniatis,

WHEREFORE, whosoever shall eat this bread, or drink the chalice of the Lord unworthily, shall be guilty of the body and of the blood of the Lord. But let a man prove himself, and so let him eat of that bread, and drink of the chalice. For he that eateth and drinketh unworthily, eateth and drinketh judgment to himself, not discerning the body of the Lord. Therefore are there many infirm and weak among you, and many sleep. But if we would judge ourselves, we should not be judged. But whilst we are judged, we are chastised by the Lord ; that we be not condemned with this world. Wherefore. my brethren! when you come together

Cetera autem, cum venero disponam.

to eat, wait for one another. If any man be hungry, let him eat at home ; that you come not together unto judgment. And the rest I will set in order, when I come.

R. Seniores populi consilium fecerunt, * Ut Jesum dolo tenerent, et occiderent : cum gladiis et fustibus exierunt tanquam ad latronem.

R. The ancients of the people consulted together that by subtilty they might apprehend Jesus and put him to death : they went out with swords and clubs as against a robber.

V. Collegerunt pontifices et Pharisæi concilium, * Ut Jesum, etc. Seniores, etc.

V. The priests and Pharisees held a council, how they might, etc. The ancients, etc.

The Lauds.

Ant. JUSTIFICERIS Domine in sermonibus tuis, et vincas cum judicaris.

Ant. THAT thou mayest be justified, O Lord ! in thy words, and mayest overcome, when thou art judged.

PSALM 50.

MISERERE mei, Deus, * secun-

HAVE mercy on me, O God ! ac-

dum magnam misericordiam tuam.

Et secundum multitudinem miserationum tuarum, * dele iniquitatem meam.

Amplius lava me ab iniquitate mea : * et a peccato meo munda me.

Quoniam iniquitatem meam ego cognosco : * et peccatum meum contra me est semper.

Tibi soli peccavi, et malum coram te feci : * ut justificeris in sermonibus tuis, et vincas cum judicaris.

Ecce enim in iniquitatibus conceptus sum : * et in peccatis concepit me mater mea.

Ecce enim veritatem dilexisti : * incerta et occulta sapientiæ tuæ manifestasti mihi.

Asperges me hyssopo, et mundabor : * lavabis

cording to thy great mercy.

And according to the multitude of thy tender mercies, blot out my iniquity.

Wash me yet more from my iniquity, and cleanse me from my sin.

For I know my iniquity, and my sin is always before me.

To thee only have I sinned, and have done evil before thee ; that thou mayest be justified in thy words, and mayest overcome when thou art judged.

For behold I was conceived in iniquities : and in sins did my mother conceive me.

For behold thou hast loved truth : the uncertain and hidden things of thy wisdom thou hast made manifest to me.

Thou shalt sprinkle me with hyssop, and I shall

me, et super nivem dealbabor.

Auditui meo dabis gaudium et lætitiam : * et exultabunt ossa humiliata.

Averte faciem tuam a peccatis meis : * et omnes iniquitates meas dele.

Cor mundum crea in me, Deus : * et spiritum rectum innova in visceribus meis.

Ne projicias me a facie tua : * et spiritum sanctum tuum ne auferas a me.

Redde mihi lætitiam salutaris tui : * et spiritu principali confirma me.

Docebo iniquos vias tuas : * et impii ad te convertentur.

Libera me de sanguinibus Deus, Deus salutis meæ : * et exultabit lingua mea justitiam tuam.

be cleansed : thou shalt wash me, and I shall be made whiter than snow.

To my hearing tnou shalt give joy and gladness; and the bones that have been humbled shall rejoice.

Turn away thy face from my sins, and blot out all my iniquities.

Create a clean heart in me, O God ! and renew a right spirit within my bowels.

Cast me not away from thy face; and take not thy holy Spirit from me.

Restore unto me the joy of thy salvation, and strengthen me with a perfect spirit.

I will teach the unjust thy ways : and the wicked shall be converted to thee.

Deliver me from blood, O God ! thou God of my salvation, and my tongue shall extol thy justice.

Domine, labia mea aperies : * et os meum annuntiabit laudem tuam.

O Lord ! thou wilt open my lips : and my mouth shall declare thy praise.

Quoniam si voluisses sacrificium, dedissem utique : * holocaustis non delactaberis.

For if thou hadst desired sacrifice, I would indeed have given it : with burnt-offerings thou wilt not be delighted.

Sacrificium Deo spiritus contribulatus : * cor contritum et humiliatum Deus non despicies.

A sacrifice to God is an afflicted spirit ; a contrite and humbled heart, O God ! thou wilt not despise.

Benigne fac Domine in bona voluntate tua Sion : * ut ædificentur muri Jerusalem.

Deal favorably, O Lord ! in thy good-will with Sion : that the walls of Jerusalem may be built up.

Tunc acceptabis sacrificium justitiæ, oblationes, et holocausta : * tunc imponent super altare tuum vitulos.

Then shalt thou accept the sacrifice of justice, oblations, and whole burnt-offerings : then shall they lay calves upon thy altar.

Here a candle is extinguished.

Ant. Justificeris Domine in sermonibus tuis, et vincas cum iudicaris.

Ant. That thou mayest be justified, O Lord ! in thy words, and mayest overcome, when thou art judged.

Ant. Dominus tanquam ovis ad victimam ductus est, et non aperuit os suum.

Ant. The Lord was led like a sheep to the slaughter, and he opened not his mouth.

PSALM 89.

DOMINE refugium factus es nobis, * a generatione in generationem.

Priusquam montes fierent, aut formaretur terra et orbis : * a sæculo et usque in sæculum tu es Deus.

Ne avertas hominem in humilitatem : * et dixisti : Convertimini filii hominum.

Quoniam mille anni ante oculos tuos, * tanquam dies hesterna quæ præteriit.

Et custodia in nocte, * quæ pro nihilo habentur, eorum anni erunt.

Mane sicut herba transeat, mane floreat, et transeat : * vespere

LORD ! thou hast been our refuge, from generation to generation.

Before the mountains were made, or the earth and the world were formed ; from eternity and to eternity, thou art God.

Turn not man away to be brought low ; and thou hast said : Be converted, O ye sons of men !

For a thousand years in thy sight, are but as yesterday which is past and gone.

And as a watch in the night ; as things that are counted nothing, so shall their years bè.

In the morning, man shall grow up like grass : in the morning he shall

decidat, induret, et arescat.

flourish, and pass away ; in the evening he shall fall, grow dry, and wither.

Quia defecimus in ira tua : * et in furore tuo turbati sumus.

For in thy wrath we are quickly consumed, and are troubled in thy indignation.

Posuisti iniquitates nostras in conspectu tuo : * sæculum nostrum in illuminatione vultus tui.

Thou hast set our iniquities before thy eyes, our life in the light of thy countenance.

Quoniam omnes dies nostri defecerunt : * et in ira tua defecimus.

For all our days are spent ; and in thy wrath we have fainted away.

Anni nostri sicut aranea meditabuntur : * dies annorum nostrorum in ipsis, septuaginta anni.

Our years shall be considered as a spider ; the days of our years in them are threescore and ten years.

Si autem in potentatibus, octoginta anni : * et amplius eorum, labor et dolor.

But if in the strong, they be fourscore years ; and what is more of them is labor and sorrow.

Quoniam supervenit mansuetudo : * et corripiemur.

For mildness is come upon us ; and we shall be corrected.

Quis novit potestatem iræ tuæ : * et præ timore tuo iram tuam dinumerare ?

Who knoweth the power of thy anger : and for thy fear can number thy wrath ?

Dexteram tuam sic notam fac: * et eruditos corde in sapientia.

So make thy right hand known : and make us learned in heart, in wisdom.

Convertere Domine usquequo ? * et deprecabilis esto super servos tuos.

Return, O Lord! how long ? and be entreated in favor of thy servants.

Repleti sumus mane misericordia tua : * et exultavimus, et delectati sumus omnibus diebus nostris.

We are filled in the morning with thy mercy ; and we have rejoiced, and are delighted all our days.

Lætati sumus pro diebus quibus nos humiliasti : * annis, quibus vidimus mala.

We have rejoiced for the days in which thou hast humbled us : for the years in which we have seen evils.

Respice in servos tuos, et in opera tua : * et dirige filios eorum.

Look upon thy servants, and upon their works : and direct their children.

Et sit splendor Domini Dei nostri super nos, et opera manuum nostrarum dirige super nos : * et opus manuum nostrarum dirige.

And let the brightness of the Lord our God be upon us ; and direct thou the works of our hands over us ; yea, the work of our hands do thou direct.

Here a candle is extinguished.

Ant. Dominus tanquam ovis ad victimam

Ant. The Lord was led like a sheep to the

ductus est, et non aperuit os suum.

slaughter, and he opened not his mouth.

Ant. Contritum est cor meum in medio mei, contremuerunt omnia ossa mea.

Ant. My heart is broken within me, all my bones tremble.

PSALM 62.

DEUS, Deus meus, * ad te de luce vigilo.

O GOD, my God! to thee do I watch at break of day.

Sitivit in te anima mea, * quam multipliciter tibi caro mea.

For thee my soul hath thirsted ; for thee my flesh, O how many ways!

In terra deserta, et invia, et inaquosa : * sic in sancto apparui tibi, ut viderem virtutem tuam, et gloriam tuam.

In a desert land, and where there is no way, and no water : so in the sanctuary have I come before thee, to see thy power and thy glory.

Quoniam melior est misericordia tua super vitas : * labia mea laudabunt te.

For thy mercy is better than lives : thee my lips shall praise.

Sic benedicam te in vita mea: * et in nomine tuo levabo manus meas.

Thus will I bless thee all my life long : and in thy name I will lift up my hands.

Sicut adipe et pinguedine repleatur anima mea : * et labiis exultationis laudabit os meum.

Let my soul be filled as with marrow and fatness ; and my mouth shall praise thee with joyful lips.

Si memor fui tui super stratum meum, in matutinis meditabor in te : * quia fuisti adjutor meus.

If I have remembered thee upon my bed, I will meditate on thee in the morning : because thou hast been my helper.

Et in velamento alarum tuarum exultabo: adhæsit anima mea post te : * me suscepit dextera tua.

And I will rejoice under the covert of thy wings : my soul hath stuck close to thee: thy right hand hath received me.

Ipsi vero in vanum quæsierunt animam meam, introibunt in inferiora terræ : * tradentur in manus gladii, partes vulpium erunt.

But they have sought my soul in vain, they shall go into the lower parts of the earth : they shall be delivered into the hands of the sword ; they shall be the portions of foxes.

Rex vero lætabitur in Deo, laudabuntur omnes qui jurant in eo : * quia obstructum est os loquentium iniqua.

But the king shall rejoice in God ; all they shall be praised that swear by him : because the mouth is stopped of them that speak wicked things.

PSALM 66.

DEUS misereatur nostri, et benedicat nobis : * illuminet

MAY God have mercy on us, and bless us : may he

vultum suum super nos, et misereatur nostri.

cause the light of his countenance to shine upon us, and may he have mercy on us.

Ut cognoscamus in terra viam tuam : * in omnibus gentibus salutare tuum.

That we may know thy way upon earth, thy salvation in all nations.

Confiteantur tibi populi Deus : * confiteantur tibi populi omnes.

Let people confess to thee, O God ! let all people give praise to thee.

Lætentur et exultent gentes : * quoniam judicas populos in æquitate, et gentes in terra dirigis.

Let the nations be glad and rejoice ; for thou judgest the people with justice, and directest the nations upon earth.

Confiteantur tibi populi Deus, confiteantur tibi populi omnes : * terra dedit fructum suum.

Let the people, O God! confess to thee, let all the people give praise to thee. The earth hath yielded her fruit.

Benedicat nos Deus, Deus noster, benedicat nos Deus : * et metuant eum omnes fines terræ.

May God, our own God, bless us : may God bless us : and all the ends of the earth fear him.

Here a candle is extinguished.

Ant. Contritum est cor meum in medio mei, contremuerunt omnia ossa mea.

Ant. My heart is broken within me, all my bones tremble.

Ant. Exhortatus es in virtute tua, et in refectione sancta tua Domine

Ant. Thou hast encouraged us with thy power and thy holy refreshment, O Lord!

THE CANTICLE OF MOSES. *Exod.* xv.

CANTEMUS Domino; gloriose enim magnificatus est : .* equum et ascensorum dejecit in mare.

LET us sing to the Lord; for he is gloriously magnified; the horse and its rider he hath thrown into the sea.

Fortitudo mea et laus mea Dominus, * et factus est mihi in salutem.

The Lord is my strength and my praise; and he is become a salvation to me.

Iste Deus meus et glorificabo eum : * Deus patris mei, et exaltabo eum.

He is my God, and I will glorify him; the God of my father, and I will exalt him.

Dominus quasi vir pugnator, omnipotens nomen ejus. * Currus Pharaonis, et exercitum ejus projecit in mare.

The Lord is like a man of war Almighty is his name. Pharao's chariots and his army he hath cast into the sea.

Electi principes ejus submersi sunt in Mari Rubro : * abyssi operuerunt eos, descenderunt in profundum quasi lapis.

His chosen captains are drowned in the Red Sea; the paths have covered them; they are sunk to the bottom like a stone.

Dextera tua Domine

Thy right hand, O

magnificata est in fortitudine ; dextera tua Domine percussit inimicum : * et in multitudine gloriæ tuæ deposuisti adversarios tuos.

Lord ! is magnified in strength; thy right hand, O Lord ! hath slain the enemy. And in the multitude of thy glory, thou hast put down the adversaries.

Misisti iram tuam, quæ devoravit eos sicut stipulam. * Et in spiritu furoris tui congregatæ sunt aquæ.

Thou hast sent thy wrath, which hath devoured them like stubble. And by the blast of thy anger the waters were gathered together.

Stetit unda fluens, * congregatæ sunt abyssi in medio mari.

The flowing water stood, the depths were gathered together in the midst of the sea.

Dixit inimicus : Persequar et comprehendam, * dividam spolia, implebitur anima mea.

The enemy said : I will pursue, and overtake : I will divide the spoils ; my soul shall have its fill.

Evaginabo gladium meum, * interficiet eos manus mea.

I will draw my sword; my hand shall slay them.

Flavit spiritus tuus, et operuit eos mare : * submersi sunt quasi plumbum in aquis vehementibus.

Thy wind blew, and the sea covered them ; they sunk as lead in the mighty waters.

Quis similis tui in fortibus Domine ? * quis similis tui, magnificus

Who is like thee among the strong, O Lord ! who is like to

in sanctitate, terribilis atque laudabilis, faciens mirabilia?

Extendisti manum tuam, et devoravit eos terra. * Dux fuisti in misericordia tua populo quem redemisti.

Et portasti eum in fortitudine tua, * ad habitaculum sanctum tuum.

Ascenderunt populi, et irati sunt: * dolores obtinuerunt habitatores Philisthiim.

Tunc conturbati sunt principes Edom, robustos Moab obtinuit tremor : * obriguerunt omnes habitatores Chanaan.

Irruat super eos formido et pavor, * in magnitudine brachii tui.

Fiant immobiles quasi lapis, donec pertranseat populus tuus Domine : * donec pertranseat populus tuus istc, quem possedisti.

thee, glorious in holiness, terrible and praiseworthy, doing wonders?

Thou stretchedst forth thy hand, and the earth swallowed them. In thy mercy thou hast been a leader to the people, which thou hast redeemed.

And in thy strength, thou hast carried them to thy holy habitation.

Nations rose up, and were angry; sorrow took hold on the inhabitants of Philistiim.

Then were the princes of Edom troubled, trembling seized on the stout men of Moab; and all the inhabitants of Chanaan became stiff.

Let fear and dread fall upon them in the greatness of thy arm.

Let them become unmovable as a stone, until thy people, O Lord! pass by; until this thy people pass by, which thou hast possessed.

Introduces eos, et plantabis in monte hæreditatis tuæ, * firmissimo habitaculo tuo quod operatus es Domine.

Thou shalt bring them in, and plant them in the mountain of thy inheritance, in thy most firm habitation, which thou hast made, O Lord!

Sanctuarium tuum Domine, quod firmaverunt manus tuæ : * Dominus regnabit in æternum, et ultra.

Thy sanctuary, O Lord! which thy hands have established ; the Lord shall reign for ever and ever.

Ingressus est enim eques Pharao cum curribus et equitibus ejus in mare : * et reduxit super eos Dominus aquas maris.

For Pharao went in on horseback, with his chariots and horsemen into the sea ; and the Lord brought back upon them the waters of the sea.

Filii autem Israel ambulaverunt per siccum * in medio ejus.

But the children of Israel walked on dry ground in the midst thereof.

Here a candle is extinguished.

Ant. Exhortatus es in virtute tua, et in refectione sancta tua Domine.

Ant. Thou hast encouraged us with thy power and thy holy refreshments, O Lord!

Ant. Oblatus est quia ipse voluit, et peccata nostra ipse portavit.

Ant. He was offered because it was his own will, and he himself hath carried our sins.

PSALM 148.

LAUDATE Domi-num de cœlis : *
laudate eum in excelsis.

Laudate eum omnes Angeli ejus : * laudate eum omnes virtutes ejus.

Laudate eum sol et luna : * laudate eum omnes stellæ et lumen.

Laudate eum cœli cœlorum : * et aquæ omnes, quæ super cœlos sunt, laudent nomen Domini.

Quia ipse dixit, et facta sunt : * ipse mandavit, et creata sunt.

Statuit ea in æternum, et in sæculum sæculi : * præceptum posuit, et non præteribit.

Laudate Dominum de terra : * dracones, et omnes abyssi.

Ignis, grando, nix,

PRAISE ye the Lord from the heavens : praise ye him in the high places.

Praise ye him, all his Angels : praise ye him, all his hosts !

Praise ye him, O sun and moon ! praise him, all ye stars, and light !

Praise him, ye heavens of heavens ! and let all the waters, that are above the heavens, praise the name of the Lord !

For he spoke, and they were made ; he commanded, and they were created.

He hath established them for ever, and for ages of ages : he hath made a decree, and it shall not pass away.

Praise the Lord from the earth, ye dragons, and all ye deeps.

Fire, hail, snow, ice,

glacies, spiritus procellarum : * quæ faciunt verbum ejus.

Montes et omnes colles : * ligna fructifera, et omnes cedri.

Bestiæ, et universa pecora : * serpentes, et volucres pennatæ.

Reges terræ, et omnes populi : * principes, et omnes judices terræ.

Juvenes et virgines, senes cum junioribus laudent nomen Domini : * quia exaltatum est nomen ejus solius.

Confessio ejus super cœlum et terram : * et exaltavit cornu populi sui.

Hymnus omnibus sanctis ejus : * filiis Israel, populo appropinquanti sibi.

stormy winds, which fulfil his word :

Mountains and all hills, fruitful trees and all cedars :

Beasts and all cattle ; serpents and feathered fowls :

Kings of the earth, and all people, princes and all judges of the earth :

Young men and maidens : let the old with the younger praise the name of the Lord : for his name alone is exalted.

The praise of him is above heaven and earth : and he hath exalted the horn of his people.

A hymn to all his saints ; to the children of Israel, a people approaching to him.

PSALM 149.

CANTATE Domino canticum novum : * laus ejus in ecclesia sanctorum.

SING ye to the Lord a new canticle ; let his praise be in the church of the saints.

Lætetur Israel in eo, qui fecit eum : * et filii Sion exultent in rege suo.

Laudent nomen ejus in choro : * in tympano et psalterio psallant ei.

Quia beneplacitum est Domino in populo suo : * et exaltabit mansuetos in salutem.

Exultabunt sancti in gloria : * lætabuntur in cubilibus suis.

Exaltationes Dei in gutture eorum : * et gladii ancipites in manibus eorum :

Ad faciendam vindictam in nationibus, * increpationes in populis.

Ad alligandos reges eorum in compedibus : * et nobiles eorum in manicis ferreis.

Ut faciant in eis judicium conscriptum : * gloria hæc est omnibus sanctis ejus.

Let Israel rejoice in him that made him : and let the children of Sion be joyful in their king.

Let them praise his name in choir : let them sing to him with the timbrel and the psaltery.

For the Lord is well pleased with his people. and he will exalt the meek unto salvation.

The saints shall rejoice in glory : they shall be joyful in their beds.

The high praises of God shall be in their mouth : and two-edged swords in their hands :

To execute vengeance upon the nations, chastisements among the people :

To bind their kings with fetters, and their nobles with manacles of iron.

To execute upon them the judgment that is written : this glory is to all his saints.

PSALM 150.

LAUDATE Domi-
num in sanctis
ejus : * laudate eum in
firmamento virtutis ejus.

Laudate eum in vir-
tutibus ejus : * laudate
eum secundum multi-
tudinem magnitudinis
ejus.

Laudate eum in sono
tubæ : * laudate eum in
psalterio et cithara.

Laudate eum in tym-
pano et choro : * lau-
date eum in chordis et
organo.

Laudate eum in cym-
balis benesonantibus ;
laudate eum in cymba-
lis jubilationis : * omnis
spiritus laudet Domi-
num.

PRAISE ye the Lord
in his holy places :
praise ye him in the fir-
mament of his power.

Praise ye him for his
mighty acts : praise ye
him according to the
multitude of his great-
ness.

Praise him with sound
of trumpet : praise him
with psaltery and harp.

Praise him with tim-
brel and choir : praise
him with strings and
organs.

Praise him on high-
sounding cymbals :
praise him on cymbals
of joy : let every spirit
praise the Lord.

Here a candle is extinguished.

Ant. Oblatus est quia
ipse voluit, et peccata
nostra ipse portavit.

V. Homo pacis meæ,
in quo speravi.

℟. Qui edebat panes

Ant. He was offered,
because it was his own
will, and he himself hath
carried our sins.

V. The man of my
peace, in whom I trusted.

℟. Who ate my bread

meos, ampliavit adversum me supplantationem.

hath greatly supplanted me.

Ant. Traditor autem dedit eis signum, dicens: Quem osculatus fuero, ipse est, tenete eum.

Ant. He that betrayed him, gave them a sign, saying : Whomsoever I shall kiss, that is he, lay hold on him.

THE CANTICLE OF ZACHARY. *Luke* i.

BENEDICTUS Dominus Deus Israel, * quia visitavit, et fecit redemptionem plebis suæ :

BLESSED be the Lord God of Israel, because he hath visited, and wrought the redemption of his people :

Et erexit cornu salutis nobis, * in domo David pueri sui.

And hath raised up a horn of salvation to us, in the house of David, his servant.

Sicut locutus est per os sanctorum, * qui a sæculo sunt, prophetarum ejus.

As he spoke by the mouth of his holy prophets, who are from the beginning.

Salutem ex inimicis nostris, * et de manu omnium qui oderunt nos :

Salvation from our enemies, and from the hand of all that hate us:

Ad faciendam misericordiam cum patribus nostris : * et memorari testamenti sui sancti.

To perform mercy to our fathers ; and to remember his holy covenant.

Jusjurandum, **quod**

The oath which he

juravit ad Abraham patrem nostrum, * daturum se nobis :

swore to Abraham, our father, that he would grant to us :

Here the last candle on the Gospel side of the Altar is extinguished, and at the next verse the last on the Epistle side, and so on, alternating one at each verse.

Ut sine timore, de manu inimicorum nostrorum liberati, * serviamus illi.

That being delivered from the hand of our enemies, we may serve him without fear.

In sanctitate et justitia coram ipso, * omnibus diebus nostris.

In holiness and justice before him, all our days.

Et tu puer, propheta Altissimi vocaberis : * præibis enim ante faciem Domini parare vias ejus.

And thou, child, shalt be called the prophet of the Highest ; for thou shalt go before the face of the Lord to prepare his ways ;

Ad dandam scientiam salutis plebi ejus : * in remissionem peccatorum eorum :

To give knowledge of salvation to his people, unto the remission of their sins ;

Per viscera misericordiæ Dei nostri : * in quibus visitavit nos, oriens ex alto :

Through the bowels of the mercy of our God ; in which the Orient from on high hath visited us ;

Illuminare his, qui in tenebris et in umbra mortis sedent : * ad dirigendos pedes nostros in viam pacis.

To enlighten them that sit in darkness, and in the shadow of death ; to direct our feet in the way of peace.

Here the candle which was left burning at the top of the triangular candlestick is taken down, and concealed under the Epistle side of the Altar.

Ant. Traditor autem dedit eis signum, dicens: Quem osculatus fuero, ipse est, tenete eum.

Ant. He that betrayed him, gave them a sign, saying: Whomsoever I shall kiss, that is he, lay hold on him.

Here all kneel.

V. CHRISTUS factus est pro nobis obediens usque ad mortem.

V. CHRIST became obedient for us unto death.

Pater noster, *totum sub silentio.*

Our Father, *privately.*

The Psalm Miserere, *p. 230, is recited in a low voice; and in the end, the following prayer, without the* Oremus.

RESPICE, quæsumus Domine, super hanc familiam tuam, pro qua Dominus noster Jesus Christus non dubitavit manibus tradi nocentium, et crucis subire tormentum. *Sed dicitur sub silentio:* Qui tecum vivit et regnat in unitate Spiritus sancti Deus, per omnia sæcula sæculorum. Amen.

LOOK down, O Lord! we beseech thee, on this thy family, for which our Lord Jesus Christ was pleased to be delivered into the hands of the wicked, and to suffer the torment of the cross. *But say in a low voice:* Who with thee and the Holy Ghost, liveth and reigneth, one God, world without end. Amen.

At the end of the prayer a little noise is made: the lighted candle is brought from under the Altar, and all rise and retire in silence.

MAUNDY THURSDAY.

THE Roman Missal and Breviary call this day *Feria quinta in Cana Domini;* this is, *The Thursday of the Lord's Supper*, being the day when our Lord, at his last supper, instituted the Sacrament of the *Eucharist.* It is called by the French *Jeudi Absolut*, or *Absolution Thursday;* because the sentence of Absolution was then pronounced over the public penitents. We call it *Maunday Thursday*, from the ceremony of washing the feet, called in the Rubric *Mandatum*, which is the first *Antiphon* sung during the ceremony.

The Mass on this day differs from the rest of the Office. That of the Holy Eucharist is celebrated, a subject, therefore, of joy and thanksgiving, expressed by the ringing of bells and the white color of the vestments and ornaments of the Altar. For, though the Church is wholly taken up during this week with the passion of *Christ*, and for that reason has appointed the feast of *Corpus Christi* as a day of thanksgiving for the institution of that Sacrament, yet she could not refrain from some expressions of her joy and gratitude on the very day when our Lord was pleased to give us so wonderful a pledge of his love. But after the *Gloria in Excelsis* the bells are silent during the remainder of this day, all *Good Friday* and *Holy Saturday*, until the recurrence of the same Angelical hymn on the last-mentioned day. This is intended to honor the wonderful silence of our Saviour during his passion, and to express the astonishment and mourning of the Church for the death of her Spouse.

The Rubric prescribes the consecration of two Hosts—one for the sacrifice of this day, the other to be carried in solemn procession to a place adorned with lights, where it is kept with great splendor for the office of the next day. The reason of this solemn worship of God in the B. Sacrament is to give the people an opportunity of returning thanks to God for this inestimable blessing on the very day itself of its institution; and this sentiment is strikingly evinced by them in their frequent visits to the places where it is reserved. The B. Sacrament is removed from the principal Altar, that the devotion of the passion, which was there commenced the evening before, at the *Tenebræ*, may be continued without pomp or magnificence. The custom of visiting the B. Sacrament on this day is commonly called *Visiting Sepulchres*, but very improperly and contrary to the intention of the Church, which, in her Rubric, ordains the honor given to it to be expressed by lights and the richest ornaments—things very unbecoming a Sepulchre Besides, it would be preposterous to pay our devotions to *Jesus Christ* in his grave

before the Church commemorates his crucifixion. For this reason representations of that kind, made under the Altar where the Holy Eucharist is kept, must be esteemed a devotion of private persons or particular countries, not in accordance with the original design of the Church of *Rome.*

After the vespers, the Priest with his ministers divest the Altars of the church of their coverings and other ornaments. The Antiphon *Diviserunt* and the Psalm *Deus, Deus meus,* said by the Priest and sung by the choir during the ceremony, sufficiently show that it represents the stripping of our Saviour of his garments, for which the soldiers cast lots, and which they divided among themselves. The nakedness of the Altar signifies that Christ in his passion lost all his beauty and majesty, and was in a manner deprived of the glory of his divine nature.

On this day the clergy of some churches meet to perform the ceremony of washing the feet, called in the Rubric *Mandatum,* or the *Commandment,* because it is commanded by the example and words of *Jesus Christ,* in the gospel sung before the Priest begins to wash the feet. Hence, in each church the superior washes the feet of his inferiors; many rich do the same to the poor; and kings disdain not to stoop to the feet of their subjects. And it teaches us to imitate the humility of our Saviour, and to cleanse our souls from the stains of the smallest sins.

The Mass.

The Priest begins the Mass at the foot of the Altar, as at page 13. *down to* Peccata mea—My sins, *p.* 17.

THE INTROIT.

NOS autem gloriari oportet in cruce Domini nostri Jesu Christi; in quo est salus, vita et resurrectio nostra, per quem salvati et liberati sumus. *Psal.* Deus misereatur nostri, et benedicat nobis: illuminet vultum suum su-

WE ought to glory in the cross of our Lord Jesus Christ; in whom is our salvation, life, and resurrection; by whom we have been saved, and delivered. *The Psalm.* May God have mercy on us, and bless us: may he cause

per nos, et misereatur nostri.—Nos autem, etc.

the light of his countenance to shine upon us, and may he have mercy on us.—We ought, etc.

[*The* Kyrie, Gloria, *and* Dominus Vobiscum, *page* 17.]

The bells are rung during the Gloria in Excelsis, *but no more till Holy Saturday.*

THE COLLECT.

Oremus.

Let us pray.

DEUS, a quo et Judas reatus sui pœnam, et confessionis suæ latro præmium sumpsit: concede nobis tuæ propitiationis effectum: ut, sicut in passione sua Jesus Christus Dominus noster diversa utrisque intulit stipendia meritorum; ita nobis, ablato vetustatis errore, resurrectionis suæ gratiam largiatur. Qui tecum vivit et regnat in unitate Spiritus sancti Deus, per omnia sæcula sæculorum.

O GOD! from whom Judas received the punishment of his sin, and the thief the reward of his confession: grant us the effects of thy mercy; that, as our Lord Jesus Christ, at the time of his passion, dispensed on both different rewards of their merits; so having destroyed the old man in us, he may give us the grace of his resurrection; who with thee, and the Holy Ghost, 'iveth and reigneth, one 'd, world without end.

R. Amen.

R. Amen.

THE EPISTLE.

Lectio Epistolæ beati Pauli Apostoli ad Corinthios. 1 Cor. xi. 20–32.

FRATRES, convenientibus vobis in unum, jam non est Dominicam cœnam manducare. Unusquisque enim suam cœnam præsumit ad manducandum. Et alius quidem esurit, alius autem ebrius est. Numquid domos non habetis ad manducandum et bibendum? Aut Ecclesiam Dei contemnitis, et confunditis eos qui non habent? Quid dicam vobis? Laudo vos? In hoc non laudo. Ego enim accepi a Domino quod et tradidi vobis, quoniam Dominus Jesus in qua nocte tradebatur, accepit panem, et gratias agens fregit, et dixit: Accipite, et manducate: hoc est corpus meum, quod pro vobis tradetur: hoc fa-

The Lesson from the Epistle of St. Paul the Apostle, to the Corinthians. 1 Cor. xi. 20–32.

BRETHREN, when you come together into one place, it is not now to eat the Lord's supper. For every one taketh before his supper to eat. And one indeed is hungry, and another is drunk. What! have you not houses to eat and drink in? Or despise ye the Church of God, and put them to shame that have not? What shall I say to you? Do I praise you? In this I praise you not. For I have received of the Lord, that which also I delivered to you: that the Lord Jesus, the same night in which he was betrayed, took bread, and giving thanks, broke it, and said: Take ye, and eat; this is my body. which shall be de-

cite in meam commemorationem. Similiter et calicem, postquam cœnavit, dicens : Hic calix novum testamentum est in meo sanguine. Hoc facite, quotiescumque bibetis, in meam commemorationem : quotiescumque enim manducabitis panem hunc, et calicem bibetis, mortem Domini annuntiabitis, donec veniat. Itaque quicumque manducaverit panem hunc, vel biberit calicem Domini indigne, reus erit corporis et sanguinis Domini. Probet autem seipsum homo, et sic de pane illo edat, et de calice bibat. Qui enim manducat et bibit indigne, judicium sibi manducat et bibit, non dijudicans corpus Domini. Ideo inter vos multi infirmi et imbecilles, et dormiunt multi. Quod si nosmetipsos dijudicaremus, non utique judicaremur. Dum judica-

livered for you : this do for the commemoration of me. In like manner, also, the chalice, after he had supped, saying : This chalice is the new testament in my blood. This do ye, as often as you shall drink it, for the commemoration of me. For as often as you shall eat this bread, and drink this chalice, you shall show the death of the Lord, until he come. Wherefore, whoever shall eat this bread, or drink the chalice of the Lord unworthily, shall be guilty of the body and of the blood of the Lord. But let a man prove himself, and so let him eat of that bread and drink of the chalice. For he that eateth and drinketh unworthily, eateth and drinketh judgment to himself, not discerning the body of the Lord. Therefore are there many infirm and weak

mur autem, a Domino corripimur, ut non cum hoc mundo damnemur.

among you, and many sleep. But if we would judge ourselves, we should not be judged. But while we are judged, we are chastised by the Lord, that we be not condemned with this world.

THE GRADUAL.

CHRISTUS factus est pro nobis obediens usque ad mortem, mortem autem crucis.

V. Propter quod et Deus exaltavit illum, et dedit illi nomen, quod est super omne nomen.

Munda cor meum, etc., as p. 19.

CHRIST became obedient for us unto death, even the death of the cross.

V. Wherefore, God also hath exalted him, and hath given him a name, which is above every name.

Cleanse my heart, etc., as p. 19.

THE GOSPEL.

Sequentia sancti Evangelii secundum Joannem. Cap. xiii. 1–15.

Continuation of the holy Gospel, according to St. John. Chap. xiii. 1–15.

ANTE diem festum paschæ, sciens Jesus quia venit hora ejus, ut transeat ex hoc mundo ad Patrem: cum dilexisset suos, qui erant

BEFORE the festival day of the pasch, Jesus knowing that his hour was come, that he should pass out of this world to the Fa-

in mundo, in finem dilexit eos. Et cœna facta, cum diabolus jam misisset in cor ut traderet eum Judas Simonis Iscariotæ; sciens quia omnia dedit ei Pater in manus, et quia a Deo exivit, et ad Deum vadit, surgit a cœna, et ponit vestimenta sua : et cum accepisset linteum, præcinxit se. Deinde mittit aquam in pelvim, et cœpit lavare pedes discipulorum, et extergere linteo, quo erat præcinctus. Venit ergo ad Simonem Petrum. Et dicit ei Petrus: Domine, tu mihi lavas pedes! Respondit Jesus, et dixit ei: Quod ego facio, tu nescis modo, scies autem postea. Dicit ei Petrus : Non lavabis mihi pedes in æternum. Respondit ei Jesus : Si non lavero te, non habebis partem mecum. Dicit ei Simon Petrus: Domine, non tantum pedes meos, sed et ma-

ther; having loved his own who were in the world, he loved them to the end. And when supper was done, the devil having now put into the heart of Judas, the son of Simon the Iscariot, to betray him; knowing that the Father had given him all things into his hands, and that he came from God, and goeth to God: he riseth from supper, and layeth aside his garments : and having taken a towel, he girded himself. After that, he poureth water into a basin, and began to wash the feet of the disciples, and to wipe them with the towel, wherewith he was girt. He cometh therefore to Simon Peter. And Peter saith to him : Lord! dost thou wash my feet? Jesus answered, and said to him : What I do thou knowest not now, but thou shalt know hereafter. Peter saith

nus et caput. Dicit ei Jesus: Qui lotus est, non indiget nisi ut pedes lavet, sed est mundus totus. Et vos mundi estis, sed non omnes. Sciebat enim quisnam esset qui traderet eum: propterea dixit: Non estis mundi omnes. Postquam ergo lavit pedes eorum, et accepit vestimenta sua, cum recubuisset iterum, dixit eis: Scitis quid fecerim vobis? Vos vocatis me Magister, et Domine; et bene dicitis: sum etenim. Si ergo ego lavi pedes vestros, Dominus et Magister; et vos debetis alter alterius lavare pedes. Exemplum enim dedi

to him: Thou shalt never wash my feet. Jesus answered him: If I wash thee not, thou shalt have no part with me. Simon Peter saith to him: Lord! not only my feet, but also my hands and my head. Jesus saith to him: He that is washed, needeth not but to wash his feet, but is clean wholly. And you are clean, but not all. For he knew who he was that would betray him: therefore he said: You are not all clean. Then after he had washed their feet, and taken his garments, being sat down again, he said to them: Know you what I have done to you? You call me Master, and Lord; and you say well, for so I am. If then I, being your Lord and Master, have washed your feet: you also ought to wash one another's feet. For I have given you an

vobis, ut quemadmodum ego feci vobis, ita et vos faciatis.

example, that as I have done to you, so you do also.

The Credo, *p.* 20.

THE OFFERTORY.

DEXTERA Domini fecit virtutem, dextera Domini exaltavit me : non moriar, sed vivam, et narrabo opera Domini.

THE right hand of the Lord hath wrought strength ; the right hand of the Lord hath exalted me : I shall not die, but live, and shall declare the works of the Lord.

Suscipe, *etc., p.* 22, *down to* Then the priest says Amen, *p.* 23.

THE SECRET.

IPSE tibi, quæsumus, Domine sancte, Pater omnipotens, æterne Deus, sacrificium nostrum reddat acceptum, qui discipulis suis in sui commemorationem hoc fieri hodierna traditione monstravit, Jesus Christus Filius tuus Dominus noster : Qui tecum vivit et regnat, etc.

WE beseech thee, O holy Lord, Almighty Father, eternal God ! that our Lord Jesus Christ, thy Son, may make our sacrifice acceptable to thee, who on this day commanded his disciples to celebrate it in memory of him; who liveth, etc.

The Preface, p. 94. *The Canon, p.* 28, *as far as* Communicantes.

COMMUNICAN- TES, et diem sacratissimum celebrantes,

PARTAKING of the same communion, and celebrating this

quo Dominus noster Jesus Christus pro nobis est traditus : sed et memoriam venerantes imprimis gloriosæ semper virginis Mariæ, genitricis ejusdem Dei et Domini nostri Jesu Christi : sed et beatorum apostolorum ac martyrum tuorum, Petri et Pauli, Andreæ, Jacobi, Joannis, Thomæ, Jacobi, Philippi, Bartholomæi, Matthæi, Simonis et Thaddæi : Lini, Cleti, Clementis, Xysti, Cornelii, Cypriani, Laurentii, Chrysogoni, Joannis et Pauli, Cosmæ et Damiani, et omnium Sanctorum tuorum : quorum meritis precibusque concedas ut in omnibus protectionis tuæ muniamur auxilio. Per eundem Christum Dominum nostrum. Amen.

Hanc igitur oblationem servitutis nostræ, sed et cunctæ familiæ tuæ, quam tibi offerimus

most sacred day, on which our Lord Jesus Christ was betrayed for us ; and also honoring, in the first place, the memory of the glorious ever Virgin Mary, mother of the same God, and our Lord Jesus Christ ; as also of thy blessed apostles and martyrs Peter and Paul, Andrew, James, John, Thomas, James, Philip, Bartholomew, Matthew, Simon and Thaddeus, Linus, Cletus, Clement, Xystus, Cornelius, Cyprian, Laurence, Chrysogonus, John and Paul, Cosmas and Damian, and of all thy saints : by whose merits and prayers grant that we may in all things be defended by the help of thy protection ; through the same Christ our Lord. Amen.

We therefore beseech thee to accept this oblation of our servitude, and of thy whole family

ob diem in qua Dominus noster Jesus Christus tradidit discipulis suis corporis et sanguinis sui mysteria celebranda: quæsumus Domine, ut placatus accipias: diesque nostros in tua pace disponas: atque ab æterna damnatione nos eripi, et in electorum tuorum jubeas grege numerari. Per eundem Christum Dominum nostrum. Amen.

which we make to thee in memory of the day on which our Lord Jesus Christ commanded his disciples to celebrate the mysteries of his body and blood: dispose our days in thy peace: preserve us from eternal damnation, and place us in the number of thy elect; through the same Christ our Lord. Amen.

Quam oblationem tu Deus in omnibus, quæsumus, benedictam, adscriptam, ratam, rationabilem, acceptabilemque facere digneris: ut nobis corpus et sanguis fiat dilectissimi Filii tui Domini nostri Jesu Christi.

Vouchsafe, we beseech thee, O God! to make this oblation, in all things, blessed, approved, ratified, reasonable, and acceptable; that it may be made for us the body and blood of thy most beloved Son, our Lord Jesus Christ.

Qui pridie quam pro nostra omniumque salute pateretur, hoc est, hodie, accepit panem, etc.

Who, on the day before he suffered for the salvation of us and of all men, that is, on this day, took bread, etc.

All the rest to the Communion, as p. 31, etc., except that the kiss of peace is not given, in detestation of the treacherous kiss of Judas.

On this day the Priest consecrates two Hosts, reserving one for the next day, when there is no consecration. Before he washes his fingers, he puts the reserved Host into another chalice, which is placed in the middle of the Altar, and covered with the pall, paten, and veil.

THE COMMUNION.

DOMINUS Jesus, postquam cœnavit cum discipulis suis, lavit pedes eorum, et ait illis : Scitis quid fecerim vobis ego Dominus et magister ? Exemplum dedi vobis, ut et vos ita faciatis.

THE Lord Jesus, after he had supped with his disciples, washed their feet, and said to them : Know you what I, your Lord and master, have done to you ? I have given you an example, that you do so also.

THE POST-COMMUNION.

Oremus.

REFECTI vitalibus alimentis, quæsumus Domine Deus noster, ut quod tempore nostræ mortalitatis exequimur, immortalitatis tuæ munere consequamur. Per Dominum nostrum, etc.

V. Dominus vobiscum.

R. Et cum spiritu tuo.

V. Ite, missa est.

R. Deo gratias.

Let us pray.

WE beseech thee, O Lord, our God ! that being nourished with this life-giving food, we may receive by thy grace in immortal glory what we celebrate in this mortal life · through our Lord, etc.

V. The Lord be with you.

R. And with thy spirit.

V. Depart, Mass is done.

R. Thanks be to God

The rest of the Mass as on p. 42.

On this day a proper place is prepared in some Chapel or Altar of the Church, and decently adorned with hangings and lights, where the chalice with the reserved Host is to be kept until the next day. At the end of the Mass, the Priest carries the B. Sacrament, in solemn procession, to the said place, being accompanied with lights and fuming censers. Being come to the place, the B. Sacrament is placed on the Altar, fumed thrice with incense, and placed in a Tabernacle. During the procession the following Hymn is sung:

THE HYMN.

PANGE, lingua! gloriosi
   Corporis mysterium,
Sanguinisque pretiosi,
Quem in mundi pretium
Fructus ventris generosi,
Rex effudit gentium.

Nobis datus, nobis natus
Ex intacta Virgine,
Et in mundo conversatus,
Sparso verbi semine,
Sui moras incolatus
Miro clausit ordine.

In supremæ nocte cœnæ
Recumbens cum fratribus
Observata lege plene
Cibis in legalibus,
Cibum turbæ duodenæ
Se dat suis manibus.

Verbum caro, panem verum
Verbo carnem efficit,
Fitque sanguis Christi merum,
Et si sensus deficit,

Ad firmandum cor sincerum
Sola fides sufficit.

Tantum ergo Sacramentum
Veneremur cernui,
Et antiquum documentum
Novo cedat ritui :
Præstet fides supplementum
Sensuum defectui.

Genitori, Genitoque
Laus et jubilatio,
Salus, honor, virtus quoque
Sit et benedictio :
Procedenti ab utroque
Compar sit laudatio.   Amen.

The same in English.

SING, O my tongue! adore and praise
The depth of God's mysterious ways;
How Christ, the world's great King, bestow'd
His flesh, conceal'd in human food,
And left mankind the blood, that paid
The ransom for the souls he made.

Giv'n from above, and born for man,
From Virgin's womb his life began;
He liv'd on earth, and preach'd, to sow
The seeds of heav'nly truth below;
Then seal'd his mission from above
With strange effects of pow'r and love.

'Twas on that ev'ning, when the last
And most mysterious supper past;

When Christ with his disciples sat
To close the law with legal meat;
Then to the twelve himself bestow'd,
With his own hands, to be their food.

The Word, made flesh for love of man,
His word turns bread to flesh again,
And wine to blood, unseen by sense,
By virtue of Omnipotence;
And here the faithful rest secure,
Whilst God can vouch, and faith ensure.

To this mysterious table now
Our knees, our hearts, and sense we bow;
Let ancient rites resign their place
To nobler elements of grace,
And faith for all defects supply,
While sense is lost in mystery.

To God the Father, born of none,
To Christ, his co-eternal Son,
And Holy Ghost, whose equal rays
From both proceed, one equal praise,
One honor, jubilee, and fame,
For ever bless his glorious name. **Amen**

The Vespers.

Pater Noster and Ave Maria are said in a low voice,

Ant. CALICEM salutaris accipiam, et nomen Domini invocabo

Ant. I WILL take the chalice of salvation, and I will call upon the name of the Lord.

PSALM 115.

CREDIDI, propter quod locutus sum : * ego autem humiliatus sum nimis.

I HAVE believed, therefore have I spoken : but I have been humbled exceedingly.

Ego dixi in excessu meo : * Omnis homo mendax.

I said in my excess : Every man is a liar.

Quid retribuam Domino, * pro omnibus quæ retribuit mihi ?

What shall I render to the Lord, for all the things that he hath rendered to me ?

Calicem salutaris accipiam, * et nomen Domini invocabo.

I will take the chalice of salvation, and I will call upon the name of the Lord.

Vota mea Domino reddam coram omni populo ejus : * pretiosa in conspectu Domini mors sanctorum ejus.

I will pay my vows to the Lord before all his people : precious in the sight of the Lord is the death of his saints.

O Domine, quia ego servus tuus : * ego servus tuus, et filius ancillæ tuæ.

O Lord ! for I am thy servant : I am thy servant, and the son of thy handmaid.

Dirupisti vincula mea : * tibi sacrificabo hostiam laudis, et nomen Domini invocabo.

Thou hast broken my bonds. I will sacrifice to thee the sacrifice of praise, and I will call upon the name of the Lord.

Vota mea Domino reddam in conspectu omnis populi ejus : * in atriis domus Domini, in medio tui, Jerusalem.

I will pay my vows to the Lord in the sight of all his · people, in the courts of the house of the Lord : in the midst of thee, O Jerùsalem !

Ant. Calicem salutaris accipiam, et nomen Domini invocabo.

Ant. I will take thè chalice of salvation, and I will call upon the name of the Lord.

Ant. Cum his qui oderunt pacem, eram pacificus : dum loquebar illis, impugnabant me gratis.

Ant. With them that hated peace, I was peaceable ; when I spoke to them, they fought against me without cause.

PSALM 119.

AD Dominum, cum tribularer, clamavi : * et exaudivit me.

IN my trouble I cried to the Lord ; and he heard me.

Domine, libera animam meam a labiis iniquis, * et a lingua dolosa.

O Lord ! deliver my soul from wicked lips, and a deceitful tongue.

Quid detur tibi, aut

What shall be given to thee, or what shall be

quid apponatur tibi, * ad linguam dolosam?

added to thee, to a deceitful tongue?

Sagittæ potentis acutæ, * cum carbonibus desolatoriis.

The sharp arrows of the mighty, with coals that lay waste.

Heu mihi, quia incolatus meus prolongatus est: habitavi cum habitantibus cedar:`*` multum incola fuit anima mea.

Wo is me that my sojourning is prolonged! I have dwelt with the inhabitants of Cedar. My soul hath been long a sojourner.

Cum his qui oderunt pacem, eram pacificus: * cum loquebar illis, impugnabant me gratis.

With them that hated peace, I was peaceable: when I spoke to them, they fought against me without cause.

Ant. Cum his qui oderunt pacem, eram pacificus: dum loquebar illis, impugnabant me gratis.

Ant. With them that hated peace, I was peaceable; when I spoke to them, they fought against me without cause.

Ant. Ab hominibus iniquis libera me, Domine.

Ant. From unjust men deliver me, O Lord!

PSALM 139.

ERIPE me Domine, ab homine malo: * a viro iniquo eripe me.

DELIVER me, O Lord! from the evil man; rescue me from the unjust man.

Qui cogitaverunt ini-

Who have devised iniquities in their hearts:

quitates in corde : * tota die constituebant prœlia.

Acuerunt linguas suas sicut serpentis : * venenum aspidum sub labiis eorum.

Custodi me Domine, de manu peccatoris : * et ab hominibus iniquis eripe me.

Qui cogitaverunt supplantare gressus meos : * absconderunt superbi laqueum mihi.

Et funes extenderunt in laqueum : * juxta iter scandalum posuerunt mihi.

Dixi Domino : Deus meus es tu : exaudi, Domine, vocem deprecationis meæ.

Domine, Domine virtus salutis meæ : * obumbrasti super caput meum in die belli.

Ne tradas me Domine, a desiderio meo peccatori : * cogitaverunt contra me, ne dere-

all the day long they designed battles.

They have sharpened their tongues like a serpent : the venom of asps is under their lips.

Keep me, O Lord ! from the hand of the wicked ; and from unjust men deliver me.

Who have proposed to supplant my steps ; the proud have hidden a net for me.

And they have stretched out cords for a snare : they have laid for me a stumbling-block by the wayside.

I said to the Lord : Thou art my God : hear, O Lord ! the voice of my supplication.

O Lord, Lord ! the strength of my salvation : thou hast overshadowed my head in the day of battle.

Give me not up, O Lord ! from my desire to the wicked : they have plotted against me; do not thou forsake

linquas me, ne forte exaltentur.

Caput circuitus eorum : * labor labiorum ipsorum operiet eos.

Cadent super eos carbones, in ignem dejicies eos : * in miseriis non subsistent.

Vir linguosus non dirigetur in terra : * virum injustum mala capient in interitu.

Cognovi quia faciet Dominus judicium inopis : * et vindictam pauperum.

Verumtamen justi confitebuntur nomini tuo : * et habitabunt recti cum vultu tuo.

Ant. Ab hominibus iniquis libera me, Domine.

Ant. Custodi me a laqueo, quem statuerunt mihi, et a scandalis operantium iniquitatem.

me, lest they should triumph.

The head of their compassing me about : the labor of their lips shall overwhelm them.

Burning coals shall fall upon them; thou wilt cast them down into the fire; in miseries they shall not be able to stand.

A man full of tongue shall not be established in the earth : evils shall catch the unjust man unto destruction.

I know that the Lord will do justice to the needy, and will revenge the poor.

But as for the just, they shall give glory to thy name; and the upright shall dwell with thy countenance.

Ant. From unjust men deliver me, O Lord!

Ant. Keep me from the snare, which they have laid for me, and from the stumblingblocks of them that work iniquity

PSALM 140.

DOMINE clamavi ad te, exaudi me : * intende voci meæ, cum clamavero ad te.

Dirigatur oratio mea sicut incensum in conspectu tuo : * elevatio manuum mearum sacrificium vespertinum.

Pone, Domine, custodiam ori meo, * et ostium circumstantiæ labiis meis.

Non declines cor meum in verba malitiæ, * ad excusandas excusationes in peccatis.

Cum hominibus operantibus iniquitatem, * et non communicabo cum electis eorum.

Corripiet me justus in misericordia, et increpabit me : * oleum autem peccatoris non impinguet caput meum.

Quoniam adhuc et oratio mea in beneplacitis eorum : * absorpti sunt juncti petræ judices eorum.

I HAVE cried to thee, O Lord ! hear me ; hearken to my voice when I cry to thee.

Let my prayer be directed as incense in thy sight ; the lifting up of my hands as evening sacrifice.

Set a watch, O Lord ! before my mouth, and a door round about my lips.

Incline not my heart to evil words, to make excuses in sins.

With men that work iniquity, I will not communicate with the choicest of them.

The just man shall correct me in mercy, and reprove me ; but let not the oil of the sinner fatten my head.

For my prayer also shall still be against the things with which they are well pleased ; *their judges falling upon the rock have been swallowed up.*

Audient verba mea quoniam potuerunt : * sicut crassitudo terræ erupta est super terram.

They shall hear my words, for they have prevailed ; as when the thickness of earth is broken up upon the ground.

Dissipata sunt ossa nostra secus infernum : * quia ad te Domine, Domine, oculi mei : in te speravi, non auferas animam meam.

Our bones are scattered by the side of hell : but to thee, O Lord, Lord ! are my eyes ; in thee have I put my trust, take not away my soul.

Custodi me a laqueo, quem statuerunt mihi : * et a scandalis operantium iniquitatem.

Keep me from the snare, which they have laid for me, and from the stumbling - block of them that work iniquity.

Cadent in retiaculo ejus peccatores : * singulariter sum ego, donec transeam.

The wicked shall fall in his net ; I am alone until I pass.

Ant. Custodi me a laqueo, quem statuerunt mihi, et a scandalis operantium iniquitatem.

Ant. Keep me from the snare, which they have laid for me, and from the stumbling-blocks of them that work iniquity.

Ant. Considerabam ad dexteram, et videbam, et non erat qui cognosceret me.

Ant. I looked on my right hand, and beheld, and there was no one that would know me.

PSALM 141.

VOCE mea ad Dominum clamavi : * voce mea ad Dominum deprecatus sum.

Effundo in conspectu ejus orationem meam, * et tribulationem meam ante ipsum pronuntio.

In deficiendo ex me spiritum meum, * et tu cognovisti semitas meas.

In via hac qua ambulabam, * absconderunt laqueum mihi.

Considerabam ad dexteram, et videbam : * et non erat qui cognosceret me.

Periit fuga a me, * et non est qui requirat animam meam.

Clamavi ad te Domine ; * dixi : Tu es spes mea, portio mea in terra viventium.

Intende ad deprecationem meam : * quia humiliatus sum nimis.

Libera me a persequentibus me : * quia confortati sunt super me.

I CRIED to the Lord with my voice : with my voice I made supplication to the Lord.

In his sight I pour out my prayer, and before him I declare my trouble.

When my spirit failed me, then thou knewest my paths.

In this way wherein I walked, they have hidden a snare for me.

I looked on my right hand, and beheld, and there was no one that would know me.

Flight hath perished from me : and there is no one that hath regard to my soul.

I cried to thee, O Lord! I said : Thou art my hope, my portion in the land of the living.

Attend to my supplication : for I am brought very low.

Deliver me from my persecutors, for they are stronger than I.

Educ de custodia animam meam ad confitendum nomini tuo : * me expectant justi, donec retribuas mihi.

Bring my soul out of prison, that I may praise thy name : the just wait for me, until thou reward me.

Ant. Considerabam ad dexteram, et videbam, et non erat qui cognosceret me.

Ant. I looked on my right hand, and beheld, and there was no one that would know me.

Ant. Cœnantibus autem illis, accepit Jesus panem, et benedixit, ac fregit, deditque discipulis suis.

Ant. Whilst they were at supper, Jesus took bread, and blessed, and broke, and gave to his disciples.

THE CANTICLE OF THE B. V. MARY. *Luke* i.

MAGNIFICAT * anima mea Dominum :

MY soul doth magnify the Lord :

Et exultavit spiritus meus * in Deo salutari meo.

And my spirit hath rejoiced in God, my Saviour.

Quia respexit humilitatem ancillæ suæ : * ecce enim ex hoc beatam me dicent omnes generationes.

Because he hath regarded the humility of his handmaid ; for behold, from henceforth, all generations shall call me blessed.

Quia fecit mihi magna qui potens est : * et sanctum nomen ejus.

For he that is mighty, hath done great things to me; and holy is his name.

Et misericordia ejus a

And his mercy is from generation to genera-

progenie in progenies * timentibus eum.

Fecit potentiam in brachio suo : * dispersit superbos mente cordis sui.

Deposuit potentes de sede, * et exaltavit humiles.

Esurientes implevit bonis : * et divites dimisit inanes.

Suscepit Israel puerum suum, * recordatus misericordiæ suæ.

Sicut locutus est ad patres nostros, * Abraham, et semini ejus in sæcula.

Ant. Cœnantibus autem illis, accepit Jesus panem, et benedixit, ac fregit, deditque discipulis suis.

tion, to them that fear him.

He hath shewed might in his arms; he hath scattered the proud in the conceit of their heart.

He hath put down the mighty from their seat, and hath exalted the humble.

He has filled the hungry with good things ; and the rich he hath sent empty away.

He hath received Israel his servant, being mindful of his mercy.

As he spoke to our fathers, to Abraham, and to his seed for ever.

Ant. While they were at supper, Jesus took bread, and blessed, and broke, and gave to his disciples.

The rest is said kneeling.

V. Christus factus est pro nobis obediens usque ad mortem.

V. Christ became obedient for us unto death.

Pater noster, *sub silentio.*

Our Father, *privately*

Miserere, *p.* 230 *and the prayer* Respice, *p.* 250.

The Divesting of the Altars.

Then the Priest, with his Ministers, divests the Altars of their coverings and ornaments, saying the Antiphon Diviserunt, *with the Psalm* Deus, Deus meus, respice in me, *which is the second Psalm of the Matins for Good Friday, as at p.* 284.

The Washing of the Feet.

After the divesting of the Altars, the Clergy at a convenient hour meet to perform the ceremony of the washing of the feet. The Prelate, or Superior, comes to the place appointed, in his alb, stole, and cope of a violet color, accompanied by the Deacon and Sub-deacon in white vestments. Then the gospel Ante diem festum Paschæ, *p.* 256, *is sung by the Deacon, with the usual ceremony of incense and lights. After the gospel, the Prelate puts off his cope, takes a towel, and then on his knees, and bareheaded, he washes, wipes, and kisses the right foot of those who are chosen for the ceremony. Whilst he is doing this, the following anthems are sung:*

Ant. MANDATUM novum do vobis : ut diligatis invicem, sicut dilexi vos, dicit Dominus. *Psalm.* Beati immaculati in via : qui ambulant in lege Domini.

Ant. I GIVE you a new commandment; that you love one another, as I have loved you, saith the Lord. *Ps.* Blessed are the undefiled in the way ; who walk in the law of the Lord.

The Ant. Mandatum novum *is repeated. This is observed with the other Antiphons, to which Psalms are attached. The first verse only of the Psalm is sung.*

Ant. POSTQUAM surrexit Dominus a cœna, misit aquam in pelvim, et cœpit lavare pedes discipulorum suorum : hoc exemplum reliquit eis. *Psalm.* Magnus Domi-

Ant. AFTER the Lord had risen from supper, he poured water into a basin; and began to wash the feet of his disciples : to whom he gave that example. *Psalm.* Great

nus et laudabilis nimis : in civitate Dei nostri, in monte sancto ejus.

Ant. Dominus Jesus postquam cœnavit cum discipulis suis, lavit pedes eorum, et ait illis : Scitis quid fecerim vobis ego Dominus et magister ? Exemplum dedi vobis, ut et vos ita faciatis. *Psalm.* Benedixisti, Domine, terram tuam : avertisti captivitatem Jacob.

Ant. Domine, tu mihi lavas pedes ? Respondit Jesus, et dixit ei : Si non lavero tibi pedes, non habebis partem mecum.

V. Venit ergo ad Simonem Petrum, et dixit ei Petrus :
Ant. Domine, tu mihi, etc.
V. Quod ego facio, tu nescis modo : scies autem postea.

is the Lord, and exceedingly to be praised, in the city of our God, in his holy mountain.

Ant. The Lord Jesus after he had supped with his disciples, washed their feet, and said to them : Know you what I, your Lord and master, have done to you ? I have given you an example, that you also may do the same. *Psalm.* Lord ! thou hast blessed thy land ; thou hast turned away the captivity of Jacob.

Ant. Lord ! dost thou wash my feet ? Jesus answered and said to him : If I wash not thy feet, thou shalt have no part with me.

V. He came to Simon Peter, and Peter said to him :
Ant. Lord ! dost thou, etc.
V. What I do, thou knowest not now : but thou shalt know hereafter.

Ant. Domine, tu mihi, etc.

V. Si ego Dominus et magister vester lavi vobis pedes, quanto magis debetis alter alterius lavare pedes?

Psalm. Audite hæc, omnes gentes: auribus percipite qui habitatis orbem.

Ant. In hoc cognoscent omnes quia discipuli mei estis, si dilectionem habueritis ad invicem.

V. Dixit Jesus discipulis suis:

Ant. Maneant in vobis fides, spes, charitas, tria hæc: major autem horum est charitas.

V. Nunc autem manent fides, spes, charitas, tria hæc: major horum est charitas.

Ant. Benedicta sit sancta Trinitas, atque indivisa Unitas: confitebimur ei, quia fecit nobiscum misericordiam suam.

Ant. Lord! dost thou, etc.

V. If I, being Lord and master, have washed your feet; how much more ought you to wash one another's feet?

Psalm. Hear these things, all ye nations! give ear, all ye inhabitants of the world!

Ant. By this shall all men know that you are my disciples, if you have love one for another.

V. Said Jesus to his disciples:

Ant. Let there remain in you faith, hope, and charity, these three; but the greatest of these is charity.

V. And now there remain faith, hope, and charity, these three; but the greatest of these is charity.

Ant. Blessed be the holy Trinity and undivided Unity; we will praise him, because he has showed us his mercy

V. Benedicamus Patrem, et Filium, cum sancto Spiritu. *Psalm.* Quam dilecta tabernacula tua, Domine virtutum : concupiscit et deficit anima mea in atria Domini.

Ant. Ubi charitas et amor, Deus ibi est.

V. Congregavit nos in unum Christi amor.

V. Exultemus, et in ipso jucundemur.

V. Timeamus et amemus Deum vivum.

V. Et ex corde diligamus nos sincero.

Ant. Ubi charitas et amor, Deus ibi est.

V. Simul ergo cum in unum congregamur.

V. Ne nos mente dividamur, caveamus.

V. Cessent jurgia maligna, cessent lites.

V. Et in medio nostri sit Christus Deus.

V. Let us bless the Father and the Son, with the Holy Ghost. *Psalm.* How lovely are thy tabernacles, O Lord of hosts! my soul longeth and fainteth after the courts of the Lord.

Ant. Where charity and love are, there is God.

V. The love of Christ hath gathered us together.

V. Let us rejoice in him and be glad.

V. Let us fear and love the living God.

V. And let us love one another with a sincere heart.

Ant. Where charity, etc.

V. When therefore we are assembled.

V. Let us take heed we be not divided in mind.

V. Let malicious quarrels and contentions cease.

V. And let Christ our God dwell among us.

Ant. Ubi charitas, etc.

V. Simul quoque cum beatis videamus.

V. Glorianter vultum tuum, Christe Deus.

V. Gaudium quod est immensum, atque probum.

V. Sæcula per infinita sæculorum. Amen.

After the feet are washed, the wipes them, and, putting on uncovered, and says:

Pater noster, *secreto.*

V. Et ne nos inducas in tentationem.

R. Sed libera nos a malo.

V. Tu mandasti mandata tua, Domine.

R. Custodiri nimis.

V. Tu lavasti pedes discipulorum tuorum.

R. Opera manuum tuarum ne despicias.

V. Domine, exaudi orationem meam.

R. Et clamor meus ad se veniat.

V. Dominus vobis-cum.

Ant. Where charity, etc.

V. Let us also with the blessed see.

V. Thy face in glory, O Christ, our God!

V. There to possess an immense and happy joy.

V. For infinite ages of ages. Amen.

Superior washes his hands, and his cope, he stands with his head

Our Father, *privately.*

V. And lead us not into temptation.

R. But deliver us from evil.

V. Thou has commanded, O Lord!

R. That thy precepts be exactly observed.

V. Thou hast washed the feet of thy disciples.

R. Despise not the works of thy hands.

V. O Lord! hear my prayer.

R. And let my cry come unto thee.

V. The Lord be with you.

R. Et cum spiritu tuo.
Oremus.

Adesto Domine, quæsumus, officio servitutis nostræ : et quia tu discipulis tuis pedes lavare dignatus es, ne despicias opera manuum tuarum, quæ nobis retinenda mandasti ; ut sicut hic nobis, et a nobis exteriora abluuntur inquinamenta, sic a te omnium nostrum interiora laventur peccata ; quod ipse præstare digneris, qui vivis et regnas, Deus per omnia sæcula sæculorum.

R. Amen.

R. And with thy spirit.
Let us pray.

Accept, O Lord! we beseech thee, this duty of our service : and since thou didst vouchsafe to wash the feet of thy disciples, despise not the work of thy hands, which thou hast commanded us to imitate ; that as here the outward stains are washed away by us, and from us, so the inward sins of us all may be blotted out by thee ; which be pleased to grant ; who livest and reignest one God, for ever and ever.

R. Amen.

TENEBRÆ ON THURSDAY,

GOOD FRIDAY.

The Matins.

Aperi Domine, Pater, Ave, *and* Credo, *in a low voice.*

THE FIRST NOCTURN.

Antiphona. ASTITERUNT reges terræ, et principes convenerunt in unum, adversus Dominum, et adversus Christum ejus.

The Ant. THE kings of the earth stood up, and the princes met together against the Lord, and against his Christ.

PSALM 2.

QUARE fremuerunt Gentes, * et populi meditati sunt inania?

Astiterunt reges terræ, et principes convenerunt in unum, * adversus Dominum, et adversus Christum ejus.

Dirumpamus vincula eorum : * et projiciamus a nobis jugum ipsorum.

Qui habitat in cœlis

WHY have the Gentiles raged, and the people devised vain things?

The kings of the earth stood up, and the princes met together against the Lord, and against his Christ.

Let us break their bonds asunder ; and let us cast away their yoke from us.

He that dwelle in

irridebit eos: * et Dominus subsannabit eos.

heaven shall laugh at them; and the Lord shall deride them.

Tunc loquetur ad eos in ira sua: * et in furore suo conturbabit eos.

Then shall he speak to them in his anger, and trouble them in his rage.

Ego autem constitutus sum rex ab eo super Sion montem sanctum ejus: * prædicans præceptum ejus.

But I am appointed by him king over Sion his holy mountain, preaching his commandment.

Dominus dixit ad me: * Filius meus es tu, ego hodie genui te.

The Lord said to me: Thou art my Son, to-day have I begotten thee.

Postula a me, et dabo tibi gentes hæreditatem tuam: * et possessionem tuam terminos terræ.

Ask of me, and I will give thee the Gentiles for thy inheritance; and the utmost parts of the earth for thy possession.

Reges eos in virga ferrea: * et tanquam vas figuli confringes eos.

Thou shalt rule them with a rod of iron, and shalt break them in pieces like a potter's vessel.

Et nunc reges intelligite: * erudimini qui judicatis terram.

And now, O ye kings! understand; receive instruction, you that judge the earth.

Servite Domino in timore: * et exultate ei cum tremore.

Serve ye the Lord with fear, and rejoice unto him with trembling.

Apprehendite disci-

Embrace discipline

plinam, ne quando iras-catur Dominus : * et pereatis de via justa.

lest at any time the Lord be angry, and ye perish from the just way.

Cum exarserit in bre-vi ira ejus, * beati om-nes qui confidunt in eo.

When his wrath shall be kindled in a short time, blessed are all that trust in him.

Here the lowest candle on the left side of the triangle is extinguished.

Ant. Astiterunt reges terræ, et principes con-venerunt in unum, ad-versus Dominum, et ad-versus Christum ejus.

Ant. The kings of the earth stood up, and the princes met together against the Lord, and against his Christ.

Ant. Diviserunt sibi vestimenta mea, et super vestem meam miserunt sortem.

Ant. They parted my garments amongst them ; and upon my vesture they cast lots.

PSALM 21.

DEUS, Deus meus, respice in me : quare me dereliquisti ? * longe a salute mea verba delictorum meorum.

O GOD, my God ! look upon me : why hast thou forsaken me ? Far from my sal-vation are the words of my sins.

Deus meus, clamabo per diem, et non exau-dies : * et nocte, et non ad insipientiam mihi.

O my God ! I shall cry by day, and thou wilt not hear ; and by night, and it shall not be re-puted as folly in me.

Tu autem in sancto habitas, * laus Israel.

But thou dwellest in the holy place, the praise of Israel.

In te speraverunt patres nostri : * speraverunt, et liberasti eos.

Ad te clamaverunt, et salvi facti sunt : * in te speraverunt, et non sunt confusi.

Ego autem sum vermis, et non homo : * opprobrium hominum, et abjectio plebis.

Omnes videntes me, deriserunt me : * locuti sunt labiis, et moverunt caput.

Speravit in Domino, eripiat eum : * salvum faciat eum, quoniam vult eum.

Quoniam tu es, qui extraxisti me de ventre : * spes mea ab uberibus matris meæ. In te projectus sum ex utero.

De ventre matris meæ Deus meus es tu : * ne discesseris a me.

Quoniam tribulatio proxima est : * quoniam non est qui adjuvet.

In thee have our fathers hoped : they have hoped, and thou hast delivered them.

They cried to thee, and they were saved ; they trusted in thee, and were not confounded.

But I am a worm, and no man : the reproach of men, and the outcast of the people.

All they that saw me have laughed me to scorn ; they have spoken with the lips, and wagged the head.

He hoped in the Lord, let him deliver him : let him save him, seeing he delighteth in him.

For thou art he that hast drawn me out of the womb : my hope from the breasts of my mother. I was cast upon thee from the womb.

From my mother's womb thou art my God ; depart not from me.

For tribulation is very near : for there is none to help me.

Circumdederunt me vituli multi : * tauri pingues obsederunt me.

Many calves have surrounded me: fat bulls have besieged me.

Aperuerunt super me os suum, * sicut leo rapiens et rugiens.

They have opened their mouths against me, as a lion ravening and roaring.

Sicut aqua effusus sum : * et dispersa sunt omnia ossa mea.

I am poured out like water; and all my bones are scattered.

Factum est cor meum tamquam cera liquescens * in medio ventris mei.

My heart is become like wax melting in the midst of my bowels.

Aruit tamquam testa virtus mea, et lingua mea adhæsit faucibus meis : * et in pulverem mortis deduxisti me.

My strength was dried up like a potsherd, and my tongue hath cleaved to my jaws; and thou hast brought me down into the dust of death.

Quoniam circumdederunt me canes multi : * concilium malignantium obsedit me.

For many dogs have encompassed me; the council of the malignant hath besieged me.

Foderunt manus meas et pedes meos : * dinumeraverunt omnia ossa mea.

They have dug my hands and my feet : they have numbered all my bones.

Ipsi vero consideraverunt et inspexerunt me : * diviserunt sibi vestimenta mea, et super

And they have looked and stared upon me : they parted my garments amongst them,

vestem meam miserunt sortem.

Tu autem, Domine, ne elongaveris auxilium tuum a me : * ad defensionem meam conspice.

Erue a framea, Deus, animam meam : * et de manu canis unicam meam.

Salva me ex ore leonis : * et a cornibus unicornium humilitatem meam.

Narrabo nomen tuum fratribus meis : * in medio ecclesiæ laudabo te.

Qui timetis Dominum, laudate eum : * universum semen Jacob, glorificate eum.

Timeat eum omne semen Israel : * quoniam non sprevit, neque despexit deprecationem pauperis.

Nec avertit faciem suam a me : * et cum clamarem ad eum, exaudivit me.

Apud te laus mea in ecclesia magna : * vota

and upon my vesture they cast lots.

But thou, O Lord ! remove not thy help from me ; look towards my defence.

Deliver, O God ! my soul from the sword, and my only one from the hand of the dog.

Save me from the lion's mouth, and my lowness from the horns of unicorns.

I will declare thy name to my brethren ; in the midst of the church will I praise thee.

Ye that fear the Lord praise him : all ye the seed of Jacob, glorify him.

Let all the seed of Israel fear him; because he hath not slighted nor despised the supplication of the poor man.

Neither hath he turned away his face from me ; and when I cried to him he heard me.

With thee is my praise in a great church ; I will

mea reddam in conspectu timentium eum.

pay my vows in the sight of them that fear him.

Edent pauperes, et saturabuntur ; et laudabunt Dominum qui requirunt eum : * vivent corda eorum in sæculum sæculi.

The poor shall eat and shall be filled ; and they shall praise the Lord, that seek him ; their hearts shall live for ever and ever.

Reminiscentur et convertentur ad Dominum * universi fines terræ.

All the ends of the earth shall remember, and shall be converted to the Lord.

Et adorabunt in conspectu ejus * universæ familiæ gentium.

And all the kindreds of the Gentiles shall adore in his sight.

Quoniam Domini est regnum : * et ipse dominabitur gentium.

For the kingdom is the Lord's ; and he shall have dominion over the nations.

Manducaverunt et adoraverunt omnes pingues terræ : * in conspectu ejus cadent omnes qui descendunt in terram.

All the fat ones of the earth have eaten and have adored ; all that go down to the earth shall fall before him.

Et anima mea illi vivet : * et semen meum serviet ipsi.

And to him my soul shall live ; and my seed shall serve him.

Annuntiabitur Domino generatio ventura : * et annuntiabunt cœli justitiam ejus populo

There shall be declared to the Lord a generation to come ; and the heavens shall show forth

ʚui nascetur, quem fecit Dominus.

his justice to a people that shall be born, which the Lord hath made.

Here the lowest candle on the right side of the triangle is extinguished.

Ant. Diviserunt sibi vestimenta mea, et super vestem meam miserunt sortem.

Ant. They parted my garments amongst them; and upon my vesture they cast lots.

Ant. Insurrexerunt in me testes iniqui, et mentita est iniquitas sibi.

Ant. Unjust witnesses have risen up against me, and iniquity hath lied to itself.

PSALM 26.

DOMINUS illuminatio mea, et salus mea : * quem timebo ?

THE Lord is my light and my salvation ; whom shall I fear ?

Dominus protector vitæ meæ : * a quo trepidabo ?

The Lord is the protector of my l :: of whom shall I be afraid ?

Dum appropiant super me nocentes, * ut edant carnes meas.

Whilst the wicked draw near against me, to eat my flesh.

Qui tribulant me inimici mei, * ipsi infirmati sunt, et ceciderunt.

My enemies that troubled me, have themselves been weakened, and have fallen.

Si consistant adversum me castra, * non timebit cor meum.

If armies in camp should stand together against me, my heart shall not fear.

Si exurgat adversum me prœlium, * in hoc ego sperabo.

Unam petii a Domino, hanc requiram : * ut inhabitem in domo Domini omnibus diebus vitæ meæ.

Ut videam voluptatem Domini, * et visitem templum ejus.

Quoniam abscondit me in tabernaculo suo ; * in die malorum protexit me in abscondito tabernaculi sui.

In petra exaltavit me : * et nunc exaltavit caput meum super inimicos meos.

Circuivi, et immolavi in tabernaculo ejus hostiam vociferationis : * cantabo, et psalmum dicam Domino.

Exaudi, Domine, vocem meam, qua clamavi ad te : * miserere mei, et exaudi me.

Tibi dixit cor meum, exquisivit te facies mea :

If a battle should rise up against me, in this will I be confident.

One thing I have asked of the Lord, this will I seek after : that I may dwell in the house of the Lord all the days of my life.

That I may see the delight of the Lord, and may visit his temple.

For he hath hidden me in his tabernacle ; in the day of evils, he hath protected me in the secret place of his tabernacle.

He hath exalted me upon a rock : and now he hath lifted up my head above my enemies.

I have gone round, and have offered up in his tabernacle a sacrifice of jubilation ; I will sing and recite a psalm to the Lord.

Hear, O Lord ! my voice, with which I have cried to thee : have mercy on me and hear me.

My heart hath said to thee, my face hath

* faciem tuam, Domine, requiram.

Ne avertas faciem tuam a me : * ne declines in ira a servo tuo.

Adjutor meus esto : * ne derelinquas me, neque despicias me, Deus salutaris meus.

Quoniam pater meus et mater mea dereliquerunt me : * Dominus autem assumpsit me.

Legem pone mihi, Domine, in via tua : * et dirige me in semitam rectam propter inimicos meos.

Ne tradideris me in animas tribulantium me: * quoniam insurrexerunt in me testes iniqui, et mentita est iniquitas sibi.

Credo videre bona Domini * in terra viventium.

Expecta Dominum, viriliter age : * et confortetur cor tuum, et sustine Dominum.

sought thee : thy face, O Lord! will I seek.

Turn not away thy face from me ; decline not in thy wrath from thy servant.

Be thou my helper; forsake me not; do not thou despise me, O God, my Saviour!

For my father and my mother have left me; but the Lord hath taken me up.

Set me, O Lord! a law in thy way; and guide me in the right path, because of my enemies.

Deliver me not over to the will of them that trouble me; for unjust witnesses have risen up again me, and iniquity ha lied to itself.

I believe to see the good things of the Lord, in the land of the living.

Expect the Lord, do manfully : and let thy heart take courage, and wait thou for the Lord.

Here a candle is extinguished.

Ant. Insurrexerunt in me testes iniqui, et mentita est iniquitas sibi.

V. Diviserunt sibi vestimenta mea.

R. Et super vestem meam miserunt sortem.

Pater noster, *secreto.*

Ant. Unjust witnesses have risen up against me, and iniquity hath lied to itself.

V. They parted my garments amongst them.

R. And upon my vesture they cast lots.

Our Father, *privately.*

THE FIRST LESSON.

De Lamentatione Jeremiæ Prophetæ, cap. ii.

From the Lamentation of Jeremias the Prophet, chap. ii.

Heth. COGITAVIT Dominus dissipare murum filiæ Sion: tetendit funiculum suum, et non avertit manum suam a perditione: luxitque antemurale, et murus pariter dissipatus est.

Heth. THE Lord hath purposed to destroy the wall of the daughter of Sion; he hath stretched out his line, and hath not withdrawn his hand from destroying: and the bulwark hath mourned, and the wall hath been destroyed together.

Teth. Defixæ sunt in terra portæ ejus: perdidit et contrivit vectes ejus: regem ejus et principes ejus in gentibus: non est lex, et prophetæ ejus non invene-

Teth. Her gates are sunk into the ground: he hath destroyed and broken her bars: her king and her princes are among the Gentiles: the law is no more, and her

runt visionem a Domino.

Jod. Sederunt in terra, conticuerunt senes filiæ Sion: consperserunt cinere capita sua, accincti sunt ciliciis: abjecerunt in terram capita sua virgines Jerusalem.

Caph. Defecerunt præ lacrymis oculi mei, conturbata sunt viscera mea: effusum est in terra jecur meum super contritione filiæ populi mei, cum deficeret parvulus, et lactens in plateis oppidi.

Jerusalem, Jerusalem, convertere ad Dominum Deum tuum.

R. Omnes amici mei dereliquerunt me, et prævaluerunt insidiantes mihi; tradidit me quem diligebam: * Et terribilibus oculis plaga

prophets have found no vision from the Lord.

Jod. The ancients of the daughter of Sion sit upon the ground; they have held their peace: they have sprinkled their heads with dust, they are girded with hair-cloth; the virgins of Jerusalem hang down their heads to the ground.

Caph. My eyes have failed with weeping, my bowels are troubled: my liver is poured out upon the earth, for the destruction of the daughter of my people, when the children and the sucklings fainted away in the streets of the city.

Jerusalem! Jerusalem! be converted to the Lord thy God.

R. All my friends have forsaken me, and they that lay in ambush for me prevailed: he whom I love has betrayed me: * And they with

crudeli percutientes, aceto potabant me.

terrible looks, striking me with a cruel wound, gave me vinegar to drink.

V. Inter iniquos pro-jecerunt me, et non pe-percerunt animæ meæ. * Et terribilibus oculis.

V. They cast me out among the wicked, and spared not my life. * And they.

THE SECOND LESSON.

Lamed. M ATRI-BUS suis dixerunt : Ubi est triti-cum et vinum ? cum de-ficerent quasi vulnerati in plateis civitatis : cum exhalarent animas suas in sinu matrum suarum.

Lamed. T HEY said to their mo-thers : Where is corn and wine ? when they fainted away as the wounded in the streets of the city : when they breathed out their souls in the bosoms of their mothers.

Mem. Cui comparabo te ? vel cui assimilabo te, filia Jerusalem ? cui ex-æquabo te, et consolabor te, virgo filia Sion ? mag-na est enim velut mare contritio tua : quis mede-bitur tui ?

Mem. To what shall I compare thee ? or to what shall I liken thee, O daughter of Jerusa-lem ? to what shall I equal thee, that I may comfort thee, O virgin daughter of Sion ? For great as the sea is thy destruction : who shall heal thee ?

Nun. Prophetæ tui viderunt tibi falsa et stulta, nec aperiebant

Nun. Thy prophets have seen false and fool-ish things for thee : and

iniquitatem tuam, ut te ad pœnitentiam provocarent: viderunt autem tibi assumptiones falsas, et ejectiones.

they have not laid open their iniquity, to excite thee to penance: but they have seen for thee false revelations and banishments.

Samech. Plauserunt super te manibus omnes transeuntes per viam: sibilaverunt, et moverunt caput suum super filiam Jerusalem: Hæccine est urbs, dicentes, perfecti decoris, gaudium universæ terræ?

Samech. All they that passed by the way, have clapped their hands at thee; they have hissed, and wagged their heads at the daughter of Jerusalem, saying: Is this the city of perfect beauty, the joy of all the earth?

Jerusalem, Jerusalem, convertere ad Dominum Deum tuum.

Jerusalem! Jerusalem! be converted to the Lord thy God.

R. Velum templi scissum est, * Et omnis terra tremuit: latro de cruce clamabat, dicens: Memento mei, Domine, dum veneris in regnum tuum.

R. The veil of the temple was rent, * And all the earth quaked: the thief from the cross cried out, saying: Lord! remember me when thou shalt come into thy kingdom.

V. Petræ scissæ sunt, et monumenta aperta sunt, et multa corpora sanctorum, qui dormierant, surrexerunt. * Et omnis terra, etc.

V. The rocks were rent, and the graves were opened, and many bodies of the saints that had slept, arose. * And all the earth.

THE THIRD LESSON.

Aleph. EGO vir videns paupertatem meam in virga indignationis ejus.

Aleph. Me minavit, et adduxit in tenebras, et non in lucem.

Aleph. Tantum in me vertit, et convertit manum suam tota die.

Beth. Vetustam fecit pellem meam, et carnem meam; contrivit ossa mea.

Beth. Ædificavit in gyro meo, et circumdedit me felle et labore.

Beth. In tenebrosis collocavit me, quasi mortuos sempiternos.

Ghimel. Circumædificavit adversum me, ut non egrediar: aggravavit compedem meum.

Ghimel. Sed et cum clamavero et rogavero, exclusit orationem meam.

Aleph. I AM the man that see my poverty by the rod of his indignation.

Aleph. He hath led me, and brought me into darkness, and not into light.

Aleph. Only against me he hath turned and turned again his hand all the day.

Beth. My skin and my flesh he hath made old, he hath broken my bones.

Beth. He hath built round about me, and hath compassed me with gall and labor.

Beth. He hath set me in dark places as those that are dead for ever.

Ghimel. He hath built against me round about, that I may not get out; he hath made my fetters heavy.

Ghimel. Yea, and when I cry, and entreat, he hath shut out my prayer.

Ghimel. Conclusit vias meas lapidibus quadris, semitas meas subvertit.

Jerusalem, Jerusalem, convertere ad Dominum tuum.

R. Vinea mea electa, ego te plantavi : * Quomodo conversa es in amaritudinem, ut me crucifigeres, et Barabbam dimitteres?

V. Sepivi te, et lapides elegi ex te, et ædificavi turrim. * Quomodo conversa es, etc. Vinea mea, etc.

Ghimel. He hath shut up my ways with square stones, he hath turned my paths upside down.

Jerusalem! Jerusalem! be converted to the Lord thy God.

R. O my chosen vineyard! it is I that have planted thee: * How art thou become so bitter that thou shouldst crucify me and dismiss Barabbas?

V. I have fenced thee in and picked the stones out of thee, and have built a tower. * How art thou, etc. O my chosen! etc.

THE SECOND NOCTURN.

Ant. VIM faciebant, qui quærebant animam meam.

Ant. THEY that sought my soul used violence.

PSALM 37.

DOMINE, ne in furore tuo arguas me : * neque in ira tua corripias me.

Quoniam sagittæ tuæ infixæ sunt mihi : * et

REBUKE me not, O Lord! in thy indignation, nor chastise me in thy wrath.

For thy arrows are fastened in me: and thy

confirmasti super me manum tuam.

hand hath been strong upon me.

Non est sanitas in carne mea a facie iræ tuæ : * non est pax ossibus meis a facie peccatorum meorum.

There is no health in my flesh because of thy wrath : there is no peace for my bones because of my sins.

Quoniam iniquitates meæ supergressæ sunt caput meum : * et sicut onus grave gravatæ sunt super me.

For my iniquities are gone over my head : and as a heavy burden are become heavy upon me.

Putruerunt et corruptæ sunt cicatrices meæ, * a facie insipientiæ meæ.

My sores are putrefied and corrupted, because of my foolishness.

Miser factus sum, et curvatus sum usque in finem : * tota die contristatus ingrediebar.

I am become miserable, and am bowed down even to the end : I walked sorrowful all the day long.

Quoniam lumbi mei impleti sunt illusionibus : * et non est sanitas in carne mea.

For my loins are filled with illusions : and there is no health in my flesh.

Afflictus sum, et humiliatus sum nimis : * rugiebam a gemitu cordis mei.

I am afflicted and humbled exceedingly : I roared with the groaning of my heart.

Domine, ante te omne desiderium meum : * et gemitus meus a te non est absconditus.

Lord, all my desire is before thee, and my groaning is not hidden from thee.

Cor meam conturbatum est, dereliquit me virtus mea : * et lumen oculorum meorum, et ipsum non est mecum.

Amici mei et proximi mei * adversum me appropinquaverunt, et steterunt.

Et qui juxta me erant, de longe steterunt : * et vim faciebant qui quærebant animam meam.

Et qui inquirebant mala mihi, locuti sunt vanitates : * et dolos tota die meditabantur.

Ego autem tamquam surdus non audiebam : * et sicut mutus non aperiens os suum.

Et factus sum sicut homo non audiens : * et non habens in ore suo redargutiones.

Quoniam in te, Domine, speravi : * tu exaudies me, Domine Deus meus.

Quia dixi : Nequando supergaudeant mihi inimici mei : * et dum

My heart is troubled, my strength hath left me, and the light of my eyes itself is not with me.

My friends and my neighbors have drawn near, and stood against me.

And they that were near me stood afar off : and they that sought my soul used violence.

And they that sought evils to me spoke vain things, and studied deceits all the day long.

But I, as a deaf man, heard not : and was as a dumb man not opening his mouth.

And I became as a man that heareth not ; and that hath no reproofs in his mouth.

For in thee, O Lord ! have I hoped : thou wilt hear me, O Lord, my God !

For I said : Lest at any time my enemies rejoice over me : and whilst my

commoventur pedes mei, super me magna locuti sunt.

Quoniam ego in flagella paratus sum : * et dolor meus in conspectu meo semper.

Quoniam iniquitatem meam annuntiabo : * et cogitabo pro peccato meo.

Inimici autem mei vivunt, et confirmati sunt super me : * et multiplicati sunt qui oderunt me inique.

Qui retribuunt mala pro bonis, detrahebant mihi : * quoniam sequebar bonitatem.

Ne derelinquas me, Domine Deus meus : * ne discesseris a me.

Intende in adjutorium meum, * Domine Deus salutis meæ.

feet are moved, they speak great things against me.

For I am ready for scourges : and my sorrow is continually before me.

For I will declare my iniquity : and I will think for my sin.

But my enemies live, and are stronger than I : and they that hate me wrongfully are multiplied.

They that render evil for good have detracted me, because I followed goodness.

Forsake me not, O Lord, my God ! do not thou depart from me.

Attend unto my help, O Lord, the God of my salvation !

Here a candle is extinguished.

Ant. Vim faciebant, qui quærebant animam meam.

Ant. Confundantur et revereantur, qui quæ-

Ant. They that sought my soul used violence.

Ant. Let them be confounded and ashamed

runt animam meam, ut auferant eam.

that seek after my soul. to take it away.

PSALM 39.

EXPECTANS expectavi Dominum, * et intendit mihi.

Et exaudivit preces meas : * et eduxit me de lacu miseriæ, et de luto fæcis.

Et statuit super petram pedes meos : * et direxit gressus meos.

Et immisit in os meum canticum novum, * carmen Deo nostro.

Videbunt multi, et timebunt : * et sperabunt in Domino.

Beatus vir, cujus est nomen Domini spes ejus : * et non respexit in vanitates et insanias falsas.

Multa fecisti tu, Domine Deus meus, mirabilia tua : * et cogitationibus tuis non est qui similis sit tibi.

WITH expectation I have waited for the Lord, and he was attentive to me.

And he heard my prayers ; and prought me out of the pit of misery and the mire of dregs.

And he set my feet upon a rock ; and directed my steps.

And he put a new canticle into my mouth, a song to our God.

Many shall see this, and shall fear : and they shall hope in the Lord.

Blessed is the man whose trust is in the name of the Lord : and who hath not had regard to vanities and lying follies.

Thou hast multiplied thy wonderful works, O Lord, my God ! and in thy thoughts there is no one like to thee.

Annuntiavi, et locutus sum : * multiplicati sunt super numerum.

I have declared and I have spoken : they are multiplied above number.

Sacrificium et oblationem noluisti : * aures autem perfecisti mihi.

Sacrifice and oblation thou didst not desire; but thou hast pierced ears for me.

Holocaustum et pro peccato non postulasti :* tunc dixi: Ecce venio.

Burnt-offering and sin-offering thou didst not require : then said I : Behold I come.

In capite libri scriptum est de me ut facerem voluntatem tuam : * Deus meus, volui, et legem tuam in medio cordis mei.

In the head of the book it is written of me, that I should do thy will : O my God! I have desired it, and thy law in the midst of my heart.

Annuntiavi justitiam tuam in ecclesia magna, * ecce labia mea non prohibebo : Domine tu scisti.

I have declared thy justice in a great church : lo, I will not restrain my lips, O Lord! thou knowest it.

Justitiam tuam non abscondi in corde meo : * veritatem tuam et salutare tuum dixi.

I have not hid thy justice within my heart : I have declared thy truth and thy salvation.

Non abscondi misericordiam tuam, et veritatem tuam, * a concilio multo.

I have not concealed thy mercy and thy truth from a great council.

Tu autem, Domine, ne longe facias misera-

Withhold not thou, O Lord! thy tender mer

tiones tuas a me : * misericordia tua et veritas tua semper susceperunt me.

cies from me : thy mercy and thy truth have always upheld me.

Quoniam circumdederunt me mala, quorum non est numerus : * comprehenderunt me iniquitates meæ, et non potui ut viderem.

For evils without number have surrounded me; my iniquities have overtaken me, and I was not able to see.

Multiplicatæ sunt super capillos capitis mei : * et cor meum dereliquit me.

They are multiplied above the hairs of my head, and my heart hath forsaken me.

Complaceat tibi, Domine, ut eruas me : * Domine, ad adjuvandum me respice.

Be pleased, O Lord ! to deliver me ; look down, O Lord ! to help me.

Confundantur et revereantur simul, qui quærunt animam meam, * ut auferant eam.

Let them be confounded and ashamed together, that seek after my soul to take it away.

Convertantur retrorsum et revereantur, * qui volunt mihi mala.

Let them be turned backward and be ashamed that desire evil to me.

Ferant confestim confusionem suam, * qui dicunt mihi : Euge, euge.

Let them immediately bear their confusion, that say to me : 'Tis well, 'tis well.

Exultent et lætentur super te omnes quærentes : * et dicant semper : Magnificetur Dominus :

Let all that seek thee rejoice and be glad in thee : and let such as love thy salvation say

qui diligunt salutare tuum.

always: The Lord be magnified.

Ego autem mendicus sum, et pauper : * Dominus sollicitus est mei.

But I am a beggar and poor ; the Lord is careful for me.

Adjutor meus et protector meus tu es : * Deus meus, ne tardaveris.

Thou art my helper and my protector : O my God ! be not slack.

Here a candle is extinguished.

Ant. Confundantur et revereantur, qui quæ-runt animam meam, ut auferant eam.

Ant. Let them be confounded and ashamed, that seek after my soul to take it away.

Ant. Alieni insurrexerunt in me, et fortes quæsierunt animam meam.

Ant. Strangers have risen up against me, and the mighty have sought after my soul.

PSALM 53.

DEUS, in nomine tuo salvum me fac : * et in virtute tua judica me.

SAVE me, O God ! by thy name, and judge me in thy strength.

Deus, exaudi orationem meam : * auribus percipe verba oris mei.

O God ! hear **my** prayer : give ear to the words of my mouth.

Quoniam alieni insurrexerunt adversum me, et fortes quæsierunt animam meam : * et non proposuerunt Deum ante conspectum suum.

For strangers have risen up against me ; and the mighty have sought after my soul ; and they have not set God before their eyes.

Ecce enim Deus adju-

For behold God is my

vat me: * et Dominus susceptor est animæ meæ.

helper: and the Lord is the protector of my soul.

Averte mala inimicis meis: * et in veritate tua disperde illos.

Turn back the evils upon my enemies: and cut them off in thy truth.

Voluntarie sacrificabo tibi, * et confitebor nomini tuo Domine: quoniam bonum est.

I will freely sacrifice to thee, and will give praise, O God! to thy name: because it is good.

Quoniam ex omni tribulatione eripuisti me: * et super inimicos meos despexit oculus meus.

For thou hast deliver- ed me out of all trouble: and my eye hath looked down upon my enemies.

Here a candle is extinguished.

Ant. Alieni insurrexerunt in me, et fortes quæsierunt animam meam.

Ant. Strangers have risen up against me, and the mighty have sought after my soul.

V. Insurrexerunt in me testes iniqui.

V. Unjust witnesses have risen up against me.

R. Et mentita est iniquitas sibi.

R. And iniquity hath lied to itself.

Pater noster, *secreto.*

Our Father, *privately.*

THE FOURTH LESSON.

Ex Tractatu sancti Augustini Episcopi super Psalmos. *In Psalm.*63.

From the treatise of St. Augustine, the Bishop, on the Psalms. *On the 63d Psalm.*

PROTEXISTI me, Deus, a conventu

THOU hast protect- ed me, O God!

malignantium, a multitudine operantium iniquitatem. Jam ipsum caput nostrum intueamur. Multi martyres talia passi sunt, sed nihil sic elucet, quomodo caput martyrum : ibi melius intuemur, quod illi experti sunt. Protectus est a multitudine malignantium, protegente se Deo, protegente carnem suam ipso Filio, et homine quem gerebat; quia filius hominis est, et Filius Dei est. Filius Dei, propter formam Dei; filius hominis, propter formam servi, habens in potestate ponere animam suam, et recipere eam. Quid ei potuerunt facere inimici ? Occiderunt corpus, animam non occiderunt. Intendite. Parum ergo erat Dominum hortari mar-

from the assembly of the malignant; from the multitude of the workers of iniquity. Now let us behold our head himself. Many martyrs have suffered such torments; but nothing is so conspicuous as the head of martyrs; there we see better what they endured. He was protected from the multitude of the malignant; that is, God protected himself, the Son, and the Man assumed by the Son, protected his own flesh. For he is the Son of Man, and the Son of God : the Son of God because of the form of God; the Son of Man because of the form of a servant, having in his power to lay down his life, and take it up again. What could his enemies do against him ? They killed his body, but they did not kill his soul. Take notice then. It signified little, for our

tyres verbo, nisi firmaret exemplo.

Lord to exhort the martyrs by word, if he had not fortified them by his example.

R. Tamquam ad latronem existis cum gladiis et fustibus comprehendere me : * Quotidie apud vos eram in templo docens, et non me tenuistis : et ecce flagellatum ducitis ad crucifigendum.

R. You are come out as against a robber, with swords and clubs to apprehend me : * I was daily with you, teaching in the temple, and you laid not hands on me, yet now you scourge me and lead me to be crucified.

V. Cumque injecissent manus in Jesum, et tenuissent eum, dixit ad eos : * Quotidie apud vos, etc.

V. And when they had laid hands on Jesus, and held him, he said to them : * I was daily, etc.

THE FIFTH LESSON.

NOSTIS qui conventus erat malignantium Judæorum, et quæ multitudo erat operantium iniquitatem. Quam iniquitatem? Quia voluerunt occidere Dominum Jesum Christum. Tanta opera bona, inquit, ostendi vobis : propter quod horum me vultis occidere? Pertu-

YOU know what was the assembly of the malignant Jews, and what the multitude of the workers of iniquity. But what was that iniquity? It was, that they intended to kill our Lord Jesus Christ. I have shown, saith he, so many good works to you; for which

lit omnes infirmos eorum, curavit omnes languidos eorum, prædicavit regnum cœlorum, non tacuit vitia eorum ; ut ipsa potius eis displicerent, non medicus a quo sanabantur. His omnibus curationibus ejus ingrati, tamquam multa febre phrenetici, insanientes in medicum qui venerat curare eos, excogitaverunt consilium perdendi eum : tamquam ibi volentes probare, utrum vere homo sit, qui mori possit ; an aliquid super homines sit, et mori se non permittat. Verbum ipsorum agnoscimus in Sapientia Salomonis : Morte turpissima, inquiunt, condemnemus eum. Interrogemus eum : erit enim respectus in sermonibus illius. Si enim vere Filius Dei est, liberet eum.

of these will you kill me ? He bore with all their weaknesses, he healed all their sick, he preached the kingdom of heaven, he concealed not their crimes, that they might rather hate them than the physician who healed them. Yet such was their ingratitude for all these cures, that, like men raving in a high fever, they raged against the physician who came to cure them, and formed a design of destroying him ; as if they had a mind to try whether he was a real man that could die, or something above men, and would not die. We find their words in the Wisdom of Solomon. Let us condemn him, say they, to a most shameful death. Let us examine him : for regard will be had to his words. If he be truly the Son of God, let him deliver him.

R. Tenebræ factæ sunt, dum crucifixissent Jesum Judæi; et circa horam nonam, exclamavit Jesus voce magna: Deus meus, ut quid me dereliquisti? * Et inclinato capite, emisit spiritum.

R. Darkness covered the earth whilst the Jews crucified Jesus, and about the ninth hour Jesus cried out with a loud voice: My God! why hast thou forsaken me? * And bowing down his head, he gave up the ghost.

V. Exclamans Jesus voce magna, ait: Pater, in manus tuas commendo spiritum meum. * Et inclinato, etc.

V. Jesus crying with a loud voice, said: Father! into thy hands I commend my spirit. * And bowing down, etc.

THE SIXTH LESSON.

EXACUERUNT tamquam gladium linguas suas. Non dicant Judæi: Non occidimus Christum. Etenim propterea eum dederunt judici Pilato, ut quasi ipsi a morte ejus viderentur immunes. Nam cum dixisset eis Pilatus: Vos eum occidite, responderunt: Nobis non licet occidere quemquam. Iniquitatem facinoris sui in judicem hominem refundere volebant: sed

THEY have whetted their tongues like a sword. Let not the Jews say: We did not kill Christ, under pretence that therefore they delivered him up to Pilate, the judge, that they might seem innocent of his death; and that when Pilate had said to them: Put him to death yourselves, they answered: It is not lawful for us to put any man to death. Thus

numquid Deum judicem fallebant? Quod fecit Pilatus, in eo ipso quod fecit, aliquantum particeps fuit; sed in comparatione illorum, multo ipse innocentior. Institit enim quantum potuit, ut illum ex eorum manibus liberaret: nam propterea flagellatum produxit ad eos. Non persequendo Dominum flagellavit, sed eorum furori satisfacere volens: ut vel sic jam mitescerent, et desinerent velle occidere, cum flagellatum viderent. Fecit et hoc. At ubi perseveraverunt, nostis illum lavisse manus, et dixisse, quod ipse non fecisset, mundum se esse a morte illius. Fecit tamen. Sed si reus quia fecit vel invitus, illi innocentes qui coegerunt ut faceret? nullo modo. Sed ille dixit in eum sententiam, et jussit eum crucifigi, et quasi ipse occidit: et vos, o Judæi, oc-

they pretended to throw the injustice of their crime upon the judge who was a man; but could they deceive a Judge who is God? What Pilate did made him partaker of their crime; but in comparison of them he was much more innocent. For he did what he could to rescue him from their hands; and for that reason ordered him to be scourged and shown to them. This he did to our Lord, not by way of persecution, but to satisfy their rage; that the sight of him in that condition might move them to pity, and make them desist from desiring his death. All this he did. But when they still persisted, you know that he washed his hands, and said that he was innocent of his death. And yet he put him to death. But if he was guilty for do-

cidistis. Unde occidis-
tis? Gladio linguæ;
acuistis enim linguas
vestras. Et quando per-
cussistis, nisi quando
clamastis: Crucifige, crucifige!

ing so against his will,
are they innocent who
forced him to it? Not
at all. He pronounced
sentence upon him, and
commanded him to be
crucified, and so might
be said to kill him; but
you also, O Jews! have
killed him. How have
you killed him? With
the sword of your
tongues: for you whet-
ted your tongues. And
when gave you the
stroke, but when you
cried out: Crucify him,
crucify him!

R. Animam meam di-
lectam tradidi in manus
iniquorum, et facta est
mihi hæreditas mea si-
cut leo in silva: dedit
contra me voces adver-
sarius, dicens: Congre-
gamini, et properate ad
devorandum illum: po-
suerunt me in deserto
solitudinis, et luxit su-
per me omnis terra: *
Quia non est inventus
qui me agnosceret, et
faceret bene.

R. I have given my
dear soul into the hands
of the wicked, and my in-
heritance is become to me
as a lion in the wood: my
adversary gave out words
against me, saying: Come
together, and make haste
to devour him: they
placed me in a solitary
desert, and all the earth
mourned for me: * Be-
cause there was none
that would know me
and do me any good.

V. Insurrexerunt in me viri absque misericordia, et non pepercerunt animæ meæ. * Quia non est, etc. Animam meam, etc.

V. Men without mercy rose up against me, and they spared not my life. * Because, etc. I have given, etc.

THIRD NOCTURN.

Ant. AB insurgentibus in me libera me, Domine, quia occupaverunt animam meam.

Ant. DEFEND me from them that rise up against me, O Lord! for they are in possession of my soul.

PSALM 58.

ERIPE me de inimicis meis, Deus meus : * et ab insurgentibus in me libera me.

DELIVER me from my enemies, O my God! and defend me from them that rise up against me.

Eripe me de operantibus iniquitatem : * et de viris sanguinum salva me.

Deliver me from them that work iniquity, and save me from bloody men.

Quia ecce ceperunt animam meam : * irruerunt in me fortes.

For behold they have caught my soul; the mighty have rushed in upon me.

Neque iniquitas mea, neque peccatum meum, Domine; * sine iniquitate cucurri, et direxi.

Neither is it for my iniquity, nor for my sin, O Lord; without iniquity have I run, and directed my steps.

Exurge in occursum meum, et vide : * et tu, Domine Deus virtutum, Deus Israel,

Rise up thou to meet me, and behold; even thou, O Lord the God of hosts, the God of Israel!

Intende ad visitandas omnes gentes : * non miserearis omnibus qui operantur iniquitatem.

Attend to visit all the nations : have no mercy on all them that work iniquity.

Convertentur ad vesperam, et famem patientur ut canes : * et circuibunt civitatem.

They shall return at evening and shall suffer hunger like dogs: and shall go round about the city.

Ecce loquentur in ore suo, et gladius in labiis eorum : * quoniam quis audivit ?

Behold, they shall speak with their mouth, and a sword is in their lips : for who, say they, hath heard us ?

Et tu Domine, deridebis eos : * ad nihilum deduces omnes gentes.

But thou, O Lord! shalt laugh at them; thou shalt bring all the nations to nothing.

Fortitudinem meam ad te custodiam, quia Deus susceptor meus es. * Deus meus, misericordia ejus præveniet me.

I will keep my strength to thee: for thou art my protector : my God, his mercy shall prevent me.

Deus ostendet mihi super inimicos meos, ne occidas eos ; * ne quando obliviscantur populi mei.

God shall let me see over my enemies : slay them not, lest at any time my people forget.

Disperge illos in virtute tua: * et depone eos, protector meus Domine.

Delictum oris eorum, sermonem labiorum ipsorum : * et comprehendantur in superbia sua.

Et de execratione et mendacio annuntiabuntur in consummatione : * in ira consummationis, et non erunt.

Et scient quia Deus dominabitur Jacob, * et finium terræ.

Convertentur ad vesperam, et famem patientur ut canes : * et circuibunt civitatem.

Ipsi dispergentur ad manducandum : * si vero non fuerint saturati, et murmurabunt.

Ego autem cantabo fortitudinem tuam : * et exultabo mane misericordiam tuam.

Quia factus es suscep-

Scatter them by thy power ; and bring them down, O Lord, my protector !

For the sin of their mouth, and the word of their lips: and let them be taken in their pride.

And for their cursing and lying they shall be talked of, when they are consumed : when they are consumed by thy wrath, and they shall be no more.

And they shall know that God will rule Jacob, and all the ends of the earth.

They shall return at evening, and shall suffer hunger like dogs : and shall go round about the city.

They shall be scattered abroad to eat, and shall murmur if they be not filled.

But I will sing thy strength ; and will extol thy mercy in the morning.

For thou art become

tor meus, * et refugium meum, in die tribulationis meæ.

my support, and my refuge, in the day of my trouble.

Adjutor meus, tibi psallam, quia Deus susceptor meus es : * Deus meus misericordia mea.

Unto thee, O my helper! will I sing, for thou art God, my defence: my God, my mercy.

Here a candle is extinguished.

Ant. Ab insurgentibus in me libera me, Domine, quia occupaverunt animam meam.

Ant. Defend me from them that rise up against me, O Lord! for they are in possession of my soul.

Ant. Longe fecisti notos meos a me : traditus sum, et non egrediebar.

Ant. Thou hast put away my acquaintance far from me ; I was delivered up, and came not forth.

PSALM 87.

DOMINE Deus salutis meæ, * in die clamavi, et nocte coram te.

O LORD, the God of my salvation! I have cried in the day and in the night before thee.

Intret in conspectu tuo oratio mea : * inclina aurem tuam ad precem meam :

Let my prayer come in before thee ; incline thy ear to my petition.

Quia repleta est malis anima mea: * et vita mea inferno appropinquavit

For my soul is filled with evils; and my life hath drawn nigh to hell.

Æstimatus sum cum descendentibus in lacum; * factus sum sicut homo sine adjutorio, inter mortuos liber.

I am counted among those that go down to the pit; I am become as a man without help, free among the dead.

Sicut vulnerati dormientes in sepulchris, quorum non es memor amplius: * et ipsi de manu tua repulsi sunt.

Like the slain sleeping in the sepulchres, whom thou rememberest no more : and they are cast off from thy hand.

Posuerunt me in lacu inferiori: * in tenebrosis et in umbra mortis.

They have laid me in the lower pit; in the dark places, and in the shadow of death.

Super me confirmatus est furor tuus: * et omnes fluctus tuos induxisti super me.

Thy wrath is strong over me; and all thy waves thou hast brought in upon me.

Longe fecisti notos meos a me : * posuerunt me abominationem sibi.

Thou has put away my acquaintance far from me; they have set me an abomination to themselves.

Traditus sum, et non egrediebar: * oculi mei languerunt præ inopia.

I was delivered up, and came not forth: my eyes languished through poverty.

Clamavi ad te, Domine, tota die : * expandi ad te manus meas.

All the day I cried to thee, O Lord ! I stretched out my hands to thee.

Numquid mortuis facies mirabilia: * aut

Wilt thou show wonders to the dead ? or

medici suscitabunt, et confitebuntur tibi?

Numquid narrabit aliquis in sepulchro misericordiam tuam, * et veritatem tuam in perditione?

Numquid cognoscentur in tenebris mirabilia tua, * et justitia tua in terra oblivionis?

Et ego ad te, Domine, clamavi: * et mane oratio mea præveniet te.

Ut quid Domine repellis orationem meam: * avertis faciem tuam a me?

Pauper sum ego, et in laboribus a juventute mea: * exaltatus autem, humiliatus sum, et conturbatus.

In me transierunt iræ tuæ: * et terrores tui conturbaverunt me.

Circumdederunt me sicut aqua tota die: * circumdederunt me simul.

shall physicians raise to life, and give praise to thee?

Shall any one in the sepulchre declare thy mercy, and thy truth in destruction?

Shall thy wonders be known in the dark; and thy justice in the land of forgetfulness?

But I, O Lord! have cried to thee: and in the morning my prayer shall prevent thee.

Lord! why castest thou off my prayer? why turnest thou away thy face from me?

I am poor, and in labors from my youth; and being exalted, have been humbled and troubled.

Thy wrath hath come upon me: and thy terrors have troubled me.

They have come round about me like water all the day: they have compassed me about together.

Elongasti a me amicum et proximum, * et notos meos a miseria.

Friend and neighbor thou hast put far from me: and my acquaintance, because of misery.

Here a candle is extinguished.

Ant. Longe fecisti notos meos a me: traditus sum, et non egrediebar.

Ant. Thou hast put away my acquaintance far from me; I was delivered up, and came not forth.

Ant. Captabunt in animam justi, et sanguinem innocentem condemnabunt.

Ant. They will hunt after the soul of the just, and will condemn innocent blood.

PSALM 93.

DEUS ultionum Dominus: * Deus ultionum libere egit.

THE Lord is the God to whom revenge belongeth: the God of revenge hath acted freely.

Exaltare qui judicas terram: * redde retributionem superbis.

Lift up thyself, thou that judgest the earth: render a reward to the proud.

Usquequo peccatores, Domine,* usquequo peccatores gloriabuntur?

How long shall the wicked, O Lord! how long shall the wicked make their boast?

Effabuntur et loquentur iniquitatem: * loquentur omnes, qui operantur injustitiam?

How long shall they utter and speak wrong things? How long shall all speak who work injustice?

Populum tuum, Domine, humiliaverunt : * et hæreditatem tuam vexaverunt.

Viduam et advenam interfecerunt : * et pupillos occiderunt.

Et dixerunt : Non videbit Dominus, * nec intelliget Deus Jacob.

Intelligite, insipientes in populo : * et stulti, aliquando sapite.

Qui plantavit aurem, non audiet? * aut qui finxit oculum, non considerat?

Qui corripit gentes, non arguet : * qui docet hominem scientiam?

Dominus scit cogitationes hominum, * quoniam vanæ sunt.

Beatus homo, quem tu erudieris, Domine : * et de lege tua docueris eum.

Thy people, O Lord! they have brought low ; and they have afflicted thy inheritance.

They have slain the widow and the stranger : and they have murdered the fatherless.

And they have said : The Lord shall not see : neither shall the God of Jacob understand.

Understand, ye senseless among the people! and, you fools! be wise at last.

He that planted the ear, shall he not hear? or he that formed the eye, doth he not con sider?

He that chastiseth na tions, shall he not rebuke : he that teacheth man knowledge?

The Lord knoweth the thoughts of men, that they are vain.

Blessed is the man whom thou shalt instruct, O Lord! and shalt teach him out of thy law

Ut mitiges ei a diebus malis : * donec fodiatur peccatori fovea.

That thou mayest give him rest from the evil days : till a pit be dug for the wicked.

Quia non repellet Dominus plebem suam : * et hæreditatem suam non derelinquet.

For the Lord will not cast off his people : neither will he forsake his own inheritance.

Quoadusque justitia convertatur in judicium; * et qui juxta illam, omnes qui recto sunt corde.

Until justice be turned into judgment : and they that are near it are all the upright in heart.

Quis consurget mihi adversus malignantes ? * aut quis stabit mecum adversus operantes iniquitatem ?

Who shall rise up for me against the evil doers ? or who shall stand with me against the workers of iniquity ?

Nisi quia Dominus adjuvit me : * paulo minus habitasset in inferno anima mea.

Unless the Lord had been my helper, my soul had almost dwelt in hell.

Si dicebam : Motus est pes meus: * misericordia tua, Domine, adjuvabat me.

If I said : My foot is moved : thy mercy, O Lord ! assisted me.

Secundum multitudinem dolorum meorum in corde meo, * consolationes tuæ lætificaverunt animam meam.

According to the multitude of my sorrows in my heart, thy comforts have given joy 'to my soul.

Numquid adhæret tibi sedes iniquitatis : * qui

Doth the seat of iniquity stick to thee : who

fingis laborem in præ-
cepto?

framest labor in com-
mandment?

Captabunt in animam
justi : * et sanguinem
innocentem condemna-
bunt.

They will hunt after
the soul of the just, and
will condemn innocent
blood.

Et factus est mihi Do-
minus in refugium, * et
Deus meus in adjuto-
rium spei meæ.

But the Lord is my
refuge : and my God
the help of my hope.

Et reddet illis iniqui-
tatem ipsorum ; et in
malitia eorum disperdet
eos : * disperdet illos
Dominus Deus noster.

And he will render to
them their iniquity : and
in their malice he will
destroy them : yea, the
Lord our God will de-
stroy them.

Here a candle is extinguished.

Ant. Captabunt in ani-
mam justi, et sanguinem
innocentem condemna-
bunt.

Ant. They will hunt
after the soul of the just,
and will condemn inno-
cent blood.

V. Locuti sunt adver-
sum me lingua dolosa.

V. They have spoken
·against me with deceit-
ful tongues.

R. Et sermonibus odii
circumdederunt me, et
expugnaverunt me gra-
tis.

R. And they have
compassed me about
with words of hatred ;
and have fought against
me without cause.

Pater noster, *secreto.*

Our Father, *privately.*

THE SEVENTH LESSON.

De Epistola beati Pauli Apostoli ad Hebræos, cap. iv. et v.

FESTINEMUS ingredi in illam requiem, ut ne in idipsum quis incidat incredulitatis exemplum. Vivus est enim sermo Dei, et efficax, et penetrabilior omni gladio ancipiti, et pertingens usque ad divisionem animæ ac spiritus, compagum quoque ac medullarum, et discretor cogitationum et intentionum cordis. Et non est ulla creatura invisibilis in conspectu ejus : omnia autem nuda et aperta sunt oculis ejus, ad quem nobis sermo. Habentes ergo Pontificem magnum, qui penetravit cœlos, Jesum filium Dei, teneamus confessionem. Non enim habemus Pontificem, qui non possit compati infirmitatibus nostris : tentatum autem

From the Epistle of St Paul the Apostle to the Hebrews, chaps. iv and v.

LET us hasten therefore to enter into that rest : lest any man fall into the same example of unbelief. For the word of God is living and effectual, and more piercing than any two-edged sword : and reaching unto the division of the soul and spirit, of the joints also, and the marrow, and is a discerner of the thoughts and intentions of the heart. Neither is there any creature invisible in his sight ; but all things are naked and open to the eyes of him, to whom our speech is. Seeing then that we have a great high-priest that hath passed into the heavens, Jesus the Son of God : let us hold fast our confession. For we have not a high-

per omnia pro similitudine, absque peccato.

priest, who cannot have compassion on our infirmities : but one tempted in all things like as we are, yet without sin.

R. Tradiderunt me in manus impiorum, et inter iniquos projecerunt me, et non pepercerunt animæ meæ : congregati sunt adversum me fortes : * Et sicut gigantes steterunt contra me.

R. They delivered me into the hands of the impious, and cast me out amongst the wicked, and spared not my life : the powerful gathered together against me : * and like giants they stood against me.

V. Alieni insurrexerunt adversum me, et fortes quæsierunt animam meam. * Et sicut, etc.

V. Strangers have risen up against me, and the mighty have sought after my soul. * And like giants.

THE EIGHTH LESSON.

ADEAMUS ergo cum fiducia ad thronum gratiæ, ut misericordiam consequamur, et gratiam inveniamus in auxilio opportuno. Omnis namque pontifex ex hominibus assumptus, pro hominibus constituitur in iis quæ sunt ad Deum, ut offerat do-

LET us go therefore with confidence to the throne of grace ; that we may obtain mercy, and find grace in seasonable aid. For every high-priest taken from among men is appointed for men in the things that appertain to God, that he may offer up

na et sacrificia pro pec-
catis : qui condolere possit iis, qui ignorant et
errant, quoniam et ipse
circumdatus est infir-
mitate. Et propterea de-
bet, quemadmodum pro
populo, ita etiam et pro
semetipso offerre pro
peccatis.

R. Jesum tradidit im-
pius summis principi-
bus sacerdotum, et se-
nioribus populi : * Pe-
trus autem sequebatur
eum a longe, ut videret
finem.

V. Adduxerunt autem
eum ad Caipham prin-
cipem sacerdotum, ubi
Scribæ et Pharisæi con-
venerant. * Petrus au-
tem, etc.

gifts and sacrifices for
sins ; who can have com-
passion on them that
are ignorant, and that
err : because he himself
also is encompassed
with infirmity : and
therefore he ought, as
for the people, so also
for himself, to offer for
sins.

R. The wicked man
betrayed Jesus to the
chief priests and an-
cients of the people : *
but Peter followed him
afar off, to see the end.

V. And they led him
to Caiphas, the high-
priest, where the Scribes
and Pharisees were met
together. * But Peter.

THE NINTH LESSON.

NEC quisquam su-
mit sibi hono-
rem, sed qui vocatur a
Deo, tamquam Aaron.
Sic et Christus non se-
metipsum clarificavit ut
Pontifex fieret, sed qui

NEITHER doth
any man take
the honor to himself,
but he that is called by
God, as Aaron was. So
also Christ did not
glorify himself to be

locutus est ad eum: Filius meus es tu, ego hodie genui te. Quemadmodum et in alio loco dicit : Tu es sacerdos in æternum, secundum ordinem Melchisedech. Qui in diebus carnis suæ preces supplicationesque ad eum, qui possit illum salvum facere a morte, cum clamore valido et lacrymis offerens, exauditus est pro sua reverentia. Et quidem cum esset Filius Dei, didicit ex iis quæ passus est obedientiam ; et consummatus, factus est omnibus obtemperantibus sibi, causa salutis æternæ, appellatus a Deo Pontifex juxta ordinem Melchisedech.

made a high-priest : but he that said to him : Thou art my Son, this day have I begotten thee. As he saith also in another place : Thou art a priest for ever, according to the order of Melchisedech. Who in the days of his flesh, offering up prayers and supplications, with a strong cry and tears, to him that was able to save him from death, was heard for his reverence. And whereas indeed he was the Son of God, he learned obedience by the things which he suffered : and being consummated, he became the cause of eternal salvation to all that obey him. Called by God a high-priest according to the order of Melchisedech.

R. Caligaverunt oculi mei a fletu meo : quia elongatus est a me, qui consolabatur me. Videte omnes populi, * Si

R. My eyes are darkened by my tears ; for he is far from me that comforted me. See, all people ! * if there be

est dolor similis sicut dolor meus.

V. O vos omnes, qui transitis per viam, attendite et videte. * Si est dolor, etc. Caligaverunt, etc.

any sorrow like to my sorrow.

V. O all ye that pass by the way! attend and see. * If there be, etc. My eyes, etc.

The Lauds.

Ant. PROPRIO Filio suo non pepercit Deus, sed pro nobis omnibus tradidit illum.

Ant. GOD spared not his own Son, but delivered him up for us all.

PSALM 50.

MISERERE mei, Deus, *p.* 230.

HAVE mercy on me, *p.* 230.

Here a candle is extinguished.

Ant. Proprio Filio suo non pepercit Deus, sed pro nobis omnibus tradidit illum.

Ant. God spared not his own Son, but delivered him up for us all.

Ant. Anxiatus est super me spiritus meus, in me turbatum est cor meum.

Ant. My spirit is in anguish within me, my heart within me is troubled.

PSALM 142.

DOMINE, exaudi orationem meam; auribus percipe obsecrationem meam in veritate tua : * exaudi me in tua justitia.

Et non intres in judicium cum servo tuo : * quia non justificabitur in conspectu tuo omnis vivens.

Quia persecutus est inimicus animam meam : * humiliavit in terra vitam meam.

Collocavit me in obscuris sicut mortuos sæculi : * et anxiatus est super me spiritus meus, in me turbatum est cor meum.

Memor fui dierum antiquorum, meditatus sum in omnibus operibus tuis : * in factis manuum tuarum meditabar.

Expandi manus meas

HEAR, O Lord! my prayer : give ear to my supplication in thy truth; hear me in thy justice.

And enter not into judgment with thy servant; for in thy sight no man living shall be justified.

For the enemy hath persecuted my soul: he hath brought down my life to the earth.

He hath made me to dwell in darkness, as those that have been dead of old: and my spirit is in anguish within me, my heart within me is troubled.

I remembered the days of old: I meditated on all thy works; I meditated on the works of thy hands.

I stretched forth my hands to thee; my soul

ad te : * anima mea sicut terra sine aqua tibi.

is as earth without water unto thee.

Velociter exaudi me, Domine : * defecit spiritus meus.

Hear me speedily, O Lord! my spirit hath fainted away.

Non avertas faciem tuam a me : * et similis ero descendentibus in lacum.

Turn not away thy face from me; lest I be like unto them that go down into the lake.

Auditam fac mihi mane misericordiam tuam : * quia in te speravi.

Cause me to hear thy mercy in the morning; for in thee have I hoped.

Notam fac mihi viam, in qua ambulem : * quia ad te levavi animam neam.

Make the way known to me wherein I should walk : for I have lifted up my soul to thee.

Eripe me de inimicis meis, Domine, ad te confugi : * doce me facere voluntatem tuam, quia Deus meus es tu.

Deliver me from my enemies, O Lord! to thee have I fled : teach me to do thy will, for thou art my God.

Spiritus tuus bonus deducet me in terram rectam : * propter nomen tuum, Domine, vivificabis me in æquitate tua.

Thy good spirit shall lead me into the right land : for thy name's sake, O Lord! thou wilt quicken me in thy justice.

Educes de tribulatione animam meam : * et in misericordia tua disperdes inimicos meos.

Thou will bring my soul out of trouble : and in thy mercy thou will destroy my enemies.

Et perdes omnes, qui tribulant animam meam : * quoniam ego servus tuus sum.

And thou wilt cut off all them that afflict my soul : for I am thy servant.

Here a candle is extinguished.

Ant. Anxiatus est super me spiritus meus, in me turbatum est cor meum.

Ant. My spirit is in anguish within me, my heart within me is troubled.

Ant. Ait latro ad latronem : Nos quidem digna factis recipimus ; hic autem quid fecit ? Memento mei, Domine, dum veneris in regnum tuum.

Ant. One thief said to the other : We indeed receive the due reward of our deeds ; but what hath this man done ? Lord ! remember me, when thou shalt come into thy kingdom.

PSALMS.

DEUS, Deus meus, *p.* 237.
Deus misereatur, *p.* 238.

O GOD, my God ! *p.* 237.
May God have mercy, *p* 238.

Here a candle is extinguished.

Ant. Ait latro ad latronem : Nos quidem digna factis recipimus ; hic autem quid fecit ? Memento mei, Domine,

Ant. One thief said to the other : We indeed receive the due reward of our deeds ; but what hath this man

dum veneris in regnum tuum.

done? Lord! remember me when thou shalt come into thy kingdom.

Ant. Cum conturbata fuerit anima mea, Domine, misericordiæ memor eris.

Ant. When my soul shall be in trouble, O Lord! thou wilt be mindful of thy mercy.

THE CANTICLE OF HABACUC, *cap.* iii.

DOMINE, audivi auditionem tuam, * et timui.

Domine, opus tuum: * in medio annorum vivifica illud.

In medio annorum notum facies: * cum iratus fueris, misericordiæ recordaberis.

Deus ab austro veniet, * et Sanctus de monte Pharan.

Operuit cœlos gloria ejus: * et laudis ejus plena est terra.

Splendor ejus ut lux erit: * cornua in manibus ejus.

Ibi abscondita est for-

O LORD! I have heard thy hearing, and was afraid.

O Lord! thy work, in the midst of the years bring it to life.

In the midst of the years thou shalt make it known: when thou art angry, thou will remember mercy.

God will come from the south, and the Holy One from Mount Pharan.

His glory covered the heavens, and the earth is full of his praise.

His brightness shall be as the light: horns are in his hands.

There is his strength

titudo ejus: * ante faciem ejus ibit mors.

Et egredietur diabolus ante pedes ejus. * Stetit, et mensus est terram.

Aspexit, et dissolvit gentes : * et contriti sunt montes sæculi.

Incurvati sunt colles mundi, * ab itineribus æternitatis ejus.

Pro iniquitate vidi tentoria Æthiopiæ : * turbabuntur pelles terræ Madian.

Numquid in fluminibus iratus es, Domine? * aut in fluminibus furo'r tuus ? vel in mari indignatio tua ?

Qui ascendes super equos tuos : * et quadrigæ tuæ salvatio.

Suscitans suscitabis arcum tuum, * juramenta tribubus quæ locutus es.

Fluvios scindes terræ

hid : death will go before his face.

And the devil shall go forth before his feet. He stood, and measured the earth.

He beheld and melted the nations; and the ancient mountains were crushed to pieces.

The hills of the world were bowed down by the journeys of his eternity.

I saw the tents of Ethiopia for their iniquity, the curtains of the land of Madian shall be troubled.

Wast thou angry, O Lord! with the rivers? or was thy wrath upon the rivers? or thy indignation in the sea?

Who wilt ride upon thy horses, and thy chariots are salvation.

Thou wilt surely take up thy bow: according to the oaths which thou hast spoken to the tribes.

Thou wilt divide the

viderunt te, et doluerunt montes : * gurges aquarum transiit.

rivers of the earth; the mountains saw thee, and were grieved, the great body of waters passed away.

Dedit abyssus vocem suam : * altitudo manus suas levavit.

The deep put forth its voice : the deep lifted up its hands.

Sol et luna steterunt in habitaculo suo, * in luce sagittarum tuarum, ibunt in splendore fulgurantis hastæ tuæ.

The sun and the moon stood still in their habitation : in the light of thy arrows, they shall go in the brightness of thy glittering spear.

In fremitu conculcabis terram : * et in furore obstupefacies gentes.

In thy anger thou wilt tread the earth under foot : in thy wrath thou wilt astonish the nations.

Egressus es in salutem populi tui, * in salutem cum Christo tuo.

Thou wentest forth for the salvation of thy people : for their salvation with thy Christ.

Percussisti caput de domo impii : * denudasti fundamentum ejus usque ad collum.

Thou struckest the head of the house of the wicked : thou hast laid bare his foundation even to the neck.

Maledixisti sceptris ejus, capiti bellatorum ejus, * venientibus ut turbo ad dispergendum me.

Thou hast cursed his sceptres, the head of his warriors, them that came out as a whirlwind to scatter me.

Exultatio eorum * sicut ejus, qui devorat pauperem in abscondito.

Viam fecisti in mari equis tuis, * in luto aquarum multarum.

Audivi, et conturbatus est venter meus ; * a voce contremuerunt labia mea.

Ingrediatur putredo in ossibus meis, * et subter me scateat.

Ut requiescam in die tribulationis : * ut ascendam ad populum accinctum nostrum.

Ficus enim non florebit, * et non erit germen in vineis.

Mentietur opus olivæ : * et arva non afferent cibum.

Abscindetur de ovili pecus : * et non erit armentum in præsepibus.

Ego autem in Domino gaudebo : * et exultabo in Deo Jesu meo.

Their joy was like that of him that devoureth the poor man in secret.

Thou madest a way in the sea for thy horses, in the mud of many waters.

I have heard, and my bowels were troubled : my lips trembled at the voice.

Let rottenness enter into my bones, and swarm under me.

That I may rest in the day of tribulation : that I may go up to our people that are girded.

For the fig-tree shall not blossom ; and there shall be no spring in the vine.

The labor of the olive-tree shall fail ; and the fields shall yield no food.

The flock shall be cut off from the fold ; and there shall be no herd in the stalls.

But I will rejoice in the Lord : and I will joy in God my Jesus.

Deus Dominus forti-tudo mea : * et ponet pedes meos quasi cervo-rum.

The Lord God is my strength : and he will make my feet like the feet of harts.

Et super excelsa mea deducet me victor * in psalmis canentem.

And he the conqueror will lead me upon my high places singing psalms.

Here a candle is extinguished.

Ant. Cum conturbata fuerit anima mea, Do-mine, misericordiæ me-mor eris.

Ant. When my sou shall be in trouble, O Lord ! thou wilt be mindful of thy mercy.

Ant. Memento mei, Domine, dum veneris in regnum tuum.

Ant. Lord ! remember me, when thou shalt come into thy kingdom.

PSALMS.

LAUDATE Domi-num de cœlis, *p.* 244.

PRAISE ye the Lord from the heavens, *p.* 244.

Cantate Domino, *p.* 245.

Sing ye to the Lord, *p.* 245.

Laudate Dominum in sanctis ejus, *p.* 247.

Praise ye the Lord in his holy places, *p.* 247.

Here a candle is extinguished.

Ant. Memento mei, Domine, dum veneris in regnum tuum.

Ant. Lord ! remem-ber me, when thou shalt come into thy kingdom.

V. Collocavit me in obscuris.

R. Sicut mortuos sæculi.

Ant. Posuerunt super caput ejus causam ipsius scriptam : Jesus Nazarenus, Rex Judæorum.

V. He hath made me to dwell in darkness.

R. As those that have been dead of old.

Ant. They put over his head his cause written : Jesus of Nazareth, the King of the Jews.

THE CANTICLE OF ZACHARY. *Luke* i.

BENEDICTUS, *p.* 248.

BLESSED be the Lord, *p.* 248.

The candle left burning at the top of the triangular candlestick is taken down while the following Ant. is said, and concealed behind the Epistle side of the altar:

Ant. Posuerunt super caput ejus causam ipsius scriptam : Jesus Nazarenus, Rex Judæorum.

Ant. They put over his head his cause written : Jesus of Nazareth, the King of the Jews.

The following is said kneeling:

CHRISTUS factus est pro nobis obediens usque ad mortem, mortem autem crucis.

CHRIST became obedient for us unto death; even the death of the cross.

Pater noster, *totum sub silentio.*

Our Father, *privately.*

The Psalm Miserere, *p.* 230, *is recited in a low voice: and in the end the following prayer, without the* Oremus.

RESPICE, quæsumus Domine. su

LOOK down, O Lord! we beseech

per hanc familiam tuam, pro qua Dominus noster Jesus Christus non dubitavit manibus tradi nocentium, et crucis subire tormentum. *Sed dicitur sub silentio:* Qui tecum vivit et regnat in unitate Spiritus sancti Deus, per omnia sæcula sæculorum. Amen.

thee, on this thy family, for which our Lord Jesus Christ was pleased to be delivered into the hands of the wicked, and to suffer the torment of the cross. *But say in a low voice:* Who with thee and the Holy Ghost liveth and reigneth, one God, world without end. Amen.

At the end of the prayer a little noise is made; the lighted candle is brought from under the Altar, and all rise and retire in silence.

GOOD FRIDAY.

MORNING OFFICE.

THE Church commemorates every day the bloody sacrifice of Jesus Christ on the cross by a true and real unbloody sacrifice, in which she offers to God the same body and blood that were given for the sins of the world. But on Good Friday she offers no sacrifice, nor is there any consecration of the Holy Eucharist; the Priest receiving the sacred Host which he had consecrated the day before. So that, in the office which is performed, instead of the Mass, she contents herself with a bare representation of the passion, and makes it her chief business to expose to the faithful Jesus Christ crucified for them. For this end she reads such Lessons and Tracts as contain predictions of his coming for their redemption, and types of his immolation on the cross, and then she reads the history of the passion, as related by St. John, to show how the Law and the prophets were verified by the Gospel.

The faithful by these Lessons are instructed in the mystery of this day, and therefore beg with the Priest the fruit and application of this passion, by praying for all sorts of persons, even *Schismatics*, *Heretics*, *Jews*, and *Pagans*. None are excluded from the suffrages of the Church on a day when Jesus Christ prayed for his persecutors, and offered his blood to his Father for the salvation of those who shed it.

Next, both Priest and people adore *Jesus Christ* crucified, expressing their adoration by kneeling thrice before they kiss the cross. The veneration of the cross is as ancient as Christianity itself. If at the bare name of Jesus every knee should bend, what feelings should arise in a Christian breast at the sight of the sacred sign of redemption? It is not to the frail materials of the cross that we pay our adoration, but to Him who on it offered for our sins the sacrifice of propitiation.

After the ceremony, the Priest brings back to the altar the body of our Lord with the same solemnity as it was carried from thence on Thursday, and finishes the office by receiving the sacred Victim that was slain this day for the redemption of mankind.

The Mass.

The Priest and his Ministers, in black vestments, go to the altar without lights and incense, and prostrate themselves before it, while the Acolytes cover it with one linen cloth. Then the Priest, with his Minister, goes up to the altar, and a reader reads the following lesson:

THE FIRST LESSON. *Osee* vi.

HÆC dicit Domi- nus: In tribula- tione sua mane consur- gent ad me. Venite, et revertamur ad Domi- num: quia ipse cepit, et sanabit nos; percutiet, et curabit nos. Vivifi- cabit nos post duos dies: in die tertia suscitabit nos, et vivemus in con- spectu ejus. Sciemus, sequemurque ut cognos- camus Dominum. Quasi diluculum præparatus est egressus ejus, et ve- niet quasi imber nobis temporaneus et seroti- nus terræ. Quid faciam tibi, Ephraim? quid fa- ciam tibi, Juda? Mise- ricordia vestra quasi nubes matutina, et qua- si ros mane pertransiens. Propter hoc dolavi in

THUS saith the Lord: In their affliction they will rise early to me. Come, and let us return to the Lord; for he hath taken us, and he will heal us: he will strike, and he will cure us. He will revive us after two days: on the third day he will raise us up, and we shall live in his sight. We shall know, and we shall follow on, that we may know the Lord. His going forth is prepared as the morning light, and he will come to us as the early and the lat- ter rain to the earth. What shall I do to thee, O Ephraim? what shall I do to thee, O Juda? Your mercy is as a morn-

prophetis, occidi eos in verbis oris mei: et judicia tua quasi lux egredientur. Quia misericordiam volui, et non sacrificium; et scientiam Dei, plus quam holocausta

ing cloud, and as the dew that goeth away in the morning. For this reason have I hewed them by the prophets, I have slain them by the words of my mouth; and thy judgments shall go forth as the light. For I desired mercy and not sacrifice: and the knowledge of God more than holocausts.

THE TRACT.

DOMINE, audivi auditum tuum, et timui; consideravi opera tua, et expavi.

LORD! I heard what thou madest me hear, and I was afraid: I considered thy works, and trembled.

V. In medio duorum animalium innotesceris: dum appropinquaverint anni, cognosceris; dum advenerit tempus, ostenderis.

V. Thou wilt appear between two animals; when the years shall be accomplished, thou wilt make thyself known: when the time shall come, thou wilt be manifested.

V. In eo dum turbata fuerit anima mea, in ira misericordiæ memor eris.

V. When my soul shall be in trouble, thou wilt remember thy mercy, even in thy wrath.

V. Deus a Libano

V. God will come

veniet, et Sanctus de monte umbroso et condenso.

V. Operuit cœlos majestas ejus, et laudis ejus plena et terra.

from Libanus, and the Holy One from the shady and dark mountain.

V. His majesty overspreads the heavens, and the earth is full of his praise.

THE COLLECT.

Oremus.
Flectamus genua.
R. Levate.

Let us pray.
Let us bend our knees.
R. Rise up.

DEUS, a quo et Judas reatus sui pœnam, et confessionis suæ latro præmium sumpsit; concede nobis tuæ propitiationis effectum: ut sicut in passione sua Jesus Christus Dominus noster diversa utrisque intulit stipendia meritorum, ita nobis ablato vetustatis errore, resurrectionis suæ gratiam largiatur. Qui tecum vivit et regnat in unitate, etc.

O GOD! from whom Judas received the punishment of his sin, and the thief the reward of his confession; grant us the effects of thy mercy; that as our Lord Jesus Christ at the time of his passion bestowed on each a different recompense of his merits, so having destroyed the old man in us, he may give us the grace of his resurrection; who liveth, etc.

THE SECOND LESSON. *Exod.* xii.

IN diebus illis: Dixit Dominus ad Moysen et Aaron in terra Ægyp-

IN those days the Lord said to Moses and Aaron in the land

ti: Mensis iste vobis principium mensium; primus erit in mensibus anni. Loquimini ad universum cœtum filiorum Israel, et dicite eis: Decima die mensis hujus tollat unusquisque agnum per familias et domos suas. Sin autem minor est numerus ut sufficere possit ad vescendum agnum, assumet vicinum suum qui junctus est domui suæ, juxta numerum animarum, quæ sufficere possunt ad esum agni. Erit autem agnus absque macula, masculus, anniculus: juxta quem ritum, tolletis et hœdum. Et servabitis eum usque ad quartam decimam diem mensis hujus, immolabitque eum universa multitudo filiorum Israel ad vesperam. Et sument de sanguine ejus, ac ponent super utrumque postem, et in superliminaribus domorum in quibus comedent illum. Et

of Egypt: This month shall be to you the beginning of months: it shall be the first in the months of the year. Speak to the whole assembly of the children of Israel, and say to them: On the tenth day of this month let every man take a lamb by their families and houses. But if the number be less than may suffice to eat the lamb, he shall take unto him his neighbor that joineth to his house, according to the number of souls which may be enough to eat the lamb. And it shall be a lamb without blemish, a male of one year; according to which rite also you shall take a kid. And you shall keep it until the fourteenth day of this month; and the whole multitude of the children of Israel shall sacrifice it in the evening, and they shall take of the blood thereof, and

edent carnes nocte illa assas igni, et azymos panes cum lactucis agrestibus. Non comedetis ex eo crudum quid, nec coctum aqua, sed tantum assum igni. Caput cum pedibus ejus et intestinis vorabitis : nec remanebit quidquam ex eo usque mane. Si quid residuum fuerit, igne comburetis. Sic autem comedetis illum : renes vestros accingetis, et calceamenta habebitis in pedibus, tenentes baculos in manibus, et comedetis *festinanter :* est enim Phase (id est transitus) Domini.

put it on upon both the side-posts and on the upper door-posts of the houses, wherein they shall eat it. And they shall eat the flesh that night roasted at the fire, and unleavened bread with wild lettuce. You shall not eat thereof, any-thing raw, nor boiled in water, but only roasted at the fire : you shall eat the head with the feet and entrails thereof. Neither shall there remain anything of it till morning. If there be anything *left,* you shall burn it with fire. And thus you shall eat it : you shall gird your reins, and you shall have shoes on your feet, holding staves in your hands : and you shall eat in haste. For it is the Phase (that is, the passage) of the Lord.

THE TRACT.

ERIPE me Domine, ab homine

DELIVER me, O Lord ! from the

malo: a viro iniquo libera me.

V. Qui cogitaverunt malitias in corde, tota die constituebant prælia.

V. Acuerunt linguas suas sicut serpentis : venenum aspidum sub labiis eorum.

V. Custodi me, Domine, de manu peccatoris; et ab hominibus iniquis libera me.

V. Qui cogitaverunt supplantare gressus meos : absconderunt superbi laqueum mihi.

V. Et funes extenderunt in laqueum pedibus meis : juxta iter scandalum posuerunt mihi.

V. Dixi Domino : Deus meus es tu; exaudi Domine vocem orationis meæ.

V. Domine, Domine, virtus salutis meæ, obumbra caput meum in die belli.

V. Ne tradas me a

evil man, rescue me from the unjust man.

V. Who have devised iniquity in their hearts, all the day long they designed battles.

V. They have sharpened their tongues like a serpent : the venom of asps is under their lips.

V. Keep me, O Lord ! from the hand of the wicked; and from unjust men deliver me.

V. Who have proposed to supplant my steps : the proud have hidden a net for me.

V. And they have stretched out cords for a snare : they have laid for me a stumbling-block by the way side.

V. I said to the Lord : Thou art my God; hear, O Lord! the voice of my supplication.

V. O Lord, O Lord, the strength of my salvation! thou hast overshadowed my head in the day of battle.

V. Give me not up, O

desiderio meo peccato-
ri : cogitaverunt adver-
sus me, ne derelinquas
me, ne unquam exal-
tentur.

V. Caput circuitus
eorum : labor labiorum
ipsorum operiet eos.

V. Verumtamen justi
confitebuntur nomini
tuo; et habitabunt recti
cum vultu tuo.

Passio Domini nostri
Jesu Christi secun-
dum Joannem. Cap.
xviii.

IN illo tempore :
Egressus est Jesus
cum discipulis suis trans
torrentem Cedron, ubi
erat hortus : in quem
introivit ipse, et disci-
puli ejus. Sciebat autem
et Judas, qui tradebat
eum, locum, quia fre-
quenter Jesus convene-
rat illuc cum discipulis
suis. Judas ergo cum
accepisset cohortem. et

Lord ! from my desire
to the wicked ; they
have plotted against me ;
do not thou forsake me
lest they should tri-
umph.

V. The head of them
compassing me about :
the labor of their lips
shall overwhelm them.

V. But as for the just,
they shall give glory to
thy name : and the up-
right shall dwell with
thy countenance.

The passion of our Lord
Jesus Christ accord-
ing to St. John. Chap.
xviii.

AT that time, Jesus
went forth with his
disciples, over the brook
of Cedron, where there
was a garden into which
he and his disciples en-
tered. Now Judas also,
who betrayed him,
knew the place ; be-
cause Jesus had often
resorted thither together
with his disciples. Ju-
das therefore having re-

a pontificibus et Phari- ceived a band of men
sæis ministros, venit il- and servants from the
luc cum làternis, et fa- chief priests and the
cibus, et armis. Jesus Pharisees, cometh thi-
itaque sciens omnia ther with lanterns and
quæ ventura erant super torches and weapons.
eum, processit, et dixit Jesus, therefore, know-
eis : Quem quæritis? ing all things that
Responderunt ei : Je- should come upon him,
sum Nazarenum. Dicit went forth and said to
eis Jesus : Ego sum. them: Whom seek ye?
Stabat autem et Judas, They answered him :
qui tradebat eum, cum Jesus of Nazareth. Je-
ipsis. Ut ergo dixit eis, sus saith to them : I am
Ego sum, abierunt re- he. And Judas also who
trorsum, et ceciderunt betrayed him, stood
in terram. Iterum ergo with him. As soon then
interrogavit eos : Quem as he had said to them :
quæritis? Illi autem I am he ; they went
dixerunt : Jesum Naza- backward, and fell to
renum. Respondit Je- the ground. Again,
sus: Dixi vobis, quia therefore, he asked
ego sum. Si ergo me them : Whom seek ye?
quæritis, sinite hos abire. And they said : Jesus of
Ut impleretur sermo Nazareth. Jesus an-
quem dixit : Quia quos swered : I have told you
dedisti mihi, non perdi- that I am he. If there-
di ex eis quemquam. fore you seek me, let
Simon ergo Petrus ha- these go away. That
bens gladium, eduxit the word might be ful-
eum, et percussit ponti- filled which he had said :
ficis servum, et abscidit Of them whom thou hast
auriculam ejus dexte- given me, I have not lost

ram. Erat autem nomen servo Malchus. Dixit ergo Jesus Petro: Mitte gladium tuum in vaginam. Calicem quem dedit mihi Pater, non bibam illum? Cohors ergo, et tribunus, et ministri Judæorum comprehenderunt Jesum, et ligaverunt eum, et adduxerunt eum ad Annam primum, erat enim socer Caiphæ, qui erat pontifex anni illius. Erat autem Caiphas, qui consilium dederat Judæis, quia expedit unum hominem mori pro populo. Sequebatur autem Jesum Simon Petrus, et alius discipulus. Discipulus autem ille erat notus pontifici, et introivit cum Jesu in atrium pontificis. Petrus autem stabat ad ostium foris. Exivit ergo discipulus alius, qui erat notus pontifici, et dixit ostiariæ, et introduxit Petrum. Dicit ergo Petro ancilla ostia-

any one. Then Simon Peter having a sword, drew it, and struck the servant of the high-priest, and cut off his right ear. And the name of the servant was Malchus. Then Jesus said to Peter: Put up thy sword into the scabbard. The cup which my Father hath given me, shall not I drink it? Then the band, and the tribune, and the servants of the Jews took Jesus, and bound him: and they led him away to Annas first, for he was father-in-law to Caiphas, who was the high-priest of that year. Now Caiphas was he who had given the counsel to the Jews, that it was expedient that one man should die for the people. And Simon Peter followed Jesus, and so did another disciple. And that disciple was known to the high-priest, and went in with Jesus into the pa-

ria : Numquid et tu ex discipulis es hominis istius? Dicit ille : Non sum. Stabant autem servi et ministri ad prunas, quia frigus erat, et calefaciebant se. Erat autem cum eis et Petrus stans, et calefaciens se.

lace of the high-priest. But Peter stood at the door without. Then the other disciple who was known to the high-priest, went out, and spoke to her that kept the door, and brought in Peter. And the maid that waited at the door, saith to Peter : Art not thou also one of this man's disciples? He saith : I am not. Now the servants and officers stood at a fire of coals ; because it was cold, and warmed themselves. And with them was Peter also standing, and warming himself.

Pontifex ergo interrogavit Jesum de discipulis suis, et de doctrina ejus. Respondit ei Jesus : Ego palam locutus sum mundo : ego semper docui in synagoga, et in templo, quo omnes Judæi conveniunt ; et in occulto locutus sum nihil. Quid me interrogas? interroga eos qui

The high-priest then asked Jesus of his disciples, and of his doctrine. Jesus answered him : I have spoken openly to the world : I have always taught in the synagogue, and in the temple, whither all the Jews resort : and in secret I have spoken nothing. Why askest thou me?

audierunt quid locutus sim ipsis: ecce hi sciunt quæ dixerim ego. Hæc autem cum dixisset, unus assistens ministrorum dedit alapam Jesu, dicens: Sic respondes pontifici? Respondit ei Jesus: Si male locutus sum, testimonium perhibe de malo; si autem bene, quid me cædis? Et misit eum Annas ligatum ad Caipham pontificem. Erat autem Simon Petrus stans, et calefaciens se. Dixerunt ergo ei: Numquid et tu ex discipulis ejus es? Negavit ille, et dixit: Non sum. Dicit ei unus ex servis pontificis, cognatus ejus cujus abscidit Petrus auriculam: Nonne ego te vidi in horto cum illo? Iterum ergo negavit Petrus, et statim gallus cantavit. Adducunt ergo Jesum a Caipha in prætorium. Erat autem mane: et ipsi non introierunt in prætorium,

ask them who have heard what I have spoken to them : behold they know what things I have said. And when he had said these things, one of the officers standing by, gave Jesus a blow, saying: Answerest thou the high-priest so? Jesus answered him: If I have spoken evil, give testimony of the evil : but if well, why strikest thou me? And Annas sent him bound to Caiphas the high-priest. And Simon Peter was standing and warming himself. They said therefore to him : Art not thou also one of his disciples? He denied it and said : I am not. One of the servants of the high-priest, a kinsman to him whose ear Peter cut off, saith to him : Did not I see thee in the garden with him? Then Peter again denied, and immediately the cock crowed. Then they led Jesus from Caiphas to

ut non contaminarentur, sed ut manducarent Pascha. Exivit ergo Pilatus ad eos foras, et dixit: Quam accusationem affertis adversus hominem hunc? Responderunt, et dixerunt ei: Si non esset hic malefactor, non tibi tradidissemus eum. Dixit ergo eis Pilatus: Accipite eum vos, et secundum legem vestram judicate eum. Dixerunt ergo ei Judæi: Nobis non licet interficere quemquam. Ut sermo Jesu impleretur, quem dixit, significans qua morte esset moriturus. Introivit ergo iterum in prætorium Pilatus, et vocavit Jesum, et dixit ei: Tu es rex Judæorum? Respondit Jesus: A temetipso hoc dicis, an alii dixerunt tibi de me? Respondit Pilatus: Numquid ego Judæus sum? Gens tua, et pontifices tradiderunt te mihi. Quid fecisti? Respondit Jesus: Reg-

the governor's hall. And it was morning: and they went not into the hall, that they might not be defiled, but that they might eat the passover. Pilate therefore went out to them, and said: What accusation bring you against this man? They answered and said to him: If he were not a malefactor, we would not have delivered him up to thee. Pilate then said to them: Take him you, and judge him according to your law. The Jews therefore said to him: It is not lawful for us to put any man to death. That the word of Jesus might be fulfilled which he said, signifying what death he should die. Pilate therefore went into the hall again, and called Jesus, and said to him: Art thou the king of the Jews? Jesus answered: Sayest thou this thing of thyself, or have others told it thee of

num meum non est de
hoc mundo. Si ex hoc
mundo esset regnum
meum, ministri mei uti-
que decertarent, ut non
traderer Judæis: nunc
autem regnum meum
non est hinc. Dixit ita-
que ei Pilatus : Ergo rex
es tu ? Respondit Jesus :
Tu dicis quia rex sum
ego. Ego in hoc natus
sum, et ad hoc veni in
mundum, ut testimoni-
um perhibeam veritati.
Omnis qui est ex veri-
tate, audit vocem meam.
Dicit ei Pilatus : Quid
est veritas ? Et cum hoc
dixisset, iterum exivit
ad Judæos, et dicit eis :
Ego nullam invenio in
eo causam. Est autem
consuetudo vobis, ut
unum dimittam vobis in
Pascha : vultis ergo di-
mittam vobis regem
Judæorum ? Clamave-
runt ergo rursum om-
nes, dicentes : Non hunc,

me ? Pilate answered:
Am I a Jew ? Thy own
nation, and the chief
priests, have delivered
thee up to me. What
hast thou done ? Jesus
answered : My kingdom
is not of this world.
If my kingdom were
of this world, my ser-
vants would certainly
strive that I should not
be delivered to the Jews :
but now my kingdom is
not from hence. Pilate
therefore said to him :
Art thou a king then ?
Jesus answered : Thou
sayest that I am a king.
For this was I born, and
for this came I into the
world, that I should
give testimony to the
truth. Every one that
is of the truth, heareth
my voice. Pilate sayeth
to him : What is truth ?
And when he had said
this, he went out again
to the Jews, and saith
to them : I find no cause
in him. But you have
a custom that I should

sed Barabbam. Erat autem Barabbas latro.

Tunc ergo apprehendit Pilatus Jesum, et flagellavit. Et milites plectentes coronam de spinis, imposuerunt capiti ejus: et veste purpurea circumdederunt eum. Et veniebant ad eum, et dicebant: Ave, rex Judæorum; et dabant ei alapas. Exivit ergo iterum Pilatus foras, et dicit eis: Ecce adduco vobis eum foras, ut cognoscatis quia nullam invenio in eo causam. (Exivit ergo Jesus portans coronam spineam, et purpureum vestimentum.) Et dicit eis: Ecce homo. Cum ergo vidissent eum pontifices et ministri, clamabant, dicentes:

release one unto you at the passover: will you therefore that I release unto you the king of the Jews? Then cried they all again, saying: Not this man, but Barabbas. Now Barabbas was a robber.

Then, therefore, Pilate took Jesus, and scourged him. And the soldiers plaiting a crown of thorns, put it upon his head: and they put on him a purple garment, and they came to him, and said: Hail, king of the Jews! And they gave him blows. Pilate, therefore, went forth again, and saith to them: Behold I bring him forth to you, that you may know that I find no cause in him. So Jesus came forth bearing the crown of thorns, and the purple garment. And he saith to them: Behold the man. When the chief priests, therefore, and

Crucifige, crucifige eum. Dicit eis Pilatus: Accipite eum vos, et crucifigite: ego enim non invenio in eo causam. Responderunt ei Judæi: Nos legem habemus, et secundum legem debet mori, quia Filium Dei se fecit. Cum ergo audisset Pilatus hunc sermonem, magis timuit. Et ingressus est prætorium iterum, et dixit ad Jesum: Unde es tu? Jesus autem responsum non dedit ei. Dicit ergo ei Pilatus: Mihi non loqueris? nescis quia potestatem habeo crucifigere te, et potestatem habeo dimittere te? Respondit Jesus: Non haberes potestatem adversum me ullam, nisi tibi datum esset desuper. Propterea qui me tradidit tibi, majus peccatum habet. Et exinde quærebat Pilatus dimittere eum. Judæi autem clamabant, dicentes: Si hunc dimittis,

the officers had seen him, they cried out, saying: Crucify him, crucify him. Pilate saith to them: Take him you, and crucify him; for I find no cause in him. The Jews answered him: We have a law; and according to the law he ought to die, because he made himself the Son of God. When Pilate therefore had heard this saying, he feared the more. And he entered into the hall again, and he said to Jesus: Whence art thou? But Jesus gave him no answer. Pilate therefore said to him: Speakest thou not to me? knowest thou not that I have power to crucify thee, and I have power to release thee? Jesus answered: Thou shouldst not have any power against me, unless it were given thee from above. Therefore he that hath delivered me to thee, hath the greater

non es amicus Cæsaris: omnis enim qui se regem facit, contradicit Cæsari.

Pilatus autem cum audisset hos sermones, adduxit foras Jesum, et sedit pro tribunali in loco qui dicitur Lithostrotos, hebraice autem Gabbatha. Erat autem Parasceve paschæ, hora quasi sexta. Et dicit Judæis: Ecce rex vester. Illi autem clamabant: Tolle, tolle, crucifige eum. Dicit eis Pilatus: Regem vestrum crucifigam? Responderunt pontifices: Non habemus regem nisi Cæsarem. Tunc ergo tradidit eis illum ut crucifigeretur. Susceperunt autem Jesum, et eduxerunt. Et bajulans sibi crucem, exivit in eum qui dicitur Calvariæ locum, he-

sin. And from thenceforth Pilate sought to release him. But the Jews cried out, saying: If thou release this man, thou art not Cæsar's friend. For whosoever maketh himself a king, speaketh against Cæsar. Now when Pilate had heard these words, he brought Jesus forth, and sat down in the judgment-seat, in the place that is called the Pavement, and in Hebrew, Gabbatha. And it was the parasceve of the passover, about the sixth hour, and he saith to the Jews: Behold your king. But they cried out: Away with him, away with him, crucify him. Pilate saith to them: Shall I crucify your king? The chief-priests answered: We have no king but Cæsar. Then, therefore, he delivered him to them to be crucified. And they took Jesus, and led

braice autem Golgotha: him forth. And bearing his own cross, he went forth to that place which is called Calvary, but in Hebrew, Golgotha; where they crucified him, and with him two others, one on each side, and Jesus in the midst. And Pilate wrote a title also, and he put it upon the cross. And the writing was, Jesus of Nazareth, the King of the Jews. The title, therefore, many of the Jews did read, because the place where Jesus was crucified was nigh to the city: and it was written in Hebrew, in Greek, and in Latin. Then the chiefpriest of the Jews said to Pilate: Write not, the King of the Jews; but that he said, I am the King of the Jews. Pilate answered: What I have written, I have written. Then the soldiers, when they had crucified him, took his garments (and they made four parts, to

ubi crucifixerunt eum, et cum eo alios duos, hinc et hinc, medium autem Jesum. Scripsit autem et titulum Pilatus, et posuit super crucem. Erat autem scriptum: Jesus Nazarenus, Rex Judæorum. Hunc ergo titulum multi Judæorum legerunt; quia prope civitatem erat locus, ubi crucifixus est Jesus. Et erat scriptum hebraice, græce, et latine. Dicebant ergo Pilato pontifices Judæorum: Noli scribere, Rex Judæorum; sed quia ipse dixit, Rex sum Judæorum. Respondit Pilatus: Quod scripsi, scripsi. Milites ergo cum crucifixissent eum, acceperunt vestimenta ejus (et fecerunt quatuor partes, unicuique militi partem) et tunicam. Erat autem tunica inconsutilis, desuper contexta per totum. Dixerunt ergo ad invicem

Non scindamus eam, sed sortiamur de illa cujus sit. Ut Scriptura impleretur, dicens: Partiti sunt vestimenta mea sibi, et in vestem meam miserunt sortem. Et milites quidem hæc fecerunt. Stabant autem juxta crucem Jesu mater ejus, et soror matris ejus Maria Cleophæ, et Maria Magdalene. Cum vidisset ergo Jesus matrem, et discipulum stantem, quem diligebat, dicit matri suæ : Mulier, ecce filius tuus. Deinde dicit discipulo : Ecce mater tua. Et ex illa hora accepit eam discipulus in sua. Postea sciens Jesus quia omnia consummata sunt, ut consummaretur Scriptura, dixit : Sitio. Vas ergo erat positum aceto, plenum. Illi autem spongiam plenam aceto, hyssopo circumponentes, obtulerunt ori ejus. Cum ergo accepisset Jesus acetum, dixit : Con-

every soldier a part) and also his coat. Now the coat was without seam, woven from the top throughout. They said then one to another: Let us not cut it, but let us cast lots for it, whose it shall be : that the Scripture might be fulfilled which saith : They have parted my garments among them, and upon my vesture they have cast lots. And the soldiers did indeed these things. Now there stood by the cross of Jesus, his mother, and his mother's sister, Mary of Cleophas, and Mary Magdalene. When Jesus therefore saw his mother and the disciple standing, whom he loved, he saith to his mother: Woman ! behold thy son. After that, he saith to the disciple : Behold thy mother. And from that hour the disciple took her to his own. Afterwards Jesus knowing

summatum est. Et in-
clinato capite, tradidit
spiritum.

that all things were now
accomplished, that the
Scripture might be ful-
filled, said: I thirst.
Now there was a vessel
set there full of vinegar.
And they, putting a
sponge full of vinegar
about hyssop, offered it
to his mouth. When Je-
sus, therefore, had taken
the vinegar, he said : It
is consummated. And
bowing his head, he
gave up the ghost.

Here all kneel, and pause a little, to meditate on the redemption of mankind.

JUDÆI ergo (quoni-
am parasceve erat)
ut non remanerent in
cruce corpora sabbato
(erat enim magnus dies
ille sabbati), rogaverunt
Pilatum ut frangerentur
eorum crura, et tolleren-
tur. Venerunt ergo mi-
lites: et primi quidem
fregerunt crura et alte-
rius qui crucifixus est
cum eo. Ad Jesum
autem cum venissent,
ut viderunt eum jam
mortuum, non fregerunt

THEN the Jews (be-
cause it was the
parasceve), that the bo-
dies might not remain
upon the cross on the
Sabbath-day (for that
was a great Sabbath-
day), besought Pilate
that their legs might be
broken, and that they
might be taken away.
The soldiers, therefore,
came; and they broke
the legs of the first, and
of the other that was
crucified with him. But

ejus crura: sed unûs militum lancea latus ejus aperuit, et continuo exivit sanguis et aqua. Et qui vidit, testimonium perhibuit, et verum est testimonium ejus. Et ille scit quia vera dicit: ut et vos credatis. Facta sunt enim hæc, ut Scriptura impleretur: Os non comminuetis ex eo. Et iterum alia Scriptura dicit: Videbunt in quem transfixerunt.

after they were come to Jesus, when they saw that he was already dead, they did not break his legs. But one of the soldiers opened his side with a spear, and immediately there came out blood and water. And he that saw it gave testimony, and his testimony is true. And he knoweth that he saith true, that you also may believe. For these things were done that the Scripture might be fulfilled : You shall not break a bone of him. And again another Scripture saith : They shall look on him whom they pierced.

Here Munda cor meum *is said as at p.* 19, *but the blessing is not asked, nor are lights used, as in other Gospels; and the Priest at the end kisses not the book.*

POST hæc autem rogavit Pilatum Joseph ab Arimathæa (eo quod esset discipulus Jesu, occultus autem propter metum Judæorum) ut tolleret corpus Jesu. Et permisit Pila-

AND after these things, Joseph of Arimathea (because he was a disciple of Jesus, but secretly for fear of the Jews) besought Pilate that he might take away the body of Jesus.

Good Friday.

tus. Venit ergo, et tulit corpus Jesu. Venit autem et Nicodemus, qui venerat ad Jesum nocte primum, ferens mixturam myrrhæ et aloes, quasi libras centum. Acceperunt ergo corpus Jesu, et ligaverunt illud linteis cum aromatibus, sicut mos est Judæis sepelire. Erat autem in loco, ubi crucifixus est, hortus; et in horto monumentum novum, in quo nondum quisquam positus erat. Ibi ergo propter Parasceven Judæorum, quia juxta erat monumentum, posuerunt Jesum.

And Pilate gave him leave. He came therefore and took away the body of Jesus. And Nicodemus also came, he who at the first came to Jesus by night, bringing a mixture of myrrh and aloes, about a hundred pound weight. They took therefore the body of Jesus, and wrapt it in linen clothes with the spices, as the manner of the Jews is to bury. Now there was a garden in the place where he was crucified; and in the garden a new sepulchre, wherein no man yet had been laid. Therefore, because of the parasceve of the Jews, they laid Jesus there; for the sepulchre was nigh at hand.

Then the Priest, at the Epistle-corner, says the following prayers:

OREMUS, dilectissimi nobis, pro Ecclesia sancta Dei : ut eam Deus et Dominus noster pacificare. adu-

LET us pray, beloved brethren! for the holy Church of God; that our God and Lord will be pleased to give

nare, et custodire dignetur toto orbe terrarum : subjiciens ei principatus, et potestates : detque nobis quietam et tranquillam vitam degentibus, glorificare Deum Patrem omnipotentem.

it peace, maintain it in union, and preserve it over the earth ; subjecting to it the princes and potentates of the world ; and grant us, who live in peace and tranquillity, grace to glorify God the Father Almighty.

Oremus.
Flectamus genua.
R. Levate.

OMNIPOTENS sempiterne Deus, qui gloriam tuam omnibus in Christo gentibus revelasti : custodi ópera misericordiæ tuæ ; ut Ecclesia tua toto orbe diffusa, stabili fide in confessione tui nominis perseveret. Per eundem Dominum nostrum Jesum Christum, etc.

R. Amen.
Oremus et pro beatissimo Papa nostro N., ut Deus et Dominus noster, qui elegit eum in ordine Episcopatus, salvum atque incolumem custo-

Let us pray.
Let us bend our knees.
R. Rise up.

ALMIGHTY and everlasting God! who, by Christ, hast revealed thy glory to all nations ; preserve the works of thy mercy ; that thy Church, spread over the whole world, may persevere with a constant faith in the confession of thy name ; through the same Lord Jesus Christ, etc.

R. Amen.
Let us pray also for our Holy Father Pope N., that our Lord God, who elected him to the order of the Episcopacy, will preserve him in

diat Ecclesiæ suæ sanctæ, ad regendum populum sanctum Dei.

health and safety, for the good of his holy Church, to govern the holy people of God.

Oremus.
Flectamus genua.
R. Levate.

Let us pray.
Let us bend our knees.
R. Rise up.

OMNIPOTENS sempiterne Deus, cujus judicio universa fundantur; respice propitius ad preces nostras, et electum nobis Antistitem tua pietate conserva; ut Christiana plebs, quæ te gubernatur auctore, sub tanto Pontifice, credulitatis suæ meritis augeatur. Per Dominum nostrum Jesum Christum, etc.

ALMIGHTY and everlasting God! by whose judgment all things are founded; mercifully regard our prayers, and by thy goodness preserve our Bishop, chosen for us; that the Christian people, who are governed by thy authority, may increase the merits of their faith under so great a Prelate; through our Lord Jesus Christ, etc.

R. Amen.

Oremus et pro omnibus Episcopis, Presbyteris, Diaconibus, Subdiaconibus, Acolythis, Exorcistis, Lectoribus, Ostiariis, Confessoribus, Virginibus, Viduis, et pro omni populo sancto Dei.

R. Amen.

Let us pray also for all Bishops, Priests, Deacons, Sub-Deacons, Acolytes, Exorcists, Readers, Porters, Confessors, Virgins, Widows. and for all the holy people of God.

Oremus.
Flectamus genua.
R. Levate.

OMNIPOTENS sempiterne Deus, cujus spiritu totum corpus Ecclesiæ sanctificatur et regitur : exaudi nos pro universis ordinibus supplicantes ; ut gratiæ tuæ munere, ab omnibus tibi gradibus fideliter serviatur. Per Dominum nostrum, . . . in unitate ejusdem, etc.

R. Amen.

Oremus et pro catechumenis nostris : ut Deus et Dominus noster adaperiat aures præcordiorum ipsorum, januamque misericordiæ : ut per lavacrum regenerationis accepta remissione omnium peccatorum, et ipsi inveniantur in Christo Jesu Domino nostro.

Oremus.
Flectamus genua.
R. Levate.

Let us pray.
Let us bend our knees.
R. Rise up.

ALMIGHTY and everlasting God ! by whose spirit the whole body of the church is sanctified and governed ; hear our prayers for all orders ; that, by the assistance of thy grace, thou mayest be faithfully served by all degrees ; through our Lord, . . . in the unity of the same, etc.

R. Amen.

Let us pray also for our catechumens ; that our Lord God will open the ears of their hearts, and the gate of his mercy ; that having received by the laver of regeneration the remission of all their sins, they also may belong to our Lord Jesus Christ.

Let us pray.
Let us bend our knees.
R. Rise up.

OMNIPOTENS sempiterne Deus, qui Ecclesiam tuam nova semper prole fœcundas : auge fidem et intellectum catechumenis nostris ; ut renati fonte baptismatis, adoptionis tuæ filiis aggregentur. Per Dominum nostrum, etc.

R. Amen.

Oremus, dilectissimi nobis, Deum Patrem omnipotentem, ut cunctis mundum purget erroribus, morbos auferat, famem depellat, aperiat carceres, vincula dissolvat, peregrinantibus reditum, infirmantibus sanitatem, navigantibus portum salutis indulgeat.

Oremus.
Flectamus genua.
R. Levate.

OMNIPOTENS sempiterne Deus, mœstorum consolatio,

ALMIGHTY and everlasting God! who always makest thy Church fruitful in new children ; increase the faith and understanding of our catechumens ; that being regenerated in the waters of baptism, they may be admitted into the society of thy adopted children ; through our Lord.

R. Amen.

Let us pray, beloved brethren, to God the Father Almighty, that he will purge the world of all errors, cure diseases, drive away famine, open prisons, break chains, grant a safe return to travellers, health to the sick, and a secure haven to such as are at sea.

Let us pray.
Let us bend our knees.
R. Rise up.

ALMIGHTY and everlasting God! the comfort of the af·

laborantium fortitudo; perveniant ad te preces de quacumque tribulatione clamantium; ut omnes sibi in necessitatibus suis misericordiam tuam gaudeant affuisse. Per Dominum nostrum, etc.

R. Amen.

Oremus et pro hæreticis et schismaticis : ut Deus et Dominus noster eruat eos ab erroribus universis; et ad sanctam matrem Ecclesiam Catholicam atque Apostolicam revocare dignetur.

Oremus.
Flectamus genua.
R. Levate.

OMNIPOTENS sempiterne Deus, qui salvas omnes, et neminem vis perire : respice ad animas diabolica fraude deceptas, ut omni hæretica pravitate deposita, errantium corda resipiscant, et ad veritatis tuæ redeant uni-

flicted, and the strength of those that labor; let the prayers of those that call upon thee in any trouble be heard by thee ; that all may, with joy, find the effects of thy mercy in their necessities; through our Lord.

R. Amen.

Let us pray also for heretics and schismatics ; that our Lord God will be pleased to deliver them from all their errors, and recall them to our holy mother the Catholic and Apostolic Church.

Let us pray.
Let us bend our knees.
R. Rise up.

ALMIGHTY and everlasting God! who savest all, and wilt have no man perish; look on the souls that are seduced by the deceit of the devil, that the hearts of those who err, having laid aside all heretical malice, may repent and

tatem. Per Dominum nostrum, etc.

R. Amen.

Oremus et pro perfidis Judæis : ut Deus et Dominus noster auferat velamen de cordibus eorum ; ut et ipsi agnoscant Jesum Christum Dominum nostrum.

Non respondetur Amen, *sed statim dicitur :*

Omnipotens sempiterne Deus, qui etiam Judaicam perfidiam a tua misericordia non repellis : exaudi preces nostras, quas pro illius populi obcæcatione · deferimus ; ut agnita veritatis tuæ luce, quæ Christus est, a suis tenebris eruantur. Per eundem Dominum nostrum, etc.

R. Amen.

Oremus et pro Paganis : ut Deus omnipotens auferat iniquitatem a cordibus eorum ; ut, relictis idolis suis,.conver-

return to the unity of thy truth ; through our Lord.

R. Amen.

Let us pray also for the perfidious Jews ; that our Lord God will withdraw the veil from their hearts ; that they also may acknowledge our Lord Jesus Christ.

Amen *is here omitted.*

Almighty and everlasting God ! who denyest not thy mercy even to the perfidious Jews ; hear our prayers, which we pour forth for the blindness of that people : that by acknowledging the light of thy truth, which is Christ, they may be brought out of their darkness, through the same Lord.

R. Amen.

Let us pray also for the Pagans : that Almighty God will take iniquity out of their hearts : that quitting

tantur ad Deum vivum et verum, et unicum Filium ejus Jesum Christum Deum et Dominum nostrum.

their idols, they may be converted to the true and living God, and his only Son Jesus Christ, our God and Lord.

Oremus.
Flectamus genua.
R. Levate.

Let us pray.
Let us bend our knees.
R. Rise up.

OMNIPOTENS sempiterne Deus, qui non mortem peccatorum, sed vitam semper inquiris: suscipe propitius orationem nostram, et libera eos ab idolorum cultura; et aggrega Ecclesiæ tuæ sanctæ, ad laudem et gloriam nominis tui. Per Dominum nostrum, etc. Per eundem.
R. Amen.

ALMIGHTY and everlasting God! who seekest not the death but the life of sinners; mercifully hear our prayers, and deliver them from the worship of idols; and for the praise and glory of thy name, admit them into thy holy Church; through our Lord.
R. Amen.

After the prayers, the Priest puts off his vestment, and taking from the altar the cross covered with a veil, he goes to the Epistle corner, where he uncovers the top of it, and shows it to the people, singing the Antiphon:

ECCE lignum crucis,

BEHOLD the wood of the cross,

Then the Deacon and Sub-deacon join with him in singing the rest:

IN quo Salus mundi pependit.

ON which the Salvation of the world was hanged.

Good Friday.

VENITE, adore-
mus.

COME, let us
adore.

From thence the Priest proceeds to the right side of the altar, where he uncovers the right arm of the cross, singing a second time, Ecce lignum, as before. Lastly, he goes to the middle of the altar, and uncovers the whole cross, singing a third time, Ecce lignum, as before. After which he carries it to a place prepared before the altar, where he adores, first himself, and then the clergy and laity, all kneeling thrice on both knees, and kissing the feet of the crucifix. What follows may be sung wholly or in part.

During the adoration, two chanters in the middle of the choir sing the following verses:

POPULE meus, quid feci tibi? aut in quo contristavi te? responde mihi.

MY people! what have I done to thee? Or in what have I grieved thee? Answer me.

V. Quia eduxi te de terra Ægypti, parasti crucem Salvatori tuo.

V. Because I brought thee out of the land of Egypt: thou hast prepared a cross for thy Saviour.

One side of the choir sings:

Agios o Theos.

Holy God.

The other side answers:

Sanctus Deus.

Holy God.

The first side:

Agios ischyros.

Holy and strong God.

The second side:

Sanctus fortis.

Holy and strong God.

The first side:

Agios athanatos, eleison imas.

Holy and immortal God, have mercy on us.

Mass.

The second side :

Sanctus immortalis, miserere nobis.

Holy and immortal God! have mercy on us.

After this, two of the second side sing :

V. QUIA eduxi te per desertum quadraginta annis, et manna cibavi te, et introduxi te in terram satis bonam, parasti crucem Salvatori tuo.

V. BECAUSE I led thee through the desert forty years and fed thee with manna and brought thee into an excellent land ; thou hast prepared a cross for thy Saviour.

Then Agios o Theos *is repeated as before, and two of the first side sing :*

V. QUID ultra debui facere tibi, et non feci? Ego quidem plantavi te vineam meam speciosissimam ; et tu facta es mihi nimis amara : aceto namque sitim meam potasti, et lancea perforasti latus Salvatori tuo.

V. WHAT more should I have done to thee, and have not done? I have planted thee for my most beautiful vineyard : and thou hast proved very bitter to me : for in my thirst thou gavest me vinegar to drink ; and with a spear thou hast pierced the side of thy Saviour.

Agios o Theos *is repeated as before—not sung.*

The following verses are sung alternately by the two chanters on each side of the choir. Both sides repeat after each verse, Popule meus, etc., *p* 366.

V. EGO propter te flagellavi Ægyptum cum primo-

V. FOR thy sake I scourged Egypt with her first-born; and

genitis suis ; et tu me fla-gellatum tradidisti.

V. Ego eduxi te de Ægypto, demerso Pharaone in Mare Rubrum ; et tu me tradidisti principibus sacerdotum.

V. Ego ante te aperui mare ; et tu aperuisti lancea latus meum.

V. Ego ante te præivi in columna nubis ; et tu me duxisti ad prætorium Pilati.

V. Ego te pavi manna per desertum ; et tu me cecidisti alapis et flagellis.

V. Ego te potavi aqua salutis de petra ; et tu me potasti felle et aceto.

V. Ego propter te Chananæorum reges percussi ; et tu percussisti arundine caput meum.

V. Ego dedi tibi scep-

thou hast delivered me to be scourged.

V. I brought thee out of Egypt, having drowned Pharao in the Red Sea ; and thou hast delivered me over to the chief priests.

V. I opened the sea before thee ; and thou with a spear hast opened my side.

V. I went before thee in a pillar of the cloud ; and thou hast brought me to the palace of Pilate.

V. I fed thee with manna in the desert ; and thou hast beaten me with buffets and scourges.

V. I gave thee wholesome water to drink out of the rock ; and thou hast given me gall and vinegar.

V. For thy sake I struck the kings of the Chanaanites ; and thou hast struck my head with a reed.

V. I gave thee a royal

trum regale; et tu dedisti capiti meo spineam coronam.

V. Ego te exaltavi magna virtute; et tu me suspendisti in patibulo crucis.

sceptre; and thou hast given me a crown of thorns.

V. I have exalted thee with great strength; and thou hast hanged me on the gibbet of the cross.

Both sides repeat Popule meus, *and then sing the following Antiphon.*

Ant. CRUCEM tuam adoramus Domine, et sanctam resurrectionem tuam laudamus, et glorificamus: ecce enim propter lignum venit gaudium in universo mundo. *Ps.* 66. Deus misereatur nostri, et benedicat nobis: illuminet vultum suum super nos, et misereatur nostri. Crucem tuam, etc.

Ant. WE adore thy cross, O Lord! and we praise and glorify thy holy resurrection: for by the wood of the cross the whole earth is filled with joy. *Ps.* May God have mercy on us and bless us; may his countenance shine upon us, and may he have mercy on us. We adore, etc.

After this is sung the versicle Crux fidelis, *with the hymn* Pange lingua gloriosi, *and after each verse is repeated* Crux fidelis *or* Dulce lignum, *in the following manner:*

Crux fidelis, inter omnes
Arbor una nobilis:
Nulla silva talem profert,
Fronde, flore, germine.
Dulce lignum, dulces clavos,
Dulce pondus sustinet.

The same in English.

O faithful cross! O noblest tree!
In all our woods there' none like thee:

No earthly groves, no shady bowers,
Produce such leaves, such fruit, such flowers
Sweet are the nails, and sweet the wood,
That bears a weight so sweet and good.

THE HYMN.

Pange, lingua, gloriosi
Lauream certaminis,
Et super crucis trophæo
Dic triumphum nobilem ;
Qualiter Redemptor orbis,
Immolatus vicerit.

Crux fidelis *is repeated as far as* Dulce lignum.

De parentis protoplasti
Fraude factor condolens :
Quando pomi noxialis
In necem morsu ruit :
Ipse lignum tunc notavit,
Damna ligni ut solveret.

Dulce lignum *is repeated.*

Hoc opus nostræ salutis
Ordo depoposcerat :
Multiformis proditoris
Ars ut artem falleret ;
Et medelam ferret inde,
Hostis unde læserat.

Crux fidelis *is repeated.*

Quando venit ergo sacri
Plenitudo temporis,
Missus est ab arce Patris
Natus, orbis conditor ;
Atque ventre virginali,
Carne amictus, prodiit.

Dulce lignum *is repeated.*

Mass.

Vagit infans inter arcta
Conditus præsepia:
Membra pannis involuta
Virgo mater alligat,
Et Dei manus pedesque
Stricta cingit fascia.

     Crux fidelis *is repeated.*

Lustra sex qui jam peregit,
Tempus implens corporis,
Sponte libera Redemptor
Passioni deditus,
Agnus in crucis levatur
Immolandus stipite.

     Dulce lignum *is repeated.*

Felle potus ecce languet;
Spina, clavi, lancea,
Mite corpus perforarunt;
Unda manat et cruor:
Terra, pontus, astra, mundus
Quo lavantur flumine!

     Crux fidelis *is repeated.*

Flecte ramos, arbor alta,
Tensa laxa viscera,
Et rigor lentescat ille,
Quem dedit nativitas:
Et superni membra Regis
Tende miti stipite.

     Dulce lignum *is repeated.*

Sola digna tu fuisti
Ferre mundi victimam;
Atque portum præparare
Arca mundo naufrago,

Quam sacer cruor perunxit,
Fusus Agni corpore.

Crux fidelis *is repeated*.

Sempiterna sit beatæ
Trinitati gloria;
Æqua Patri, Filioque,
Par decus Paraclito :
Unius, Trinique nomen
Laudet universitas.   **Amen.**

Dulce lignum *is repeated*.

The same in English.

Sing, O my tongue! devoutly sing
The glorious laurels of our King ;
Sing the triumphant victory
Gained on a cross erected high ;
Where man's Redeemer yields his breath,
And, dying, conquers hell and death.

With pity our Creator saw
His noble work transgress his law ;
When our first parents rashly eat
The fatal tree's forbidden meat ;
He then resolved the cross' wood
Should make that wood's sad damage good.

By this wise method God designed
From sin and death to save mankind ;
Superior art with love combines,
And arts of Satan countermines ;
And where the traitor gave the wound,
There healing remedies are found.

When the full time decreed above
Was come to show this work of love,
Th' eternal Father sends his Son,
The world's Creator, from the throne;
Who on our earth, this vale of tears,
Cloth'd with a virgin's flesh appears.

Thus God made man an infant lies,
And in the manger weeping cries;
His sacred limbs, by Mary bound,
The poorest tattered rags surround;
And God incarnate's feet and hands
Are closely tied with swathing bands.

Full thirty years were freely spent
In this our mortal banishment;
And then the Son of Man decreed
For the lost sons of men to bleed;
And on the cross a victim laid,
The solemn expiation made.

Gall was his drink; his flesh they tear
With thorns and nails; a cruel spear
Pierces his sides; from whence a flood
Streams forth of water mixed with blood—
With what a tide are washed again
The sinful earth, the stars and main!

Bend, tow'ring tree! thy branches bend,
Thy native stubbornness suspend;
Let not stiff nature use its force,
To weaker sap have now recourse;
With softest arms receive thy load,
And gently bear our dying God.

On thee alone the Lamb was slain
That reconcil'd the world again ;
And when on raging seas was tost
The shipwreck'd world and mankind lost,
Besprinkled with his sacred gore,
Thou safely brought'st them to the shore.

All glory to the sacred Three,
One undivided Deity ;
To Father, Holy Ghost, and Son,
Be equal praise and homage done ;
Let the whole universe proclaim
Of one and three the glorious name. Amen.

*When the adoration of the cross is almost finished, the candles upon
the altar are lighted; and after the adoration, the cross is
placed again upon the altar. Then the Priest with his Ministers and Clergy goes in procession to the place where the B. Sacrament was put the day before : from whence he brings It back
in the same order as It was carried thither. During the procession is sung the hymn* Vexilla regis prodeunt, *as at p.* 107.

*The Priest, having come back to the altar, places the holy Sacrament
on it, fumes It with incense, on his knees, and lays the sacred
Host on the corporal. Then wine and water are put into the
chalice, which is set on the altar, and the incense is put into the
censer : with which the Priest fumes the sacred Host and the
offering of wine and water, saying:*

INCENSUM istud, a
te benedictum, as-
cendat ad te, Domine;
et descendat super nos
misericordia tua.

MAY this incense,
which thou hast
blest, ascend to thee, O
Lord! and may thy mer-
cy descend upon us.

Then he fumes the altar, saying:

DIRIGATUR, Do-
mine, oratio mea,
sicut incensum in con-

LET my prayer, O
Lord ! be directed
as incense in thy sight :

spectu tuo : elevatio manuum mearum sacrificium vespertinum. Pone, Domine, custodiam ori meo, et ostium circumstantiæ labiis meis : ut non declinet cor meum in verba malitiæ, ad excusandas excusationes in peccatis.

the lifting up of my hands, an evening sacrifice. Set a watch, O Lord! before my mouth, and a door round about my lips; that my heart may not incline to evil words, to make excuses in sins.

When he gives the censer to the Deacon, he says:

ACCENDAT in nobis Dominus ignem sui amoris, et flammam æternæ charitatis. Amen.

MAY the Lord kindle in us the fire of his love, and the flame of eternal charity. Amen.

After this, he goes down from the altar on the Epistle side, and there washes his hands. Then returning to the middle of the altar, he says, bowing down :

IN spiritu humilitatis, et in animo contrito suscipiamur a te, Domine ; et sic fiat sacrificium nostrum in conspectu tuo hodie, ut placeat tibi, Domine Deus.

IN a spirit of humility, and with contrition of heart, we pray thee, O Lord ! to make us acceptable to thee ; and let our Sacrifice be so performed this day in thy sight, that it may be pleasing to thee, O Lord, our God!

Then, turning to the people, he says :

ORATE, fratres : ut meum ac vestrum sacrificium acceptabile

PRAY, brethren, that my sacrifice and yours may be ac-

fiat apud Deum Patrem omnipotentem.

ceptable to God, the Father Almighty.

And turning again to the altar, he says:

Oremus.

Let us pray.

PRÆCEPTIS salutaribus moniti, et divina institutione formati, audemus dicere:

INSTRUCTED by thy wholesome precepts, and following thy divine institution, we presume to say:

Pater noster, qui es in cœlis: sanctificetur nomen tuum: adveniat regnum tuum: fiat voluntas tua, sicut in cœlo, et in terra. Panem nostrum quotidianum da nobis hodie: et dimitte nobis debita nostra, sicut et nos dimittimus debitoribus nostris. Et ne nos inducas in tentationem.

Our Father, who art in heaven; hallowed be thy name; thy kingdom come: thy will be done on earth, as it is in heaven. Give us this day our daily bread; and forgive us our trespasses, as we forgive them that trespass against us. And lead us not into temptation.

R. Sed libera nos a malo.

R. But deliver us from evil.

The Priest in a low tone says Amen, *and then says aloud:*

LIBERA nos, quæsumus Domine, ab omnibus malis præteritis, præsentibus, et futuris: et intercedente beata et gloriosa semper Virgine Dei genitrice Maria, cum beatis Apos-

DELIVER us, O Lord! we beseech thee, from all evils, past, present, and to come; and by the intercession of the blessed and glorious ever Virgin Mary, mother of God, of thy

olis tuis Petro et Paulo, atque Andrea, et omnibus Sanctis, da propitius pacem in diebus nostris: ut ope misericordiæ tuæ adjuti, et a peccato simus semper liberi, et ab omni perturbatione securi. Per eundem Dominum nostrum Jesum Christum Filium tuum, qui tecum vivit et regnat in unitate Spiritus sancti Deus, per omnia sæcula sæculorum.

R. Amen.

blessed Apostles Peter and Paul, and of Andrew, and all the Saints, mercifully grant peace in our days: that by the assistance of thy mercy we may be always free from sin, and secure from all disturbance; through the same Lord Jesus Christ thy Son, who liveth and reigneth with thee and the Holy Ghost, one God, for ever and ever.

R. Amen.

After this prayer, having adored on his knees, he puts the paten under the sacred Host, which with his right hand he elevates, that It may be seen by the people; and immediately divides It into three parts, putting the last into the chalice. Then he says the following prayer:

PERCEPTIO corporis tui, Domine Jesu Christe, quod ego indignus sumere præsumo, non mihi proveniat in judicium et condemnationem: sed pro tua pietate prosit mihi ad tutamentum mentis et corporis, et ad medelam percipiendam. Qui vivis et regnas cum Deo Patre in unitate Spiritus

LET not the participation of thy body, O Lord Jesus Christ! which though unworthy I presume to receive, turn to my judgment and condemnation: but through thy mercy let it be for me an effectual safeguard and remedy of soul and body; who with God the Father and the Holy Ghost

sancti Deus, per omnia sæcula sæculorum. Amen.

livest and reignest one God, world without end. Amen.

Then he kneels and takes the paten with the body of Christ, and says with the greatest humility and reverence :

PANEM cœlestem accipiam, et nomen Domini invocabo.

I WILL take the heavenly bread, and invoke the name of the Lord.

Then striking his breast, he says thrice :

DOMINE, non sum dignus ut intres sub tectum meum: sed tantum dic verbo, et sanabitur anima mea.

LORD! I am not worthy that thou shouldst enter under my roof; but only say the word, and my soul shall be healed.

After which, he signs himself with the blessed Sacrament, saying :

CORPUS Domini nostri Jesu Christi custodiat animam meam in vitam æternam. Amen.

THE body of our Lord Jesus Christ preserve my soul to life everlasting. Amen.

Then he reverently receives the Body, and immediately after the particle of the sacred Host with the wine in the chalice. And having, as usual, washed his fingers and taken the purification, bowing in the middle of the altar, with his hands joined, he says :

QUOD ore sumpsimus, Domine, pura mente capiamus : et de munere temporali fiat nobis remedium sempiternum.

GRANT, O Lord! that what we have taken with our mouth, we may receive with a pure mind, and that, of a temporal gift, it may prove an eternal remedy.

After this, the Priest, having made a reverence to the altar, departs. Vespers are then said, which are the same as the day before, p. 266, except the following:

Ad Magnificat.

Ant. CUM accepisset acetum, dixit: Consummatum est; et inclinato capite, emisit spiritum.

V. Christus factus est pro nobis obediens usque ad mortem, mortem autem crucis.

At Magnificat.

Ant. WHEN he had taken the vinegar, he said: It is consummated; and bowing his head, he gave up the ghost.

V. Christ became obedient for us unto death; even the death of the cross.

TENEBRÆ ON GOOD FRIDAY;

BEING THE MORNING OFFICE OF

HOLY SATURDAY.

The Matins.

Aperi Domine, Pater, Ave, *and* **Credo,** *are said in a low voice.*

THE FIRST NOCTURN.

Antiphona. IN pace in idipsum dormiam, et requiescam.

The Antiphon. IN peace in the self-same, I will sleep and I will rest.

PSALM 4.

CUM invocarem, exaudivit me Deus justitiæ meæ : * in tribulatione dilatasti mihi.

Miserere mei, * et exaudi orationem meam.

Filii hominum usquequo gravi corde? * ut quid diligitis vanitatem, et quæritis mendacium?

Et scitote quoniam mirificavit Dominus sanctum suum : * Dominus exaudiet me, cum clamavero ad eum.

WHEN I called upon him, the God of my justice heard me ; when I was in distress, thou hast enlarged me.

Have mercy on me, and hear my prayer.

O ye sons of men! how long will you be dull of heart? why do you love vanity, and seek after lying?

Know ye also that the Lord hath made his holy one wonderful ; the Lord will hear me, when I shall cry unto him.

Irascimini, et nolite peccare: quæ dicitis in cordibus vestris, in cubilibus vestris compungimini.

Be ye angry, and sin not ; the things you say in your hearts, be sorry for them upon your beds.

Sacrificate sacrificium justitiæ, et sperate in Domino. * Multi dicunt: Quis ostendit nobis bona?

Offer up the sacrifice of justice, and trust in the Lord ; many say : Who showeth us good things?

Signatum est super nos lumen vultus tui, Domine : * dedisti lætitiam in corde meo.

The light of thy countenance, O Lord ! shined upon us, thou hast given gladness in my heart.

A fructu frumenti, vini, et olei sui, * multiplicati sunt.

By the fruit of their corn, wine, and oil, they are multiplied.

In pace in idipsum * dormiam, et requiescam :

In peace in the selfsame, I will sleep and I will rest.

Quoniam tu Domine, singulariter in spe * constituisti me.

For thou, O Lord ! hast singularly settled me in hope.

Here the lowest candle on the left side of the triangle is extinguished.

Ant. In pace in idipsum dormiam, et requiescam.

Ant. In peace in the self-same, I will sleep and I will rest.

Ant. Habitabit in tabernaculo tuo, requiescet in monte sancto tuo.

Ant. He shall dwell in thy tabernacle, he shall rest on thy holy hill.

PSALM 14.

DOMINE, quis habitabit in taberna-

LORD ! who shall dwell in thy ta-

culo tuo? * aut quis re- bernacle? or who shall
quiescet in monte sancto rest in thy holy hill?
tuo?

Qui ingreditur sine He that walketh with-
macula, * et operatur out blemish, and work-
justitiam: eth justice.

Qui loquitur verita- He that speaketh truth
tem in corde suo, * qui in his heart, who hath
non egit dolum in lin- not used deceit in his
gua sua: tongue.

Nec fecit proximo suo Nor hath done evil to
malum: * et opprobri- his neighbor: nor taken
um non accepit adversus up a reproach against
proximos suos. his neighbors.

Ad nihilum deductus In his sight the malig-
est in conspectu ejus ma- nant is brought to no-
lignus: * timentes autem thing: but he glorifieth
Dominum glorificat: them that fear the Lord.

Qui jurat proximo suo, He that sweareth to
et non decipit: qui pe- his neighbor, and de-
cuniam suam non dedit ceiveth not, he that hath
ad usuram, et munera not put out his money
super innocentem non to usury, nor taken
accepit. bribes against the innocent.

Qui facit hæc, * non He that doeth these
movebitur in æternum. things shall not be
moved for ever.

*Here the lowest candle on the right side of the triangle is
extinguished.*

Ant. Habitabit in ta- *Ant.* He shall dwell in
bernaculo tuo, requiescet thy tabernacle, he shall
in monte sancto tuo rest on thy holy hill.

Ant. Caro mea requi-
escet in spe.

Ant. My flesh shall
rest in hope.

PSALM 15.

CONSERVA me Do-
mine, quoniam
speravi in te. * Dixi
Domino : Deus meus es
tu, quoniam bonorum
meorum non eges.

Sanctis qui sunt in
terra ejus, * mirificavit
omnes voluntates meas
in eis.

Multiplicatæ sunt in-
firmitates eorum : * pos-
tea acceleraverunt.

Non congregabo con-
venticula eorum de san-
guinibus : nec memor
ero nominum eorum per
labia mea.

Dominus pars hæredi-
tatis meæ, et calicis mei :
* tu es qui restitues hæ-
reditatem meam mihi.

Funes ceciderunt mi-
hi in præclaris : * etenim
hæreditas mea præclara
est mihi.

Benedicam Dominum,

PRESERVE me, O
Lord! for I have
put my trust in thee. I
have said to the Lord :
Thou art my God, for
thou hast no need of my
goods.

To the saints, who
are in his land, he hath
made wonderful all my
desires in them.

Their infirmities were
multiplied : afterwards
they made haste.

I will not gather to-
gether their meetings for
blood-offerings : nor will
I be mindful of their
names by my lips.

The Lord is the por-
tion of my inheritance
and of my cup; it is
thou that wilt restore
mine inheritance to me.

The lines are fallen
unto me in goodly
places ; for my inheri-
tance is goodly to me.

I will bless the Lord.

qui tribuit mihi intellectum : * insuper et usque ad noctem increpuerunt me renes mei.

who hath given me understanding: moreover my reins also have corrected me even till night.

Providebam Dominum in conspectu meo semper : * quoniam a dextris est mihi, ne commovear.

I set the Lord always in my sight : for he is at my right hand, that I be not moved.

Propter hoc lætatum est cor meum, et exultavit lingua mea : * insuper et caro mea requiescet in spe.

Therefore my heart hath been glad, and my tongue hath rejoiced : moreover my flesh also shall rest in hope.

Quoniam non derelinques animam meam in inferno : * nec dabis sanctum tuum videre corruptionem.

Because thou wilt not leave my soul in hell : nor wilt thou give thy holy one to see corruption.

Notas mihi fecisti vias vitæ, adimplebis me lætitia cum vultu tuo : delectationes in dextera tua usque in finem.

Thou hast made known to me the ways of life, thou shalt fill me with joy with thy countenance : at thy right hand are delights even to the end.

Here a candle is extinguished.

Ant. Caro mea requiescet in spe.

Ant. My flesh shall rest in hope.

V. In pace in idipsum.

V. In peace in the self-same.

R. Dormiam, et re-quiescam.

R. I will sleep and I will rest.

Pater noster, *secreto.*

Our Father, *privately.*

THE FIRST LESSON.

De Lamentatione Jere-miæ Prophetæ, *cap.* iii.

From the lamentation of Jeremias the Prophet, *chap.* iii.

Heth. MISERI-CORDIÆ Domini quia non sumus consumpti : quia non defecerunt miserationes ejus.

Heth. THE mercies of the Lord that we are not consum-ed : because his tender mercies have not failed.

Heth. Novi diluculo, multa est fides tua.

Heth. They are new every morning, great is thy faithfulness.

Heth. Pars mea Domi-nus, dixit anima mea : propterea expectabo eum.

Heth. The Lord is my portion, said my soul : therefore will I wait for him.

Teth. Bonus est Domi-nus sperantibus in eum, animæ quærenti illum.

Teth. The Lord is good to them that hope in him, to the soul that seeketh him.

Teth. Bonum est præ-stolari cum silentio salu-tare Dei.

Teth. It is good to wait with silence for the salvation of God.

Teth. Bonum est viro, cum portaverit jugum ab adolescentia sua.

Teth. It is good for a man, when he hath borne the yoke from his youth.

Jod. Sedebit solitarius, et tacebit: quia levavit super se.

Jod. He shall sit solitary and hold his peace : because he hath taken it up upon himself.

Jod. Ponet in pulvere os suum, si forte sit spes.

Jod. He shall put his mouth in the dust, if so be there may be hope.

Jod. Dabit percutienti se maxillam, saturabitur opprobriis.

Jod. He shall give his cheek to him that striketh him, he shall be filled with reproaches.

Jerusalem, Jerusalem, convertere ad Dominum Deum tuum.

Jerusalem! Jerusalem! be converted to the Lord thy God.

R. Sicut ovis ad occisionem ductus est; et dum male tractaretur, non aperuit os suum: traditus est ad mortem,* Ut vivificaret populum suum.

R. He was led as a sheep to the slaughter, and all the time of his ill-usage he opened not his mouth : he was condemned to death, * that he might give life to his people.

V. Tradidit in mortem animam suam, et inter sceleratos reputatus est. * Ut vivificaret, etc.

V. He hath delivered his soul unto death, and was reputed with the wicked. * That he might.

THE SECOND LESSON.

Aleph. QUOMODO obscuratum est aurum, mutatus est color optimus. dispersi sunt lapi-

Aleph. HOW is the gold become dim, the finest color is changed, the stones of the sanctuary are

des sanctuarii in capite omnium platearum?

scattered in the top of every street?

Beth. Filii Sion incly-ti, et amicti auro primo: quomodo reputati sunt in vasa testea, opus manuum figuli?

Beth. The noble sons of Sion, and they that were clothed with the best gold, how are they esteemed as earthen vessels, the work of the potter's hand.

Ghimel. Sed et lamiæ nudaverunt mammam, lactaverunt catulos suos; filia populi mei crudelis, quasi struthio in deserto.

Ghimel. Even the sea-monsters have drawn out the breast, they have given suck to their young, the daughter of my people is cruel, like the ostrich in the desert.

Daleth. Adhæsit lingua lactentis ad palatum ejus in siti: parvuli petierunt panem, et non erat qui frangeret eis.

Daleth. The tongue of the suckling child hath stuck to the roof of his mouth for thirst: the little ones have asked for bread, and there was none to break it unto them.

He. Qui vescebantur voluptuose, interierunt in viis: qui nutriebantur in croceis, amplexati sunt stercora.

He. They that were fed delicately have died in the streets: they that were brought up in scarlet, have embraced the dung.

Vau. Et major effecta est iniquitas filiæ populi mei peccato Sodomorum, quæ subversa est

Vau. And the iniquity of the daughter of my people is made greater than the sin of Sodom,

in momento, et non ceperunt in ea manus.

which was overthrown in a moment, and hands took nothing in her.

Jerusalem, Jerusalem, convertere ad Dominum Deum tuum.

Jerusalem! Jerusalem! be converted to the Lord thy God.

R. Jerusalem surge, et exue te vestibus jucunditatis : induere cinere et cilicio, * Quia in te occisus est Salvator Israel.

R. Arise, Jerusalem ! and put off thy garments of joy ; put on ashes and hair-cloth, * for in thee was slain the Saviour of Israel.

V. Deduc quasi torrentem lacrymas per diem et noctem, et non taceat pupilla oculi tui. * Quia.

V. Let tears run down like a torrent day and night, and let not the apple of thy eye cease. * For in thee.

THE THIRD LESSON.

Incipit Oratio Jeremiæ Prophetæ, *cap*. v.

The beginning of the Prayer of Jeremias the Prophet, *chap*. v.

RECORDARE, Domine, quid acciderit nobis : intuere, et respice opprobrium nostrum. Hæreditas nostra versa est a dalienos, domus nostræ ad extraneos. Pupilli facti sumus absque patre, matres nostræ quasi viduæ. Aquam nostram pecu-

REMEMBER, O Lord ! what is come upon us : consider and behold our reproach. Our inheritance is turned to aliens : our houses to strangers. We are become orphans without a father : our mothers are as widows. We have drunk our water for

nia bibimus, ligna nostra pretio comparavimus. Cervicibus nostris minabamur, lassis non dabatur requies. Ægypto dedimus manum, et Assyriis, ut saturaremur pane. Patres nostri peccaverunt, et non sunt; et nos iniquitates eorum portavimus. Servi dominati sunt nostri : non fuit qui redimeret de manu eorum. In animabus nostris afferebamus panem nobis, a facie gladii in deserto. Pellis nostra quasi clibanus exusta est a facie tempestatum famis. Mulieres in Sion humiliaverunt, et virgines in civitatibus Juda.

Jerusalem, Jerusalem, convertere ad Dominum Deum tuum.

R. Plange quasi virgo, plebs mea : ululate, pastores, in cinere et cilicio : * Quia venit dies

money: we have bought our wood. We were dragged by the necks, we were weary, and no rest was given us. We have given our hand to Egypt, and to the Assyrians, that we might be satisfied with bread. Our fathers have sinned, and are not; and we have borne their iniquities. Servants have ruled over us : and there was none to redeem us out of their hand. We fetched our bread at the peril of our lives, because of the sword in the desert. Our skin was burnt as an oven, by reason of the violence of the famine. They oppressed the women in Sion, and the virgins in the cities of Juda.

Jerusalem! Jerusalem! be converted to the Lord thy God.

R. Mourn as a virgin, my people! howl, ye pastors, in ashes and hair-cloth : * for the

Domini magna, et amara valde.

great and exceeding bitter day of the Lord is coming.

V. Accingite vos, sacerdotes, et plangite, ministri altaris; aspergite vos cinere. * Quia venit, etc. Plange, etc.

V. Gird yourselves, ye priests! and mourn, ye ministers of the altar! sprinkle yourselves with ashes. * For the great, etc. Mourn as a virgin, etc.

THE SECOND NOCTURN.

Ant. ELEVAMINI portæ æternales, et introibit Rex gloriæ.

Ant. BE ye lifted up, O eternal gates! and the King of glory shall enter in.

PSALM 23.

DOMINI est terra, et plenitudo ejus : * orbis terrarum, et universi qui habitant in eo.

THE earth is the Lord's and the fulness thereof; the world, and all they that dwell therein.

Quia ipse super maria fundavit eum : * et super flumina præparavit eum.

For he hath founded it upon the seas; and hath prepared it upon the rivers.

Quis ascendet in montem Domini? * aut quis stabit in loco sancto ejus?

Who shall ascend into the mountain of the Lord? or who shall stand in his holy place?

Innocens manibus, et mundo corde, * qui non

The innocent in hands, and clean of heart, who

accepit in vano animam suam, nec juravit in dolo proximo suo.

hath not taken his soul in vain, nor sworn deceitfully to his neighbor.

Hic accipiet benedictionem a Domino : * et misericordiam a Deo salutari suo.

He shall receive a blessing from the Lord, and mercy from God his Saviour.

Hæc est generatio quærentium eum, * quærentium faciem Dei Jacob.

This is the generation of them that seek him, of them that seek the face of the God of Jacob.

Attollite portas principes vestras, et elevamini portæ æternales : * et introibit Rex gloriæ.

Lift up your gates, O ye princes ! and be ye lifted up, O eternal gates ! and the King of **glory** shall enter in.

Quis est iste Rex gloriæ ? * Dominus fortis et potens, Dominus potens in prœlio.

Who is this King of glory ? the Lord who is strong and mighty, the Lord mighty in battle.

Attollite portas principes vestras, et elevamini portæ æternales : * et introibit Rex gloriæ.

Lift up your gates, O ye princes ! and be ye lifted up, O eternal gates ! and the King of glory shall enter in.

Quis est iste Rex gloriæ ? * Dominus virtutum ipse est Rex gloriæ.

Who is this King of glory ? the Lord of Hosts, he is the King of glory.

Here a candle is extinguished.

Ant. Elevamini portæ   *Ant.* Be ye lifted up,

æternales, et introibit Rex gloriæ.

O eternal gates! and the King of glory shall enter in.

Ant. Credo videre bona Domini in terra viventium.

Ant. I believe to see the good things of the Lord in the land of the living.

PSALM 26.

DOMINUS illuminatio mea, et salus mea; * quem timebo?

THE Lord is my light and my salvation, whom shall I fear?

Dominus protector vitæ meæ; * a quo trepidabo?

The Lord is the protector of my life; of whom shall I be afraid?

Dum appropiant super me nocentes, * ut edant carnes meas.

Whilst the wicked draw near against me, to eat my flesh.

Qui tribulant me inimici mei, * ipsi infirmati sunt, et ceciderunt.

My enemies that trouble me, have themselves been weakened, and have fallen.

Si consistant adversum me castra, * non timebit cor meum.

If armies in camp should stand together against me, my heart shall not fear.

Si exurgat adversum me prœlium, * in hoc ego sperabo.

If a battle should rise up against me, in this will I be confident.

Unam petii a Domino, hanc requiram: * ut inhabitem in domo Domi-

One thing I have asked of the Lord, this will J seek after; that I may

ni omnibus diebus vitæ meæ :

Ut videam voluptatem Domini, * et visitem templum ejus.

Quoniam abscondit me in tabernaculo suo : * in die malorum protexit me in abscondito tabernaculi sui.

In petra exaltavit me : * et nunc exaltavit caput meum super inimicos meos.

Circuivi, et immolavi in tabernaculo ejus hostiam vociferationis : * cantabo, et psalmum dicam Domino.

Exaudi Domine vocem meam, qua clamavi ad te : * miserere mei, et exaudi me.

Tibi dixit cor meum, exquisivit te facies mea : * faciem tuam Domine requiram.

Ne avertas faciem tuam a me : * ne declines in ira a servo tuo.

dwell in the house of the Lord all the days of my life.

That I may see the delight of the Lord, and may visit his temple.

For he hath hidden me in his tabernacle : in the day of evils, he hath protected me in the secret place of his tabernacle.

He hath exalted me upon a rock : and now he hath lifted up my head above my enemies.

I have gone round, and have offered up in his tabernacle a sacrifice of jubilation : I will sing, and recite a psalm to the Lord.

Hear, O Lord! my voice, with which I have cried to thee ; have mercy on me and hear me.

My heart hath said to thee, my face hath sought thee : thy face, O Lord! will I seek.

Turn not away thy face from me : decline not in thy wrath from thy servant.

Adjutor meus esto : * ne derelinquas me, neque despicias me, Deus salutaris meus.

Be thou my helper; forsake me not, do not thou despise me, O God, my Saviour !

Quoniam pater meus, et mater mea dereliquerunt me : * Dominus autem assumpsit me.

For my father and my mother have left me ; but the Lord hath taken me up.

Legem pone mihi Domine in via tua : * et dirige me in semitam rectam propter inimicos meos.

Set me, O Lord! a law in thy way: and guide me in the right path, because of my enemies.

Ne tradideris me in animas tribulantium me : * quoniam insurrexerunt in me testes iniqui, et mentita est iniquitas sibi.

Deliver me not over to the will of them that trouble me ; for unjust witnesses have risen up against me, and iniquity hath lied to itself.

Credo videre bona Domini * in terra viventium.

I believe to see the good things of the Lord in the land of the living.

Exspecta Dominum, viriliter age : * et confortetur cor tuum, et sustine Dominum.

Expect the Lord, do manfully ; and let thy heart take courage, and wait thou for the Lord.

Here a candle is extinguished.

Ant. Credo videre bona Domini in terra viventium.

Ant. I believe to see the good things of the Lord in the land of the living.

Ant. Domine, ab-

Ant. Thou hast

traxisti ab inferis animam meam.

brought forth, O Lord! my soul from hell

PSALM 29.

EXALTABO te Domine, quoniam suscepisti me: * nec delectasti inimicos meos super me.

Domine Deus meus, clamavi ad te, * et sanasti me.

Domine, eduxisti ab inferno animam meam: * salvasti me a descendentibus in lacum.

Psallite Domino sancti ejus: * et confitemini memoriæ sanctitatis ejus.

Quoniam ira in indignatione ejus: * et vita in voluntate ejus.

Ad vesperum demorabitur fletus, * et ad matutinum lætitia.

Ego autem dixi in abundantia mea: * Non movebor in æternum.

Domine, in voluntate tua. * præstitisti decori meo virtutem.

I WILL extol thee, O Lord! because thou hast protected me; and hast not made my enemies to rejoice over me.

O Lord, my God! I have cried to thee; and thou hast healed me.

Thou hast brought forth, O Lord! my soul from hell; thou hast saved me from them that go down into the pit.

Sing to the Lord, O ye his saints! and give praise to the memory of his holiness.

For wrath is in his indignation; and life in his good-will.

In the evening weeping shall have place, and in the morning gladness.

And in my abundance I said: I shall never be moved.

O Lord! in thy favor, thou gavest strength to my beauty.

Avertisti faciem tuam a me, * et factus sum conturbatus.

Thou turnedst away thy face from me, and I became troubled.

Ad te Domine, clamabo : * et ad Deum meum deprecabor.

To thee, O Lord! will I cry; and I will make supplication to my God.

Quæ utilitas in sanguine meo, * dum descendo in corruptionem?

What profit is there in my blood, whilst I go down to corruption?

Numquid confitebitur tibi pulvis, * aut annuntiabit veritatem tuam?

Shall dust confess to thee, or declare thy truth?

Audivit Dominus, et misertus est mei : * Dominus factus est adjutor meus.

The Lord hath heard, and hath had mercy on me : the Lord became my helper.

Convertisti planctum meum in gaudium mihi : * conscidisti saccum meum, et circumdedisti me lætitia :

Thou hast turned for me my mourning into joy : thou hast cut my sackcloth, and hast compassed me with gladness.

Ut cantet tibi gloria mea, et non compungar : * Domine Deus meus, in æternum confitebor tibi.

To the end that my glory may sing to thee, and I may not regret; O Lord, my God! I will give praise to thee for ever.

Here a candle is extinguished.

Ant. Domine, abstraxisti ab inferis animam meam.

Ant. Thou hast brought forth, O Lord! my soul from hell.

V. Tu autem, Domine, miserere mei.

R. Et resuscita me, et retribuam eis.

Pater noster, *secreto.*

V. But thou, O Lord! have mercy on me.

R. And raise me up again, and I will requite them.

Our Father, *privately.*

THE FOURTH LESSON.

Ex Tractatu sancti Augustini Episcopi super Psalmos. In Psalm 63.

From the Treatise of St. Augustine the Bishop, on the Psalms. On the 63d Psalm.

ACCEDET homo ad cor altum, et exaltabitur Deus. Illi dixerunt: Quis nos videbit? Defecerunt scrutantes scrutationes, consilia mala. Accessit homo ad ipsa consilia, passus est se teneri ut homo. Non enim teneretur nisi homo, aut videretur nisi homo, aut cæderetur nisi homo, aut crucifigereter, aut moreretur nisi homo. Accessit ergo homo ad illas omnes passiones, quæ in illo nihil valerent, nisi esset homo. Sed si ille non esset homo, non liberaretur homo. Accessit

MAN shall come to a deep heart, and God shall be exalted. They said: Who shall see us? They failed in making diligent search for wicked designs. Man came to those designs, and suffered himself to be seized on as a man. For he could not be seized on, if he were not man, or seen, if he were not man, or scourged, if he were not man, or crucified, or die, if he were not man. Man, therefore, came to all these sufferings, which could have no effect on him, if he were not man

homo ad cor altum, id est, cor secretum, objiciens aspectibus humanis hominem, servans intus Deum; celans formam Dei, in qua æqualis est Patri, et offerens formam servi, qua minor est Patre.

But if he had not been man, man could not have been redeemed. Man came to a deep heart, that is, a secret heart, exposing his humanity to human view, but hiding his divinity; concealing the form of God, by which he is equal to the Father; and offering the form of the servant, by which he is inferior to the Father.

R. Recessit pastor noster, fons aquæ vivæ, ad cujus transitum sol obscuratus est: * Nam et ille captus est, qui captivum tenebat primum hominem: hodie portas mortis et seras pariter Salvator noster dirupit.

R. Our shepherd, the fountain of living water, is gone, at whose departure the sun was darkened : * for he is taken, who made the first man a prisoner; to-day our Saviour broke forth the locks and gates of death.

V. Destruxit quidem claustra inferni, et subvertit potentias diaboli. * Nam et ille, etc.

V. He destroyed the prisons of hell, and overthrew the power of the devil. * For he, etc.

THE FIFTH LESSON.

QUO perduxerunt illas scrutationes suas, quas perscrutantes defecerunt,

HOW far did they carry this their diligent search, in which they failed so much, that,

ut etiam mortuo Domino et sepulto, custodes ponerent ad sepulchrum ? Dixerunt enim Pilato : Seductor ille. Hoc appellabatur nomine Dominus Jesus Christus, ad solatium servorum suorum, quando dicuntur seductores. Ergo illi Pilato : Seductor ille, inquiunt, dixit adhuc vivens : Post tres dies resurgam. Jube itaque custodiri sepulchrum usque in diem tertium, ne forte veniant discipuli ejus, et furentur eum, et dicant plebi, Surrexit a mortuis ; et erit novissimus error pejor priore. Ait illis Pilatus : Habetis custodiam, ite, custodite sicut scitis. Illi autem abeuntes, munierunt sepulchrum, signantes lapidem cum custodibus.

when our Lord was dead and buried, they placed guards at the sepulchre ? For they said to Pilate : This seducer ; by which name our Lord Jesus Christ was called, for the comfort of his servants, when they are called seducers. This seducer, say they to Pilate, whilst he was yet alive, said : After three days, I will rise again. Command, therefore, the sepulchre to be guarded until the third day ; lest his disciples come and steal him away, and say to the people : He is risen from the dead : so the last error shall be worse than the first. Pilate said to them : You have a guard, go, and guard it as you know. And they departing, made the sepulchre sure with guards, sealing up the stone.

R. O vos omnes, qui transitis per viam, at-

R. O all ye that pass by the way ! attend and

tendite et videte * Si est
dolor similis sicut dolor
meus.

V. Attendite, universi
populi, et videte dolorem
meum. * Si est dolor,
etc.

see, * if there be any
sorrow like to my sor-
row.

V. Attend, all ye peo-
ple! and see my grief.
* If there, etc.

THE SIXTH LESSON.

POSUERUNT cus-
todes milites ad
sepulchrum. Concussa
terra, Dominus resur-
rexit: miracula facta
sunt talia circa sepul-
chrum, ut et ipsi milites,
qui custodes advenerant,
testes fierent, si vellent
vera nuntiare. Sed ava-
ritia illa, quæ captivavit
discipulum comitem
Christi, captivavit et
militem custodem se-
pulchri. Damus, inqui-
unt, vobis pecuniam, et
dicite quia vobis dormi-
entibus venerunt disci-
puli ejus, et abstulerunt
eum. Vere defecerunt
scrutantes scrutationes.
Quid est quod dixisti,
o infelix astutia? Tan-
tumne deseris lucem

THEY placed sol-
diers to guard
the sepulchre. The
earth shook, and the
Lord rose again: such
miracles were done at
the sepulchre, that the
very soldiers who came
as guards, might be
witnesses of it, if they
would declare the truth.
But that covetousness,
which possessed the dis-
ciple, who was the com-
panion of Christ, blinded
also the soldiers who
were the guards of his
sepulchre. We will
give you money, said
they: and say, that
whilst you were asleep,
his disciples came and
took him away; they
truly failed in making

consilii pietatis, et in profunda versutiæ demergeris, ut hoc dicas: Dicite quia vobis dormientibus venerunt discipuli ejus, et abstulerunt eum? Dormientes testes adhibes: vere tu ipse obdormisti, qui scrutando talia defecisti.

diligent search. What is it thou hast said, O wretched craft? Dost thou shut thy eyes against the light of prudence and piety, and plunge thyself so deep in cunning, as to say this: Say, that whilst you were asleep, his disciples came and took him away? Dost thou produce sleeping witnesses? Certainly thou thyself sleepest who failest in making search after such things.

R. Ecce quomodo moritur justus, et nemo percipit corde; et viri justi tolluntur, et nemo considerat. A facie iniquitatis sublatus est justus, * et erit in pace memoria ejus.

R. Behold how the just man dies, and nobody takes it to heart; and just men are taken away, and nobody considers it. The just man is taken away from the face of iniquity, * and his memory shall be in peace.

V. Tamqnam agnus coram tondente se obmutuit, et non aperuit os suum: de angustia et de judicio sublatus est. * Et erit in pace

V. He was dumb as a lamb before his shearer, and opened not his mouth; he was taken away from distress, and from judgment. * And

memoria ejus. Ecce quomodo, etc.

his memory shall be in peace. Behold, etc.

THE THIRD NOCTURN.

Ant. DEUS adjuvat me, et Dominus susceptor est animæ meæ.

Ant. GOD is my helper; and the Lord is the protector of my soul.

PSALM 53.

DEUS, in nomine tuo salvum me fac : * et in virtute tua judica me.

SAVE me, O God! by thy name, and judge me in thy strength.

Deus, exaudi orationem meam : * auribus percipe verba oris mei.

O God! hear my prayer: give ear to the words of my mouth.

Quoniam alieni insurrexerunt adversum me, et fortes quæsierunt animam meam : * et non proposuerunt Deum ante conspectum suum.

For strangers have risen up against me : and the mighty have sought after my soul; and they have not set God before their eyes.

Ecce enim Deus adjuvat me : * et Dominus susceptor est animæ meæ.

For behold God is my helper : and the Lord is the protector of my soul.

Averte mala inimicis meis : * et in veritate tua disperde illos.

Turn back the evils upon my enemies; and cut them off in thy truth.

Voluntarie sacrificabo tibi, * et confitebor no-

I will freely sacrifice to thee, and will give

mini tuo Domine, quoniam bonum est.

Quoniam ex omni tribulatione eripuisti me : * et super inimicos meos despexit oculus meus.

praise, O God ! to thy name: because it is good.

For thou hast delivered me out of all trouble, and my eye hath looked down upon my enemies.

Here a candle is extinguished.

Ant. Deus adjuvat me, et Dominus susceptor est animæ meæ.

Ant. In pace factus est locus ejus, et in Sion habitatio ejus.

Ant. God is my helper, and the Lord is the protector of my soul.

Ant. His place is in peace, and his abode in Sion.

PSALM 75.

NOTUS in Judæa Deus: * in Israel magnum nomen ejus.

Et factus est in pace locus ejus : * et habitatio ejus in Sion.

Ibi confregit potentias arcuum, * scutum, gladium, et bellum.

Illuminans tu mirabiliter a montibus æternis : * turbati sunt omnes insipientes corde.

Dormierunt somnum suum : * et nihil inve-

IN Judea God is known ; his name is great in Israel.

And his place is in peace, and his abode in Sion.

There hath he broken the powers of bows, the shield, the sword, and the battle.

Thou enlightenest wonderfully from the everlasting hills : all the foolish of heart were troubled.

They have slept their sleep: and all the men

nerunt omnes viri divitiarum in manibus suis.

of riches have found nothing in their hands.

Ab increpatione tua Deus Jacob, * dormitaverunt qui ascenderunt equos.

At thy rebuke, O God of Jacob ! they have all slumbered that mounted on horseback.

Tu terribilis es, et quis resistet tibi ? * ex tunc ira tua.

Thou art terrible, and who shall resist thee? from that time thy wrath.

De cœlo auditum fecisti judicium : * terra tremuit et quievit.

Thou hast caused judgment to be heard from heaven : the earth trembled and was still.

Cum exurgeret in judicium Deus, * ut salvos faceret omnes mansuetos terræ.

When God arose in judgment, to save all the meek of the earth.

Quoniam cogitatio hominis confitebitur tibi :* et reliquiæ cogitationis diem festum agent tibi.

For the thought of man shall give praise to thee ; and the remainders of the thought shall keep holyday to thee.

Vovete, et reddite Domino Deo vestro, * omnes qui in circuitu ejus affertis munera.

Vow ye, and pay to the Lord, your God, all you that round about him bring presents.

Terribili et ei qui aufert spiritum principum, * terribili apud reges terræ.

To him that is terrible, even to him who taketh away the spirit of princes, to the terrible with the kings of the earth.

Here a candle is extinguished.

Ant. In pace factus est locus ejus, et in Sion habitatio ejus.

Ant. His place is in peace, and his abode in Sion.

Ant. Factus sum sicut homo sine adjutorio, inter mortuos liber.

Ant. I am become like a man without help, free among the dead.

PSALM 87.

DOMINE Deus salutis meæ, * in die clamavi, et nocte coram te.

O LORD, the God of my salvation! I have cried in the day and in the night before thee.

Intret in conspectu tuo oratio mea : * inclina aurem tuam ad precem meam :

Let my prayer come in before thee : incline thy ear to my petition.

Quia repleta est malis anima mea : *et vita mea inferno appropinquavit.

For my soul is filled with evils : and my life hath drawn nigh to hell.

Æstimatus sum cum descendentibus in lacum : * factus sum sicut homo sine adjutorio, inter mortuos liber.

I am counted among those that go down to the pit; I am become as a man without help, free among the dead.

Sicut vulnerati dormientes in sepulchris, quorum non es memor amplius : * et ipsi de manu tua repulsi sunt.

Like the slain sleeping in the sepulchres, whom thou rememberest no more : and they are cast off from thy hand.

Posuerunt me in lacu

They have laid me in

inferiori : * in tenebrosis, et in umbra mortis.

Super me confirmatus est furor tuus : * et omnes fluctus tuos induxisti super me.

Longe fecisti notos meos a me : * posuerunt me abominationem sibi.

Traditus sum, et non egrediebar : * oculi mei languerunt præ inopia.

Clamavi ad te Domine tota die : * expandi ad te manus meas.

Numquid mortuis facies mirabilia : * aut medici suscitabunt, et confitebuntur tibi ?

Numquid narrabit aliquis in sepulchro misericordiam tuam, * et veritatem tuam in perditione ?

Numquid cognoscentur in tenebris mirabilia tua, * et justitia tua in terra oblivionis ?

the lower pit ; in the dark places, and in the shadow of death.

Thy wrath is strong over me : and all thy waves thou hast brought in upon me.

Thou hast put away my acquaintance far from me ; they have set me an abomination to themselves.

I was delivered up, and came not forth : my eyes languished through poverty.

All the day I cried to thee, O Lord ! I stretched out my hands to thee.

Wilt thou show wonders to the dead ? or shall physicians raise to life, and give praise to thee ?

Shall any one in the sepulchre declare thy mercy ; and thy truth in destruction ?

Shall thy wonders be known in the dark ; and thy justice in the land of forgetfulness ?

Et ego ad te, Domine, clamavi : * et mane oratio mea præveniet te.

But I, O Lord! have cried to thee : and in the morning my prayer shall prevent thee.

Ut quid Domine repellis orationem meam : * avertis faciem tuam a me ?

Lord ! why castest thou off my prayer : why turnest thou away thy face from me ?

Pauper sum ego, et in laboribus a juventute mea : * exaltatus autem, humiliatus sum et conturbatus.

I am poor, and in labors from my youth; and being exalted, have been humbled and disturbed.

In me transierunt iræ tuæ : * et terrores tui conturbaverunt me.

Thy wrath hath come upon me : and thy terrors have troubled me.

Circumdederunt me sicut aqua tota die : * circumdederunt me simul.

They have come round about me like water all the day : they have compassed me about together.

Elongasti a me amicum et proximum : * et notos meos a miseria.

Friend and neighbor thou hast put far from me : and my acquaintance, because of misery.

Here a candle is extinguished.

Ant. Factus sum sicut homo sine adjutorio, inter mortuos liber.

Ant. I am become a man without help, free among the dead.

V. In pace factus est locus ejus.

V. His place is in peace.

℞. Et in Sion habitatio ejus.

Pater noster, *secreto.*

℞. And his abode in Sion.

Our Father, *privately.*

THE SEVENTH LESSON.

De Epistola beati Pauli Apostoli ad Hebræos, cap. ix.

From the Epistle of St. Paul the Apostle to the Hebrews, chap. ix.

CHRISTUS assistens pontifex futurorum bonorum, per amplius et perfectius tabernaculum non manu factum, id est, non hujus creationis, neque per sanguinem hircorum aut vitulorum, sed per proprium sanguinem introivit semel in Sancta, æterna redemptione inventa. Si enim sanguis hircorum et taurorum, et cinis vitulæ aspersus inquinatos sanctificat ad emundationem carnis; quanto magis sanguis Christi, qui per Spiritum sanctum semetipsum obtulit immaculatum Deo, emundabit conscientiam nostram ab

BUT Christ being come a high-priest of the good things to come, by a greater and more perfect tabernacle not made with hands, that is, not of this creation; neither by the blood of goats, or of calves, but by his own blood, entered once into the Holies, having obtained eternal redemption. For if the blood of goats and of oxen, and the ashes of a heifer being sprinkled, sanctify such as are defiled, to the cleansing of the flesh: how much more shall the blood of Christ, who, through the Holy Ghost, offered himself without spot to God, cleanse our consciences from dead

operibus mortuis, ad serviendum Deo viventi?

R. Astiterunt reges terræ, et principes convenerunt in ụnum * Adversus Dominum, et adversus Christum ejus.

V. Quare fremuerunt gentes, et populi meditati sunt inania? * Adversus Dominum, etc.

works, to serve the living God?

R. The kings of the earth stood up, and the princes assembled together, * against the Lord and against his Christ.

V. Why have the nations raged? and the people meditated vain things? * Against the Lord, etc.

THE EIGHTH LESSON.

ET ideo novi testamenti mediator est, ut, morte intercedente, in redemptionem earum prævaricationum, quæ erant sub priori testamento, repromissionem accipiant qui vocati sunt æternæ hæreditatis. Ubi enim testamentum est, mors necesse est intercedat testatoris. Testamentum enim in mortuis confirmatum est: alioquin nondum valet, dum vivit qui testatus est. Unde nec primum

AND therefore he is the mediator of the new testament: that, by means of his death, for the redemption of those transgressions, which were under the former testament, they that are called may receive the promise of eternal inheritance. For where there is a testament, the death of the testator must of necessity come in. For a testament is of force, after men are dead: otherwise it is as yet of no strength,

quidem sine sanguine dedicatum est.

R. Æstimatus sum cum descendentibus in lacum : * Factus sum sicut homo sine adjutorio, inter mortuos liber.

V. Posuerunt me in lacu inferiori, in tenebrosis, et in umbra mortis. * Factus sum, etc.

whilst the testator liveth. Wherefore neither was the first indeed dedicated without blood.

R. I am counted among them that go down into the pit : * I am become as a man without help, free among the dead.

V. They have laid me in the lower pit ; in the dark places and in the shadow of death. * I am become, etc.

THE NINTH LESSON.

LECTO enim omni mandato legis a Moyse universo populo, accipiens sanguinem vitulorum et hircorum, cum aqua, et lana coccinea et hyssopo, ipsum quoque librum et omnem populum aspersit, dicens : Hic sanguis testamenti, quod mandavit ad vos Deus. Etiam tabernaculum, et omnia vasa ministerii sanguine similiter aspersit. Et omnia pene in sanguine

FOR when every commandment of the law had been read by Moses to all the people, he took the blood of calves and goats, with water, scarlet wool, and hyssop ; and sprinkled both the book itself and all the people, saying : This is the blood of the testament, which God hath enjoined unto you. The tabernacle also, and all the vessels of the min-

secundum legem mundantur, et sine sanguinis effusione non fit remissio.

istry in like manner, he sprinkled with blood. And almost all things, according to the law, are cleansed with blood, and without the shedding of blood there is no remission.

R. Sepulto Domino, signatum est monumentum, volventes lapidem ad ostium monumenti; * Ponentes milites, qui custodirent illum.

R. When the Lord was buried, they sealed up the sepulchre, rolling a stone before the mouth of the sepulchre, * and placing soldiers to guard him.

V. Accedentes principes sacerdotum ad Pilatum, petierunt illum. * Ponentes, etc. Sepulto Domino, etc.

V. The chief priests went to Pilate and asked him. * And placing soldiers, etc. When the Lord, etc.

The Lauds.

Ant. O MORS, ero mors tua; morsus tuus ero, inferne.

Ant. O DEATH! I will be thy death; O hell! I will be thy bite.

PSALM 50.

MISERERE mei, Deus, *p.* 230.

HAVE mercy on me, *p.* 230.

Here a candle is extinguished.

Ant. O mors, ero mors tua; morsus tuus ero, inferne.

Ant. O death! I will be thy death; O hell! I will be thy bite.

Ant. Plangent eum quasi unigenitum, quia innocens Dominus occisus est.

Ant. They shall mourn for him as for an only son, because our innocent Lord is slain.

PSALM 42.

JUDICA me Deus, et discerne causam meam de gente non sancta, * ab homine iniquo et doloso erue me.

JUDGE me, O God! and distinguish my cause from the nation that is not holy; deliver me from the unjust and deceitful man.

Quia tu es Deus fortitudo mea : * quare me repulisti? et quare tristis incedo, dum affligit me inimicus?

For thou art God, my strength : why hast thou cast me off? and why do I go sorrowful, whilst the enemy afflicteth me?

Emitte lucem tuam et veritatem tuam : * ipsa me deduxerunt, et adduxerunt in montem sanctum tuum, et in tabernacula tua.

Send forth thy light and thy truth; they have conducted me, and brought me to thy holy mountain, and into thy tabernacles.

Et introibo ad altare

And I will go in to the altar of God: to God

Dei : * ad Deum qui læ-tificat juventutem meam.

Confitebor tibi in cithara, Deus Deus meus : * quare tristis es, anima mea? et quare conturbas me?

Spera in Deo, quoniam adhuc confitebor illi : * salutare vultus mei, et Deus meus.

wno giveth joy to my youth.

To thee, O God my God! I will give praise upon the harp : why art thou sad, O my soul? and why dost thou dis quiet me?

Hope in God, for I will still give praise to him : he is the salvation of my countenance, and my God.

Here a candle is extinguished

Ant. Plangent eum quasi unigenitum, quia innocens Dominus occisus est.

Ant. Attendite, universi populi, et videte dolorem meum.

Ant. They shall mourn for him as for an only son, because our innocent Lord is slain.

Ant. Behold, all ye people! and see my grief.

PSALMS.

DEUS Deus meus, *p.* 237.
Deus misereatur, *p.* 238.

O GOD, my God! *p.* 237.
May God have mercy, *p.* 238.

Here a candle is extinguished.

Ant. Attendite, universi populi, et videte dolorem meum.

Ant. Behold, all ye people, and see my grief.

Ant. A porta inferi erue Domine animam meam.

Ant. From the gate of hell, O Lord! deliver my soul.

THE CANTICLE OF EZECHIAS. *Is.* 38.

EGO dixi: In dimidio dierum meorum * vadam ad portas inferi.

Quæsivi residuum annorum meorum; * dixi: Non videbo Dominum Deum in terra viventium.

Non aspiciam hominem ultra, * et habitatorem quietis.

Generatio mea ablata est, et convoluta est a me, quasi tabernaculum pastorum.

Præcisa est velut a texente vita mea; dum adhuc ordirer, succidit me: * de mane usque ad vesperam finies me.

Sperabam usque ad mane: * quasi leo sic contrivit omnia ossa me .

I SAID: In the midst of my days I shall go to the gates of hell.

I sought for the residue of my years; I said: I shall not see the Lord God in the land of the living.

I shall behold no man more, the inhabitant of rest.

My generation is at an end, and it is rolled away from me as a shepherd's tent.

My life is cut off, as by a weaver: whilst I was yet but beginning, he cut me off: from morning even to night thou wilt make an end of me.

I hoped till morning, as a lion so hath he broken all my bones.

De mane usque ad vesperam finies me: * sicut pullus hirundinis sic clamabo, meditabor ut columbia.

From morning even to night thou wilt make an end of me: I will cry like a young swallow, I will meditate like a dove.

Attenuati sunt oculi mei, * suspicientes in excelsum.

My eyes are weakened with looking upward.

Domine, vim patior, responde pro me.* Quid dicam, aut quid respondebit mihi, cum ipse fecerit?

Lord! I suffer violence, answer thou for me. What shall I say, or what shall he answer for me, whereas he himself hath done it?

Recogitabo tibi omnes annos meos * in amaritudine animæ meæ.

I will recount to thee all my years in the bitterness of my soul.

Domine, si sic vivitur, et in talibus vita spiritus mei, corripies me, et vivificabis me. * Ecce in pace amaritudo mea amarissima.

O Lord! if man's life be such, and the life of my spirit be in such things as these; thou shalt correct me, and make me to live. Behold in peace, is my bitterness most bitter.

Tu autem eruisti animam meam ut non periret: * projecisti post tergum tuum omnia peccata mea.

But thou hast delivered my soul, that it should not perish; thou hast cast all my sins behind thy back.

Quia non infernus confitebitur tibi, neque mors

For hell shall not confess to thee, neither shall

laudabit te : * non ex-pectabunt qui descen-dunt in lacum, veritatem tuam.

death praise thee : not shall they that go down into the pit, look for truth.

Vivens, vivens ipse confitebitur tibi, sicut et ego hodie : * pater filiis notam faciet veritatem tuam.

The living, the living, he shall give praise to thee, as I do this day ; the father shall make thy truth known to the children.

Domine, salvum me fac ; * et psalmos nos-tros cantabimus cunctis diebus vitæ nostræ in domo Domini.

O Lord ! save me, and we shall sing our psalms, all the days of our life, in the house of the Lord.

Here a candle is extinguished.

Ant. A porta inferi erue Domine animam meam.

Ant. From the gate of hell ! O Lord ! deliver my soul.

Ant. O vos omnes qui transitis per viam, atten-dite et videte, si est do-lor sicut dolor meus.

Ant. O all ye that pass by the way ! * behold and see, if there be grief like to my grief.

PSALMS.

LAUDATE Domi-num de cœlis, *p.* 244.

PRAISE the Lord from the heavens, *p.* 244.

Cantate Domino, *p.* 149.

Sing to the Lord. *p.* 149.

Laudate Dominum in sanctis ejus, *p.* 247.

Praise the Lord in his holy places, *p.* 247.

Here a candle is extinguished

Ant. O vos omnes qui transitis per viam, attendite et videte, si est dolor sicut dolor meus.

Ant. O all ye that pass by the way! * behold and see, if there be grief like to my grief.

V. Caro mea requiescet in spe.

V. My flesh shall rest in hope.

R. Et non dabis Sanctum tuum videre corruptionem.

R. And thou wilt not give thy holy One to see corruption.

Ant. Mulieres sedentes ad monumentum lamentabantur, flentes Dominum.

Ant. The women sitting at the sepulchre lamented, weeping for our Lord.

THE CANTICLE OF ZACHARY. *Luke* i.

B ENEDICTUS, *p.* 248.

B LESSED be the Lord, *p.* 248.

The candle left burning at the top of the triangular candlestick is taken down while the following Ant. is said, and concealed behind the Epistle side of the altar:

Ant. Mulieres sedentes ad monumentum lamentabantur, flentes Dominum.

Ant. The women sitting at the sepulchre lamented, weeping for our Lord.

The following is said kneeling:

V. C HRISTUS factus est pro nobis obediens usque ad mortem, mortem autem crucis: propter quod et Deus exaltavit illum, et dedit

V. C HRIST became obedient for us unto death; even the death of the cross; wherefore God hath also exalted him. and hath

illi nomen, quod est super omne nomen.

given him a name which is above every name.

Pater noster, *totum sub silentio.*

Our Father, *privately.*

The Psalm Miserere, *p. 230, is recited in a low voice; and in the end the following prayer, without the* Oremus.

RESPICE, quæsumus Domine, super hanc familiam tuam, pro qua Dominus noster Jesus Christus non dubitavit manibus tradi nocentium, et crucis subire tormentum. *Sed dicitur sub silentio:* Qui tecum vivit et regnat in unitate Spiritus sancti Deus, per omnia sæcula sæculorum. Amen.

LOOK down, O Lord! we beseech thee, on this thy family, for which our Lord Jesus Christ was pleased to be delivered into the hands of the wicked, and to suffer the torment of the cross. *But say in a low voice:* Who with thee and the Holy Ghost liveth and reigneth, one God, world without end. Amen.

At the end of the prayer a little noise is made; the lighted candle is brought from under the Altar, and all rise and retire in silence.

HOLY SATURDAY.

The *Tenebræ* or *Matins*, with the other Canonical hours for this day, are consecrated to the memory of our Lord in his sepulchre ; at Mass, he is represented to the faithful as coming out of the grave, and triumphing over death by his resurrection. The word *Night*, used in the benediction of the Paschal Candle, in the Collect of the Mass, in the Preface and *Communicantes*, shows that the Office and Mass, now said in the middle of the day, were formerly said in the following night, to honor the time of our Saviour's resurrection, which happened in this night.

The altars, deprived of their ornaments on *Maundy-Thursday*, are again clothed with them, and a new *Fire* is blessed, to illuminate them. The Office begins with lighting a *triple Candle*, which is emblematic of the *light of Christ*, and signifies that the faith of the blessed Trinity proceeds from the light communicated to us by Christ risen from the dead. The *Paschal Candle*, blessed in the next place by the Deacon, is a figure of the body of Jesus Christ, and, not being lighted at first, represents him dead ; and the five blessed *Grains of incense* fixed in it denote the aromatic spices that embalmed him in the sepulchre. The lighting of the *Paschal Candle* is a representation of his rising again to a new life ; and the lighting of the lamps, and other candles afterwards, teaches the faithful that the resurrection of the Head will be followed by that of the members.

After this ceremony, the Church disposes the Catechumens for a worthy receiving of baptism ; for which purpose she reads twelve Lessons out of the Old Testament, called *Prophecies*, and after each says a solemn Prayer ; by both of which she not only instructs them in the effects and fruit of that sacrament, but begs for them, of Almighty God, all the advantages of it. The Church could not have appointed a more suitable time for the solemn administration of baptism, which is a lively representation of our Lord's resurrection. As he was laid in the sepulchre truly dead, and came out again truly alive, so the sinner is buried in the baptismal water, as in a mystical grave, and is taken out again animated with a new life of grace. *For we are buried together with him by baptism unto death ; that as Christ is risen from the dead by the glory of the Father, so we also may walk in newness of life* (*Rom.* vi. 4).

Before the administration of the sacrament, the *Baptismal Font* is blessed with ceremonies that are full of mysteries. 1. The Priest divides the water in the form of a cross, to teach us that it confers grace and sanctity by the merits of Christ crucified. 2. He touches the water

with his hand, praying that it may be free from all impressions of evil spirits. 3. He signs it thrice with the sign of the cross, to bless it in the name of the Holy Trinity. 4. He separates it with his hand, and casts out some of it towards the four parts of the world, to instruct us that the grace of baptism, like the rivers of paradise, flows all over the earth. 5. He breathes thrice upon it in the form of a cross, desiring God to bless it with the infusion of his holy Spirit, that it may perceive the virtue of sanctifying the soul. 6. He plunges the Paschal Candle thrice into it, praying that the Holy Ghost may descend upon it, as he did at the baptism of Christ in the waters of Jordan. 7. He mixes holy Oil and Chrism with it, to signify that baptism consecrates us to God, and gives spiritual strength to wrestle with and overcome all the enemies of our soul.

After the benediction of the font, the sacrament of baptism is solemnly administered to such as are prepared for it ; and then the Litany and Mass are sung. to obtain of God that the new baptized may persevere in the grace they have received. Incense is used at the Gospel, to represent the perfumes carried by the women to our Saviour's monument ; but no lights are carried, as at other times, because they and the Apostles did not yet believe his resurrection ; for which reason the Creed is also not said. The Offertory, the kiss of peace, and the Antiphon, called the *Communion*, are omitted, because the faithful did not receive the blessed Eucharist at this Mass, but waited till Easter-day.

The Blessing of the New Fire.

At a convenient hour, the altars are dressed ; but the candles are not lighted till the beginning of the Mass. Then, without the church, fire is struck from a flint, and coals are lighted with it ; after which the Priest (attended by the Ministers with the cross, holy-water, and incense, before the church gate, if it can be conveniently done, otherwise in the very entrance of the church, blesses the new fire, saying:

V. DOMINUS vobiscum.
R. Et cum spiritu tuo.

Oremus.

Deus, qui per Filium tuum, angularem scilicet lapidem, claritatis tuæ ignem fidelibus con-

V. THE Lord be with you.
R. And with thy spirit.

Let us pray.

O God ! who by thy Son, the corner-stone, hast bestowed on the faithful the fire of thy

tulisti : productum e silice, nostris profuturum usibus, novum hunc ignem sanctifica; et concede nobis, ita per hæc festa paschalia cœlestibus desideriis inflammari, ut ad perpetuæ claritatis, puris mentibus, valeamus festa pertingere. Per eundem Christum Dominum nostrum.

R. Amen.

Oremus.

Domine Deus Pater omnipotens, lumen indeficiens, qui es conditor omnium luminum : benedic hoc lumen, quod a te sanctificatum atque benedictum est, qui illuminasti omnem mundum ; ut ab eo lumine accendamur, atque illuminemur igne claritatis tuæ : et sicut illuminasti Moysen exeuntem de Ægypto, ita illumines corda et sensus nostros : ut ad vitam et lucem æternam pervenire mereamur. Per

brightness ; sanctify this new fire produced from a flint for our use ; and grant that during this Paschal solemnity we may be so inflamed with heavenly desires, that with pure minds we may come to the so· lemnity of eternal splendor ; through the same Christ our Lord.

R. Amen.

Let us pray.

O Lord God, Almighty Father, never - failing light! who art the author of all light ; bless this light, which is bless· ed and sanctified by thee, who hast enlightened the whole world : that we may be enlight ened by that light, and inflamed with the fire of thy brightness ; and, as thou didst give light to Moses, when he went out of Egypt, so illuminate our hearts and senses, that we may obtain light and life everlast-

Christum Dominum nostrum.

R. Amen.

Oremus.

Domine sancte, Pater omnipotens, æterne Deus : benedicentibus nobis hunc ignem in nomine tuo, et unigeniti Filii tui Dei ac Domini nostri Jesu Christi, et Spiritus sancti, co-operari digneris; et adjuva nos contra ignita tela inimici, et illustra gratia cœlesti. Qui vivis et regnas cum eodem Unigenito tuo, et Spiritu sancto Deus : per omnia sæcula sæculorum.

R. Amen.

ing; through Christ our Lord.

R. Amen.

Let us pray.

Holy Lord, Almighty Father, eternal God! vouchsafe to co-operate with us, who bless this fire in thy name, and in that of thy only Son, Jesus Christ our Lord and God, and of the Holy Ghost; assist us against the fiery darts of the enemy, and illuminate us with thy heavenly grace : who livest and reignest with the same only Son and Holy Ghost, one God for ever and ever.

R. Amen.

Then he blesses the five grains of incense that are to be fixed in the Paschal Candle, saying the following prayer :

VENIAT, quæsumus, omnipotens Deus, super hoc incensum larga tuæ benedictionis infusio, et hunc nocturnum splendorem invisibilis regenerator accende : ut non solum sacrificium, quod hac

POUR forth, we beseech thee, Almighty God! thy abundant blessing on this incense, and kindle, O invisible regenerator! the brightness of this night; that not only the sacrifice, which is offered

nocte litatum est, arcana luminis tui admixtione refulgeat ; sed in quocumque loco ex hujus sanctificationis mysterio aliquid fuerit deportatum, expulsa diabolicæ fraudis nequitia, virtus tuæ majestatis assistat. Per Christum Dominum nostrum.

this night may shine by the secret mixture of thy light ; but also, that into whatever place anything sanctified by these mystical prayers shall be carried, there, by the power of thy majesty, all the malicious artifices of the devil may be defeated ; through Christ our Lord.

R. Amen.

R. Amen.

Whilst he blesses the grains of incense, an Acolyte puts some of the blessed fire into the censer, and the Priest, after the prayer, puts incense into it, blessing it as usual, saying :

AB illo benedicaris, in cujus honore cremaberis. Amen.

MAY thou be blessed by him, in whose honor thou shalt be burnt. Amen.

Then he sprinkles the grains of incense and the fire thrice with holy-water saying :

ASPERGES me, Domine, hyssopo, et mundabor : lavabis me, et super nivem dealbabor.

THOU shalt sprinkle me, O Lord ! with hyssop, and I shall be cleansed ; thou shalt wash me, and I shall be made whiter than snow.

After which he fumes them thrice with the censer. Then the Deacon, putting on a white Dalmatic, takes the rod with the three candles fixed on the top. The Thurifer goes first with an Acolyte carrying in a plate the five grains of incense: the Subdeacon with the cross follows, and the Clergy in order : then the Deacon with the three candles, and last of all the Priest. When

*the Deacon is come into the church, an Acolyte, who carries a
candle lighted from the new fire, lights one of the three candles
on the top of the rod : and the Deacon, holding up the rod, kneels,
as do all the rest, except the Sub-deacon, and sings alone :*

L,UMEN Christi.

R̸. Deo gratias.

BEHOLD the light of Christ.

R. Thanks be to God.

*The same is done in the middle of the church, and before the altar,
when the other two candles are lighted. Being come to the
altar, the priest goes to the Epistle side, and the Deacon with
the book asks the blessing of the Priest, saying :*

JUBE, Domne, benedicere.

PRAY, Father! bless me.

Then the Priest says :

DOMINUS sit in corde tuo et in labiis tuis, ut digne et competenter annunties suum Paschale præconium: In nomine Patris, et Filii, et Spiritus sancti.

R. Amen.

THE Lord be in thy heart and lips; that thou mayest worthily and fitly proclaim his Paschal praise ; in the name of the Father, and of the Son, and of the Holy Ghost.

R. Amen.

*After this, the Deacon goes to the desk on the Gospel side, where he
fumes the book with incense : and, all standing as at the Gospel,
he blesses the Paschal Candle, saying :*

EXULTET jam angelica turba cœlorum: exultent divina mysteria ; et pro tanti regis victoria, tuba insonet salutaris. Gaudeat et tellus tantis irradiata fulgoribus; et

LET now the heavenly troop of angels rejoice ; let the divine mysteries be joyfully celebrated ; and let a sacred trumpet proclaim the victory of so great a king. Let the

æterni regis splendore illustrata, totius orbis se sentiat amisisse caliginem. Lætetur et mater Ecclesia tanti luminis adornata fulgoribus: et magnis populorum vocibus hæc aula resultet. Quapropter adstantes vos, fratres clarissimi, ad tam miram hujus sancti luminis claritatem, una mecum, quæso, Dei omnipotentis misericordiam invocate. Ut qui me non meis meritis intra Levitarum numerum dignatus est aggregare, luminis sui claritatem infundens, cerei hujus laudem implere perficiat. Per Dominum nostrum Jesum Christum Filium suum: qui cum eo vivit et regnat in unitate Spiritus sanc-

earth also be filled with joy, being illuminated with such resplendent rays; and let it see the darkness, which overspread the whole world, chased away by the splendor of our eternal king. Let our mother the Church also rejoice, being adorned by the rays of so great a light: and let this temple resound with the joyful acclamations of the people. Wherefore, beloved brethren, you who are now present at the admirable brightness of this holy light, I beseech you to invoke with me the name of the Almighty God. That he, who hath been pleased above my desert to admit me into the number of the Levites, will, by an effusion of his light upon me, enable me to celebrate the praises of this emblematic taper: through our Lord Jesus Christ, his Son: who

ti Deus, per omnia sæcula sæculorum.

R. Amen.

V. Dominus vobiscum.

R. Et cum spiritu tuo.

V. Sursum corda.

R. Habemus ad Dominum.

V. Gratias agamus Domino Deo nostro.

R. Dignum et justum est.

Vere dignum et justum est, invisibilem Deum Patrem omnipotentem, Filiumque ejus unigenitum, Dominum nostrum Jesum Christum, toto cordis ac mentis affectu, et vocis ministerio personare. Qui pro nobis æterno Patri, Adæ debitum solvit; et veteris piaculi cautionem pio cruore detersit. Hæc sunt enim festa Paschalia, in quibus verus ille Agnus occiditur, cujus sanguine postes fidelium conse-

with him and the Holy Ghost liveth and reigneth one God for ever and ever.

R. Amen.

V. The Lord be with you.

R. And with thy spirit.

V. Lift up your hearts.

R. We have them lifted up to the Lord.

V. Let us give thanks to the Lord our God.

R. It is meet and just.

It is truly meet and just to proclaim with all the affection of our heart and soul, and with the sound of our voice, the invisible God, the Father Almighty, and his only Son, our Lord Jesus Christ. Who paid for us to his eternal Father the debt of Adam; and by his sacred blood cancelled the guilt contracted by original sin. For this is the Paschal solemnity, in which the true Lamb was slain, by whose blood the doors

crantur. Hæc nox est, in qua primum patres nostros filios Israel eductos de Ægypto, Mare Rubrum sicco vestigio transire fecisti. Hæc igitur nox est, quæ peccatorum tenebras, columnæ illuminatione purgavit. Hæc nox est, quæ hodie per universum mundum, in Christo credentes, a vitiis sæculi, et caligine peccatorum segregatos reddit gratiæ, sociat sanctitati. Hæc nox est, in qua destructis vinculis mortis, Christus ab inferis victor ascendit. Nihil enim nobis nasci profuit, nisi redimi profuisset. O mira circa nos tuæ pietatis dignatio! O inæstimabilis dilectio charitatis! ut servum redimeres, filium tradidisti. O certe necessarium Adæ peccatum, quod Christi morte deletum est! O felix culpa, quæ talem ac tantum meruit habere Redemptorem! O vere

of the faithful are consecrated. This is the night in which thou formerly broughtest forth our forefathers the children of Israel out of Egypt, leading them dry-foot through the Red Sea. This then is the night which dissipated the darkness of sin, by the light of the pillar. This is the night which now delivers all over the world those that believe in Christ from the vices of the world and darkness of sin, restores them to grace, and clothes with sanctity. This is the night in which Christ broke the chains of death, and ascended conqueror from hell. O how admirable is thy goodness towards us! O how inestimable is thy love! Thou hast delivered up thy Son to redeem a slave. O truly necessary sin of Adam, which the death of Christ has blotted out!

beata nox, quæ sola me-
ruit scire tempus et
horam, in qua Christus
ab inferis resurrexit!
Hæc nox est, de qua
scriptum est : Et nox
sicut dies illuminabitur;
et nox illuminatio mea
in deliciis meis. Hujus
igitur sanctificatio noc-
tis fugat scelera culpas
iavat, et reddit innocen-
tiam lapsis, et mœstis
lætitiam. Fugat odia,
concordiam parat, et
curvat imperia.

O happy fault that mer-
ited such and so great
a Redeemer! O truly
blessed night! which
alone deserved to know
the time and hour when
Christ rose again from
hell. This is the night
of which it is written :
And the night shall be
as light as day ; and the
night shineth upon me
in my pleasures. There-
fore the sanctification
of this night blots out
crimes, washes away
sins, and restores inno-
cence to the fallen, and
joy to the sorrowful. It
banishes enmities, pro-
duces concord, and
humbles empires.

*Here the Deacon fixes the five grains of incense in the candle, in the
form of a cross.*

IN hujus igitur noctis
gratia, suscipe, sanc-
te Pater, incensi hujus
sacrificium vespertinum,
quod tibi in hac cerei
oblatione solemni, per
ministrorum manus, de
operibus apum, sacro-
sancta reddit Ecclesia.

THEREFORE, on
this sacred night,
receive, O holy Father!
the evening sacrifice of
this incense, which thy
holy Church, by the
hands of her ministers,
presents to thee in this
solemn oblation of this

Sed jam columnæ hujus præconia novimus, quam in honorem Dei rutilans ignis accendit.

wax candle, made out of the labor of bees. And now we know the excellence of this pillar, which the sparkling fire lights for the honor of God.

Here the Deacon lights the candle with one of the three candles on the rod.

QUI licet sit divisus in partes, mutuati tamen luminis detrimenta non novit. Alitur enim liquantibus ceris, quas in substantiam pretiosæ hujus lampadis, apis mater eduxit.

WHICH fire, though now divided, suffers no loss from the communication of its light. Because it is fed by the melted wax, produced by the bee, to make this taper.

Here the lamps are lighted.

O VERE beata nox, quæ expoliavit Ægyptios, ditavit Hebræos! Nox in qua terrenis cœlestia, humanis divina junguntur. Oramus ergo te, Domine, ut cereus iste in honorem tui nominis consecratus, ad noctis hujus caliginem destruendam, indeficiens perseveret; et in odorem suavitatis acceptus, supernis luminaribus **misceatur.**

O TRULY blessed night! which plundered the Egyptians, and enriched the Hebrews. A night in which heaven is united to earth, and God to man. We beseech thee, therefore, O Lord! that this candle, consecrated to the honor of thy name, may continue burning to dissipate the darkness of this night; and being accepted as a sweet

Flammas ejus lucifer matutinus inveniat. Ille, inquam, lucifer, qui nescit occasum. Ille, qui regressus ab inferis, humano generi serenus illuxit. Precamur ergo te, Domine : ut nos famulos tuos, omnemque clerum, et devotissimum populum, una cum beatissimo Papa nostro N., et Antistite nostro N., quiete temporum concessa, in his Paschalibus gaudiis, assidua protectione regere, gubernare, et conservare digneris. Per eundem Dominum nostrum Jesum Christum Filium tuum : qui tecum vivit et regnat in unitate Spiritus sancti Deus, per omni sæcula sæculorum.

R. Amen.

odor, may be united with the celestial lights. Let the morning-star find it burning. That morning-star, I mean, which never sets. Which, being returned from hell, shone with brightness on mankind. We beseech thee, therefore, O Lord ! to grant us peace during this paschal solemnity, and with thy constant protection to rule, govern, and preserve us, thy servants, all the Clergy, and the devout Laity, together with our Holy Father, Pope N.; and our Bishop, N.; through the same Lord Jesus Christ, thy Son, who with thee and the Holy Ghost liveth and reigneth one God, for ever and ever.

R. Amen.

After the benediction of the Paschal Candle, the prophecies are read, and the Catechumens are instructed and prepared to receive baptism.

THE FIRST PROPHECY.

Gen. i. IN principio creavit Deus

Gen. i. IN the beginning, God

cœlum et terram. Terra autem erat inanis et vacua, et tenebræ erant super faciem abyssi: et Spiritus Dei ferebatur super aquas. Dixitque Deus: Fiat lux. Et facta est lux. Et vidit Deus lucem quod esset bona: et divisit lucem a tenebris. Appellavitque lucem diem, et tenebras noctem: factumque est vespere et mane, dies unus. Dixit quoque Deus: Fiat firmamentum in medio aquarum, et dividat aquas ab aquis. Et fecit Deus firmamentum, divisitque aquas, quæ erant sub firmamento, ab his quæ erant super firmamentum. Et factum est ita. Vocavitque Deus firmamentum, cœlum: et factum est vespere et mane, dies secundus. Dixit vero Deus: Congregentur aquæ, quæ sub cœlo sunt, in locum unum, et appareat arida. Et factum est ita.

created heaven and earth. And the earth was void and empty, and darkness was upon the face of the deep: and the Spirit of God moved over the waters. And God said: Be light made. And light was made. And God saw the light that it was good: and he divided the light from the darkness. And he called the light day, and the darkness night: and there was evening and morning one day. And God said: Let there be a firmament made amidst the waters: and let it divide the waters from the waters. And God made a firmament, and divided the waters that were under the firmament, from those that were above the firmament. And it was so. And God called the firmament heaven: and the evening and morning were the second day

Et vocavit Deus aridam, terram, congregationesque aquarum appellavit maria. Et vidit Deus quod esset bonum. Et ait : Germinet terra herbam virentem, et facientem semen, et lignum pomiferum faciens fructum juxta genus suum, cujus semen in semetipso sit super terram. Et factum est ita. Et protulit terra herbam virentem, et facientem semen juxta genus suum, lignumque faciens fructum, et habens unumquodque sementem secundum speciem suam. Et vidit Deus quod esset bonum. Et factum est vespere et mane, dies tertius.

God also said : Let the waters that are under the heaven, be gathered together into one place : and let the dry land appear. And it was so done. And God called the dry land, earth : and the gathering together of the waters he called seas. And God saw that it was good. And he said : Let the earth bring forth the green herb, and such as may seed ; and the fruit tree yielding fruit after its kind, which may have seed in itself upon the earth. And it was so done. And the earth brought forth the green herb, and such as yieldeth seed according to its kind, and the tree that beareth fruit, having seed each one according to its kind. And God saw that it was good. And the evening and the morning were the third day.

Dixit autem Deus : And God said : Let

Fiant luminaria in firmamento cœli, et dividant diem ac noctem, et sint in signa et tempora, et dies et annos: ut luceant in firmamento cœli, et illuminent terram. Et factum est ita. Fecitque Deus duo luminaria magna: luminare majus, ut præesset diei; et luminare minus, ut præesset nocti; et stellas. Et posuit eas in firmamento cœli, ut lucerent super terram, et præessent diei ac nocti, et dividerent lucem ac tenebras. Et vidit Deus quod esset bonum. Et factum est vespere et mane, dies quartus.

Dixit etiam Deus: Producant aquæ reptile animæ viventis, et volatile super terram sub firmamento cœli. Creavitque Deus cete grandia, et omnem animam

there be lights made in the firmament of heaven, to divide the day and the night, and let them be for signs, and for seasons, and for days and years: to shine in the firmament of heaven, and to give light upon the earth. And it was so done. And God made two great lights: a greater light to rule the day; and a lesser light to rule the night; and stars. And he set them in the firmament of heaven, to shine upon the earth, and to rule the day and the night, and to divide the light and the darkness. And God saw that it was good. And the evening and morning were the fourth day.

God also said: Let the waters bring forth the creeping creature having life, and the fowl that may fly over the earth under the firmament of heaven. And

viventem atque motabilem, quam produxerant aquæ in species suas: et omne volatile secundum genus suum. Et vidit Deus quod esset bonum. Benedixitque eis, dicens: Crescite et multiplicamini, et replete aquas maris: avesque multiplicentur super terram. Et factum est vespere et mane, dies quintus. Dixit quoque Deus: Producat terra animam viventem in genere suo, jumenta, et reptilia, et bestias terræ, secundum species suas. Factumque est ita. Et fecit Deus bestias terræ juxta species suas, et jumenta, et omne reptile terræ in genere suo. Et vidit Deus quod esset bonum, et ait: Faciamus hominem ad imaginem et similitudinem nostram: et præsit piscibus maris, et volatilibus cœli, et bestiis, universæque terræ, omnique reptili quod move-

God created the great whales, and every living and moving creature, which the waters brought forth, according to their kinds, and every winged fowl according to its kind. And God saw that it was good. And he blessed them, saying: Increase and multiply, and fill the waters of the sea: and let the birds be multiplied upon the earth. And the evening and morning were the fifth day. And God said: Let the earth bring forth the living creature in its kind, cattle, and creeping things, and beasts of the earth according to their kinds: and it was so done. And God made the beasts of the earth according to their kinds, and cattle, and everything that creepeth on the earth after its kind. And God saw that it was good. And he said

tui in terra. Et creavit Deus hominem ad imaginem suam: ad imaginem Dei creavit illum, masculum et feminam creavit eos. Benedixitque illis Deus, et ait: Crescite et multiplicamini, et replete terram, et subjicite eam, et dominamini piscibus maris, et volatilibus cœli, et universis animantibus, quæ moventur super terram. Dixitque Deus: Ecce dedi vobis omnem herbam afferentem semen super terram, et universa ligna quæ habent in semetipsis sementem generis sui, ut sint vobis in escam; et cunctis animantibus terræ, omnique volucri cœli, et universis quæ moventur in terra, et in quibus est anima vivens, ut habeant ad vescendum. Et factum est ita. Viditque Deus cuncta quæ fecerat: et erant valde bona. Et factum est vespere et

Let us make man to our image and likeness: and let him have dominion over the fishes of the sea, and the fowls of the air, and the beasts, and the whole earth, and every creeping creature that moveth upon the earth. And God created man to his own image: to the image of God he created him, male and female he created them. And God blessed them, saying: Increase and multiply, and fill the earth, and subdue it, and rule over the fishes of the sea, and the fowls of the air, and all living creatures that move upon the earth. And God said: Behold I have given you every herb bearing seed upon the earth, and all trees that have in themselves seed of their own kind, to be your meat: and to all beasts of the earth, and to every fowl of the air, and to all that move

mane, dies sextus. Igitur perfecti sunt cœli et terra, et omnis ornatus eorum. Complevitque Deus die septimo opus suum, quod fecerat: et requievit die septimo ab universo opere, quod patrarat.

upon the earth, and wherein there is life that they may have to feed upon. And it was so done. And God saw all the things that he had made, and they were very good. And the evening and morning were the sixth day. So the heavens and the earth were finished, and all the furniture of them. And on the seventh day God ended his work which he had made: and he rested on the seventh day from all his work which he had done.

Oremus.
Flectamus genua.

Let us pray.
Let us bend our knees.

R. Levate.

R. Rise up.

Deus, qui mirabiliter creasti hominem, et mirabilius redemisti: da nobis, quæsumus, contra oblectamenta peccati, mentis ratione persistere, ut mereamur ad æterna gau-

O God! who hast wonderfully created man, and more wonderfully redeemed him; grant us, we beseech thee, such strength of mind and reason against the allurements of sin, that

dia pervenire. Per Dominum nostrum Jesum Christum, etc.

R. Amen.

we may deserve to obtain eternal joy; through Jesus Christ our Lord.

R. Amen.

THE SECOND PROPHECY.

Gen. v. NOE vero cum quingentorum esset annorum, genuit Sem, Cham, et Japheth. Cumque cœpissent homines multiplicari super terram, et filias procreassent; videntes filii Dei filias hominum quod essent pulchræ, acceperunt sibi uxores ex omnibus quas elegerant. Dixitque Deus: Non permanebit spiritus meus in homine in æternum, quia caro est: eruntque dies illius centum viginti annorum. Gigantes autem erant super terram in diebus illis. Postquam enim ingressi sunt filii Dei ad filias hominum, illæque genuerunt; isti sunt potentes a sæculo viri famosi. Videns autem Deus quod multa militia

Gen. v. NOE, when he was five hundred years old, begat Sem, Cham, and Japheth. And after that men began to be multiplied upon the earth, and daughters were born to them. The sons of God seeing the daughters of men, that they were fair, took to themselves wives of all, which they chose. And God said: My spirit shall not remain in man for ever, because he is flesh, and his days shall be a hundred and twenty years. Now giants were upon the earth in those days. For after the sons of God went in to the daughters of men, and they brought forth children, these are the mighty men of old,

hominum esset in terra, et cuncta cogitatio cordis intenta esset ad malum omni tempore, pœnituit eum quod hominem fecisset in terra. Et tactus dolore cordis intrinsecus: Delebo, inquit, hominem quem creavi, a facie terræ, ab homine usque ad animantia, a reptili usque ad volucres cœli: pœnitet enim me fecisse eos. Noe vero invenit gratiam coram Domino. Hæ sunt generationes Noe. Noe vir justus atque perfectus fuit in generationibus suis; cum Deo ambulavit. Et genuit tres filios, Sem, Cham, et Japheth. Corrupta est autem terra coram Deo, et repleta est iniquitate.

men of renown. And God seeing that the wickedness of men was great on the earth, and that all the thought of their heart was bent upon evil at all times, it repented him that he had made man on the earth. And being touched inwardly with sorrow of heart, he said: I will destroy man, whom I have created, from the face of the earth, from man even to beasts, from creeping things even to the fowls of the air, for it repenteth me that I have made them. But Noe found grace before the Lord. These are the generations of Noe: Noe was a just and perfect man in his generations, he walked with God. And he begat three sons, Sem, Cham, and Japheth. And the earth was corrupted before God, and was filled with iniquity

Cumque vidisset Deus terram esse corruptam (omnis quippe caro corruperat viam suam super terram), dixit ad Noe: Finis universæ carnis venit coram me: repleta est terra iniquitate a facie eorum, et ego disperdam eos cum terra. Fac tibi arcam de lignis lævigatis: mansiunculas in arca facies, et bitumine linies intrinsecus et extrinsecus. Et sic facies eam: trecentorum cubitorum erit longitudo arcæ, quinquaginta cubitorum latitudo, et triginta cubitorum altitudo illius. Fenestram in arca facies, et in cubito consummabis summitatem ejus: ostium autem arcæ pones ex latere: deorsum, cœnacula, et tristega facies in ea. Ecce ego adducam aquas diluvii super terram, ut interficiam omnem carnem, in qua spiritus vitæ est subter cœlum:

And when God had seen that the earth was corrupted (for all flesh had corrupted its way upon the earth), he said to Noe: The end of all flesh is come before me, the earth is filled with iniquity through them, and I will destroy them with the earth. Make thee an ark of timber planks: thou shalt make little rooms in the ark, and thou shalt pitch it within and without. And thus shalt thou make it: The length of the ark shall be three hundred cubits: the breadth of it fifty cubits, and the height of it thirty cubits. Thou shalt make a window in the ark, and in a cubit shalt thou finish the top of it; and the door of the ark thou shalt set in the side: with lower middle chambers and third stories shalt thou make it. Behold I will bring

universa quæ in terra sunt, consumentur. Ponamque fœdus meum tecum : et ingredieris arcam, tu, et filii tui, uxor tua, et uxores filiorum tuorum tecum. Et ex cunctis animantibus universæ carnis bina induces in arcam, ut vivant tecum ; masculini sexus et feminini. De volucribus juxta genus suum, et de jumentis in genere suo, et ex omni reptili terræ secundum genus suum : bina de omnibus ingredientur tecum, et possint vivere. Tolles igitur tecum ex omnibus escis, quæ mandi possunt, et comportabis apud te : et erunt tam

the waters of a great flood upon the earth, to destroy all flesh, wherein is the breath of life under heaven. All things that are in the earth shall be consumed. And I will establish my covenant with thee, and thou shalt enter into the ark, thou and thy sons, and thy wife, and the wives of thy sons with thee. And of every living creature of all flesh, thou shalt bring two of a sort into the ark, that they may live with thee : of the male sex, and the female. Of fowls according to their kind, and of beasts in their kind, and of everything that creepeth on the earth according to its kind ; two of every sort shall go in with thee, that they may live. Thou shalt take unto thee of all food that may be eaten, and thou shalt lay it up with thee : and

tibi, quam illis in cibum.

Fecit igitur Noe omnia quæ præceperat illi Deus. Eratque sexcentorum annorum, quando diluvii aquæ inundaverunt super terram. Rupti sunt omnes fontes abyssi magnæ, et cataractæ cœli apertæ sunt: et facta est pluvia super terram quadraginta diebus et quadraginta noctibus. In articulo diei illius ingressus est Noe, et Sem, et Cham, et Japheth, filii ejus, uxor illius, et tres uxores filiorum ejus cum eis in arcam: ipsi et omne animal, secundum genus suum, universaque jumenta in genere suo, et omne quod movetur super terram in genere suo, cunctumque volatile secundum genus suum. Porro arca ferebatur super aquas. Et aquæ prævaluerunt nimis super terram: opertique sunt omnes montes excelsi

it shall be food for thee and them.

And Noe did all things which God commanded him. And he was six hundred years old, when the waters of the flood overflowed the earth. All the fountains of the great deep were broken up, and the flood-gates of heaven were opened: and the rain fell upon the earth forty days and forty nights. In the self same day Noe, and Sem, and Cham, and Japheth, his sons, his wife, and the three wives of his sons with them went into the ark: they and every beast according to its kind, and all the cattle in their kind, and everything that moveth upon the earth according to its kind, and every fowl according to its kind. And the ark was carried upon the waters. And the waters prevailed beyond measure upon the earth:

sub universo cœlo. Quindecim cubitis altior fuit aqua super montes, quos operuerat. Consumptaque est omnis caro, quæ movebatur super terram, volucrum, animantium, bestiarum, omniumque reptilium quæ reptant super terram. Remansit autem solus Noe, et qui cum eo erant in arca. Obtinueruntque aquæ terram centum quinquaginta diebus.

and all the high mountains under the whole heaven were covered. The water was fifteen cubits higher than the mountains, which it covered. And all flesh was destroyed that moved upon the earth, both of fowl, and of cattle, and of beasts, and of all creeping things that creep upon the earth; and all men. And all things, wherein there is the breath of life on the earth, died. And he destroyed all the substance, that was upon the earth, from man even to beast, and the creeping things and fowls of the air; and they were destroyed from the earth: and Noe only remained, and they that were with him in the ark. And the waters prevailed upon the earth a hundred and fifty days.

Recordatus autem Deus Noe, cunctorumque

And God remembered Noe, and all the living

animantium, et omnium jumentorum, quæ erant cum eo in arca, adduxit spiritum super terram, et imminutæ sunt aquæ. Et clausi sunt fontes abyssi, et cataractæ cœli : et prohibitæ sunt pluviæ de cœlo. Reversæque sunt aquæ de terra euntes et redeuntes : et cœperunt minui post centum quinquaginta dies. Cumque transissent quadraginta dies, aperiens Noe fenestram arcæ, quam fecerat, dimisit corvum : qui egrediebatur, et non revertebatur, donec siccarentur aquæ super terram. Emisit quoque columbam post eum, ut videret si jam cessassent aquæ super faciem terræ. Quæ cum non invenisset ubi requiesceret pes ejus, reversa est ad eum in arcam ; aquæ enim erant super universam terram : extenditque manum, et apprehensam intulit in arcam. Ex-

creatures, and all the cattle which were with him in the ark, and brought a wind upon the earth, and the waters were abated. The fountains also of the deep, and the flood-gates of heaven, were shut up : and the rain from heaven was restrained. And the waters returned from off the earth, going and coming : and they began to be abated after a hundred and fifty days. And after that forty days were passed, Noe opening the window of the ark, which he had made, sent forth a raven. Which went forth, and did not return till the waters were dried up upon the earth. He sent forth also a dove after him to see if the waters had now ceased upon the face of the earth. But she not finding where her foot might rest, returned to him into the ark, for the

pectatis autem ultra septem diebus aliis, rursum dimisit columbam ex arca. At illa venit ad eum ad vesperam, portans ramum olivæ virentibus foliis in ore suo. Intellexit ergo Noe quod cessassent aquæ super terram. Expectavitque nihilominus septem alios dies: et emisit columbam, quæ non est reversa ultra ad eum. Locutus est autem Deus ad Noe, dicens: Egredere de arca, tu, et uxor tua, filii tui et uxores filiorum tuorum tecum. Cuncta animantia, quæ sunt apud te, ex omni carne, tam in volatilibus, quam in bestiis et universis reptilibus, quæ reptant super terram, educ tecum, et ingredimini super terram: crescite, et multiplicamini super eam. Egressus est ergo Noe, et filii ejus, uxor illius, et uxores filiorum ejus cum eo. Sed et

waters were upon the whole earth: and he put forth his hand, and caught her and brought her into the ark. And having waited yet seven other days, he again sent forth the dove out of the ark. And she came to him in the evening carrying a bough of an olive-tree, with green leaves, in her mouth. Noe therefore understood that the waters were ceased upon the earth. And he stayed yet other seven days: and he sent forth the dove, which returned not any more unto him. And God spoke to Noe, saying: Go out of the ark, thou and thy wife, thy sons and the wives of thy sons with thee. All living things that are with thee of all flesh, as well in fowls, as in beasts, and all creeping things that creep upon the earth, bring out with thee. and

omnia animantia, jumenta, et reptilia, quæ reptant super terram secundum genus suum, egressa sunt de arca. Ædificavit autem Noe altare Domino : et tollens de cunctis pecoribus et volucribus mundis, obtulit holocausta super altare. Odoratusque est Dominus odorem suavitatis.

go ye upon the earth : increase and multiply upon it. So Noe went out, he and his sons : his wife, and the wives of his sons with him. And all living things, and cattle, and creeping things that creep upon the earth, according to their kinds, went out of the ark. And Noe built an altar unto the Lord : and taking of all cattle and fowls that were clean, offered holocausts upon the altar. And the Lord smelled a sweet savor.

Oremus.
Flectamus genua.
R. Levate.
Deus incommutabilis virtus, et lumen æternum : respice propitius ad totius Ecclesiæ tuæ mirabile sacramentum, et opus salutis humanæ perpetuæ dispositionis effectu tranquillius operare : totusque mundus experiatur, et videat dejecta erigi, inveterata

Let us pray.
Let us bend our knees.
R. Rise up.
O God ! whose power is unchangeable and whose light is eternal : mercifully regard the wonderful sacrament of thy whole Church, and by an effect of thy perpetual providence, perform with tranquillity the work of human salvation : and let th

renovari, et per ipsum redire omnia in integrum, a quo sumpsere principium: Dominum nostrum Jesum Christum Filium tuum: Qui tecum vivit et regnat, etc.

whole world experience and see, that what was fallen is raised up, what was old is made new, and that all things are re-established through him that gave them their first being, our Lord Jesus Christ, who liveth and reigneth with thee, etc.

THE THIRD PROPHECY.

Gen. xxii. IN diebus illis : Tentavit Deus Abraham, et dixit ad eum: Abraham, Abraham. At ille respondit: Adsum. Ait illi : Tolle filium tuum unigenitum, quem diligis, Isaac, et vade in terram Visionis : atque ibi offeres eum in holocaustum super unum montium, quem monstravero tibi. Igitur Abraham de nocte consurgens, stravit asinum suum; ducens secum duos juvenes, et Isaac filium suum. Cumque concidisset ligna in holocaus-

Gen. xxii. IN those days: God tempted Abraham and said to him: Abraham, Abraham! And he answered: Here I am. He said to him: Take thy only-begotten son Isaac, whom thou lovest, and go into the land of Vision: and there thou shalt offer him for an holocaust upon one of the mountains which I will show thee. So Abraham rising up in the night, saddled his ass; and took with him two young men, and Isaac his son and wher

tum, abiit ad locum quem præceperat ei Deus. Die autem tertio, elevatis oculis, vidit locum procul; dixitque ad pueros suos: Expectate hic cum asino : ego et puer illuc usque properantes, postquam adoraverimus, revertemur ad vos. Tulit quoque ligna holocausti, et imposuit super Isaac filium suum: ipse vero portabat in manibus ignem et gladium. Cumque duo pergerent simul, dixit Isaac patri suo: Pater mi. At ille respondit: Quid vis fili? Ecce, inquit, ignis et ligna: ubi est victima holocausti? Dixit autem Abraham: Deus providebit sibi victimam holocausti, fili mi.

Pergebant ergo pariter, et venerunt ad locum quem ostenderat ei

he had cut wood for the holocaust, he went his way to the place, which God had commanded him. And on the third day, lifting up his eyes, he saw the place afar off. And he said to his young men : Stay you here with the ass: I and the boy will go with speed as far as yonder, and after we have worshipped, will return to you. And he took the wood for the holocaust, and laid it upon Isaac his son: and he himself carried in his hands fire and a sword. And as they two went on together, Isaac said to his father: My father! And he answered : What wilt thou, son ? Behold, saith he, fire and wood : where is the victim for the holocaust ? And Abraham said : God will provide himself a victim for a holocaust, my son.

So they went on together. And they came to the place which God

Deus, in quo ædificavit altare, et desuper ligna composuit. Cumque alligasset Isaac filium suum, posuit eum in altare super struem lignorum. Extenditque manum, et arripuit gladium, ut immolaret filium suum. Et ecce Angelus Domini de cœlo clamavit, dicens: Abraham, Abraham. Qui respondit: Adsum. Dixitque ei: Non extendas manum tuam super puerum, neque facias illi quidquam: nunc cognovi quod times Deum, et non pepercisti unigenito filio tuo propter me. Levavit Abraham oculos suos, viditque post tergum arietem inter vepres hærentem cornibus, quem assumens obtulit holocaustum pro filio. Appellavitque nomen loci illius, Dominus videt. Unde usque hodie dicitur: In monte Dominus videbit. Vocavit autem Angelus Domini Abraham se-

had showed him, where he built an altar, and laid the wood in order upon it: and when he had bound Isaac his son, he laid him on the altar upon the pile of wood. And he put forth his hand, and took the sword, to sacrifice his son. And behold an angel of the Lord from heaven called to him, saying: Abraham, Abraham! And he answered: Here I am. And he said to him: Lay not thy hand upon the boy, neither do thou anything to him: now I know that thou fearest God, and hast not spared thy only-begotten son for my sake. Abraham lifted up his eyes, and saw behind his back a ram amongst the briers, sticking fast by the horns, which he took and offered for a holocaust instead of his son. And he called the name of that place. the Lord

cundo de cœlo, dicens: Per memetipsum juravi, dicit Dominus: quia fecisti hanc rem, et non pepercisti filio tuo unigenito propter me, benedicam tibi, et multiplicabo semen tuum sicut stellas cœli, et velut arenam quæ est in littore maris. Possidebit semen tuum portas inimicorum suorum, et benedicentur in semine tuo omnes gentes terræ, quia obedisti voci meæ. Reversus est Abraham ad pueros suos, abieruntque Bersabee simul, et habitavit ibi.

seeth. Whereupon even to this day, it is said: In the mountain the Lord will see. And the angel of the Lord called to Abraham a second time from heaven, saying: By my own self have I sworn, saith the Lord: because thou hast done this thing, and hast not spared thy only-begotten son for my sake: I will bless thee, and I will multiply thy seed as the stars of heaven, and as the sand that is by the sea-shore: thy seed shall possess the gates of their enemies. And in thy seed shall all the nations of the earth be blessed, because thou hast obeyed my voice. Abraham returned to his young men, and they went to Bersabee together, and he dwelt there.

Oremus.
Flectamus genua.
R. Levate.
Deus, fidelium pater summe, qui in toto orbe

Let us pray.
Let us bend our knees.
R. Rise up.
O God, the sovereign Father of the faithful!

terrarum, promissionis tuæ filios diffusa adopti- nis gratia multiplicas; et per Paschale sacra- mentum, Abraham pue- rum tuum universarum, sicut jurasti, gentium ef- ficis patrem: da populis tuis digne ad gratiam tuæ vocationis introire. Per Dominum nostrum Jesum Christum, etc.

who throughout the world multipliest the children of thy promise, by the grace of thy adoption; and makest thy servant Abraham, according to thy oath, the father of all nations, by this Paschal Sacra- ment; grant that thy people may worthily re- ceive the grace of thy vocation; through our Lord, etc.

THE FOURTH PROPHECY.

Exod. xiv. IN diebus illis: Fac- tum est in vigilia matu- tina, et ecce respiciens Dominus super castra Ægyptiorum per colum- nam ignis et nubis, inter- fecit exercitum eorum: et subvertit rotas cur- ruum, ferebanturque in profundum. Dixerunt ergo Ægyptii: Fugiamus Israelem; Dominus en- im pugnat pro eis contra nos. Et ait Dominus ad Moysen: Extende ma- num tuam super mare.

Exod. xiv. IN those days it came to pass in the morning watch, and be- hold the Lord looking upon the Egyptian army through the pillar of fire and of the cloud, slew their host, and over- threw the wheels of the chariots, and they were carried into the deep. And the Egyptians said: Let us flee from Israel: for the Lord fighteth for them against us. And the Lord said to Moses:

ut revertantur aquæ ad Ægyptios super currus et equites eorum. Cumque extendisset Moyses manum contra mare, reversum est primo diluculo ad priorem locum: fugientibusque Ægyptiis occurrerunt aquæ, et involvit eos Dominus in mediis fluctibus. Reversæque sunt aquæ, et operuerunt currus et equites cuncti exercitus Pharaonis, qui sequentes ingressi fuerant mare: nec unus quidem superfuit ex eis. Filii autem Israel perrexerunt per medium sicci maris, et aquæ eis erant quasi pro muro a dextris et a sinistris: liberavitque Dominus in die illa Israel de manu Ægyptiorum. Et viderunt Ægyptios mortuos super litus maris, et manum magnam, quam exercuerat Dominus contra eos: timuitque populus Dominum, et crediderunt Domino, et Moysi servo ejus.

Stretch forth thy hand over the sea, that the waters may come again upon the Egyptians, upon their chariots and horsemen. And when Moses had stretched forth his hand towards the sea, it returned at the first break of day to the former place; and as the Egyptians were fleeing away, the waters came upon them, and the Lord shut them up in the middle of the waves. And the waters returned, and covered the chariots and the horsemen of all the army of Pharao, who had come into the sea after them, neither did there so much as one of them remaim. But the children of Israel marched through the midst of the sea upon dry land, and the waters were to them as a wall on the right hand and on the left. And the Lord delivered Israel

Tunc cecinit Moyses et filii Israel carmen hoc Domino, et dixerunt:

in that day out of the hands of the Egyptians. And they saw the Egyptians dead upon the sea-shore, and the mighty hand that the Lord had used against them: and the people feared the Lord, and they believed the Lord, and Moses his servant. Then Moses and the children of Israel sung this canticle to the Lord, and said

THE TRACT.

CANTEMUS Domino: gloriose enim honorificatus est: equum et ascensorem projecit in mare: adjutor et protector factus est mihi in salutem.

LET us sing to the Lord; for he is gloriously magnified, the horse and the rider he hath thrown into the sea; he hath been my help, and my protector, and Saviour.

V. Hic Deus meus, et honorificabo eum: Deus patris mei, et exaltabo eum.

V. He is my God, and I will glorify him; the God of my father, and I will exalt him.

V. Dominus conterens bella: Dominus nomen est illi.

V. The Lord putteth an end to wars; the Lord is his name.

Oremus.

Flectamus genua.

R. Levate.

Deus, cujus antiqua miracula etiam nostris sæculis coruscare sentimus: dum, quod uni populo a persecutione Ægyptiaca liberando, dexteræ tuæ potentia contulisti, id in salutem gentium per aquam regenerationis operaris: præsta, ut in Abrahæ filios, et in Israeliticam dignitatem, totius mundi transeat plenitudo. Per Dominum nostrum, etc.

Let us pray.

Let us bend our knees.

R. Rise up.

O God! whose ancient miracles we see renewed in our days; whilst, by the water of regeneration, thou performest for the salvation of the Gentiles, that which by the power of thy right hand thou didst for the deliverance of one people from the Egyptian persecution; grant that all the nations of the world may become the children of Abraham, and partake of the dignity of the people of Israel; through our Lord, etc.

THE FIFTH PROPHECY.

Isaiæ liv. HÆC est hæreditas servorum Domini, et justitia eorum apud me, dicit Dominus. Omnes sitientes venite ad aquas: et qui non habetis argentum, properate, emite, et comedite· venite emite

Isaias liv. THIS is the inheritance of the servants of the Lord, and their justice with me, saith the Lord. All you that thirst, come to the waters: and you that have no money, make haste, buy

absque argento, et absque ulla commutatione vinum et lac. Quare appenditis argentum non in panibus, et laborem vestrum non in saturitate? Audite audientes me, et comedite bonum, et delectabitur in crassitudine anima vestra. Inclinate aurem vestram, et venite ad me: audite et vivet anima vestra, et feriam vobiscum pactum sempiternum misericordias David fidelis. Ecce testem populis dedi eum, ducem ac præceptorem Gentibus. Ecce gentem, quam nesciebas, vocabis: et gentes, quæ te non cognoverunt, ad te current propter Dominum Deum tuum et Sanctum Israel, quia glorificavit te. Quærite Dominum, dum inveniri potest: invocate eum, dum prope est. Derelinquat impius viam suam, et vir iniquus cogitationes suas, et revertatur ad Dominum, et

and eat: come ye, buy wine and milk without money, and without any price. Why do you spend money for that which is not bread, and your labor for that which doth not satisfy you? Hearken diligently to me, and eat that which is good, and your soul shall be delighted in fatness. Incline your ear, and come to me; hear, and your soul shall live, and I will make an everlasting covenant with you, the mercies of David faithful. Behold I have given him for a witness to the people, for a leader and a master to the Gentiles. Behold thou shalt call a nation, which thou knewest not; and the nations that knew not thee shall run to thee, because of the Lord thy God, and for the Holy One of Israel, for he hath glorified thee. Seek ye the Lord

miserebitur ejus, et ad
Deum nostrum, quoniam
multus est ad ignoscen-
dum. Non enim cogita-
tiones meæ, cogitationes
vestræ, neque viæ ves-
træ, viæ meæ, dicit Do-
minus. Quia sicut ex-
altantur cœli a terra, sic
exaltatæ sunt viæ meæ a
viis vestris, et cogitationes meæ a cogitatio-
nibus vestris. Et quo-
modo descendit imber et
nix de cœlo, et illuc ul-
tra non revertitur, sed
inebriat terram, et infun-
dit eam, et germinare
eam facit, et dat semen
serenti, et panem come-
denti: sic erit verbum
meum, quod egredietur
de ore meo: non rever-
tetur ad me vacuum, sed

while he may be found :
call upon him while he
is near. Let the wicked
forsake his way, and
the unjust man his
thoughts, and let him
return to the Lord, and
he will have mercy on
him ; and to our God,
for he is bountiful to for·
give. For my thoughts
are not your thoughts :
nor your ways my
ways, saith the Lord.
For as the heavens are
exalted above the earth,
so are my ways exalted
above your ways, and
my thoughts above your
thoughts. And as the
rain and the snow come
down from heaven, and
return no more thither,
but soak the earth, and
water it, and make it to
spring, and give seed to
the sower, and bread to
the eater: so shall my
word be, which shall go
forth from my mouth :
it shall not return to me
void, but it shall do
whatsoever I please, and

faciet quæcumque volui, et prosperabitur in his, ad quæ misi illud, dicit Dominus omnipotens.

shall prosper in the things for which I sent it, saith the Lord Almighty.

Oremus.

Let us pray.

Flectamus genua.

Let us bend our knees.

R. Levate.

R. Rise up.

Omnipotens sempiterne Deus, multiplica in honorem nominis tui, quod patrum fidei spopondisti, et promissionis filios sacra adoptione dilata: ut quod priores sancti non dubitaverunt futurum, Ecclesia tua magna jam ex parte cognoscat impletum. Per Dominum nostrum Jesum Christum, etc.

Almighty and eternal God! multiply for the honor of thy name what thou didst promise to the faith of our forefathers; and increase, by thy sacred adoption, the children of that promise; that, what the ancient saints doubted not would come to pass, thy Church may now find in great part accomplished; through our Lord, etc.

THE SIXTH PROPHECY.

Baruch iii. AUDI, Israel, mandata' vitæ : auribus percipe, ut scias prudentiam. Quid est, Israel, quod in terra inimicorum es? Inveterasti in terra aliena, coinquinatus es cum mortuis: de-

Baruch iii. HEAR, O Israel! the commandments of life; give ear, that thou mayest learn wisdom. How happeneth it, O Israel! that thou art in thy enemies' land? Thou art grown old in a

putatus es cum descendentibus in infernum. Dereliquisti fontem sapientiæ. Nam si in via Dei ambulasses, habitasses utique in pace sempiterna. Disce ubi sit prudentia, ubi sit virtus, ubi sit intellectus: ut scias simul ubi sit longiturnitas vitæ et victus, ubi sit lumen oculorum, et pax. Quis invenit locum ejus? Et quis intravit in thesauros ejus? Ubi sunt principes gentium, et qui dominantur super bestias quæ sunt super terram? Qui in avibus cœli ludunt, qui argentum thesaurizant, et aurum, in quo confidunt homines, et non est finis acquisitionis eorum? Qui argentum fabricant, et soliciti sunt, nec est inventio operum illorum? Exterminati

strange country, thou art defiled with the dead: thou art counted with them that go down into hell. Thou hast forsaken the fountain of wisdom: for if thou hadst walked in the way of God, thou hadst surely dwelt in peace for ever. Learn where is wisdom, where is strength, where is understanding: that thou mayest know also where is length of days and life, where is the light of the eyes, and peace. Who hath found out her place? and who hath gone into her treasures? Where are the princes of the nations, and they that rule over the beasts, that are upon the earth? That take their pastime with the birds of the air, that hoard up silver and gold, wherein men trust, and there is no end of their getting? who work in silver and are solicitous,

sunt, et ad inferos descenderunt, et alii loco eorum surrexerunt.

and their works are unsearchable. They are cut off, and are gone down to hell, and others are risen up in their place.

Juvenes viderunt lumen et habitaverunt super terram : viam autem disciplinæ ignoraverunt, neque intellexerunt semitas ejus, neque filii eorum susceperunt eam, a facie ipsorum longe facta est : non est audita in terra Chanaan, neque visa est in Theman. Filii quoque Agar, qui exquirunt prudentiam quæ de terra est, negotiatores Merrhæ et Theman, et fabulatores, et exquisitores prudentiæ et intelligentiæ : viam autem sapientiæ nescierunt, neque commemorati sunt semitas ejus. O Israel, quam magna est domus Dei, et ingens locus possessionis ejus ! Magnus est, et non habet finem; excelsus et immensus. Ibi

Young men have seen the light, and dwelt upon the earth : but the way of knowledge they have not known, nor have they understood the paths thereof, neither have their children received it, it is far from their face. It hath not been heard in the land of Chanaan, neither hath it been seen in Theman. The children of Agar also, that search after the wisdom that is of the earth, the merchants of Merrha, and of Theman, and the tellers of fables, and searchers of prudence and understanding: but the way of wisdom they have not known, neither have they remembered her paths. O Israel! how great is the house

fuerunt gigantes nominati illi, qui ab initio fuerunt, statura magna, scientes bellum. Non hos elegit Dominus, neque viam disciplinæ invenerunt: propterea perierunt. Et quoniam non habuerunt sapientiam, interierunt propter suam insipientiam.

of God, and how vast is the place of his possession! It is great, and hath no end: it is high and immense. There were the giants, those renowned men, that were from the beginning, of great stature, expert in war. The Lord chose not them, neither did they find the way of knowledge: therefore did they perish. And because they had not wisdom, they perished through their folly.

Quis ascendit in cœlum, et accepit eam, et eduxit eam de nubibus? Quis transfretavit mare, et invenit illam, et attulit illam super aurum electum? Non est qui possit scire vias ejus, neque qui exquirat semitas ejus: sed qui scit universa, novit eam, et adinvenit eam prudentia sua: qui præparavit terram in æterno tempore, et replevit eam

Who hath gone up into heaven, and taken her, and brought her down from the clouds? Who hath passed over the sea, and found her, and brought her preferably to chosen gold? There is none that is able to know her ways, nor that can search out her paths. But he that knoweth all things, knoweth her, and hath found her out with his

pecudibus, et quadrupedibus: qui emittit lumen, et vadit; et vocavit illud, et obedit illi in tremore. Stellæ autem dederunt lumen in custodiis suis, et lætatæ sunt: vocatæ sunt, et dixerunt: Adsumus; et luxerunt ei cum jucunditate, qui fecit illas. Hic est Deus noster, et non æstimabitur alius adversus eum. Hic adinvenit omnem viam disciplinæ, et tradidit illam Jacob puero suo, et Israel dilecto suo. Post hæc in terris visus est, et cum hominibus conversatus est.

understanding: he that prepared the earth for evermore, and filled it with cattle and four-footed beasts: he that sendeth forth light, and it goeth: and hath called it, and it obeyed him with trembling. And the stars have given light in their watches, and rejoiced: they were called, and they said: Here we are: and with cheerfulness they have shined forth to him, that made them. This is our God, and there shall no other be accounted of in comparison to him. He found out all the way of knowledge, and gave it to Jacob, his servant, and to Israel, his beloved. Afterwards he was seen upon earth, and conversed with men.

Oremus.
Flectamus genua.
R. Levate.
Deus, qui Ecclesiam tuam semper gentium

Let us pray.
Let us bend our knees.
R. Rise up.
O God! who continually multipliest thy

vocatione multiplicas: concede propitius, ut quos aqua baptismatis abluis, continua protectione tuearis. Per Dominum nostrum, etc.

Church by the vocation to the Gentiles ; mercifully grant thy perpetual protection to those, whom thou washest with the water of baptism ; through our Lord, etc.

THE SEVENTH PROPHECY.

Ezech. xxxvii. IN diebus illis : Facta est super me manus Domini, et eduxit me in spiritu Domini : et dimisit me in medio campi, qui erat plenus ossibus : et circumduxit me per ea in gyro : erant autem multa valde super faciem campi, siccaque vehementer. Et dixit ad me : Fili hominis, putasne vivent ossa ista? Et dixi : Domine Deus, ut nosti. Et dixit ad me : Vaticinare de ossibus istis ; et dices eis : Ossa arida audite verbum Domini. Hæc dicit Dominus Deus ossibus his : Ecce ego intromittam in vos spiritum, et

Ezech. xxxvii. IN those days, the hand of the Lord was upon me, and brought me forth in the spirit of the Lord : and set me down in the midst of a plain that was full of bones. And he led me about through them on every side : now they were very many upon the face of the plain. And they were exceeding dry. And he said to me : Son of man ! dost thou think these bones shall live? And I answered : O Lord God ! thou knowest. And he said to me : Prophesy concerning these bones : and say to them : Ye

vivetis. Et dabo super vos nervos, et succrescere faciam super vos carnes, et superextendam in vobis cutem, et dabo vobis spiritum, et vivetis, et scietis quia ego Dominus. Et prophetavi sicut præceperat mihi : factus est autem sonitus, prophetante me, et ecce commotio, et accesserunt ossa ad ossa, unumquodque ad juncturam suam. Et vidi, et ecce super ea nervi et carnes ascenderunt : et extenta est in eis cutis desuper, et spiritum non habebant. Et dixit ad me : Vaticinare ad spiritum, vaticinare, fili hominis, et dices ad spiritum : Hæc dicit Dominus Deus : A quatuor ventis veni spiritus, et insuffla super interfectos istos, et reviviscant. Et prophetavi sicut præceperat mihi : et ingressus est in ea spiritus, et vixerunt : steteruntque super pedes

dry bones! hear the word of the Lord. Thus saith the Lord God to these bones Behold, I will send spirit into you, and you shall live. And I will lay sinews upon you, and will cause flesh to grow over you, and will cover you with skin : and I will give you spirit, and you shall live, and you shall know that I am the Lord. And I prophesied as he had commanded me : and as I prophesied, there was a noise, and behold a commotion : and the bones came together, each one to his joint. And I saw, and behold the sinews, and the flesh came up upon them : and the skin was stretched out over them, but there was no spirit in them. And he said to me : Prophesy to the spirit, prophesy, O son of man ! and say to the spirit : Thus saith the Lord God : Come

suos exercitus grandis nimis valde.

spirit from the four winds, and blow upon these slain, and let them live again. And I prophesied as he had commanded me: and the spirit came into them, and they lived: and they stood up upon their feet, an exceeding great army.

Et dixit ad me: Fili hominis, ossa hæc universa, domus Israel est: ipsi dicunt: Aruerunt ossa nostra, et periit spes nostra, et abscissi sumus. Propterea vaticinare, et dices ad eos: Hæc dicit Dominus Deus: Ecce ego aperiam tumulos vestros, et educam vos de sepulchris vestris, populus meus: et inducam vos in terram Israel, et scietis quia ego Dominus, cum aperuero sepulchra vestra, et eduxero vos de tumulis vestris, popule meus: et dedero spiritum meum in vobis, et vixeritis, et requiescere

And he said to me: Son of man! all these bones are the house of Israel. They say: Our bones are dried up, and our hope is lost, and we are cut off. Therefore prophesy, and say to them: Thus saith the Lord God: Behold, I will open your graves, and will bring you out of your sepulchres, O my people! and will bring you into the land of Israel. And you shall know that I am the Lord, when I shall have opened your sepulchres, and shall have brought you out of your graves, O my people!

vos faciam super humum vestram : dicit Dominus omnipotens.

and shall have put my spirit in you, and you shall live, and I shall make you rest upon your own land, saith the Lord Almighty.

Oremus.

Flectamus genua.

R. Levate.

Deus, qui nos ad celebrandum Paschale sacramentum, utriusque Testamenti paginis instruis : da nobis intelligere misericordiam tuam ; ut ex perceptione præsentium munerum, firma sit expectatio futurorum. Per Dominum nostrum, etc.

Let us pray.

Let us bend our knees.

R. Rise up.

O God ! who by the Scriptures of both Testaments, teachest us to celebrate the Paschal Sacrament ; give us such a sense of thy mercy, that by receiving thy present graces, we may have a firm hope of thy future blessings ; through our Lord, etc.

THE EIGHTH PROPHECY.

Isaiæ iv. APPREhendent septem mulieres virum unum in die illa, dicentes : Panem nostrum comedemus, et vestimentis nostris operiemur : tantummodo invocetur nomen tuum super nos, aufer opprobrium nostrum. In die

Isaias iv. IN that day seven women shall take hold of one man, saying : We will eat our own bread, and wear our own apparel : only let us be called by thy name, take away our reproach. In that day the bud of the Lord shall be in

illa, erit germen Domini in magnificentia et gloria, et fructus terræ sublimis, et exultatio his qui salvati fuerint de Israel. Et erit: Omnis qui relictus fuerit in Sion, et residuus in Jerusalem, sanctus vocabitur, omnis qui scriptus est in vita in Jerusalem. Si abluerit Dominus sordes filiarum Sion, et sanguinem Jerusalem laverit de medio ejus, in spiritu judicii, et spiritu ardoris. Et creabit Dominus super omnem locum montis Sion, et ubi invocatus est, nubem per diem, et fumum et splendorem ignis flammantis in nocte: super omnem enim gloriam protectio. Et tabernaculum erit in umbraculum diei ab æs-

magnificence and glory, and the fruit of the earth shall be high, and a great joy to them that shall have escaped of Israel. And it shall come to pass, that every one that shall be left in Sion, and that shall remain in Jerusalem, shall be called holy, every one that is written in life in Jerusalem. If the Lord shall wash away the filth of the daughters of Sion, and shall wash away the blood of Jerusalem, out of the midst thereof, by the spirit of judgment, and by the spirit of burning. And the Lord will create upon every place of Mount Sion, and where he is called upon, a cloud by day, and a smoke, and the brightness of a flaming fire in the night: for over all the glory shall be a protection. And there shall be a tabernacle for a shade in the day-time from the heat, and for

tu, et in securitatem et absconsionem a turbine, et a pluvia.

a security and covert from the whirlwind, and from rain.

THE TRACT.

VINEA facta est dilecto in cornu, in loco uberi.

V. Et maceriam circumdedit, et circumfodit: et plantavit vineam Sorec, et ædificavit turrim in medio ejus.

V. Et torcular fodit in ea: vinea enim Domini Sabaoth, domus Israel est.

Oremus.
Flectamus genua.
R. Levate.
Deus, qui in omnibus Ecclesiæ tuæ filiis, sanctorum prophetarum voce manifestasti, in omni loco dominationis tuæ, satorem te bonorum seminum, et electorum palmitum esse cultorem: tribue populis tuis, qui et vinearum apud te nomine censen-

MY beloved had a vineyard on a hill in a fruitful place.

V. And he fenced it in, and digged it about, and planted it with the choicest vines, and built a tower in the midst theroof.

V. And he set up a wine-press therein; for the vineyard of the Lord of Hosts is the house of Israel.

Let us pray.
Let us bend our knees.
R. Rise up.
O God! who by the mouths of thy holy prophets hast declared, that through the whole extent of thy empire it is thou that sowest the good seed, and improvest the choicest branches that are found in all the children of thy church; grant to thy people who

tur et segetum; ut spi-
narum, et tribulorum
squalore resecato, digna
efficiantur fruge fœcun-
di. Per Dominum nos-
trum Jesum Christum,
etc.

are called by the name
of vines and corn; that
they may root out all
thorns and briers, and
bring forth good fruit in
abundance; through our
Lord, etc.

THE NINTH PROPHECY.

Exod. xii. IN diebus
illis: Dix-
it Dominus ad Moysen
et Aaron, in terra Ægyp-
ti: Mensis iste, vobis
principium mensium:
primus erit in mensibus
anni. Loquimini ad
universum cœtum filio-
rum Israel, et dicite eis:
Decima die mensis hujus
tollat unusquisque ag-
num per familias et do-
mos suas. Sin autem
minor est numerus ut
sufficere possit ad ves-
cendum agnum, assumet
vicinum suum qui junc-
tus est domui suæ, jux-
ta numerum animarum
quæ sufficere possunt ad
esum agni. Erit autem
agnus absque macula,
masculus, - anniculus:

Exod. xii. IN those
days, the
Lord said to Moses and
Aaron, in the land of
Egypt; this month shall
be to you the begin-
ning of months; it shall
be the first in the
months of the year.
Speak to the whole as-
sembly of the children
of Israel, and say to
them: On the tenth day
of this month let every
man take a lamb by
their families and
houses. But if the
number be less than
may suffice to eat the
lamb, he shall take unto
him his neighbor that
joineth to his house, ac-
cording to the number
of souls which may be

juxta quem ritum tolletis et hœdum. Et servabitis eum usque ad quartamdecimam diem mensis hujus: immolabitque eum universa multitudo filiorum Israel ad vesperam. Et sument de sanguine ejus, ac ponent super utrumque postem, et in superliminaribus domorum, in quibus comedent illum. Et edent carnes nocte illa assas igni, et azymos panes cum lactucis agrestibus. Non comedetis ex eo crudum quid, nec coctum aqua, sed tantum assum igni: caput cum pedibus ejus et intestinis vorabitis: nec remanebit quidquam ex eo usque mane. Si quid residuum fuerit, igne comburetis. Sic autem comedetis illum: Renes vestros accingetis, et calceamenta habebitis in pedibus, tenentes baculos in manibus, et comedetis festinanter:

enough to eat the lamb. And it shall be a lamb without blemish, a male of one year; according to which rite also you shall take a kid. And you shall keep it until the fourteenth day of this month; and the whole multitude of the children of Israel shall sacrifice it in the evening: and they shall take of the blood thereof, and put it upon both the side-posts and on the upper door-posts of the houses wherein they shall eat it. And they shall eat the flesh that night, roasted at the fire, and unleavened bread with wild lettuce. You shall not eat thereof, anything raw, nor boiled in water, but only roasted at the fire: you shall eat the head with the feet and entrails thereof. Neither shall there remain anything of it till morning. If there be anything left, you

esc enim Phase (id est transitus) Domini.

shall burn it with fire. And thus you shall eat it : you shall gird your reins, and you shall have shoes on your feet, holding staves in your hands; and you shall eat in haste. For it is the Phase, that is, the passage of the Lord.

Oremus.

Flectamus genua.

R. Levate.

Omnipotens sempiterne Deus, qui in omnium operum tuorum dispensatione mirabilis es : intelligant redempti tui, non fuisse excellentius, quod initio factus est mundus, quam quod in fine sæculorum Pascha nostrum immolatus est Christus : Qui tecum vivit et regnat, etc.

Let us pray.

Let us bend our knees.

R. Rise up.

O Almighty and eternal God ! who art wonderful in the performance of all thy works : let thy servants whom thou hast redeemed, understand, that the creation of the world in the beginning was not more excellent, than the immolation of Christ, our Passover, at the end of the world : who with thee, etc.

THE TENTH PROPHECY.

Jonæ iii. IN diebus illis : Factum est verbum Domini ad Jonam Prophetam se-

Jonas iii. IN those days, the word of the Lord came to Jonas the second

cundo, dicens: Surge, et
vade in Niniven civita-
tem magnam, et prædica
in ea prædicationem,
quam ego loquor ad te.
Et surrexit Jonas, et
abiit in Niniven juxta
verbum Domini.   Et
Ninive erat civitas mag-
na itinere trium dierum.
Et cœpit Jonas introire
in civitatem itinere diei
unius; et clamavit, et
dixit: Adhuc quadra-
ginta dies, et Ninive
subvertetur.   Et credi-
derunt viri Ninivitæ in
Deum, et prædicaverunt
jejunium, et vestiti sunt
saccis, a majore usque
ad minorem.   Et per-
venit verbum ad regem
Ninive: et surrexit de
solio suo, et abjecit vestimentum, suum a se, et
indutus est sacco, et se-
dit in cinere.   Et cla-
mavit, et dixit in Ninive
ex ore regis, et princi-
pum ejus, dicens: Ho-
mines, et jumenta, et
boves, et pecora non
gustent quidquam: nec

time, saying: Arise, and
go to Ninive the great
city: and preach in it
the preaching that I
bid thee.   And Jonas
arose, and went to
Ninive according to the
word of the Lord: now
Ninive was a great city
of three days' journey.
And Jonas began to
enter into the city one
day's journey: and he
cried and said: Yet
forty days, and Ninive
will be destroyed.   And
the men of Ninive be-
lieved in God: and they
proclaimed a fast, and
put on sackcloth from
the greatest to the least.
And the word came to
the king of Ninive: and
he rose up out of his
throne, and cast away
his robe from him, and
was clothed with sack-
cloth and sat in ashes.
And he caused it to be
proclaimed and pub-
lished in Ninive from
the mouth of the king
and of his princes, say-

pascantur, et aquam non bibant. Et operiantur saccis homines, et jumenta, et clament ad Dominum in fortitudine, et convertatur vir a via sua mala, et ab iniquitate, quæ est in manibus eorum. Quis scit si convertatur, et ignoscat Deus: et revertatur a furore iræ suæ, et non peribimus? Et vidit Deus opera eorum, quia conversi sunt de via sua mala: et misertus est populo suo Dominus Deus noster.

ing: Let neither men nor beasts, oxen nor sheep, taste anything; let them not feed, nor drink water. And let men and beasts be covered with sackcloth, and cry to the Lord with all their strength, and let them turn every one from his evil way, and from the iniquity that is in their hands. Who can tell if God will turn, and forgive: and will turn away from his fierce anger, and we shall not perish? And God saw their works, that they were turned from their evil way : and the Lord, our God, had mercy on his people.

Oremus.

Flectamus genua.

R. Levate.

Deus, qui diversitatem Gentium in confessione tui nominis adunasti: da nobis et velle et posse quæ præcipis; ut populo ad æternitatem vo-

Let us pray.

Let us bend our knees.

R. Rise up.

O God! who hast united the several nations of the Gentiles in the profession of thy name : give us both the will and the power to

cato, una sit fides mentium, et pietas actionum. Per Dominum nostrum, Jesum Christum, etc.

obey thy command; that thy people called to eternity may have the same faith in their minds, and piety in their actions; through our Lord, etc.

THE ELEVENTH PROPHECY.

Deut. xxxi. IN diebus illis: Scripsit Moyses canticum, et docuit filios Israel. Præcepitque Dominus Josue filio Nun, et ait: Confortare, et esto robustus: tu enim introduces filios Israel in terram quam pollicitus sum, et ego ero tecum. Postquam ergo scripsit Moyses verba legis hujus in volumine, atque complevit, præcepit Levitis, qui portabant arcam fœderis Domini, dicens: Tollite librum istum, et ponite eum in latere arcæ fœderis Domini Dei vestri, ut sit ibi contra te in testimonium. Ego enim scio contentionem tuam, et

Deut. xxxi. IN those days, Moses wrote a canticle, and taught it the children of Israel. And the Lord commanded Josue the son of Nun, and said: Take courage. and be valiant: for thou shalt bring the children of Israel into the land, which I have promised, and I will be with thee. Therefore after Moses had wrote the words of this law in a volume, and finished it, he commanded the Levites, who carried the ark of the covenant of the Lord, saying: Take this book, and put it in the side of the ark of the covenant of the Lord

cervicem tuam durissimam. Adhuc vivente me, et ingrediente vobiscum, semper contentiose egistis contra Dominum: quanto magis cum mortuus fuero? Congregate ad me omnes majores natu per tribus vestras, atque doctores, et loquar audientibus eis sermones istos, et invocabo contra eos cœlum et terram. Novi enim quod post mortem meam inique agetis, et declinabitis cito de via, quam præcepi vobis. Et occurrent vobis mala in extremo tempore, quando feceritis malum in conspectu Domini, ut irritetis eum per opera manuum vestrarum. Locutus est ergo Moyses, audiente universo cœtu Israel,

your God, that it may be there for a testimony against thee. For I know thy obstinacy, and thy most stiff neck. While I am yet living, and going in with you, you have always been rebellious against the Lord: how much more when I shall be dead? Gather unto me all the ancients of your tribes, and your doctors, and I will speak these words in their hearing, and will call heaven and earth to witness against them. For I know that, after my death, you will do wickedly, and will quickly turn aside from the way that I have commanded you: and evils shall come upon you in the latter times, when you shall do evil in the sight of the Lord, to provoke him by the works of your hands. Moses therefore spoke, in the hearing of the whole assembly of Is·

verba carminis hujus, et ad finem usque complevit.

rael, the words of this canticle, and finished it even to the end.

THE TRACT.

ATTENDE cœlum, et loquar: et audiat terra verba ex ore meo.

HEAR, O ye heavens! and I will speak: let the earth give ear to the words of my mouth.

V. Expectetur sicut pluvia eloquium meum: et descendant sicut ros verba mea.

V. Let what I say be looked for like rain; and let my words drop down like dew.

V. Sicut imber super gramen, et sicut nix super fœnum: quia nomen Domini invocabo.

V. Like the shower upon the grass, and the snow upon the dry herb; for I will call upon the name of the Lord.

V. Date magnitudinem Deo nostro · Deus, vera opera ejus, et omnes viæ ejus, judicia.

V. Publish the greatness of our God: he is God; his works are perfect, and all his ways are justice.

V. Deus fidelis, in quo non est iniquitas: justus et sanctus Dominus.

V. God is faithful, in whom there is no iniquity: the Lord is just and holy.

Oremus.
Flectamus genua.
R. Levate.

Let us pray.
Let us bend our knees.
R. Rise up.

Deus, celsitudo humilium, et fortitudo recto-

O God, the exaltation of the humble, and the

rum : qui per sanctum Moysen puerum tuum, ita erudire populum tuum sacri carminis tui decantatione voluisti, ut illa legis iteratio fieret etiam nostra directio : excita in omnem justificatarum Gentium plenitudinem potentiam tuam, et da lætitiam, mitigando terrorem ; ut omnium peccatis tua remissione deletis, quod denuntiatum est in ultionem, transeat in salutem. Per Dominum nostrum, etc.

fortitude of the righteous ! who by thy holy servant Moses didst please so to instruct thy people by the singing of the sacred canticle, that the repetition of the law might be also our direction ; show thy power to all the multitude of Gentiles justified by thee, and by mitigating thy terrors grant them joy ; that, all their sins being pardoned by thee, the threatened vengeance may contribute to their salvation ; through our Lord, etc.

THE TWELFTH PROPHECY.

Daniel iii. IN diebus illis : Nabuchodonosor rex fecit statuam auream, altitudine cubitorum sexaginta, latitudine cubitorum sex, et statuit eam in campo Dura provinciæ Babylonis. Itaque Nabuchodonosor rex misit ad congregandos satrapas, magistratus et ju-

Daniel iii. IN those days, King Nabuchodonosor made a statue of gold, of sixty cubits high, and six cubits broad, and he set it up in the plain of Dura, of the province of Babylon. Then Nabuchodonosor the king sent to call together the nobles.

dices, duces et tyrannos, et præfectos, omnesque principes regionum, ut convenirent ad dedicationem statuæ, quam erexerat Nabuchodonosor rex. Tunc congregati sunt satrapæ, magistratus et judices, duces et tyranni, et optimates qui erant in potestatibus constituti, et universi principes regionum, ut convenirent ad dedicationem statuæ, quam erexerat Nabuchodonosor rex. Stabant autem in conspectu statuæ, quam posuerat Nabuchodonosor rex: et præco clamabat valenter: Vobis dicitur populis, tribubus et linguis: in hora, qua audieritis sonitum tubæ, et fistulæ, et citharæ, sambucæ, et psalterii, et symphoniæ, et universi generis musicorum, cadentes adorate statuam auream, quam constituit Nabuchodonosor rex. Si quis autem non prostratus

the magistrates, and the judges, the captains, the rulers, and governors, and all the chief men of the provinces, to come to the dedication of the statue, which King Nabuchodonosor had set up. Then the nobles, the magistrates, and the judges, the captains, and rulers, and the great men that were placed in authority, and all the princes of the provinces were gathered together to come to the dedication of the statue, which King Nabuchodonosor had set up. And they stood before the statue, which King Nabuchodonosor had set up. Then a herald cried with a strong voice: To you it is commanded, O nations, tribes, and languages! that in the hour that you shall hear the sound of the trumpet, and of the flute, and of the harp, of the sackbut,

adoraverit, eadem hora mittetur in fornacem ignis ardentis. Post hæc igitur, statim ut audierunt omnes populi sonitum tubæ, fistulæ, et citharæ, sambucæ, et psalterii, et symphoniæ, et omnis generis musicorum ; cadentes omnes populi, tribus, et linguæ, adoraverunt statuam auream, quam constituerat Nabuchodonosor rex. Statimque in ipso tempore accedentes viri Chaldæi accusaverunt Judæos, dixeruntque Nabuchodonosor regi : Rex, in æternum vive : tu rex posuisti decretum, ut omnis homo, qui audierit sonitum tubæ, fistulæ, et citharæ, sambucæ, et psalterii, et symphoniæ, et universi generis musicorum, prosternat se, et adoret statuam auream. Si quis autem non procidens adoraverit, mittatur in fornacem ignis ardentis. Sunt ergo viri

and of the psaltery, and of the symphony, and of all kind of music ; ye fall down and adore the golden statue, which King Nabuchodonosor hath set up. But if any man shall not fall down and adore, he shall the same hour be cast into a furnace of burning fire. Upon this therefore, at the time when all the people heard the sound of the trumpet, the flute, and the harp, of the sackbut, and the psaltery, of the symphony, and of all kinds of music : all the nations, tribes, and languages fell down and adored the golden statue, which King Nabuchodonosor had set up. And presently, at that very time, some Chaldeans came and accused the Jews, and said to King Nabuchodonosor : O king ! live for ever : thou O king ! hast made a decree that every man,

Judæi, quos constituisti super opera regionis Babylonis, Sidrach, Misach, et Abdenago : viri isti contempserunt, rex, decretum tuum : deos tuos non colunt ; et statuam auream, quam erexisti, non adorant.

that shall hear the sound of the trumpet, the flute, and the harp, of the sackbut, and the psaltery, of the symphony, and of all kind of music, shall prostrate himself, and adore the golden statue : and that if any man shall not fall down and adore, he should be cast into a furnace of burning fire. Now, there are certain Jews, whom thou hast set over the works of the province of Babylon, Sidrach, Misach, and Abdenago : these men, O king ! have slighted thy decree : they worship not thy gods, nor do not they adore the golden statue which thou hast set up.

Tunc Nabuchodonosor in furore et in ira præcepit ut adducerentur Sidrach, Misach, et Abdenago : qui confestim adducti sunt in conspectu regis. Pronuntiansque Nabuchodonosor rex, ait eis : Verene,

Then Nabuchodonosor in fury, and in wrath, commanded that Sidrach, Misach, and Abdenago should be brought : who immediately were brought before the king. And Nabuchodonosor the king

Sidracn, Misach, et Abdenago, deos meos non colitis, et statuam auream, quam constitui, non adoratis? nunc ergo, si estis parati, quacumque hora audieritis sonitum tubæ, fistulæ, citharæ, sambucæ, et psalterii, et symphoniæ, omnisque generis musicorum, prosternite vos, et adorate statuam quam feci. Quod si non adoraveritis, eadem hora mittemini in fornacem ignis ardentis: et quis est Deus qui eripiet vos de manu mea? Respondentes Sidrach, Misach, et Abdenago, dixerunt regi Nabuchodonosor: Non oportet nos de hac re respondere tibi. Ecce enim Deus noster, quem colimus, potest eripere nos de camino ignis ardentis, et de manibus tuis, o rex, liberare. Quod si noluerit, notum sit tibi, rex, quia deos tuos non colimus, et statuam auream.

spoke to them, and said: Is it true, O Sidrach, Misach, and Abdenago! that you do not worship my gods, nor adore the golden statue that I have set up? Now therefore if you be ready, at what hour soever you shall hear the sound of the trumpet, flute, harp, sackbut, and psaltery, and symphony, and of all kind of music, prostrate yourselves, and adore the statue which I have made: but if you do not adore, you shall be cast the same hour into the furnace of burning fire: and who is the God that shall deliver you out of my hands? Sidrach, Misach, and Abdenago answered and said to King Nabuchodonosor: We have no occasion to answer thee concerning this matter. For behold our God whom we worship, is able to save us from the furnace of burning fire.

quam erexisti, non adoramus. Tunc Nabuchodonosor repletus est furore, et aspectus faciei illius immutatus est super Sidrach, Misach, et Abdenago. Et præcepit ut succenderetur fornax septuplum quam succendi consueverat. Et viris fortissimis de exercitu suo jussit, ut ligatis pedibus Sidrach, Misach, et Abdenago, mitterent eos in fornacem ignis ardentis. Et confestim viri illi vincti, cum braccis suis, et tiaris, calceamentis, et vestibus, missi sunt in medium fornacis ignis ardentis : nam jussio regis urgebat. Fornax autem succensa erat nimis. Porro viros illos, qui miserant Sidrach, Misach, et Abdenago, interfecit flamma ignis. Viri autem hi tres, id est, Sidrach, Misach, et Abdenago, ceciderunt in medio camino ignis ardentis, colligati. Et

and to deliver us out of thy hands, O king! But if he will not, be it known to thee, O king! that we will not worship thy gods, nor adore the golden statue, which thou hast set up. Then was Nabuchodonosor filled with fury : and the countenance of his face was changed against Sidrach, Misach, and Abdenago, and he commanded that the furnace should be heated seven times more than it had been accustomed to be heated. And he commanded the strongest men that were in his army, to bind the feet of Sidrach, Misach, and Abdenago, and to cast them into the furnace of burning fire. And immediately these men were bound and were cast into the furnace of burning fire, with their coats, and their caps, and their shoes, and

ambulabant in medio flammæ, laudantes Deum, et benedicentes Domino.

their garments, for the king's commandment was urgent, and the furnace was heated exceedingly. And the flame of the fire slew those men that had cast in Sidrach, Misach, and Abdenago But these three men, that is, Sidrach, Misach, and Abdenago, fell down bound in the midst of the furnace of burning fire. And they walked in the midst of the flame, praising God, and blessing the Lord.

Oremus.

Omnipotens sempiterne Deus, spes unica mundi, qui prophetarum tuorum præconio, præsentium temporum declarasti mysteria: auge populi tui vota placatus; quia in nullo fidelium, nisi ex tua inspiratione, proveniunt quarumlibet incrementa virtutum. Per Dominum nostrum Jesum Christum, etc.

Let us pray.

Almighty and everlasting God! the only hope of the world, who by the voice of thy prophets hast manifested the mysteries of this present time; graciously increase the desires of thy people: since none of the faithful can advance in any virtue without thy inspiration: through our Lord, etc.

If the Church has no baptismal Font, the following benediction of the Font is omitted, and the Litany is said immediately after the Prophecies, in the manner hereafter prescribed, at p. 491. But where there is a Font, the Priest, with his Ministers and the Clergy, goes in procession to the Font, singing:

THE TRACT.

SICUT cervus deside- rat ad fontes aqua- rum: ita desiderat ani- ma mea ad te, Deus.

AS the hart panteth after the fountains of waters; so my soul panteth after thee, O God!

V. Sitivit anima mea ad Deum vivum: quan- do veniam, et apparebo ante faciem Dei?

V. My soul hath thirsted after the living God; when shall I come and appear before the face of God?

V. Fuerunt mihi la- crymæ meæ panes die ac nocte, dum dicitur mihi per singulos dies: Ubi est Deus tuus?

V. My tears have been my bread day and night, whilst it is said to me daily: **Where is** thy God?

Before the blessing of the Font, the Priest says this prayer:

V. DOMINUS vobis- cum.

V. THE Lord be with you.

R. Et cum spiritu tuo.
Oremus.

R. And with thy spirit.
Let us pray.

Omnipotens sempiter- ne Deus, respice propi- tius ad devotionem po- puli renascentis, qui si- cut cervus, aquarum tuarum expetit fontem: et concede propitius, ut fidei ipsius sitis, baptis-

O Almighty and ever- lasting God! mercifully regard the devotion of the people who are to be regenerated, and who, like the hart, pant after the fountain of thy waters; and mercifully

matis mysterio, animam corpusque sanctificet. Per Dominum nostrum, etc.

R. Amen.

The Priest begins the blessing of the Font, saying:

V. DOMINUS vobiscum.

R. Et cum spiritu tuo.

Oremus.

Omnipotens sempiterne Deus, adesto magnæ pietatis tuæ mysteriis, adesto sacramentis: et ad recreandos novos populos, quos tibi fons baptismatis parturit, spiritum adoptionis emitte; ut quod nostræ humilitatis gerendum est ministerio, virtutis tuæ impleatur effectu. Per Dominum nostrum Jesum Christum Filium tuum: qui tecum vivit et regnat in unitate ejusdem Spiritus sancti Deus, per omnia sæcula sæculorum

grant, that the thirst of their faith may, by the Sacrament of baptism, sanctify their souls and bodies; through our Lord, etc.

R. Amen.

V. THE Lord be with you.

R. And with thy spirit.

Let us pray.

O Almighty and everlasting God! be present at these mysteries, be present at these sacraments of thy great goodness; and send forth the spirit of adoption, to regenerate the new people, whom the font of baptism brings forth; that what is to be done by the ministry of our weakness may be accomplished by the effect of thy power; through our Lord Jesus Christ, thy Son, who with thee and the same Holy Spirit liveth and reigneth one God for ever and ever.

R. Amen.

V. Dominus vobiscum.

R. Et cum spiritu tuo.

V. Sursum corda.

R. Habemus ad Dominum.

V. Gratias agamus Domino Deo nostro.

R. Dignum et justum est.

Vere dignum et justum est, æquum et salutare, nos tibi semper, et ubique gratias agere, Domine sancte, Pater omnipotens, æterne Deus: qui invisibili potentia, sacramentorum tuorum mirabiliter operaris effectum; et licet nos tantis mysteriis exequendis simus indigni, tu tamen gratiæ tuæ dona non deserens, etiam ad nostras preces aures tuæ pietatis inclinas. Deus, cujus spiritus super aquas, inter ipsa mundi primordia ferebatur: ut jam tunc virtutem sanctificatio-

R. Amen.

V. The Lord be with you.

R. And with thy spirit.

V. Lift up your hearts.

R. We have them lifted up to the Lord.

V. Let us give thanks to the Lord our God.

R. It is meet and just.

It is truly meet and just, right and profitable to salvation, that we should at all times, and in all places, give thanks to thee, O holy Lord, Almighty Father, and eternal God! who by thy invisible power dost wonderfully produce the effects of thy sacraments; and, though we are unworthy to administer so great mysteries; yet, as thou dost not forsake the gifts of thy grace, so thou inclinest the ears of thy goodness even to our prayers. O God! whose Spirit in the very be-

nis, aquarum natura conciperet. Deus, qui nocentis mundi crimina per aquas abluens, regenerationis speciem in ipsa diluvii effusione signasti; ut unius ejusdemque elementi mysterio, et finis esset vitiis, et origo virtutibus. Respice, Domine, in faciem Ecclesiæ tuæ, et multiplica in ea regenerationes tuas, qui gratiæ tuæ affluentis impetu lætificas civitatem tuam, fontemque baptismatis aperis toto orbe terrarum Gentibus innovandis: ut tuæ majestatis imperio, sumat Unigeniti tui gratiam de Spiritu sancto.

ginning of the world moved over the waters; that even then the nature of water might receive the virtue of sanc-tification; O God! who by water didst wash away the crimes of the guilty world, and by the overflowing of the deluge didst give us a figure of regeneration; that one and the same element might in a mystery be the end of vice, and the origin of virtue. Look, O Lord! on the face of thy Church, and multiply in her thy regenerations, who by the streams of thy abundant grace fillest thy city with joy, and openest the fonts of baptism all over the world, for the renewing of the Gentiles: that by the command of thy majesty, she may receive the grace of thy only Son from the Holy Ghost.

Here the Priest divides the water in the form of a cross.

QUI hanc aquam regenerandis hominibus præparatam, arcana sui numinis admixtione fœcundet: ut sanctificatione concepta, ab immaculato divini fontis utero, in novam renata creaturam progenies cœlestis emergat: et quos aut sexus in corpore, aut ætas discernit in tempore, omnes in unam pariat gratia mater infantiam. Procul ergo hinc, jubente te Domine, omnis spiritus immundus abscedat: procul tota nequitia diabolicæ fraudis absistat. Nihil hic loci habeat contrariæ virtutis admixtio: non insidiando circumvolet: non latendo subrepat: non inficiendo corrumpat.

WHO, by a secret mixture of his divine virtue, may render this water fruitful for the regeneration of men; to the end that those who have been sanctified in the immaculate womb of this divine font, being born again new creatures, may come forth a heavenly offspring; and that all, however distinguished by sex in body, or age in time, may be brought forth to the same infancy, by grace their spiritual mother. Therefore may all unclean spirits, by thy command, O Lord! depart far from hence; may the whole malice of diabolical deceit be entirely banished; may no power of the enemy prevail here; may he not fly about to lay his snares; may he not creep in by his secret artifices: may he not corrupt with his infection.

Here he touches the water with his hand.

SIT hæc sancta et innocens creatura libera ab omni impugnatoris incursu, et totius nequitiæ purgata discessu. Sit fons vivus, aqua regenerans, unda purificans: ut omnes hoc lavacro salutifero diluendi, operante in eis Spiritu sancto, perfectæ purgationis indulgentiam consequantur.

MAY this holy and innocent creature be free from all the assaults of the en·my, and purified by the destruction of all his malice. May it become a living fountain, a regenerating water, a purifying stream; that all those who are to be washed in this saving bath, may obtain, by the operation of the Holy Ghost, the grace of a perfect purification.

Here he makes the sign of the cross thrice over the Font, saying:

UNDE benedico te creatura aquæ, per Deum vivum, per Deum verum, per Deum sanctum: per Deum, qui te in principio, verbo separavit ab arida: cujus spiritus super te ferebatur.

WHEREFORE I bless thee, O creature of water! by the living God, by the true God, by the holy God; by that God who in the beginning separated thee by his word from the dry land; whose spirit moved over thee.

Here he divides the water with his hand, and throws some of it out towards the four parts of the world, saying:

QUI te de paradisi fonte manare fecit, et in quatuor

WHO made thee flow from the fountain of Paradise, and

fluminibus totam terram rigare præcepit. Qui te in deserto amaram, suavitate indita, fecit esse potabilem, et sitienti populo de petra produxit. Benedico te et per Jesum Christum Filium ejus unicum Dominum nostrum: qui te in Cana Galilææ, signo admirabili, sua potentia convertit in vinum. Qui pedibus super te ambulavit: et a Joanne in Jordane in te baptizatus est. Qui te una cum sanguine de latere suo produxit; et discipulis suis jussit, ut credentes baptizarentur in te, dicens: Ite, docete omnes gentes, baptizantes eos in nomine Patris, et Filii, et Spiritus sancti.

commanded thee to water the whole earth with thy four rivers. Who changing thy bitterness, in the desert, unto sweetness, made thee fit to drink, and produced thee out of a rock to quench the thirst of the people. I bless thee also by our Lord Jesus Christ, his only Son; who in Cana of Galilee changed thee into wine, by a wonderful miracle of his power. Who walked upon thee dry foot, and was baptized in thee by John in the Jordan. Who made thee flow out of his side together with his blood, and commanded his disciples, that such as believed, should be baptized in thee, saying: Go, teach all nations, baptizing them in the name of the Father, and of the Son, and of the Holy Ghost.

Hæc nobis præcepta servantibus, tu Deus

Do thou, Almighty God! mercifully assist

omnipotens, clemens adesto; tu benignus adspira.

us who observe this commandment; do thou graciously inspire us.

He breathes thrice upon the water in the form of a cross, saying:

TU has simplices aquas tuo ore benedicito: ut præter naturalem emundationem, quam lavandis possunt adhibere corporibus, sint etiam purificandis mentibus efficaces.

DO thou with thy mouth bless these clear waters; that besides their natural virtue of cleansing the body, they may also be effectual for purifying the soul.

Here the Priest sinks the Paschal-candle into the water three different times, saying each time:

DESCENDAT in hanc plenitudinem fontis virtus Spiritus sancti.

MAY the virtue of the Holy Ghost descend into all the water of this font.

Then breathing thrice upon the water, he goes on:

TOTAMQUE hujus aquæ substantiam regenerandi fœcundet effectu.

AND make the whole substance of this water fruitful, and capable of regenerating.

Here the Paschal-candle is taken out of the water, and he goes on:

HIC omnium peccatorum maculæ deleantur, hic natura, ad imaginem tuam condita, et ad honorem sui reformata principii, cunctis vetustatis squaloribus emundetur: ut omnis

HERE may the stains of all sins be washed out; here may human nature, created to thy image, and reformed to the honor of its author, be cleansed from all the filth of the

homo sacramentum hoc regenerationis ingressus, in veræ innocentiæ novam infantiam renascatur. Per Dominum nostrum Jesum Christum Filium tuum: qui venturus est judicare vivos et mortuos, et sæculum per ignem.

 R. Amen.

old man; that all who receive this sacrament of regeneration, may be born again new children of true innocence; through our Lord Jesus Christ, thy Son: who is to come to judge the living and the dead, and the world by fire.

 R. Amen.

Then the people are sprinkled with the blessed water, some of which is reserved to be distributed to the Faithful for use in their houses. After this the Priest pours some oil of Catechumens into the water, in the form of a cross, saying:

SANCTIFICETUR, et fœcundetur fons iste oleo salutis renascentibus ex eo, in vitam æternam.

 R. Amen.

MAY this font be sanctified and made fruitful by the oil of salvation, for such as are regenerated in it, unto life everlasting.

 R. Amen.

Then he pours Chrism into it in the same manner, saying:

INFUSIO Chrismatis Domini nostri Jesu Christi, et Spiritus sancti Paracliti, fiat in nomine sanctæ Trinitatis.

 R. Amen.

MAY this infusion of the Chrism of our Lord Jesus Christ. and of the Holy Ghost the Comforter, be made in the name of the Holy Trinity.

 R. Amen

Lastly, he pours the Oil and Chrism both together into the water, in the form of a cross, saying :

COMMIXTIO Chrismatis sanctificationis, et olei unctionis, et aquæ baptismatis, pariter fiat, in nomine Patris, et Filii, et Spiritus sancti.

MAY this mixture of the Chrism of sanctification, and of the oil of unction, and of the water of baptism, be made in the name of the Father, and of the Son, and of the Holy Ghost.

R. Amen.

R. Amen.

Then he mingles the oil with the water, and with his hand spreads it all over the Font. If there are any to be baptized, they may be baptized after the usual manner. After the blessing of the Font, he returns to the altar, where he and his Ministers lie prostrate before it, and all the rest kneel, whilst the Litany is sung by two Chanters in the middle of the choir, both sides repeating the same.

KYRIE eleison.

LORD! have mercy on us.

Christe eleison.

Christ ! have mercy on us.

Kyrie eleison.

Lord ! have mercy on us.

Christe audi nos.

Christ ! hear us.

Christe exaudi nos.

Christ ! graciously hear us.

Pater de cœlis Deus, miserere nobis.

God the Father of heaven, have mercy on us.

Fili Redemptor mundi Deus, miserere nobis.

God the Son, Redeemer of the world, have mercy on us.

Spiritus sancte Deus, miserere nobis.

God the Holy Ghost, have mercy on us.

Sancta Trinitas unus Deus, miserere nobis.

Holy Trinity, one God, have mercy on us.

Sancta Maria, ora pro nobis.

Holy Mary, pray for us

Sancta Dei genitrix, ora.

Holy mother of God, pr'y.

Sancta Virgo virginum, ora.

Holy Virgin of virgins. pray.

Sancte Michael, ora.

St. Michael, pray.

Sancte Gabriel, ora.

St. Gabriel, pray.

Sancte Raphael, ora.

St. Raphael, pray.

Omnes sancti Angeli et Archangeli, orate.

All ye holy Angels and Archangels, pray.

Omnes sancti beatorum Spirituum ordines, orate.

All ye holy orders of blessed Spirits, pray.

S. Joannes Baptista, ora.

St. John the Baptist, pray.

S. Joseph, ora.

St. Joseph, pray.

Omnes sancti Patriarchæ et Prophetæ, orate.

All ye holy Patriarchs and Prophets, pray.

S. Petre, ora.

St. Peter, **pray.**

S. Paule, ora.

St. Paul, pray.

S. Andrea, ora.

St. Andrew, pray.

S. Joannes, ora.

St. John, pray.

Omnes sancti Apostoli et Evangelistæ, orate.

All ye holy Apostles and Evangelists, pray.

Omnes sancti Discipuli Domini, orate.

All ye holy disciples of our Lord, pray.

S. Stephane, ora.

St. Stephen. pray.

S. Laurenti, ora.

St. Laurence, pray

S. Vincenti,	ora.	St. Vincent,	pray.
Omnes sancti Martyres,		All ye holy Martyrs,	
	orate.		pray.
S. Silvester,	ora.	St. Silvester,	pray.
S. Gregori,	ora.	St. Gregory,	pray.
S. Augustine,	ora.	St. Augustin,	pray.
Omnes sancti Pontifices et Confessores, orate.		All ye holy Bishops and Confessors, pray.	
Omnes sancti Doctores,		All ye holy doctors,	
	orate.		pray.
S. Antoni,	ora.	St. Anthony,	pray.
S. Benedicte,	ora.	St. Benedict,	pray.
S. Dominice,	ora.	St. Dominick,	pray.
S. Francisce,	ora.	St. Francis,	pray.
Omnes sancti Sacerdotes et Levitæ, orate.		All ye holy Priests and Levites, pray.	
Omnes sancti Monachi et Eremitæ, orate.		All ye holy Monks and Hermits, pray.	
Sancta Maria Magdalena, ora.		St. Mary Magdalen, pray.	
S. Agnes,	ora.	St. Agnes,	pray.
S. Cæcilia,	ora.	St. Cecily,	pray.
S. Agatha,	ora.	St. Agatha,	pray.
S. Anastasia,	ora.	St. Anastasia,	pray.
Omnes sanctæ virgines et viduæ, orate.		All ye holy virgins and widows, pray.	
Omnes sancti et sanctæ Dei, intercedite pro nobis.		All ye men and women, Saints of God, make intercession for us.	
Propitius esto, parce nobis Domine.		Be merciful to us; spare us, O Lord.	
Propitius esto, exaudi nos Domine.		Be merciful to us; hear us, O Lord.	

Ab omni malo, libera nos Domine.

From all evil, O **Lord!** deliver us.

Ab omni peccato, libera nos Domine.

From all sin, O **Lord!** deliver us.

A morte perpetua, libera nos Domine.

From everlasting death, O Lord! deliver us.

Per mysterium sanctæ incarnationis tuæ, libera nos Domine.

Through the mystery of thy holy incarnation, O Lord! deliver us.

Per adventum tuum, libera nos Domine.

Through thy coming, O Lord! deliver us.

Per nativitatem tuam, libera nos Domine.

Through thy nativity, O Lord! deliver us.

Per baptismum et sanctum jejunium tuum libera nos Domine.

Through thy baptism and holy fasting, O Lord! deliver us.

Per crucem et passionem tuam, libera nos Domine.

Through thy cross and passion, O Lord! deliver us.

Per mortem et sepulturam tuam, libera nos Domine.

Through thy death and burial, O Lord! deliver us.

Per sanctam resurrectionem tuam, libera nos Domine.

Through thy holy resurrection, O Lord! deliver us.

Per admirabilem ascensionem tuam, libera nos Domine.

Through thy admirable ascension, O Lord! deliver us.

Per adventum Spiritus sancti Paracliti, libera nos Domine.

Through the coming of the Holy Ghost, the Comforter, O Lord deliver us.

In die judicii, libera nos Domine.

In the day of judgment, O Lord! deliver us.

Peccatores, te rogamus audi nos.

We sinners, do beseech thee to hear us.

Here the Priest and his Ministers go into the Sacristy, to vest themselves in white for the celebration of the Mass ; and the candles are lighted upon the altar, the Litany being continued by the Choir.

Ut nobis parcas, te rogamus audi nos.

That thou spare us, we beseech thee to hear us.

Ut Ecclesiam tuam sanctam regere et conservare digneris, te rogamus audi nos.

That thou vouchsafe to govern and preserve thy holy Church, we beseech thee to hear us.

Ut Domnum Apostolicum, et omnes Ecclesiasticos ordines in sancta religione conservare digneris, te rogamus audi nos.

That thou vouchsafe to preserve our Apostolic Prelate, and all the orders of the Church in thy holy religion, we beseech thee to hear us.

Ut inimicos sanctæ Ecclesiæ humiliare digneris, te rogamus audi nos.

That thou vouchsafe to humble the enemies of thy holy church, we beseech thee to hear us.

Ut regibus et principibus Christianis pacem et veram concordiam donare digneris, te rogamus audi nos.

That thou vouchsafe to give peace and true concord to Christian kings and princes, we beseech thee to hear us.

Ut nosmetipsos in tuo sancto servitio confortare et conservare digneris, te rogamus audi nos.

That thou vouchsafe to confirm and preserve us in thy holy service, we beseech thee to hear us.

Ut omnibus benefactoribus nostris sempiterna bona retribuas, te rogamus audi nos.

That thou render eternal good things to all our benefactors, we beseech thee to hear us.

Ut fructus terræ dare et conservare digneris, te rogamus audi nos.

That thou vouchsafe to give and preserve the fruits of the earth, we beseech thee to hear us.

Ut omnibus fidelibus defunctis requiem æternam donare digneris, te rogamus audi nos.

That thou vouchsafe to give eternal rest to all the faithful departed, we beseech thee to hear us.

Ut nos exaudire digneris, te rogamus audi nos.

That thou vouchsafe graciously to hear us, we beseech thee to hear us.

Agnus Dei, qui tollis peccata mundi, parce nobis Domine.

Lamb of God, who takest away the sins of the world, spare us, O Lord!

Agnus Dei, qui tollis peccata mundi, exaudi nos Domine.

Lamb of God, who takest away the sins of the world, hear us, O Lord!

Agnus Dei, qui tollis

Lamb of God, who tak-

peccata mundi, mise- est away the sins of
rere nobis. the world, have mercy
on us.

Christe audi nos. Christ, hear us.
Christe exaudi nos. Christ, graciously hear
us.

Here the Chanters solemnly intone the Kyrie eleison. *In the mean-
time the Priest goes to the altar, beginning the Mass in the ac-
customed manner, as at p.* 18, *inserting the Psalm* Judica me
Deus, *with* Gloria Patri. *Having kissed the altar, he begins the*
Gloria in excelsis, *as at p.* 18; *during which the bells are rung.
After which, the Priest says:*

V. DOMINUS vobis- *V.* THE Lord be
cum. with you.
R. Et cum spiritu tuo. *R.* And with thy spirit.

THE COLLECT.

Oremus. Let us pray.

DEUS, qui hanc sa- O GOD! who mak-
cratissimam noc- est this most sa-
tem gloria Dominicæ cred night illustrious by
resurrectionis illustras: the glory of the resur-
conserva in nova familiæ rection of our Lord:
tuæ progenie adoptionis preserve in the new off-
spiritum, quem dedisti; spring of thy family, the
ut corpore et mente spirit of adoption, which
renovati, puram tibi thou hast given them;
exhibeant servitutem. that being renewed in
Per eundem Dominum body and soul, they may
nostrum Jesum Chris- serve thee with purity
tum Filium tuum: qui of heart, through the
tecum vivit et regnat in same Lord Jesus Christ
unitate ejusdem Spiritus

sancti Deus, per om-
nia, etc.

R. Amen.

. . . in the unity of the
same Holy Ghost, etc.

R. Amen.

THE EPISTLE.

Lectio Epistolæ beati
Pauli Apostoli ad Co-
lossenses, cap. iii.

The Lesson from the
Epistle of St. Paul the
Apostle to the Colos-
sians, chap. iii.

FRATRES: Si con-
surrexistis cum
Christo, quæ sursum
sunt quærite, ubi Chris-
tus est in dextera Dei
sedens : quæ sursum
sunt sapite, non quæ
super térram. Mortui
enim estis, et vita vestra
est abscondita cum
Christo in Deo. Cum
Christus apparuerit vita
vestra : tunc et vos ap-
parebitis cum ipso in
gloria.

BRETHREN, if you
be risen with Christ,
seek the things that are
above, where Christ is
sitting at the right hand
of God: mind the things
that are above, not the
things that are on the
earth. For you are dead,
and your life is hidden
with Christ in God.
When Christ shall ap-
pear, who is your life,
then shall you appear
with him in glory.

After the Epistle, the Priest sings thrice Alleluia, *which is thrice
repeated by the choir ; after the third, he sings the following
verse :*

*V.*CONFITEMINI
Domino quoni-
am bonus : quoniam in
sæculum misericordia
ejus.

*V.*GIVE praise to the
Lord, for he is
good ; for his mercy en-
dureth for ever.

THE TRACT.

LAUDATE Dominum omnes gentes: et collaudate eum omnes populi.

V. Quoniam confirmata est super nos misericordia ejus, et veritas Domini manet in æternum.

PRAISE the Lord, all ye nations, and praise him, all ye people!

V. For his mercy is confirmed upon us; and the truth of the Lord remaineth for ever.

At the Gospel, lights are not carried, but incense only. The **Munda** cor meum, *as at p.* **19.**

THE GOSPEL.

Sequentia sancti Evangelii secundum Matthæum, cap. xxviii. 1–7.

VESPERE autem sabbati, quæ lucescit in prima sabbati, venit Maria Magdalene, et altera Maria, videre sepulchrum. Et ecce terræ motus factus est magnus. Angelus enim Domini descendit de cœlo: et accedens revolvit lapidem, et sedebat super eum: erat autem aspectus ejus sicut fulgur, et vestimentum ejus sicut nix. Præ ti-

A continuation of the holy Gospel according to St. Matthew, chap. xxviii. 1–7.

IN the end of the sabbath, when it began to dawn towards the first day of the week, came Mary Magdalene, and the other Mary, to view the sepulchre. And behold there was a great earthquake. For an angel of the Lord descended from heaven: and coming, rolled back the stone, and sat upon it. And his countenance was as lightning

more autem ejus exterriti sunt custodes, et facti sunt velut mortui. Respondens autem angelus, dixit mulieribus: Nolite timere vos: scio enim quod Jesum, qui crucifixus est, quæritis: non est hic; surrexit enim, sicut dixit. Venite, et videte locum, ubi positus erat Dominus. Et cito euntes, dicite discipulis ejus quia surrexit: et ecce præcedit vos in Galilæam; ibi eum videbitis. Ecce prædixi vobis.

and his raiment as snow. And for fear of him, the guards were struck with terror, and became as dead men. And the angel answering, said to the women: Fear not you: for I know that you seek Jesus, who was crucified. He is not here, for he is risen, as he said. Come, and see the place where the Lord was laid. And going, quickly tell ye his disciples that he is risen: and behold he will go before you into Galilee; there you shall see him. Lo, I have foretold it to you.

V. Dominus vobiscum.

R. Et cum spiritu tuo.

Oremus.

V. The Lord be with you.

R. And with thy spirit.

Let us pray.

The Offertory is omitted. Suscipe, etc., *p.* 22, *down to* **Then the** Priest says Amen, *p.* 28.

THE SECRET.

SUSCIPE, quæsumus Domine, preces populi tui, cum oblationibus hostiarum: ut

RECEIVE, O Lord! we beseech thee, the prayers of thy people, together with the

paschalibus initiata mysteriis, ad æternitatis nobis medelam, te operante, proficiant. Per Dominum nostrum Jesum Christum, etc.

offering of these hosts: that being consecrated by these paschal mysteries, they may, by the help of thy grace, avail us to eternal life; through our Lord Jesus Christ, thy Son, etc.

THE PREFACE.

V. PER omnia sæcula sæculorum.

R. Amen.

V. Dominus vobiscum.

R. Et cum spiritu tuo.

V. Sursum corda.

R. Habemus ad Dominum.

V. Gratias agamus Domino Deo nostro.

R. Dignum et justum est.

Vere dignum et justum est, æquum et salutare, te quidem Domine omni tempore, sed in hac potissimum nocte gloriosius prædicare, cum Pascha nostrum immolatus est Christus. Ipse enim verus est Agnus, qui abstulit pec-

V. FOR ever and ever.

R. Amen.

V. The Lord be with you.

R. And with thy spirit.

V. Lift up your hearts

R. We have them lifted up to the Lord.

V. Let us give thanks to the Lord, our God.

R. It is meet and just.

It is truly meet and just, right and profitable to salvation to praise thee, O Lord! at all times, but chiefly and more gloriously on this night when Christ our Paschal Lamb was sacrificed. For he is the true Lamb, that hath

cata mundi. Qui mortem nostram moriendo destruxit, et vitam resurgendo reparavit. Et ideo cum Angelis et Archangelis, cum Thronis et Dominationibus cumque omni militia cœlestis exercitus, hymnum gloriæ tuæ canimus, sine fine dicentes :

taken away the sins of the world. Who, by dying, destroyed our death, and, by rising again, restored our life. And therefore with the Angels and Archangels, with the thrones and dominations, and with all the troops of the celestial army, we sing the hymn of thy glory, incessantly saying :

Sanctus, *p.* 28. *The Canon of the Mass, p.* 29, *as far as* Communicantes.

COMMUNICAN-TES, et noctem sacratissimam celebrantes resurrectionis Domini nostri Jesu Christi secundum carnem : sed et memoriam venerantes, in primis gloriosæ semper Virginis Mariæ, genitricis ejusdem Dei et Domini nostri Jesu Christi, etc., *p. 30.*

PARTAKING of the same communion, and celebrating the most sacred night of the resurrection of our Lord Jesus Christ according to the flesh ; and also honoring the memory, in the first place, of the glorious ever Virgin Mary, mother of the same God and our Lord Jesus Christ, etc., *p. 30.*

Hanc igitur oblationem servitutis nostræ, sed et cunctæ familiæ tuæ, quam tibi offerimus

We therefore beseech thee, O Lord ! graciously to accept this oblation of our servitude, which

pro his quoque, quos re- generare dignatus es ex aqua et Spiritu sancto, tribuens eis remissio- nem omnium peccato- rum, quæsumus Do- mine, ut placatus acci- pias, diesque nostros in tua pace disponas, atque ab æterna damnatione nos eripi, et in electo- rum tuorum jubeas grege numerari: Per Christum Dominum nos- trum. Amen.

is also that of thy whole family, and which we of- fer to thee for these also, whom thou hast been pleased to regenerate by water and the Holy Ghost, granting them the remission of all their sins; dispose our days in thy peace; preserve us from eternal damna- tion, and place us in the number of thy elect: through Christ, our Lord. Amen.

Quam oblationem, *p.* 31, *until* **Agnus Dei,** *which is not said: but the Priest says the three prayers before the Communion, and the rest to the ablution inclusively, as from p.* 39 *to* 42: *after which the Vespers are sung by the Choir.*

THE VESPERS.

Ant. ALLELUIA, al- leluia, alleluia.   *Ant.* ALLELUIA, al- leluia, alleluia.

PSALM 116.

LAUDATE Domi- num, omnes gentes: * laudate eum omnes populi.

PRAISE the Lord, all ye nations! praise him, all ye people!

Quoniam confirmata est super nos misericordia ejus, * et veritas Domini manet in æternum.

Gloria Patri, etc.

Ant. Alleluia, alleluia, alleluia.

Because his mercy is confirmed upon us ; and the truth of the Lord remaineth for ever.

Glory, etc.

Ant. Alleluia, alleluia, alleluia.

Then the Priest at the altar begins the following Antiphon, which is continued by the Choir :

VESPERE autem sabbati, quæ lucescit in prima sabbati, venit Maria Magdalene, et altera Maria, videre sepulchrum, alleluia.

IN the end of the Sabbath, when it began to dawn towards the first day of the week, came Mary Magdalen and the other Mary to view the sepulchre, alleluia.

After this Antiphon, the Magnificat, *as at p. 109, is sung, and terminated with* Gloria Patri. *The altar is fumed with incense, with the ceremonies used at Vespers. After which, the Antiphon* Vespere autem sabbati *being repeated, the Priest at the altar turns to the people, saying:*

V. DOMINUS vobiscum.

R. Et cum spiritu tuo.

Oremus.

Spiritum nobis, Domine, tuæ charitatis infunde : ut quos sacramentis paschalibus satiasti, tua fācias pietate concordes. Per Dominum . . . in unitate ejusdem Spiritus sancti Deus, etc.

V. THE Lord be with you.

R. And with thy spirit.

Let us pray.

Pour on us, O Lord! the spirit of thy charity : that those, whom thou hast replenished with the paschal sacraments, may by thy goodness live in perfect concord; through our Lord, etc.

Then he says:

V. DOMINUS vobis-
cum.

R. Et cum spiritu tuo.

V. THE Lord be with
you.

R. And with thy spirit.

And the Deacon turning to the people, sings:

V. ITE, Missa est, al-
leluia, alleluia.

R. Deo gratias, alle-
luia, alleluia.

V. GO, Mass is end-
ed, alleluia, al-
leluia.

R. Thanks be to God,
alleluia, alleluia.

Placeat tibi, *and the rest, as p. 48.*

COMPLINE.

Jube Domne, *p.* 119. Fratres, sobrii estote. Adjutorium nostrum. Paternoster. Confiteor, etc. Converte nos, etc. Deus in adjutorium. Gloria Patri. Alleluia. *Then the four usual Psalms, as at page* 114 ; *after which is said the following:*

Ant. VESPERE au-
tem sabbati.

Ant. IN the end of the
sabbath.

THE CANTICLE OF SIMEON. *St. Luke* ii.

NUNC dimittis ser-
vum tuum Do-
mine, * secundum ver-
bum tuum in pace.

Quia viderunt oculi mei * salutare tuum,

Quod parasti * ante faciem omnium populorum :

NOW thou dost dis-
miss thy servant,
O Lord ! according to thy word, in peace :

Because my eyes have seen thy salvation,

Which thou hast pre-
pared before the face of all people :

Lumen ad revelationem Gentium, * et gloriam plebis tuæ Israel.

A light to the revelation of the Gentiles, and the glory of thy people of Israel.

Gloria, etc.

Glory, etc.

Ant. Vespere autem sabbati, quæ lucescit in prima sabbati, venit Maria Magdalene, et altera Maria, videre sepulchrum, alleluia.

Ant. In the end of the Sabbath, when it began to dawn towards the first day of the week, came Mary Magdalen, and the other Mary, to view the sepulchre, alleluia.

V. Dominus vobiscum.

V. The Lord be with you.

R. Et cum spiritu tuo.

R. And with thy spirit.

Oremus.

Let us pray.

Visita, quæsumus Domine, habitationem istam, et omnes insidias inimici ab ea longe repelle : Angeli tui sancti habitent in ea, qui nos in pace custodiant ; et benedictio tua sit super nos semper. Per Dominum, etc.

Visit, we beseech thee, O Lord ! this habitation, and drive from it all the snares of the enemy; let thy holy Angels dwell in it, to preserve us in peace ; and may thy blessing be upon us for ever. Through our Lord, etc.

V. Dominus vobiscum.

V. The Lord be with you.

R. Et cum spiritu tuo.

R. And with thy spirit.

V. Benedicamus Domino.

V. Let us bless the Lord.

R. Deo gratias.

R. Thanks be to God.

Benedictio. Benedicat et custodiat nos omnipotens et misericors Dominus, Pater, et Filius, et Spiritus sanctus.
R. Amen.

The blessing : May the Almighty and merciful Lord, the Father, Son, and Holy Ghost, bless and preserve us.
R. Amen.

THE ANTHEM.

REGINA cœli lætare, alleluia;

Quia quem meruisti portare, alleluia;

Resurrexit sicut dixit, alleluia.
Ora pro nobis Deum, alleluia.
V. Gaude et lætare, Virgo Maria, alleluia.

R. Quia surrexit Dominus vere, alleluia.

O QUEEN of heaven! rejoice, alleluia;

For he, whom thou didst deserve to bear, alleluia ;

Is risen again as he said, alleluia.
Pray for us to God, alleluia.
V. Rejoice and be glad, O Virgin Mary! alleluia.

R. Because our Lord is truly risen, alleluia.

Oremus.

DEUS, qui per resurrectionem Filii tui Domini nostri Jesu Christi mundum lætificare dignatuses: præsta, quæsumus; ut per ejus_

Let us pray.

O GOD! who by the resurrection of thy Son, our Lord Jesus Christ, hast been pleased to fill the world with joy: grant, we beseech thee,

genitricem Virginem Mariam, perpetuæ capiamus gaudia vitæ. Per eundem Christum Dominum nostrum.

℞. Amen.

℣. Divinum auxilium maneat semper nobiscum.

℞. Amen.

that by the Virgin Mary, his mother, we may receive the joys of eternal life. Through the same Christ, our Lord.

℞. Amen.

℣. May the divine assistance always remain with us.

℞. Amen.

Pater, Ave, Credo.

EASTER DAY.

The Mass.

The Priest begins the Mass, as at page 13, *down to* Peccata mea—My sins, *p.* 17.

THE INTROIT.

RESURREXI, et adhuc tecum sum, alleluia: posuisti super me manum tuum, alleluia: mirabilis facta est scientia tua, alleluia, alleluia.

Psal. Domine probasti me, et cognovisti me: tu cognovisti sessionem meam, et resurrectionem meam.

V. Gloria Patri, etc.
Resurrexi, etc.

I HAVE risen, and am yet with thee, alleluia: thou hast laid thy hand upon me, alleluia: thy knowledge is become wonderful, alleluia, alleluia.

Psal. Lord! thou hast proved me, and known me; thou hast known my sitting down, and my rising up.

V. Glory, etc.
I have risen, etc.

Kyrie eleison, Gloria in Excelsis, *and* Dominus vobiscum, *as at p.* 17.

THE COLLECT.

Oremus.

DEUS, qui hodierna die per Unigenitum tuum, æternitatis nobis aditum devicta morte reserasti: vota

Let us pray.

O GOD! who on this day, by the victory of thy only-begotten Son over death, hast opened for us the

nostra, quæ præveni- passage to eternity :
endo aspiras, etiam grant that our prayers
adjuvando prosequere. which thy preventing
Per eundem Dominum grace inspireth, may by
nostrum, etc. thy help become effectual ; through the same
Lord, etc.

THE EPISTLE.

Lectio Epistolæ beati The Lesson from the
Pauli Apostoli ad Co- Epistle of St. Paul the
rinthios, 1 Cor. v. 7, 8. Apostle to the Corinthians, 1 Cor. v. 7, 8.

FRATRES : Expur- BRETHREN, purge
gate vetus fermen- out the old leaven,
tum, ut sitis nova con- that you may be a new
spersio, sicut estis azymi. paste, as you are unlea-
Etenim Pascha nostrum vened. For Christ our
immolatus est Christus. Pasch is sacrificed.
Itaque epulemur, non in Therefore let us feast,
fermento veteri, neque not with old leaven, nor
in fermento malitiæ et with the leaven of ma-
nequitiæ : sed in azymis lice and wickedness ;
sinceritatis, et veritatis. but with the unleavened
bread of sincerity and
truth.

THE GRADUAL.

HÆC dies, quam THIS is the day
fecit Dominus : which the Lord
exultemus et lætemur in hath made ; let us be
ea. glad and rejoice therein.

V. Confitemini Domino, quoniam bonus: quoniam in sæculum misericordia ejus. Alleluia, alleluia.

V. Give praise to the Lord, for he is good; for his mercy endureth for ever. Alleluia, alleluia.

V. Pascha nostrum immolatus est Christus.

V. Christ, our Pasch, is sacrificed.

THE PROSE.

VICTIMÆ Paschali laudes immolent Christiani.

LET Christians offer a sacrifice of praise to the Paschal victim.

Agnus redemit oves: Christus innocens Patri reconciliavit peccatores.

The Lamb redeemed the sheep; the innocent Christ reconciled sinners to his Father.

Mors et vita duello conflixere mirando: dux vitæ mortuus, regnat vivus.

Life and death have struggled in sharp conflict. The ruler of life who was dead, now liveth and reigneth.

Dic nobis, Maria, quid vidisti in via?

Tell us, Mary, what thou hast seen in the way?

Sepulchrum Christi viventis, et gloriam vidi resurgentis:

The sepulchre of Christ, who lives, and the glory of him, who is risen.

Angelicos testes, sudarium et vestes.

The angelic witnesses; the linen and the clothes.

Surrexit Christus spes mea: præcedet vos in Galilæam.

Christ, my hope, is risen; he goeth before you into Galilee

Scimus Christum sur-
rexisse a mortuis vere:
tu nobis victor Rex mi-
serere. Amen. Alle-
luia.

We know Christ to
have truly risen. Do
thou, victorious King!
have mercy on us.
Amen. Alleluia.

The foregoing Prose is said every day this week.

Munda cor meum, *etc.*, *p.* 19—Cleanse my heart, *etc.*, *p.* 19.

THE GOSPEL.

Sequentia sancti Evan-
gelii secundum Mar-
cum, cap. xvi. 1–7.

A continuation of the
holy Gospel accord-
ing to St. Mark, chap.
xvi. 1–7.

IN illo tempore: Ma-
ria Magdalene, et
Maria Jacobi, et Salome
emerunt aromata, ut ve-
nientes ungerent Jesum.
Et valde mane una sab-
batorum, veniunt ad
monumentum, orto jam
sole. Et dicebant ad
invicem: Quis revolvet
nobis lapidem ab ostio
monumenti? Et respi-
cientes viderunt revo-
lutum lapidem. Erat
quippe magnus valde.
Et introeuntes in monu-
mentum, viderunt juve-
nem sedentem in dex-
tris, coopertum stola

AT that time, Mary
Magdalene and
Mary the mother of
James and Salome
brought sweet spices,
that coming they might
anoint Jesus. And very
early in the morning, the
first day of the week,
they come to the sepul-
chre. the sun being now
risen. And they said
one to another: Who
shall roll back the stone
from the door of the se-
pulchre? And looking,
they saw the stone rolled
back. For it was very
great. And entering

candida, et obstupue-runt. Qui dixit illis : Nolite expavescere ; Jesum quæritis Nazarenum, crucifixum : surrexit, non est hic : ecce locus ubi posuerunt eum. Sed ite, dicite discipulis ejus, et Petro, quia præcedit vos in Galilæam : ibi eum videbitis, sicut dixit vobis.

into the sepulchre, they saw a young man sitting on the right side, clothed with a white robe ; and they were astonished. And he saith to them : Be not affrighted ; you seek Jesus of Nazareth, who was crucified ; he is risen, he is not here. Behold the place where they laid him. But go tell his disciples and Peter, that he goeth before you into Galilee : there you shall see him, as he told you.

Credo, *p*. 20.

THE OFFERTORY.

TERRA tremuit, et quievit, dum resurgeret in judicio Deus, alleluia.

THE earth trembled, and war still, when God arose in judgment, alleluia.

Suscipe, *etc.*, *p*. 22, *down to* Then the Priest says Amen, *p*. 23.

THE SECRET.

SUSCIPE, quæsumus Domine, preces populi tui cum oblationibus hostiarum : ut Paschalibus initiata myste-

RECEIVE, O Lord ! we beseech thee, the prayers of thy people, together with the offerings of these hosts ;

riis ad æternitatis nobis medelam, te operante, proficiant. Per Dominum, etc.

that being consecrated by these Paschal mysteries, they may, by the help of thy grace, avail us to eternal life; through our Lord, etc.

THE PREFACE.

V. PER omnia sæcula sæculorum.

R. Amen.

V. Dominus vobiscum.

R. Et cum spiritu tuo.

V. Sursum corda.

R. Habemus ad Dominum.

V. Gratias agamus Domino Deo nostro.

R. Dignum et justum est.

Vere dignum et justum est, æquum et salutare, te quidem, Domine, omni tempore, sed in hac potissimum die gloriosius prædicare, cum Pascha nostrum immolatus est Christus. Ipse enim verus est Agnus, qui abstulit peccata mundi. Qui mortem nostram moriendo destruxit, et

V. FOR ever and ever.

R. Amen.

V. The Lord be with you.

R. And with thy spirit.

V. Lift up your hearts.

R. We have them lifted up to the Lord.

V. Let us give thanks to the Lord, our God.

R. It is meet and just.

It is truly meet and just, right and profitable to salvation, to praise thee, O Lord! at all times; but chiefly, and more gloriously, on this day, when Christ our Paschal Lamb is sacrificed. For he is the true Lamb that hath taken away the sins of the world. Who by dying

vitam resurgendo reparavit. Et ideo cum Angelis et Archangelis, cum Thronis et Dominationibus, cumque omni militia cœlestis exercitus, hymnum gloriæ tuæ canimus, sine fine dicentes :

destroyed our death, and by rising again, restored our life. And therefore with the Angels and Archangels, with the Thrones and Dominations, and with all the troops of the celestial army, we sing the hymn of thy glory, incessantly saying :

Sanctus, *p.* 28. *The Canon of the Mass, p.* 29, *as far as* Communicantes.

COMMUNICAN-TES, et diem sacratissimum celebrantes resurrectionis Domini nostri Jesu Christi secundum carnem : sed et memoriam venerantes, in primis gloriosæ semper Virginis Mariæ, genitricis ejusdem Dei et Domini nostri Jesu Christi, etc., *p.* 30.

PARTAKING of the same communion, and celebrating the most sacred day of the resurrection of our Lord Jesus Christ according to the flesh ; also honoring the memory, in the first place, of the glorious ever Virgin Mary, mother of the same God and our Lord Jesus Christ, etc., *p.* 30.

Hanc igitur oblationem servitutis nostræ, sed et cunctæ familiæ tuæ, quam tibi offerimus pro his quoque, quos regenerare dignatus es

We therefore beseech thee, O Lord ! graciously to accept this oblation of our servitude, which is also that of thy whole family, and which we

ex aqua et Spiritu sancto, tribuens eis remissionem omnium peccatorum, quæsumus Domine, ut placatus accipias, diesque nostros in tua pace disponas, atque ab æterna damnatione nos eripi, et in electorum tuorum jubeas grege numerari. Per Christum Dominum nostrum. Amen.

offer to thee for these also, whom thou hast been pleased to regenerate by water and the Holy Ghost, granting the remission of all their sins; dispose our days in thy peace; preserve us from eternal damnation, and place us in the number of thy elect; through Christ our Lord. Amen.

Quam oblationem, *etc.*, *p.* 31, *down to end of prayer* Corpus tuum—Let thy, *etc.*, *p.* 42.

THE COMMUNION.

PASCHA nostrum immolatus est Christus, alleluia : itaque epulemur in azymis sinceritatis et veritatis, alleluia, alleluia, alleluia.

CHRIST, our Pasch, is sacrificed, alleluia ; therefore let us feast with the unleavened bread of sincerity and truth, alleluia, alleluia, alleluia.

V. Dominus vobiscum.

V. The Lord be with you.

R. Et cum spiritu tuo.

R. And with thy spirit.

THE POST-COMMUNION.

Oremus.

Let us pray.

SPIRITUM nobis, Domine, tuæ charitatis infunde : ut quos

POUR on us, O Lord! the spirit of thy charity; that those whom

sacramentis paschalibus satiasti, tua facias pietate concordes. Per Dominum nostrum Jesum Christum Filium tuum : qui tecum vivit et regnat in unitate ejusdem Spiritus sancti Deus, etc.

V. Ite, Missa est, alleluia, alleluia.

R. Deo gratias, alleluia, alleluia.

thou hast replenished with the paschal sacraments, may by thy goodness live in perfect concord; through our Lord, etc., in the unity of the same Holy Ghost, etc.

V. Go, Mass is ended, alleluia, alleluia.

R. Thanks be to God, alleluia, alleluia.

Placeat tibi, *and the rest, as at p. 43.*

THE VESPERS.

DEUS in adjutorium, etc., *p.* 97. *Instead of* Laus tibi, etc., *say* Alleluia.

Ant. Angelus autem Domini descendit de cœlo, et accedens revolvit lapidem, et sedebat super eum, alleluia, alleluia.

Ps. Dixit Dominus, etc., *p.* 97.

Ant. Et ecce terræ motus factus est magnus : Angelus enim Domini descendit de cœlo, alleluia.

Ps. Confitebor tibi, etc., *p.* 99.

Ant. Erat autem aspectus ejus sicut fulgur, vestimenta autem ejus sicut nix, alleluia, alleluia.

Ps. Beatus vir, etc., *p.* 100.

Ant. Præ timore autem ejus exterriti sunt custodes, et facti sunt velut mortui, alleluia.

INCLINE unto my aid, etc., *p.* 97. *Instead of* Praise be to thee, etc., *say* Alleluia.

Ant. An angel of the Lord descended from heaven ; and coming rolled back the stone and sat upon it ; alleluia.

Ps. The Lord said, etc., *p.* 97.

Ant. And behold there was a great earthquake ; for an Angel of the Lord descended from heaven ; alleluia.

Ps. I will praise thee etc., *p.* 99.

Ant. And his countenance was as lightning ; and his raiment as snow ; alleluia, alleluia.

Ps. Blessed is the man etc., *p.* 100.

Ant. And for fear of him, the guards were struck with terror, and became as dead men ; alleluia.

Ps. Laudate, pueri, etc., *p.* 102.

Ps. Praise the Lord etc., *p.* 102.

Ant. Respondens autem Angelus, dixit mulieribus : Nolite timere ; scio enim quod Jesum quæritis, alleluia.

Ant. And the Angel answering, said to the women : Fear not you ; for I know that you seek Jesus ; alleluia.

Ps. In exitu Israel, etc., *p.* 103.

Ps. When Israel went, etc., *p.* 103.

Instead of the hymn, the following Anthem is said :

HÆC dies, quam fecit Dominus : exultemus et lætemur in ea.

THIS is the day, which the Lord hath made ; let us be glad and rejoice therein.

The Magnificat, *p.* 109.

Ant. ET respicientes viderunt revolutum lapidem : erat quippe magnus valde, alleluia.

Ant. AND looking, they saw the stone rolled back ; for it was very great ; alleluia.

Oremus.

Let us pray.

Deus, qui hodierna die per Unigenitum tuum æternitatis nobis aditum devicta morte reserasti : vota nostra, quæ præveniendo aspiras, etiam adjuvando prosequere. Per eundem Dominum nostrum, etc.

O God ! who on this day, by the victory of thy only-begotten Son over death, hast opened for us the passage to eternity ; grant that our prayers which thy preventing grace inspireth, may by thy help become effectual ; through the same Lord, etc.

The Anthem Regina Cœli, *as at p.* 507.

EASTER MONDAY.

The Priest begins Mass at the foot of the Altar, as at page 11, down to Peccata mea—My sins, *p.* 17.

THE INTROIT.

INTRODUXIT vos Dominus in terram fluentem lac et mel, alleluia : et ut lex Domini semper sit in ore vestro, alleluia, alleluia. *Psal.* Confitemini Domino, et invocate nomen ejus : annuntiate inter gentes opera ejus.

V. Gloria Patri, etc. Introduxit, etc.

THE Lord hath brought you into a land that floweth with milk and honey, alleluia; that the law of the Lord be always in your mouth, alleluia, alleluia. *Psal.* Give glory to the Lord, and call upon his name; declare his deeds among the Gentiles.

V. Glory, etc. The Lord hath brought, etc.

Kyrie eleison, Gloria in Excelsis, *and* Dominus vobiscum, *as at p.* 17.

THE COLLECT.

Oremus.

DEUS, qui solemnitate Paschali, mundo remedia contulisti : populum tuum, quæsumus, cœlesti dono prosequere ; ut et perfectam libertatem con-

Let us pray.

O GOD ! who, by the mystery of the Paschal solemnity, hast given to the world a remedy against all evils, pour forth, we beseech thee, on thy peo-

sequi mereatur, et ad vitam proficiat sempiternam. Per Dominum, etc.

ple thy celestial grace; that they may obtain perfect liberty, and advance daily in the way to everlasting life; through our Lord, etc.

THE EPISTLE.

Lectio Actuum Apostolorum, cap. x. 37–43.

The Lesson from the Acts of the Apostles, chap. x. 37–43.

IN diebus illis: Stans Petrus in medio plebis, dixit: Viri fratres, vos scitis quod factum est verbum per universam Judæam: incipiens enim a Galilæa post baptismum, quod prædicavit Joannes, Jesum a Nazareth: quomodo unxit eum Deus Spiritu sancto, et virtute; qui pertransiit benefaciendo, et sanando omnes oppressos a diabolo, quoniam Deus erat cum illo. Et nos testes sumus omnium quæ fecit in regione Judæorum, et Jerusalem, quem occiderunt suspendentes in ligno. Hunc Deus sus-

IN those days, Peter standing up in the midst of the people, said: You know the word which hath been published through all Judea; for it began from Galilee, after the baptism which John preached, Jesus of Nazareth: how God anointed him with the Holy Ghost, and with power, who went about doing good, and healing all that were oppressed by the devil, for God was with him. And we are witnesses of all things that he did in the land of the Jews and in Jerusalem; whom they killed, hang-

citavit tertia die, et dedit eum manifestum fieri, non omni populo, sed testibus præordinatis a Deo ; nobis, qui manducavimus et bibimus cum illo, postquam resurrexit a mortuis. Et præcepit nobis prædicare populo, et testificari, quia ipse est, qui constitutus est a Deo judex vivorum et mortuorum. Huic omnes Prophetæ testimonium perhibent, remissionem peccatorum accipere per nomen ejus omnes, qui credunt in eum.

ing him upon a tree. Him God raised up the third day, and gave him to be made manifest. Not to all the people, but to witnesses preordained by God, even to us who did eat and drink with him after he arose again from the dead. And he commanded us to preach to the people, and to testify that it is he who was appointed by God to be judge of the living and of the dead. To him all the prophets give testimony, that through his name all receive remission of sins, who believe in him.

THE GRADUAL.

HÆC dies, quam fecit Dominus : exultemus, et lætemur in ea.

V. Dicat nunc Israel, quoniam bonus : quoniam in sæculum misericordia ejus. Alleluia, alleluia.

THIS is the day which the Lord hath made ; let us be glad and rejoice therein.

V. Let Israel now say, that he is good ; that his mercy endureth for ever. Alleluia, alleluia.

V. Angelus Domini descendit de cœlo, et accedens revolvit lapidem, et sedebat super eum.

V. An angel of the Lord descended from heaven, and coming, rolled back the stone, and sat upon it.

Victimæ Paschali, *p.* 511. Munda cor meum, *etc.*, *p.* 19.

THE GOSPEL.

Sequentia sancti Evangelii secundum Lucam, cap. xxiv. 13–35.

A continuation of the holy Gospel according to St. Luke, chap. xxiv. 13–35.

IN illo tempore: Duo ex discipulis Jesu ibant ipsa die in castellum, quod erat in spatio stadiorum sexaginta ab Jerusalem, nomine Emmaus. Et ipsi loquebantur ad invicem de his omnibus, quæ acciderant. Et factum est, dum fabularentur, et secum quærerent; et ipse Jesus appropinquans ibat cum illis: oculi autem illorum tenebantur ne eum agnoscerent. Et ait ad illos: Qui sunt hi sermones, quos confertis ad invicem ambulantes, et estis

AT that time, two of the disciples of Jesus went, that same day, to a town, sixty furlongs from Jerusalem, named Emmaus. And they talked together of all these things, which had happened. And it came to pass, that while they talked, and reasoned with one another, Jesus himself also drew near, and went with them. But their eyes were held that they should not know him. And he said to them: What are these discourses, that you hold

tristes ? Et respondens unus, cui nomen Cleophas, dixit ei : Tu solus peregrinus es in Jerusalem, et non cognovisti quæ facta sunt in illa his diebus? Quibus ille dixit : Quæ? Et dixerunt : De Jesu Nazareno, qui fuit vir propheta, potens in opere et sermone, coram Deo et omni populo : et quomodo eum tradiderunt summi sacerdotes, et principes nostri in damnationem mortis, et crucifixerunt eum. Nos autem sperabamus quia ipse esset redempturus Israel : et nunc super hæc omnia, tertia dies est hodie quod hæc facta sunt. Sed et mulieres quædam ex nostris terruerunt nos, quæ ante lucem fuerunt ad monumentum, et non invento corpore ejus, venerunt, dicentes se etiam visionem Angelorum vidisse, qui dicunt eum vivere. Et abierunt quidam ex

with one another, as you walk, and are sad? And the one of them, whose name was Cleophas, answering, said to him : Art thou only a stranger in Jerusalem, and hast not known the things that have been done there in these days? And he said to them : What things? And they said : Concerning Jesus of Nazareth, who was a prophet, mighty in work and word, before God, and all the people. And how our chief priests and rulers delivered him to be condemned to death, and crucified him. But we hoped that it was he that should have redeemed Israel; and now besides all this, to-day is the third day since these things were done. Yea, and certain women also of our company affrighted us, who before it was light were at the sepulchre, and not finding his

nostris ad monumentum, et ita invenerunt sicut mulieres dixerunt, ipsum vero non invenerunt. Et ipse dixit ad eos : O stulti, et tardi corde ad credendum in omnibus, quæ locuti sunt prophetæ ! Nonne hæc oportuit pati Christum, et ita intrare in gloriam suam ? Et incipiens a Moyse, et omnibus Prophetis, interpretabatur illis in omnibus Scripturis quæ de ipso erant. Et appropinquaverunt castello, quo ibant : et ipse se finxit longius ire. Et coegerunt illum, dicentes : Mane nobiscum, quoniam advesperascit, et inclinata est jam dies. Et intravit cum illis. Et factum est, dum recumberet cum eis, accepit panem, et benedixit, ac fregit, et porrigebat illis. Et aperti sunt oculi eorum, et cognoverunt eum : et ipse evanuit ex oculis eorum. Et dixerunt ad invicem :

body, came, saying that they had also seen a vision of Angels, who say that he is alive. And some of our people went to the sepulchre : and found it so as the women had said, but him they found not. Then he said to them : O foolish, and slow of heart to believe in all the things which the prophets have spoken ! Did it not behoove Christ to suffer these things, and so to enter his glory ? And beginning at Moses, and all the prophets, he expounded to them in all the Scriptures the things that were concerning him. And they drew nigh to the town whither they were going : and he made as though he would go farther. But they constrained him, saying : Stay with us, because it is towards evening, and the day is now far spent. And he went in with them. And it came to

Nonne cor nostrum ardens erat in nobis, dum loqueretur in via, et aperiret nobis Scripturas? Et surgentes eadem hora regressi sunt in Jerusalem: et invenerunt congregatos undecim, et eos qui cum illis erant, dicentes : Quod surrexit Dominus vere, et apparuit Simoni. Et ipsi narrabant quæ gesta erant in via : et quomodo cognoverunt eum in fractione panis.

pass, whilst he· was at table with them, he took bread, and blessed, and brake, and gave to them. And their eyes were opened, and they knew him; and he vanished out of their sight. And they said one to the other : Was not our hearts burning within us, whilst he was speaking in the way, and opened to us the Scriptures? And they rose up the same hour, and went back to Jerusalem; and they found the eleven gathered together, and those that were with them, saying : The Lord is risen indeed, and hath appeared to Simon. And they told what things were done in the way; and how they knew him in the breaking of bread.

Credo, *p.* 20.

THE OFFERTORY.

ANGELUS Domini descendit de cœlo.

AN Angel of the Lord descended

et dixit mulieribus : Quem quæritis, surrexit, sicut dixit, alleluia.

from heaven, and said to the woman : He, whom you seek, is risen, as he said : alleluia.

Suscipe, *etc., p.* 22, *down to* Then the Priest says Amen, *p.* 29.

THE SECRET.

SUSCIPE, quæsumus Domine, preces populi tui cum oblationibus hostiarum : ut paschalibus initiata mysteriis, ad æternitatis nobis medelam, te operante, proficiant. Per Dominum nostrum Jesum Christum, etc.

RECEIVE, O Lord! we beseech thee, the prayers of thy people, together with the offerings of these hosts; that being initiated in the paschal mysteries, they may, by thy operation, obtain us eternal life; through our Lord, etc.

The Preface and Communicantes, *as at p* 514. *The Canon, as at p.* 29, *down to end of prayer* Corpus tuum, *p.* 42.

THE COMMUNION.

SURREXIT Dominus, et apparuit Petro, alleluia.

V. Dominus vobiscum.

R. Et cum spiritu tuo.

THE Lord is risen, and hath appeared to Peter ; alleluia.

V. The Lord be with you.

R. And with thy spirit.

THE POST-COMMUNION.

Oremus.

SPIRITUM nobis, Domine, tuæ charitatis infunde : ut quos

Let us pray.

POUR forth on us, O Lord ! the spirit of thy charity ; that

sacramentis paschalibus satiasti, tua facias pietate concordes. Per Dominum nostrum, etc., in unitate ejusdem Spiritus sancti Deus, etc.

those, whom thou hast replenished with the paschal sacraments, may by thy goodness live in perfect concord ; through our Lord, etc., in the unity of the same Holy Ghost, etc.

Rest of Mass as p. 42.

Vespers are said as yesterday, p. 517, *except the following:*

Ad Magnificat.

Ant. QUI sunt hi sermones, quos confertis ad invicem ambulantes, et estis tristes? Alleluia.

At Magnificat.

Ant. WHAT are these discourses, that you hold with one another, as you walk, and are sad? Alleluia.

Oremus.

Deus, qui solemnitate, V. 520.

Let us pray.

O God! who by the mystery, p. 520

EASTER TUESDAY.

The Priest begins Mass at the foot of the Altar, as at page 13, *down to* Peccata mea—My sins, *p.* 17.

THE INTROIT.

AQUA sapientiæ potavit eos, alleluia: firmabitur in illis, et non flectetur, alleluia: et exaltabit eos in æternum, alleluia, alleluia. *Psal.* Confitemini Domino, et invocate nomen ejus: annuntiate inter Gentes opera ejus.

HE hath given them the water of wisdom to drink, alleluia; he shall be made strong in them, and he shall not be moved, alleluia; and he shall exalt them for ever, alleluia, alleluia. *Psalm.* Give glory to the Lord, and call upon his name; declare his deeds among the Gentiles.

V. Gloria Patri, etc. Aqua sapientiæ, etc.

V. Glory, etc. He hath given, etc.

Kyrie eleison. Gloria in Excelsis, *and* Dominus vobiscum, *as at p.* 17.

THE COLLECT.

Oremus.

DEUS, qui Ecclesiam tuam novo semper fœtu multiplicas: concede famulis tuis, ut sacramentum

Let us pray.

O GOD! who by a new increase dost continually enlarge thy Church; grant that thy servants may, by a

529

vivendo teneant, quod fide perceperunt. Per Dominum nostrum, etc.

holy life, retain that sacrament, which they have received by faith ; through our Lord, etc.

THE EPISTLE.

Lectio Actuum Apostolorum, cap. xiii. 26–33.

The Lesson from the Acts of the Apostles, chap. xiii. 26–33.

IN diebus illis : Surgens Paulus, et manu silentium indicens, ait : Viri fratres, filii generis Abraham, et qui in vobis timent Deum, vobis verbum salutis hujus missum est. Qui enim habitabant Jerusalem, et principes ejus, ignorantes Jesum, et voces prophetarum, quæ per omne Sabbatum leguntur, judicantes impleverunt ; et nullam causam mortis invenientes in eo, petierunt a Pilato, ut interficerent eum. Cumque consummassent omnia, quæ de eo scripta erant, deponentes eum de ligno, posuerunt eum in monu-

IN those days, Paul rising up, and with his hand bespeaking silence, said : Men brethren ! children of the race of Abraham, and whosoever among you fear God, to you the word of this salvation is sent. For they that inhabited Jerusalem, and the rulers thereof, not knowing him, nor the voice of the prophets, which are read every Sabbath, judging him have fulfilled them. And finding no cause of death in him, they desired of Pilate that they might kill him. And when they had fulfilled all things that were written

mento. Deus vero suscitavit eum a mortuis tertia die : qui visus est per dies multos his, qui simul ascenderant cum eo de Galilæa in Jerusalem : qui usque nunc sunt testes ejus ad plebem. Et nos vobis annuntiamus eam, quæ ad patres nostros repromissio facta est : quoniam hanc Deus adimplevit filiis nostris, resuscitans Jesum Christum, Dominum nostrum.

of him, taking him down from the tree, they laid him in a sepulchre. But God raised him up from the dead the third day ; and he was seen for many days, by them who came up with him from Galilee to Jerusalem, who are to this present time his witnesses to the people. And we declare to you that the promise which was made to our fathers, this same hath God fulfilled to our children, raising up Jesus Christ, our Lord.

THE GRADUAL.

HÆC dies, quam fecit Dominus : exultemus et lætemur in ea.

V. Dicant nunc, qui redempti sunt a Domino, quos redemit de manu inimici, et de regionibus congregavit eos. Alleluia, alleluia.

V. Surrexit Dominus

THIS is the day, which the Lord hath made ; let us be glad and rejoice therein.

V. Let them say so that have been redeemed by the Lord ; whom he hath redeemed from the hand of the enemy, and gathered out of the countries. Alleluia, alleluia.

V. The Lord is risen

de sepulchro, qui pro from the sepulchre, whe
nobis pependit in ligno. for us hung upon the
tree of the cross.

Victimæ Paschali, *p.* 511. Munda cor meum, *etc.*, *p.* 19—Cleanse my
heart, *etc.*, *p.* 19.

THE GOSPEL.

Sequentia sancti Evan- A continuation of the
gelii secundum Lu- holy Gospel accord-
cam, cap. xxiv. 36–47. ing to St. Luke, chap.
xxiv. 36–47.

IN illo tempore : Ste-
tit Jesus in medio
discipulorum suorum, et
dicit eis : Pax vobis ;
ego sum, nolite timere.
Conturbati vero et con-
territi, existimabant se
spiritum videre. Et
dixit eis : Quid turbati
estis, et cogitationes as-
cendunt in corda vestra?
Videte manus meas, et
pedes, quia ego ipse
sum : palpate et videte ;
quia spiritus carnem et
ossa non habet, sicut me
videtis habere. Et cum
hoc dixisset, ostendit eis
manus et pedes. Adhuc
autem illis non creden-
tibus, et mirantibus præ
gaudio, dixit : Habetis

AT that time, Jesus
stood in the midst
of his disciples, and saith
to them : Peace be to
you ; it is I, fear not.
But they being troubled
and affrighted, supposed
they saw a spirit. And
he said to them : Why
are you troubled, and
why do thoughts arise
in your hearts? See my
hands and my feet, that
it is I myself : handle
me, and see ; for a spirit
hath not flesh and bones,
as you see me to have.
And when he had said
this, he showed them his
hands and his feet. But
while they yet believed
not and wondered for

hic aliquid, quod manducetur? At illi obtulerunt ei partem piscis assi, et favum mellis. Et cum manducasset coram eis, sumens reliquias, dedit eis. Et dixit ad eos: Hæc sunt verba, quæ locutus sum ad vos, cum adhuc essem vobiscum, quoniam necesse est impleri omnia quæ scripta sunt in lege Moysi, et prophetis, et psalmis de me. Tunc aperuit illis sensum, ut intelligerent Scripturas. Et dixit eis: Quoniam sic scriptum est, et sic oportebat Christum pati, et resurgere a mortuis tertia die; et prædicari in nomine ejus pœnitentiam, et remissionem peccatorum in omnes gentes.

joy, he said: Have you here anything to eat? And they offered him a piece of broiled fish, and a honeycomb. And when he had eaten before them, taking the remains he gave to them. And he said to them: These are the words, which I spoke to you, while I was yet with you, that all things must needs be fulfilled, which are written in the law of Moses, and in the prophets, and in the psalms, concerning me. Then he opened their understanding, that they might understand the Scriptures. And he said to them: Thus it is written, and thus it behooved Christ to suffer, and to rise again from the dead the third day: and that penance, and remission of sins, should be preached in his name among all nations.

Credo, *p.* 20.

THE OFFERTORY.

INTONUIT de cœlo Dominus, et Altissimus dedit vocem suam: et apparuerunt fontes aquarum, alleluia.

THE Lord thundered from heaven, and the Highest gave his voice; and fountains of water appeared, alleluia.

Suscipe, *etc.*, *p.* 22, *down to* Then the Priest says Amen, *p.* 28.

THE SECRET.

SUSCIPE, Domine, fidelium preces cum oblationibus hostiarum: ut per hæc piæ devotionis officia, ad cœlestem gloriam transeamus. Per Dominum, etc.

RECEIVE, O Lord! we beseech thee, the prayers of the faithful, together with these oblations; that by these offices of piety, we may obtain eternal glory; through our Lord, etc.

The Preface and Communicantes, *p.* 514. *The rest of the Canon, as on p.* 29, *down to end of prayer* Corpus tuum, *p.* 42.

THE COMMUNION.

SI consurrexistis cum Christo, quæ sursum sunt quærite, ubi Christus est in dextera Dei sedens, alleluia: quæ sursum sunt sapite, alleluia.

V. Dominus vobiscum.

R. Et cum spiritu tuo.

IF you be risen with Christ, seek the things that are above, where Christ is sitting at the right hand of God, alleluia. Mind the things that are above, alleluia.

V. The Lord be with you.

R. And with thy spirit.

THE POST-COMMUNION.

Oremus.

CONCEDE, quæsumus, omnipotens Deus : ut Paschalis perceptio sacramenti, continua in nostris mentibus perseveret. Per Dominum, etc.

Let us pray.

GRANT, we beseech thee, O Almighty God ! that the virtue of the Paschal sacrament which we have received, may always remain in our minds; through our Lord, etc.

The rest of the Mass from Dominus vobiscum, *as on p.* 43.

HYMNS.

THE PLAINT OF THE BLESSED VIRGIN.

Stabat Mater dolorosa
Juxta crucem lacrymosa,
   Dum pendebat Filius.
Cujus animam gementem,
Contristatam, et dolentem,
   Pertransivit gladius.

O quam tristis et afflicta
Fuit illa benedicta
   Mater Unigeniti !
Quæ mœrebat, et dolebat,
Pia Mater dum videbat
   Nati pœnas inclyti.

Quis est homo qui non fleret,
Christi matrem si videret
   In tanto supplicio ?

Quis posset non contristari,
Piam Matrem contemplari
   Dolentem cum Filio ?

Pro peccatis suæ gentis,
Vidit Jesum in tormentis,
   Et flagellis subditum.
Vidit suum dulcem Natum,
Morientem, desolatum,
   Dum emisit spiritum.

Eia, Mater, fons amoris,
Me sentire vim doloris
   Fac, ut tecum lugeam.
Fac ut ardeat cor meum
In amando Christum Deum,
   Ut sibi complaceam.

Sancta Mater, istud agas,
Crucifixi fige plagas
   Cordi meo valide.
Tui Nati vulnerati,
Tam dignati pro me pati,
   Pœnas mecum divide.

Fac me tecum pie flere,
Crucifixo condolere,
   Donec ego vixero.
Juxta crucem tecum stare,
Et me tibi sociare,
   In planctu desidero.

Virgo virginum præclara,
Mihi jam non sis amara :
   Fac me tecum plangere.

Fac ut portem Christi mortem,
Passionis fac consortem,
  Et plagas recolere.

Fac me plagis vulnerari,
Fac me cruce inebriari,
  Et cruore filii.
Inflammatus et accensus,
Per te, Virgo, sim defensus
  In die judicii.

Fac me cruce custodiri,
Morte Christi præmuniri,
  Confoveri gratia.
Quando corpus morietur,
Fac ut animæ donetur
  Paradisi gloria.   Amen.

The same in English.

Under the world's redeeming wood
The most afflicted Mother stood,
Mingling her tears with her Son's blood,
As that streamed down from ev'ry part;
Of all his wounds she felt the smart—
What pierced his body, pierced her heart.

Who can with tearless eyes look on,
When such a Mother, such a Son,
Wounded and gasping, does bemoan i
O worse than Jewish heart, that could
Unmovèd see the double flood
Of Mary's tears and Jesus' blood

They are our sins, alas! not his,
For which he bleeds, for which he dies,
In this atoning sacrifice.
When graves did open, rocks were rent;
When nature and each element
His torments and his griefs resent,

Shall man, the cause of all his pain
And all his grief—shall sinful man
Alone insensible remain?
Ah! pious Mother, teach my heart
Of sighs and tears the holy art,
And in thy grief to bear a part.

That sword of grief that did pass through
Thy very soul, oh! may it now
One kind wound on my heart bestow.
Great Queen of Sorrows! in thy train
Let me a mourner's place obtain,
With tears to cleanse all sinful stain.

Refuge of sinners! grant that we
May tread thy steps; and let it be
Our sorrow not to grieve like thee.
Oh! may the wounds of thy dear Son
Our contrite heart possess alone,
And all terrene affections drown!

And on us such impressions make
That we of suff'ring for his sake
May joyfully our portion take!
Let us his proper badge put on,
Let's glory in the cross alone
By which he marks us for his own.

That when the dreadful day shall come
For ev'ry man to hear his doom,
On his right hand we may find room.
Pray for us, Mary ! Jesus ! hear
Our humble prayers ; secure our fear,
When thou in judgment shalt appear.

Now give us sorrow, give us love,
That, so prepared, we may remove,
When called to the blest seats above. **Amen**

AN EASTER HYMN.

O Filii, et Filiæ,
Rex cœlestis, Rex gloriæ
Morte surrexit hodie.
         Alleluia, alleluia, alleluia,

Et Maria Magdalene,
Et Jacobi, et Salome
Venerunt corpus ungere.   Alleluia.

A Magdalene moniti,
Ad ostium monumenti
Duo currunt discipuli.   Alleluia.

Sed Joannes Apostolus
Concurrit Petro citius,
Ad sepulchrum venit prius.   Alleluia.

In albis sedens Angelus,
Respondit mulieribus
Quia surrexit Dominus.   Alleluia

Discipulis astantibus,
In medio stetit Christus,
Dicens : Pax vobis omnibus   Alleluia

Postquam audivit Didymus
Quia surrexerat Jesus,
Remansit fide dubius.   Alleluia

Vide, Thoma, vide latus,
Vide pedes, vide manus :
Noli esse incredulus.   Alleluia.

Quando Thomas Christi latus,
Pedes vidit, atque manus,
Dixit : Tu es Deus meus.   Alleluia.

Beati qui non viderunt,
Et firmiter crediderunt :
Vitam æternam habebunt.   Alleluia.

In hoc festo sanctissimo,
Sit laus et jubilatio :
Benedicamus Domino.   Alleluia

De quibus nos humillimas,
Devotas atque debitas
Deo dicamus gratias.   Alleluia.

The same in English.

Young men and maids ! rejoice and sing,
The King of heaven, the glorious King,
This day from death rose triumphing.
                    Alleluia, alleluia, alleluia

And Magdalen, in company
With Mary of James, and Salome,
T' embalm the corpse came zealously.   Alleluia

By Mary told, at break of day,
His dear disciples haste away
Unto the tomb, wherein he lay.   Alleluia

The much-belov'd Apostle John
Much swifter than Saint Peter ran,
And first arrivèd at the tomb.   Alleluia

An angel clothed in white they see
When thither come ; and thus spoke he :
The Lord you'll meet in Galilee.   Alleluia

While in a room the Apostles were,
Our Lord among them did appear,
And said : Peace be unto all here.   Alleluia

To Didymus when all declar'd
That Christ had risen and appear'd,
He doubted still the truth he heard.   Alleluia

O Thomas ! view my hands, my side,
My feet ; my wounds still fresh abide ;
Set incredulity aside.   Alleluia

When Thomas his dear Saviour saw,
And touched his wounds with trembling awe.
Thou art my God, said he, I know.   Alleluia

Blessed are they who have not seen,
And yet who firm in faith have been ;
With me they shall for ever reign.   Alleluia

In this most solemn feast let's raise
Our hearts to God in hymns of praise,
And let us bless the Lord always.   Alleluia

Our grateful thanks to God let's give,
In humble manner, while we live,
For all the favors we receive.   Alleluia

THE OFFICE OF THE

BLESSING OF THE HOLY OILS

ON THURSDAY IN HOLY WEEK.

FROM THE ROMAN PONTIFICAL.

On this day every year takes place the blessing of the Oil of Catechumens, and of the Oil of Unction for the sick, and the Holy Chrism is made.

In the morning, due preparation having been made before by the Sacristan, the Bishop comes into the church, where he vests for Mass with all his Pontifical attire, rich and of a white color. The attendants of the Bishop also vest, and besides them twelve Priests, seven Deacons, seven Subdeacons, Acolytes, and others, all in the vestures proper to their several orders, of a white color. Which done, a procession is formed to the Altar. All taking their places in the Choir, the Bishop, having reached the front of the Altar, says the *Confiteor*, and proceeds with the Mass, until the words in the Canon, *Per quem hæc omnia, Domine, semper bona creas,* etc

Before the Bishop pronounces these words, having made a genuflexion to the Blessed Sacrament already consecrated upon the Altar, he retires to the Epistle side of the Altar, where he purifies his fingers over an empty chalice, and wipes them with the purifier. Then a second time genuflecting to the Blessed Sacrament, he descends the first step of the Altar, and there receiving his mitre, goes to a seat prepared for him in the Presbytery, over against the Altar, and there sits, with his face towards the Altar, at a table previously set there, with the twelve Priests, and others in their respective vestments. Then the Priests and others standing round, the Archdeacon at the side of the Bishop says with a loud voice, "*Oleum Infirmorum,*" i.e., "the Oil for the Sick" which one of the Subdeacons, accompanied by two Acolytes, proceeds to bring from the Sacristy (where it has been previously got in readiness), and gives it into the hands of the Archdeacon, saying distinctly, "*Oleum Infirmorum.*"

The Archdeacon presents it to the Bishop to be blessed, saying the same words, and placing it on the table. The Bishop rising, with his mitre, says in a low voice:

The Blessing of the Oil for the Sick.

Exorcizo te, immundissime spiritus, omnisque incursio Satanæ, et omne phantasma, in nomine Pa✝tris, et Fi✝lii, et Spiritus ✝ sancti; ut recedas ab hoc oleo, ut possit effici unctio spiritalis ad corroborandum templum Dei vivi; ut in eo possit Spiritus sanctus habitare, per nomen Dei, Patris Omnipotentis, et per nomen dilectissimi Filii ejus, Domini nostri, Jesu Christi, qui venturus est judicare vivos et mortuos, et sæculum per ignem.

I exorcise and adjure thee, O unclean spirit' and every assault and illusion of Satan, in the name of the Father✝, and of the Son✝, and of the Holy✝Ghost; to depart from this Oil, that it may be made an unction of grace to strengthen the Temple of the living God; that in it the Holy Ghost may dwell, through the name of God, the Father Almighty, and through the name of his most dearly beloved Son, our Lord Jesus Christ, who shall come to judge the quick and the dead and the world by fire.

R. Amen.　　　　　*R.* Amen.

Then putting off his mitre, he blesses the Oil, saying in the same tone:

V. Dominus vobiscum.

R. Et cum spiritu tuo.

Oremus.

Emitte, quæsumus, Domine. Spiritum sanc-

V. The Lord be with you.

R. And with thy spirit.

Let us pray.

Send forth, we beseech thee. O Lord! thy Holy

tum, tuum paraclitum de cœlis, in hanc pinguedinem olivæ, quem de viridi ligno producere dignatus es, ad refectionem mentis, et corporis ; ut tua sancta bene✝dictione, sit omni hoc unguento cœlestis medicinæ peruncto, tutamen mentis et corporis, ad evacuandos omnes dolores, omnes infirmitates, omnemque ægritudinem mentis, et corporis, unde unxisti Sacerdotes, Reges, Prophetas, et Martyres; sit Chrisma tuum perfectum, Domine, nobis a te benedictum, permanens in visceribus nostris, in nomine Domini nostri, Jesu Christi.

Ghost, the paraclete from Heaven, upon this fatness of the olive which thou hast vouchsafed to bring forth out of a green tree, for the strengthening and refreshing of soul and body: that by thy grace and bene✝diction whosoever is anointed with this oil of heavenly virtue may receive protection of soul and body, and deliverance from all pains, all infirmities, and all ills of soul and body ; whereby thou didst anoint Priests, Kings, Prophets, and Martyrs: grant, O Lord. it may be thy true and perfect Chrism, blessed by thee, dwelling in our hearts ; in the name of our Lord Jesus Christ.

After this, the Oil is carried back to the Sacristy, and kept most carefully. Then the Bishop, resuming his mitre, sits, washes his hands, rises, and with his mitre goes, accompanied by his attendants, to the step of the Altar, where putting off his mitre, he genu· flects, goes up to the Altar, and proceeds with the Mass, until the Communion, which the Bishop receives only. The Deacon then puts the consecrated Host to be reserved for the morrow into a chalice, and reverently places it in the midst of the Altar. · Then the Bishop communicates the Deacon and Subdeacon and the rest

of the clergy; and after receiving the ablutions, he genuflects to the Blessed Sacrament upon the Altar, and returning sits as before; the attendants and others standing.

Then the Archdeacon, standing near the Bishop, says with a loud voice: "Oleum ad sanctum Chrisma," *i.e., the Oil for the holy Chrism. And after, in the same tone, he adds,* "Oleum Catechumenorum."

After which, a thurible being presented to the Bishop, he puts incense into it, and blesses it after the accustomed manner. Then the Priests, Deacons, and Subdeacons go in procession to the Sacristy to fetch with all solemnity the Oil of Chrism and the Oil of Catechumens, which are brought in, carried in the procession by two Deacons, preceded by a Subdeacon, carrying a vessel of balsam, and followed by the Priests, Deacons, and Subdeacons

As the procession moves from the Sacristy, two Cantors chant the verses following:

Consecration of the Holy Chrism.

O Redemptor, sume carmen temet concinentium.

Hear our hymn, Redeemer Lord : thee we praise with one accord.

The Choir repeat the same, and the Cantors then say:

Cantores. Audi judex mortuorum, una spes mortalium, audi voces proferentum donum pacis prævium.

Cantors. Hear us, Judge of dead and living, Hope of mortals, hear us singing :

Hear us, tribute to thee from the peaceful olive bringing.

Chorus. O Redemptor.

Choir. Hear our hymn.

Cantores. Arbor fœta alma luce hoc sacrandum protulit : fert hoc prona præsens turba Salvatori sæculi.

Cantors. Fruit of light the tree did yield, that gave this hallowed store : worshipping the world's Redeemer, this we offer, and adore.

Chorus. O Redemptor.

Cantores. Stans ad aram imo supplex infulatus pontifex, debitum persolvit omne, consecrato Chrismate.

Chorus. O Redemptor.

Cantores. Consecrare tu dignare, Rex perennis patriæ, hoc olivum, signum vivum, jura contra dæmonum.

Chorus. O Redemptor.

Choir. Hear our hymn.

Cantors. There before the altar standing prays the mitred pontiff lowly:
Duly he performs the rite, to bless the Chrism holy.

Choir. Hear our hymn.

Cantors. Consecrate, thou Christ eternal, King of Heaven our home,
This our Chrism a living seal, against the powers of doom.

Choir. Hear our hymn.

When all have reached their places in the Choir, the Deacon who carries the Oil of Chrism comes before the Bishop: and the Archdeacon, receiving it from him, places it, covered with a white cloth, on the table before the Bishop. Then the Subdeacon, carrying the vessel with balsam, gives it to the Archdeacon, who places it in like manner upon the table. The Bishop then rises, puts off his mitre, and first blesses the balsam, saying:

V. Dominus vobiscum.

R. Et cum spiritu tuo.

Oremus.

Deus, mysteriorum cœlestium et virtutum omnium præparator, nostras, quæsumus, preces exaudi, hanc odoriferam sicci corticis lacrymam

V. The Lord be with you.

R. And with thy spirit

Let us pray.

O God, who art the author and giver of heavenly mysteries, and of all graces, we beseech thee to hear our prayers: grant that these balmy

(quæ felicis virgæ pro-fluendo sudorem, sacerdotali nos opimat unguento) acceptabilem tuis præsta mysteriis, et concessa benedictione sancti✠fica. Per Dominum nostrum, Jesum Christum, Filium tuum, qui tecum vivit et regnat in unitate Spiritus sancti Deus, per omnia sæcula sæculorum.

tears of sapless wood (which, exuding from a fruitful branch, make fat our souls with sacerdotal unction) may be made acceptable to thee in thy sacraments, and be graciously sancti✠fied by thy blessing, through our Lord Jesus Christ, thy Son; who liveth and reigneth with thee, in the unity of the Holy Ghost, God, world without end.

R. Amen.

R. Amen.

Oremus.

Let us pray.

Creaturarum omnium, Domine, procreator, qui per Moysen famulum tuum permistis herbis aromatum fieri præcepisti sanctificationem unguenti; clementiam tuam suppliciter deposcimus, ut huic unguento, quod radix produxit stirpea, spiritualem gratiam largiendo, plenitudinem sancti✠ficationis infundas: sit nobis, Domine, fidei hilaritate

O Lord, the maker of all creatures! who by thy servant Moses didst command, a mixture being made of sweet spices, the hallowing of anointing oil: we humbly beseech thy clemency, that upon this oil, which the root of a tree hath yielded, thou wouldst bestow the grace of thy Spirit, and the fulness of conse✠cration: make it unto us, O Lord!

conditum ; sit sacerdo-
talis unguenti Chrisma
perpetuum ; sit ad cœ-
lestis vexilli impressio-
nem dignissimum ; ut
quicumque Baptismate
sacro renati isto fuerint
liquore peruncti, corpo-
rum atque animarum,
benedictionem plenissi-
mam consequantur, et
beatæ fidei collato mu-
nere perenniter ampli-
entur. Per Dominum
nostrum, Jesum Chris-
tum, Filium tuum, qui
tecum vivit et regnat in
unitate Spiritus sancti,
Deus, per omnia sæcula
sæculorum.

a savor of faith and
gladness, an everlast-
ing Chrism of sacer-
dotal unction ; make it
worthy of the sign of thy
heavenly banner ; that
whosoever being born
again by holy Baptism
shall have been anoint-
ed with this oil, may re-
ceive the fullest bene-
diction, both of body
and soul, and may be
everlastingly fulfilled
with the blessed grace
of faith, through our
Lord Jesus Christ, thy
Son, who liveth and
reigneth with thee in
the unity of the Holy
Ghost, God, world with-
out end.

R. Amen.   *R*. Amen.

*Then taking his mitre, the Bishop still standing, mixes, in a paten,
balsam with a little of the oil from the vessel, containing the
Chrism, saying:*

Oremus Dominum De-
um nostrum Omnipo-
tentem, qui incompre-
hensibilem unigeniti Fi-
lii sui sibique coæterni
divinitatem mirabili dis-

Let us beseech our
Lord God Almighty
(who hath joined to-
gether the infinite God-
head of his only-begot-
ten and co-eternal Son

positione veræ humani-
tati inseparabiliter con-
junxit, et co-operante
gratia Spiritus sancti,
oleo exultationis præ
participibus suis lini-
vit, ut homo fraude
diaboli perditus, ge-
mina et singulari con-
stans materia, perenni
redderetur de qua exci-
derat hereditati ; qua-
tenus hos ex diversis
creaturarum speciebus
liquores creatos sanctæ
Trinitatis perfectione
bene✠dicat, et bene-
dicendo sancti✠ficet,
concedatque, ut simul
permisti unum fiant ;
et quicumque exterius
inde perunctus fuerit,
ita interius liniatur,
quod omnibus sordibus
corporalis materiæ ca-
rens, se participem reg-
ni cœlestis effici gratu-
letur. Per eundem Do-
minum nostrum, Jesum
Christum, Filium suum,
qui cum eo vivit et reg-
nat in unitate ejusdem
Spiritus sancti Deus,

inseparably unto a true
and very humanity, and
with the grace of the
Holy Ghost co-operat-
ing, hath anointed him
with the oil of gladness
above his fellows, in or-
der that man, undone
by the fraud and malice
of the devil, consisting
of a twofold, yet singu-
lar nature, might be re-
stored to the everlasting
inheritance, from which
he had fallen), that he
will be pleased to➡✠bless
these creatures of oil, of
two different natures,
with the full blessing of
the Holy Trinity, and in
blessing to sanc➡✠tify
them, and grant that
being commingled to-
gether they may be-
come one; and that who-
soever shall be outward-
ly anointed therewith,
may be so inwardly
anointed that, being
freed from all soil of
bodily matter, he may
rejoice in being made
partaker of the kingdom

per omnia sæcula sæ-
culorum.

of Heaven, through the
same our Lord Jesus
Christ, his Son, who
liveth and reigneth with
him in the unity of the
Holy Ghost, God, world
without end.

R. Amen.   *R.* Amen.

*After which, the Bishop sits, with his mitre still on, and breathes
thrice, in the form of a cross, over the Chrism.*
*Then the twelve Priests in order bowing lowly to the Blessed Sacra-
ment on the Altar, and to the Bishop, approach the table, and each
in turn breathes, as the Bishop had done, over the Chrism. Then
lowly bowing, as before, they return to their places. Which done,
the Bishop standing, with his mitre, pronounces at once the Exorcism of the Chrism, saying:*

Exorcizo te, creatura
olei, per Deum Patrem
omnipotentem, qui fecit
cœlum et terram, mare,
et omnia quæ in eis
sunt; ut omnis virtus
adversarii, omnis exer-
citus diaboli, omnisque
incursio et omne phan-
tasma satanæ eradicetur,
et effugetur a te; ut fias
omnibus qui ex te un-
gendi sunt, in adoptio-
nem filiorum per Spiri-
tum sanctum. In no-
mine Dei, Pa✝tris Om-
nipotentis, et Jesu ✝
Christi, Filii ejus, Do-

I exorcise thee, O crea-
ture of oil! by God the
Father Almighty, who
hath made heaven and
earth, and all that therein is, that all the power
of the enemy, all the
host of Satan, and all
the wiles and illusions
of the devil may be ex-
pelled, and vanish from
thee; that thou mayest
be, to all who shall be
anointed with thee, for
their adoption as sons
through the Holy Ghost;
in the name of God the
Fa✝ther Almighty, and

mini nostri, qui cum eo vivit et regnat Deus, in unitate ejusdem Spiritus ✠ sancti.

of Jesus ✠ Christ his Son, our Lord, who liveth and reigneth one God, in the unity of the same Holy ✠ Spirit.

Then putting off his mitre, and extending his hands before his breast, he says the Preface:

V. Per omnia sæcula sæculorum.

R. Amen.

V. Dominus vobiscum.

R. Et cum spiritu tuo.

V. Sursum corda.

R. Habemus ad Dominum.

V. Gratias agamus Domino Deo nostro.

R. Dignum et justum est.

Vere dignum et justum est, æquum, et salutare, nos tibi semper, et ubique gratias agere, Domine Sancte, Pater Omnipotens, æterne Deus. Qui in principio inter cetera bonitatis tuæ munera, terram producere fructifera ligna justisti, inter quæ hujus pinguissimi liquoris mi-

V. World without end.

R. Amen.

V. The Lord be with you.

R. And with thy spirit.

V. Lift up your hearts.

R. We lift them up unto the Lord.

V. Let us give thanks unto our Lord God.

R. It is meet and right so to do.

It is very meet, right, and our bounden duty, that we should at all times, and in all places, give thanks unto thee, Holy Father, Almighty, everlasting God. Who in the beginning among other blessings of thy bounty, didst command the earth to bring forth trees yielding fruit, and

nistræ olivæ nasceren-
tur, quarum fructus sa-
cro Chrismati deserviret
Nam et David prophe-
tico spiritu gratiæ tuæ
Sacramenta prænoscens,
vultus nostros in oleo
exhilarandos esse can-
tavit. Et cum mundi
crimina diluvio quon-
dam expiarentur effuso,
similitudinem futuri mu-
neris columba demon-
strans per olivæ ramum,
pacem terris redditam
nuntiavit. Quod in no-
vissimis temporibus ma-
nifestis est effectibus
declaratum, cum baptis-
matis aquis omnium cri-
minum commissa delen-
tibus, hæc olei unctio
vultus nostros jucundos
efficit, ac serenos. Inde
etiam Moysi famulo tuo
mandatum dedisti, ut
Aaron fratrem suum
prius aqua lotum per in-
fusionem hujus unguen-
ti constitueret Sacerdo-
tem. Accessit ad hoc
amplior honori, cum Fi-
lius tuus, Jesus Christus,

that among these the
olive, yielding this fat-
ness of oil, should grow,
whose fruit should serve
to holy Chrism.   For
David also, foreknowing
by prophetic spirit the
sacraments of thy grace,
sang of oil to make man
of a cheerful counte-
nance; and when of old
the crimes of the world
were punished by the
flood of waters, a dove
declaring the image of
the future blessing by an
olive branch, announced
the return of peace to
the earth.   Which has
been shown by the ma-
nifest effects of grace, in
these last days, wherein
the waters of baptism
washing away all guilt
of sin, this unction of oil
maketh us of a cheerful
and glad countenance.
Then to Moses also thy
servant thou didst com-
mand, that he should or-
dain Aaron his brother,
first washed with water,
priest by affusion of this

Dominus noster lavari se a Joanne undis Jordanicis exegisset ; ut Spiritu sancto in columbæ similitudine desuper misso, unigenitum tuum in quo tibi optime complacuisse testimonio subsequentis vocis ostenderes, et hoc illud esse manifestissime comprobares, quod eum oleo lætitiæ præ consortibus suis ungendum David propheta cecinisset. Te igitur deprecamur, Domine Sancte, Pater Omnipotens, æterne Deus, per eundem Jesum Christum, Filium tuum, Dominum nostrum, ut hujus creaturæ pinguedinem sancti✠ficare tua bene✠dictione digneris, et sancti ✠ Spiritus ei admiscere virtutem, cooperante Christi Filii tui potentia, a cujus nomine sancto Chrisma nomen accepit, unde unxisti sacerdotes, reges, prophetas, et martyres ; ut spiritualis lavacri baptismo oil. Hereunto was added higher honor, when thy Son, our Lord Jesus Christ, had demanded to be baptized of John in the waters of Jordan ; that the Holy Ghost descending in the likeness of a dove upon thine only-begotten, in whom thou didst, by the testimony of thy voice which followed, declare thyself well pleased, and most manifestly prove this to be that of which the prophet David had sung, that he should be anointed with the oil of gladness above his fellows. We therefore pray thee, O Lord, holy Father, Almighty, everlasting God, through the same Jesus Christ our Lord, that thou wouldst vouchsafe to sanc✠tify with thy bless✠ing this creature of oil, and to infuse into it the virtue of thy Holy ✠ Spirit, with the power of Christ thy Son co-operating, from whose

renovandis, creaturam Chrismatis in sacramentum perfectæ salutis vitæque confirmes ; ut sanctificatione unctionis infusa, corruptione primæ nativitatis absorpta, sanctum uniuscujusque templum acceptabilis vitæ innocentiæ odore redolescat ; ut secundum constitutionis tuæ sacramentum, regio, et sacerdotali, propheticoque honore perfusi, vestimento incorrupti muneris induantur; ut sit his, qui renati fuerint ex aqua, et Spiritu sancto, Chrisma salutis, eosque æternæ vitæ participes, ;t cœlestis gloriæ faciat esse consortes.

holy name it has received the name of Chrism, with which thou hast anointed thy kings, priests, and martyrs; that to all who shall be renewed in the spiritual laver of baptism, thou wouldst confirm this Chrism for a sacrament of perfect health and life, that by the infusion of sanctifying grace, and the destruction of our original corruption, each one as an holy temple may breathe the fragrance of an holy and acceptable life ; that according to the sacrament of thy institution, being anointed to the dignity of kings and priests and prophets, they may be clad with the robe of the undying gift, that it may be to all who shall be born again of water and the Holy Ghost, the Chrism of salvation, and may make them partakers of eternal life and heirs together of celestial glory.

Then in a lower tone :

Per eundem Dominum nostrum, Jesum Christum, Filium tuum, qui tecum vivit et regnat in unitate ejusdem Spiritus sancti Deus, per omnia sæcula sæculorum.

R. Amen.

Through the same Jesus Christ, thy Son our Lord, who with thee liveth and reigneth in the unity of the same Holy Spirit, one God, world without end.

R. Amen.

The Preface being ended, the Bishop mingles the balsam and oil, mixed on the paten, with the holy Chrism in the vessel, saying :

Hæc commistio liquorum fiat omnibus ex ea perunctis propitiatio, et custodia salutaris in sæcula sæculorum.

R. Amen.

Let this mixture of oils be to all anointed therewith a means of grace, and a defence unto salvation, world without end.

R. Amen.

The Deacon then removes the veil which hitherto covered the vessel, and the Bishop, bowing his head, salutes the Chrism, saying :

Ave sanctum Chrisma.   Hail ! Holy Chrism.

This he does a second and a third time, saying it louder each time : and after saying it the third time, he kisses the lip of the vessel. Afterwards the twelve Priests in order make the same salutation, thrice repeating :

Ave sanctum Chrisma.   Hail ! Holy Chrism.

And having kissed the lip of the vessel, return to their places. Presently the Deacon approaches with the other vessel, containing the Oil of Catechumens, which he presents to the Archdeacon

who places it on the table before the Bishop. The Bishop and the twelve Priests breathe over it, as before was done in the case of the vessel of Chrism Which done, the Bishop rises, and with his mitre at once pronounces in a low tone the Exorcism of the Oil of Catechumens, saying:

The Blessing of the Oil of Catechumens.

Exorcizo te, creatura olei, in nomine Dei Pa✠tris Omnipotentis, et in nomine Jesu ✠ Christi, et Spiritus ✠ sancti, ut in hac invocatione individuæ Trinitatis, atque unius virtute Deitatis, omnis nequissima virtus adversarii, omnis inveterata malitia diaboli, omnis violenta incursio, omne confusum et cæcum phantasma eradicetur, et effugetur, et discedat a te; ut divinis Sacramentis purificata fias in adoptionem carnis et spiritus, eis qui ex te ungendi sunt, in remissionem omnium peccatorum; ut efficiantur eorum corpora ad omnem gratiam spiritualem accipiendam sanctificata. Per eundem Dominum nostrum, Jesum

I exorcise thee, O creature of oil ! in the name of God the Fa✠ther Almighty, and in the name of Jesus✠Christ, and of the Holy ✠ Ghost, that by this invocation of the undivided Trinity, in unity of operation, and of Godhead, all the most *wicked powers of the* enemy, all the inveterate malice of the devil, every violent assault, every hidden and dark illusion may be rooted out, and chased away, and dispelled from thee ; that thou mayest be hallowed to the use of holy sacraments for the adoption both of flesh and spirit to those who shall be anointed with thee, for the forgiveness of all sins : that their bodies may be sanctified to re

Christum, qui venturus est judicare vivos et mortuos, et sæculum per ignem.

ceive all spiritual grace, through the same our Lord Jesus Christ, who shall come to judge the quick and the dead, and the world by fire.

R. Amen.

R. Amen.

Then the Bishop, putting off his mitre, blesses the Oil of Catechumens, saying :

V. Dominus vobiscum.

V. The Lord be with you.

R. Et cum spiritu tuo.

R. And with thy spirit.

Oremus.

Let us pray.

Deus incrementorum omnium et profectuum spiritualium remunerator, qui virtute sancti Spiritus imbecillarum mentium rudimenta confirmas, te oramus, Domine, ut emittere digneris tuam bene✠dictionem super hoc oleum, et venturis ad beatæ regenerationis lavacrum, tribuas per unctionem hujus creaturæ purgationem mentis et corporis; ut si quæ illis adversantium spirituum inhæsere maculæ, ad tactum sancti-

O God ! the giver of all spiritual growth and advancement, who by the power of the Holy Ghost dost strengthen the first beginnings of weak minds, we beseech thee, O Lord ! that thou wouldst vouchsafe to send thy bless✠ing upon this oil, and to all who come to the blessed laver of regeneration, wouldst give by the use of this anointing oil, absolution of mind and body : that if any stains have sunk into them by the work of

ficati olei hujus abscedant; nullus spiritualibus nequitiis locus, nulla refugis virtutibus sit facultas, nulla insidiantibus malis latendi licentia relinquatur. Sed venientibus ad fidem servis tuis, et sancti Spiritus tui operatione mundandis, sit unctionis hujus præparatio utilis ad salutem, quam etiam cœlestis regenerationis nativitate in sacramento sunt baptismatis adepturi. Per Dominum nostrum, Jesum Christum, Filium tuum, qui venturus est judicare vivos et mortuos, et sæculum per ignem.

the enemy, at the touch of this hallowed oil, they may be done away; that there be no place for spiritual wickedness, no occasion given to relapsing virtue, no power of concealment left to lurking sins. But to thy servants, coming to the faith, and to be cleansed by the grace of thy Holy Spirit, let the preparation of this unction be availing towards the salvation which they will receive in the sacrament of baptism by the birth of a heavenly regeneration, through our Lord Jesus Christ, thy Son, who shall come to judge the quick and the dead, and the world by fire.

R. Amen.   *R.* Amen.

Then the Bishop and the twelve Priests, in order, reverently salute the Oil of Catechumens, saying thrice:

Ave sanctum Oleum.   Hail! Holy Oil.

And when they have done this the third time, they kiss the mouth of the vessel, as before was directed for the Chrism. After this, the two vessels are carried by the two Deacons back to the Sacristy, in the same form and order as they were brought in procession; the two Cantors chanting the following verses:

Ut novetur sexus omnis unctione Chrismatis, ut sanetur sauciata dignitatis gloria.

That by this most sacred unction, either sex may be renewed,

And our wounded glory rescued through the Spirit's plenitude.

Chorus. O Redemptor.

Choir. Hear our hymn.

Cantores. Lota mente sacro fonte aufugantur crimina; uncta fronte sacrosancta influunt charismata.

Cantors. By this fountain's hallowed waters may the soul be cleansed from sin,

And the brows with oil anointed heavenly graces gain within.

Chorus. O Redemptor.

Choir. Hear our hymn.

Cantores. Corde natus ex parentis alvum implens virginis, præsta lucem, claude mortem Chrismatis consortibus.

Cantors. Son of the Eternal Father, virgin-born, afford us light,

Who receive this holy unction; save us from death's gloomy night.

Chorus. O Redemptor.

Choir. Hear our hymn.

Cantores. Sit hæc dies festa nobis sæculorum sæculis : sit sacrata digna laude, nec senescal tempore.

Cantors. May this day of festal gladness, keep its holy joys in store,

Dignified with joyful praises, blooming now and evermore.

Chorus. O Redemptor.

Choir. Hear our hymn.

Meanwhile the Bishop, sitting with his mitre, washes his hands, then returns to the Altar, and proceeds with the Mass as in the Missal.

LAUS DEO.

CPSIA information can be obtained
at www.ICGtesting.com
Printed in the USA
LVHW040221130420
653218LV00016B/1464